Sheffield Hallam University
Learning and IT Services
Adsetts Centre City Campus
Sheffield   S1 1WB

TELEPEN

D1145131

Key Text

REFERENCE

Sheffield Hallam University
Learning and Information Services
WITHDRAWN FROM STOCK

The Abolition of the Atlantic Slave Trade

The Abolition of the Atlantic Slave Trade

Origins and Effects in Europe, Africa, and the Americas

edited by **David Eltis and James Walvin**

with the collaboration of SVEND E. GREEN-PEDERSEN
and with an Introduction by STANLEY L. ENGERMAN

The University of Wisconsin Press

Published 1981

The University of Wisconsin Press
114 North Murray Street
Madison, Wisconsin 53715

The University of Wisconsin Press, Ltd.
1 Gower Street
London WC1E 6HA, England

Copyright © 1981
The Board of Regents of the University of Wisconsin System
All rights reserved

First printing

Printed in the United States of America

For LC CIP information see the colophon

ISBN 0–299–08490–6

CONTRIBUTORS AND CONFERENCE PARTICIPANTS

Roger T. Anstey, Eliot College, University of Kent

Ralph A. Austen, Committee on African Studies, University of Chicago

Henrik Becker-Christensen, Institut for Grænseregionsforskning, Abenrå

Philip D. Curtin, Department of History, The Johns Hopkins University

Troels Dahlerup, Institut for Historie, Aarhus Universitet

Serge Daget, U.E.R. des sciences historiques, Université de Nantes

Christian Degn, Niemannsweg 30, Kiel

David Eltis, Department of Economics, Algonquin College

Pieter C. Emmer, Centre for the History of European Expansion, University of Leiden

Poul Enemark, Institut for Historie, Aarhus Universitet

Stanley L. Engerman, Department of Economics, University of Rochester

Henry A. Gemery, Department of Economics, Colby College

Svend E. Green-Pedersen, Institut for Historie, Aarhus Universitet

Jan S. Hogendorn, Department of Economics, Colby College

Stiv Jakobsson, Malma Ringväg 32, Uppsala

Jens V. Jensen, Institut for Historie, Aarhus Universitet

Henrik Jeppesen, Georgrafisk Centralinstitut, Københavns Universitet

Hans Christian Johansen, Odense Universitet

Ole Justesen, Institut for økonomisk Historie, Københavns Universitet

Axsel Kjær Sørensen, Institut for Historie, Aarhus Universitet

Henning Højlund Knap, Granlysstien 25, Kalundborg

Franklin W. Knight, Department of History, The Johns Hopkins University

Walter E. Minchinton, Department of Economic History, University of Exeter

Magnus Mörner, Latinamerika-Institutet, Stockholm

Georg Nørregård, Dag Hammarskjëlds Allé 1, København

Edward E. Reynolds, Department of History, University of California

Patricia Romero, Department of History, The Johns Hopkins University

Richard B. Sheridan, Department of Economics, University of Kansas

Jarle Simensen, Historisk Institut, Universitetet Trondheim

Howard Temperley, School of English and American Studies, University of East Anglia

James Walvin, Department of History, University of York

P. C. Willemoes-Jørgensen, Historisk Institut, Aarhus Universitet

Contents

Maps

Figures and Tables

FIGURES

TABLES

Preface

This volume of essays is the fruit of a symposium held between October 16 and 19, 1978, at Aarhus University, Denmark, as part of the celebration of the fiftieth anniversary of the University. The symposium and the proceedings were made possible by the generosity and assistance of both the Faculty of Humanities and the Institute of History of Aarhus University. Financial help was also forthcoming from the Danish Research Council for the Humanities and the Danish Ministry of Education, enabling scholars from three continents to gather and discuss work of mutual interest. What follows are the main proceedings of that gathering, greatly refined and revised for publication. It needs to be stressed, however, that many of the essays were improved by comments and discussion with conference participants who did not contribute an essay to this collection.

These essays not only represent a collection of distinct essays grouped around the themes in the abolition of the Atlantic slave trade but also provide a statement of the current historiographical debate, drawing its substance and inspiration from a much wider body of scholarship. In recent years, the upsurge in scholarship on the slave trade has made it increasingly difficult for any single person to keep in contact with all contemporary work. It is hoped that this volume, even if it cannot overcome that difficulty, will at least bring into sharper focus current work in the field.

Throughout the discussions at the Aarhus conference, Roger Anstey played a key role, but he did not live to see the publication of his work. His influence on the study of the slave trade was enormous and will, of course, continue. It is therefore fitting that the editors and contributors to this book should record our collective intellectual and personal debts to him.

David Eltis
Svend E. Green-Pedersen
James Walvin

January 27, 1981

Introduction

CHAPTER 1: **Some Implications of the Abolition of the Slave Trade**

Stanley L. Engerman

The recent outpouring of scholarly work on slavery and abolition has added much to our knowledge of the specifics of the rise, nature, and fall of the slave system and its impact on Europe, Africa, the Americas, and Asia. In part this reflects new research and the new information generated. In part, however, it reflects the convergence of the study of slavery and abolition with other historical currents, and a shift toward placing these topics within the mainstream of the historical developments in the modern world. Slavery is seen as an important aspect of the expansion of Europe after the fifteenth century, while abolition is increasingly regarded as part of the process of the rise of free labor and industry during the "modernization" of Western Europe and North America. Although specific relationships may seem more complex than they appeared to an earlier generation of scholars, no longer is slavery regarded as a minor or aberrant component in geographic and economic expansion, nor is abolition seen as a movement isolated from emerging social and political patterns in the major slaveowning areas. While the transatlantic slave trade has regained a more central role in the study of Western history, rather ironically its role in the study of African history has become somewhat muted in comparison with its treatment in the earlier Eurocentric historiography. For with the emergence of the study of African history as a discipline, recent work has focused on the indigenous developments within Africa, and no longer concentrates solely on the

3

responses of African societies to European penetration into slave markets. Moreover, with the reinterpretations of the slave experience, studies of the social and cultural life of slave populations have generated much richer interpretations than was possible earlier, when polar presentations of either docility or rebellion were provided as the only possible patterns of slave behavior.

Recent studies have, however, made for great ideological as well as historical complexity, and raised havoc with attempts to reach easy historical and moral answers. If abolition is now seen as related to the emergence of new attitudes toward labor, property, and society, then earlier debates trying to argue the case for morality as opposed to narrow economic interest appear to be somewhat artificial. If the study of the African slave trade and African slavery points to a major role for Africans, then it would seem that the establishment of this role leads to some deflection of the contrast between "European immorality" and the innocence of Africans exploited by Europeans. If the study of slave culture suggests that the experience of enslavement did not have the fully disastrous consequences earlier argued for, then perhaps specific aspects of the abolitionist descriptions of slavery need modification, while the defenses provided by slaveowners are themselves severely weakened.

The papers in this volume represent extensions of recent studies dealing with the slave trade and abolition on five continents, tracing through several traditional themes as well as important emerging ones. Slavery is seen as a system which was important in many regions and which influenced the entire range of interactions among these areas. Yet slavery and abolition are presented as only one part of the national and international experience, influenced by other aims and never being the single, all-encompassing aim in any country or region. The present collection of articles is concerned mainly with the British slave trade and its abolition, with some attention given to the Danish, Dutch, and French experiences. The Danes were the first people to end their international slave trade (in 1803); British abolition of the trade occurred in 1808, the same year that it was abolished in the United States.

In the study of British history, the slave trade and abolition are accorded more central roles than they are in the histories of the first slave-trading nations—Portugal and Spain—or the first to experience a large-scale ending of slavery in the New World—the French. By the start of the nineteenth century Britain had begun its industrial growth, the monarchy was limited, and parliamentary action was the necessary means to achieve most legislative changes. The British West

Indies had received over 1.7 million of the slaves sent from Africa, and the black population ca. 1800 was about 600,000. Denmark, at the time of the ending of the slave trade, was still an agricultural nation ruled by an absolute monarch. It should be noted, moreover, that antislavery was not the first Danish reform discussed after the political changes in 1784. Serfdom was abolished in 1788, and other liberal and "modern" measures were similarly discussed and introduced. The Danish West Indies received less than 4 percent of the number of slaves received by the British, and the black population of the Danish possessions at the start of the nineteenth century was below 40,000.[1]

The political circumstances in France, and French legislation regarding the slave trade and slavery in French colonies, were part of a rather complex situation. The legal slave trade was officially ended by decree in 1815; the illegal trade, however, persisted for several decades and became the basis for prolonged disputes between the British and the French. The French Caribbean colonies, overall, received about as many slaves as did the British, but after slavery ended and Saint Domingue gained its independence, their slave population fell to less than one-third that of the British colonies. The Dutch abolished their slave trade by a royal decree in 1814, after their colonies had received about one-half million slaves. The number of blacks in the 1800 population was, however, considerably below that number.

In all of these Caribbean colonies the slave populations experienced rates of natural population decrease; all were involved primarily in sugar production, although the extent of trade with the metropolis and the political and economic importance of the colonies differed markedly. With this European focus, however, it might seem nationalistic to point out that the United States ended its international slave trade in the same year as did England (the expected outcome of agreements reached twenty years earlier), and that several of the northern states had ended slavery before the start of the nineteenth century.

The papers are arranged in four sections, reflecting coincidentally the phases of the typical slave-trading voyage. The first section is concerned with the European metropolis and, specifically, with an examination of the movements for abolition. The second deals with the African response to the slave trade and to its abolition. In the third section the operations of, and reactions to, the illegal slave trade between Africa and the New World in the early nineteenth century are examined. The last section deals with demographic and cultural patterns among the slave populations of the West Indies.

EUROPEAN ABOLITION

The discussion of British abolition must begin with the issues raised by Eric Williams in his reaction to the earlier purely humanitarian interpretation of the ending of the slave trade in 1808 and of slavery in 1834.[2] In contrast with the view of abolition as a disinterested action undertaken in the interests of morality, Williams argued that it was basically the outcome of the economic interest of British industrialists in ending a costly encumbrance. His separation of the two motives was quite clear-cut. Underlying the Williams thesis was the implication that slavery was not only becoming less important to the British economy, but that it was inefficient and unprofitable.

Work on British antislavery, concentrating mainly on the initial breakthrough of ending the slave trade, has cast doubt on several of the specifics of the Williams argument. Slavery, according to Seymour Drescher, was an expanding economic force in the early nineteenth century—efficient, viable, and of increasing importance to the British economy.[3] Both Roger Anstey and Drescher point to the absence of any indication that emerging industrial capitalists either stood to gain from or were instrumental in the votes against the slave trade.[4] While these points raise significant reservations about the applicability of the Williams analysis, there is one key fact which permits his work to continue as a central focus and starting point. The fact remains that Britain did not end the slave trade until industrial expansion had begun; and it seems to many that such a temporal congruence could not have been accidental. Some might point to the earlier Danish abolition as raising further questions, but it seems that that move was made mainly in anticipation of British abolition and was itself related to fundamental socioeconomic changes in Denmark, although based upon a rather different set of political relationships.

Recent work on British antislavery has confronted two important questions. First, what, if any, was the relationship between the rise and success of the antislavery movement and the development of industrial capitalism? Second, where did the major impetus for the success of antislavery come from—what groups and classes in society were instrumental in making antislavery a key domestic political issue?[5] Work on the first of these questions argues that the previous separation of economics from morality now seems quite artificial, ignoring the complexity with which social, political, religious, and other movements evolved, and the fact that each pointed to the desirability of ending unfree labor. What seems striking is that once the issue came to the fore in the late 1780s there were few defenders of slavery on moral grounds. Religion, economics, philosophy, and political studies all pointed to the undesirability of slavery. It was a system with relatively few defenders, the word itself generating pejorative emotive connotations. And, while the examination of day-to-day events suggests hard struggle, perhaps it is most striking that within about one century after a centuries-long institution was first questioned it has virtually disappeared. Howard Temperley notes the relationship of several emerging (and, on the issue of slavery, converging) beliefs at the time, pointing out the significant impact of the economic expansion in England and in New England, where both economies were based on free labor. This spurt of economic growth not only provided a comparative framework within which to discuss (however accurately) relative labor efficiency, but also supported the argument that slavery could be eliminated at little (or no) cost. Anstey, in seeming contrast, stresses more the religious motive in the activity which ended slavery, as well as in the generation of the antislavery idea.

Yet puzzles remain in regard both to timing and to exactly why these economic and religious movements had to take the particular antislavery tinge they did. Little is said in these essays about racial attitudes, or why similar critiques of unfree labor developed in regard not only to slavery but to serfdom in Russia and the rest of Eastern Europe as well. England may be unique in its relatively early and successful abolition—a point obviously of great importance—but it remains useful to separate explanations for the origins of the attack on unfree labor from those factors which led to its success.

Anstey, Temperley, and most explicitly James Walvin point to a much wider base of antislavery support than did either Williams, with his emphasis on the interests of the industrial capitalists, or the humanitarians, with their stress on those noble few who triumphed over adverse forces. Emphasis is placed on the broad-based, mass appeal of antislavery as a political movement, and the involvement of middle-class voters as well as of the working class in generating pressures for abolition and emancipation. Clearly the numbers and interests of those involved in the petitions seem high, but the puzzle suggested by David Brion Davis remains: why should the working class have been so involved in antislavery, given that it might have better concentrated its efforts to improve its own position in England? While an English working-class movement to free slaves would seem less directly costly to laborers than such a working-class movement would have been in the United States, our cynical age might question such a presumed disinterested set of actions by individuals who had their own important problems. And, of course, it is not just the present cynical age: Cobbett, among others, attacked the abolitionist leaders and presented the campaign against "West Indian slavery" as a diversion from the attack on "wage slavery." Nevertheless, this recent emphasis on the implications of voting patterns, petitions, and mass meetings reveals that antislavery was seen by many contemporaries as an important cause, among the first of the major reforms of the nineteenth century world.

The discussions about abolition of the slave trade on the European continent are to be seen as reflections of the debates in England, with many of the arguments being the same. In Denmark, for example, a debate similar to that raised by Williams does exist, although here it is focussed on the behavior of one individual rather than that of various classes. The dual role of Ernst Schimmelmann as government minister and plantation owner, in conjunction with the decade-long delay between the decision to end the slave trade and its actual ending, generates controversy over the importance of humanitarianism versus economic interest in explaining Schimmelmann's behavior. Perhaps this controversy will be resolved in the same manner as that of the British—the recognition that any attempt to separate motives involves an artificial attempt to separate beliefs that are consistent, not conflicting.

There is one curious irony to be noted in the Anstey and Walvin discussions of the ending of British slavery in 1834: while the economic interpretation of the ending of the slave trade in 1808 has been weakened, both authors point to a very strong role of economic forces in the final abolition of 1834. Walvin notes the introduction of arguments about the level of sugar costs and the price paid for slave-grown British West Indian sugar, and the increased attention being paid to implications of the inefficiency of slave labor. Anstey goes even further, arguing that despite the increased West Indian political role in Parliament in the 1820s, the islands were seen as having decreasing economic importance to Britain, and slavery was seen as an institution no longer economically necessary. Indeed, Anstey further argues that the planters were eager to accept compensation to end the system because of these dire economic prospects.

In many ways, therefore, recent views of abolition in the 1830s have taken on a more Williams-like explanation than even Williams applied to the period, although, of course, there is a conspicuous absence of a significant, unique role for British capitalists. While these Williams-like views of otherwise extreme critics of Williams are of great interest, perhaps their depiction of economic trends is overly pessimistic. It seems clear that growth was continuing in many West

Indian islands, profitable new areas in Guyana and Trinidad were opening up and a search for additional labor was already under way before the end of slavery, and that the primary response to the ending of slavery was to import forced labor from India and China under various indenture schemes. It is possible that more work on the post-1808 West Indian economy might indicate a paucity of evidence for the loss of slavery's economic viability even after the end of the slave trade, thus extending the findings of recent work on the period before abolition further into the nineteenth century. If so, attempts to find explanations along the line here suggested by Temperley become more interesting and important.

AFRICA

The recent emphasis on the study of indigenous African history has led to a revaluation of the relationship between the slave trade and African social and economic development. This work on the African role in slave trading and the relationship between African and American slavery has provided quite a different view of the impact of European trade with Africa than those held earlier. As Philip Curtin notes, it is now possible to discuss movements within Africa without giving exclusive, or even primary, attention to the slave trade. Without downgrading the slave trade's impact, it is seen that while slaves may have been a major export, they did not form the only basis of trade either within Africa or among the continents. Abolition of the slave trade posed the problem within Africa of generating new export commodities with which to acquire desired imports. Moreover, more attention is now given to the relationship between the ending of the international slave trade and the expansion of slavery in Africa, particularly East Africa, in the second half of the nineteenth century. Indeed, this relationship presents a rather significant historical and moral paradox involving the impact of European expansion and cultural hegemony and the desirability of permitting antislavery attitudes to override concerns for noninterference in the religions, customs, and practices within Africa.

African slavery has been a difficult topic for historians (as well as contemporaries) because of the role to which it was assigned by earlier defenders of the transatlantic slave trade. For if this defense was that enslavement in Africa was as harsh as enslavement elsewhere, it was necessary for antislavery advocates to argue that African slavery was more benevolent and benign than American. And if the defense of the slave trade was that the alternative was death in Africa, anti-slavery advocates could not comfortably argue that captives were only enslaved, not killed, unless they could also present a benign view of the institution. It was in reaction to this dilemma that some historians were led to argue either that slavery (and warfare) in Africa were limited before European penetration, or, at the least, that the impor-tance and nature of these institutions changed significantly under Eu-ropean influence. While these views of African slavery have some plausibility, it should be noted that carried to an extreme they can ignore much of the nature of internal class conflict within African states, as well as the external power relations among those states.

Curtin's paper, drawing on his recent book on Senegambia, clearly indicates the usefulness of the shift in focus in the study of African society.[6] While not denying the impact of the slave trade and Euro-pean contact, it traces out those developments in the region which influenced the nature and magnitude of various commercial interac-tions, both with Europeans and with other Africans inland. Senegam-bia's slave trade peaked before the ending of the transatlantic slave trade, and the search for new export commodities began, and to some degree succeeded, before the British abolition of the trade. The same overlap of slave and commodity trades is to be seen elsewhere in Africa. To some extent the new commodity trade used the existing networks generated by the slave trade, and the impact of the ending of the slave trade upon the coastal economies is now seen to have been frequently overstated.

In his analysis Curtin calls attention to one significant figure relat-ing to the mechanism of the slave trade and to the argument that high economic returns were sufficient to lead to a desire for forced enslavement of others. By tracing through the extent of the transport and distribution network, he shows that the return to actual enslavers was a rather small part of the final American slave price. This sug-gests that economic returns to enslavers were relatively low (at least compared to what some might expect). Some, of course, might em-phasize that these returns were positive, while others might argue that the paucity of returns from the slave trade is a further indication of the pernicious European impact on Africa. Yet clearly the esti-mates provide important information whose implications need fur-ther exploration; the distinctions suggested by Curtin between politi-cal and economic factors in enslavement should be examined, as well as the choices made concerning sales of the enslaved within Africa and to other continents.

The argument for the negative impact of the transatlantic slave trade upon Africa is further extended by Gemery and Hogendorn. They point to the high social costs within Africa of the disruptions caused by the acquisition of manpower to be sent overseas, as well as to the losses resulting from the reduction in productive power within Africa. And they argue that the African enslavers did not even use all of the proceeds to acquire needed (or at least useful) consumer and investment goods, but rather obtained cowries and other commodities to be used as forms of money. This practice further increased the costs to Africa of slavery, since the use of paper money could conceivably have met the demands for a currency without reducing the quantities of goods imported.

While the commercial penetration of West Africa has attracted much scholarly attention, the later impact of European ideas brought in by missionaries is also of considerable importance. The attack on slavery in the Americas led to an active role by missionaries in Africa, who sought similar ends in quite different social contexts. On this point some ambiguity in judgment persists. To earlier generations the attempt to spread European ideas, and particularly the drive to end slavery and the slave trade whereever it existed, were seen as obviously "good things." Moreover, as Ralph Austen points out, in East Africa this interference can be argued to have been in opposition to the political ends sought by the British. Yet, more recently, the attempt to inculcate European ideas is seen as an example of "cultural imperialism," and many of the Europeans' ideas are now seen as unworthy of emulation (although antislavery has not yet been accorded this status). This emphasis is, of course, not newly discovered, since missionaries and politicians of the time faced the same dilemma in trying to determine how far to go in interfering with African religion and customs, and, at times, the foremost critics of the missionaries were the local colonial administrators who claimed that the activities of the missionaries complicated their problems.

The first of the missionary movements, that in Sierra Leone, has been examined in detail.[7] The missionaries worked with the ex-slaves from the New World who had resettled in that area, as well as with native Africans, to convince them of the evils of the slave trade. The missionaries had mixed, if any, success in achieving their aims, although more seemed to be done in Christianizing the freedmen than in ending the African slave trade. Another aspect of missionary activity is noted by Edward Reynolds in his description of the search for new, free-labor crops which would still permit commercial success and trade with Europe after the ending of the slave trade. The search by mission groups and private entrepreneurs apparently resulted in success in the Gold Coast with the introduction of cocoa in the 1860s. Students of "dependency theory" might ask, however, if European influence had led to a rather limited search among possible alternatives, thus doing little to solve the basic economic problems generated by European expansion.

The most morally puzzling of the themes is raised in Austen's paper on slavery in East Africa. For what is striking is the great increase in the magnitude of plantation slavery there after the abolition of slavery in most of the Western world, and the role of the changing nature of slavery in the increased commercialization and development in this area compared to the rest of Africa. And despite the strong antislavery stand of Britain—a stand which operated against Britain's political interests in this region—British influence clearly played a large part in this belated expansion of slavery. In part this was because the closing of the international slave trade led to lower slave prices, but the law, order, and transport unification provided by British penetration made commercialization and trade with Asia and Europe more feasible and profitable. While direct British control and interference did not persist on a major scale, the same paradox of "modernization" and "commercialization" leading to the importance of slavery which had been seen in the Americas was to be seen in Africa. Slavery had existed earlier in Africa, but it seems that in general it lacked the large commercial element apparent in East Africa in the late nineteenth century. And, as Austen asks in his discussion of its ultimate abolition, do we have the same triumph of ideology over economics as argued for in the European case, here compounded by the conflict of Western as opposed to African and Islamic ideals?

THE ILLEGAL SLAVE TRADE

Nineteenth century writing dealing with the attempts (mainly by and at the behest of the British) to regulate the illegal slave trade tends to fall into one of two polar positions. Confirmed abolitionists saw the noble British trying to overcome the moral failings of other Europeans, and the lack of success as a reflection of a failure of will on the part of others. To many Europeans, on the other hand, the attacks on the slave trade were seen as a sign of British hypocrisy, an attempt to dominate the world and to impose British will upon other countries.

The British, it was argued, used the slave trade as a means of interfering with and controlling others under the guise of some higher, more moral, justification. Some later historians, to whom control over illegal slave trading seems to have been possible, based their attacks on British hypocrisy on Britain's failure to pursue fully the prescribed policy, and accused the British of hiding a limited attack behind high moral phrases.

Recent estimates of the magnitude of the illegal slave trade in the nineteenth century do suggest that the trade, mainly to Cuba and Brazil, remained large, and that while complications caused by the suppression policies of the British made for some reduction in the number of slaves sent, this reduction was of a somewhat limited magnitude. While not gainsaying the legal actions of Britain and others, or of a British push for greater control and limitations, it is clear that significant differences remained between legal actions and active enforcement. Yet we again confront a moral dilemma, for as Pieter Emmer, David Eltis, and Serge Daget indicate, without agreements among all parties to restrict the slave trade, and an acceptance by both metropolitan powers and receiving areas of the anti-slave-trade principle, there was a limitation on what the British could accomplish. For to end illegal activities when, for whatever ideological or economic reasons, the issue was of considerably greater concern to the British than to others, meant an attempt to "force British moral standards on others," and created an infinite number of diplomatic problems revolving around rights of search and interference with foreign shipping. Practical difficulties persisted because of possibilities of continued transatlantic trade, as well as trade within the Caribbean; these difficulties led to the implementation of slave registration in British and, somewhat later, Dutch, areas of control. In France, Daget suggests that the concern for French commerce and the need for national self-assertion in the face of British sea power meant that the official anti-slave-trade stance was often little more than a facade. In the Dutch possessions Emmer indicates that British initiatives were behind many of the Dutch moves against the slave trade and acted as an irritant between the home government and the planters. And, as Eltis points out, the importance of British commerce and manufacturing meant that much of the illegal trade was ultimately based upon British money and goods—a certain (and frequently utilized) grounds for a charge of hypocrisy, even when resulting from circumstances that could be controlled only by extreme interference with the existing structure of property rights, as well as with "legitimate" British trade.

Eltis usefully divides the analysis of the impact of the illegal slave trade into that which took place before and that which occurred after the second half of the decade of the 1830s. Before the mid-1830s there was little support by the French, the Dutch, and others in controlling the trade, and thus, Eltis argues, abolition had a limited effect on the structure of the slave trade as measured by shipping characteristics and sailing practices. Mortality on ships apparently rose, but earlier images of shifts to smaller vessels and quicker turnaround do not seem to apply in general to these years. In the late 1830s the legal and the administrative successes of the British resulted in a greater impact on the structure of the trade, if not also upon the number of slaves carried. Without an international acceptance of the desirability of ending the international slave trade, however, the accomplishments of Britain, whatever its will and intentions, could only have been limited, and even today few would agree that Britain should have behaved as the moral policeman of the entire world, even if it had possessed the power to enforce abolition unilaterally.

NEW WORLD IMPACT

Among the central themes in the debate about the abolition of the slave trade were its relationship to the demographic performance of West Indian slaves, and the expected impact of the closing of the trade upon the economic position of the owners and their treatment of the enslaved in the New World. Central to the discussion was an awareness that West Indian slave populations were not self-reproducing, that deaths exceeded births, and that the number of slaves previously imported greatly exceeded the size of the remaining slave population. This was in marked contrast to the patterns of fertility and mortality of slaves in the United States—a point frequently perceived at the time, and a subject of frequent debate and concern among contemporaries, as well as among later demographers and historians. We are now aware of some things not knowable or fully appreciated at the time of earlier writings: that in most European colonies natural decrease persisted after the slave trade closed, as was also the case in many British areas; that some British areas (for example, Barbados) possibly had a natural increase in the early nineteenth century; that while West Indian slave fertility was low compared to that of slaves (and whites) in the United States, it was generally not markedly below fertility levels in western Europe; and

that the age-sex pattern of imports meant that the actual demographic patterns of creoles were often more favorable than the raw
data indicated.[8] Nevertheless, as Hans Christian Johansen, Svend
Green-Pedersen, and Richard Sheridan indicate, those earlier debates were often extremely sophisticated in their demographic thrust.

The abolitionist view drew attention to several relationships between closing the slave trade and the economic position of the slaveowners. It was frequently argued that the demographic potential for
a natural increase was there, so that closing the slave trade would not
lead to a dying out of the slave economy. The more sophisticated
could argue that the high rate of imports obscured the fact that for
those slave populations already in the New World births exceeded
deaths, and thus the basis for a sustained population increase without
imports was already there. More, however, argued that the failure to
achieve a natural increase was a result of inappropriate (but perhaps
financially appropriate) planter policy in regard to the care of slaves,
and to a deliberate discouragement of fertility; they also suggested
that, as some frequently cited examples demonstrated, the appropriate policy of better treatment would provide for an increased number
of slaves. Some held that such a demographic adjustment would have
become not only necessary, but also profitable if the slave trade
closed. Indeed, some abolitionists could not resist the temptation to
argue that they knew better how to maximize profits than did the
slaveowners, and claimed that a policy of fertility encouragement
would have been highly profitable even while the slave trade remained open.

It may seem a weak moral argument against the slave trade that its
elimination would be costless (or even profitable) to slaveowners and
would not interfere with the continuation of slavery, but this is to
overlook the central thrust of the antislavery argument. While clearly
not yet willing to attack slavery itself—the slave trade was a more
vulnerable starting point—abolitionists saw the closing of the slave
trade as an important action which would greatly ameliorate the living conditions and improve the treatment of the enslaved. Banking
on the presumed self-interest of the planters, they argued that ending the slave trade would force owners to provide better care and
thus to reduce mortality, while taking direct and indirect steps to increase fertility. As owners responded to the closing off of slave imports and the resulting rise in the prices of slaves, the enslaved would
at least be spared the unnecessary and inhumane hardships of the
previous situation, and the worst abuses of the slave condition would
be modified. In addition to the introduction of policies to encourage

fertility and to reduce adult and infant mortality, during the few years remaining before the closing of the trade there was expected to be an adjustment in the age-sex composition of slave imports from Africa. This would provide the benefits of more equal sex ratios, and thus a greater opportunity for the stable family patterns that were expected to increase fertility. The British debates on the sex ratio of imports, and the Danish move to permit females to be imported without being subject to the taxes paid on males in this period, indicate the concern with family life and reproduction. While the high ratio of males among slave imports, as Curtin points out, may represent a greater demand for females in Africa rather than a higher demand for males in the Americas, sensitivity to factors related to slave fertility was a central feature in the debates about the impact of ending the slave trade, and in the attempts to argue that it was a mild reform which would not have a major effect as long as planters were rational people.

In retrospect, it now seems that there was some overstatement of the extent to which various planter measures could have had a significant impact on the demographic performance of the enslaved population. Tropical diseases, and the higher mortality rate among slaves on sugar plantations and among imported Africans, influenced West Indian demographic patterns; and while the increased proportion of creoles in the slave populations raised crude birth rates overall, even those incentives introduced before or with the closing of the slave trade did not seem to have led to dramatically increased fertility rates.[9] More work on patterns of infant mortality needs to be undertaken before we can satisfactorily compare fertility rates in different areas, and so little is known about African fertility patterns at that time that it remains difficult to describe the impact of enslavement on fertility.

Whatever the causes, these demographic patterns were among the major influences upon the Afro-American cultural developments which arose out of the forced migration from Africa to the New World. The relationship between Afro-American and African cultures is a topic that has generated much heated political controversy. A curious coalition of planters and proslavery defenders (arguing that the enslaved retained African patterns—"superstitions" they called them) and modern scholars (who emphasize African survivals as if that was the only way to demonstrate the humanity of slaves) have argued that a limited amount of cultural adjustment and adaptation characterized the slave experience. In discussing this issue, Franklin Knight very usefully points to certain key parameters for our consideration. The basic nature of the slave trade, the variability of African patterns, and the differing natures of life in Africa and the Americas all made the retention of the structural patterns of West African society extremely difficult and of limited possibility. Other important determinants of slave culture were the differing black-white ratios in a region, the volume, the pace, and the age-sex composition of imports, and the stage of economic development in the area receiving the slaves. Clearly these influenced, and were influenced by, the demographic factors discussed previously, and attempts to define uniform Afro-American patterns in the presence of such diverse influences remains doubtful. This is not to deny the basic role of African ideas and beliefs, but it does suggest that other factors must also be considered in the examination of slave belief and behavior.

The recent upsurge of interest in slavery and abolition shows little sign of receding. Indeed, the range of issues discussed has expanded: particularly noteworthy is the increased attention given to slavery within Africa; to the relationships between the economic growth, antislavery ideology, and abolition activities of the European and American powers; and to the patterns of belief and behavior of the Africans and Afro-Americans enslaved in the New World. The new work on these topics has generated sufficient ironies to unsettle most readers, and it is often difficult (if not impossible) to know whether an appropriate response is one of cynicism about, or of admiration for, the individuals and groups described. It is, perhaps, these complexities that make the study of history so interesting and, ultimately, rewarding. We may ask for easy answers and resolutions to historical issues, but as the study of slavery and abolition so clearly demonstrates, things are generally more complex and complicated than we should like to acknowledge.

NOTES

I should like to thank David Eltis for his help in writing this introduction. Since the essays include detailed citations to the relevant literature, it was decided to minimize the number of references here.
1 The estimates of the number of blacks enslaved by the trade and the number of blacks in the populations in the various colonies ca. 1800, in this and the following paragraph, are drawn from Philip D. Curtin, *The Atlan-*

tic Slave Trade: A Census (Madison, 1969); Michael Craton, *Sinews of Empire: A Short History of British Slavery* (Garden City, N.Y. 1974); *Revue française d'histoire d'outre-mer* 62 (1975); and essays in this volume. While subsequent investigations have suggested some possible revisions of the estimates used, the basic orders of magnitude remain unchanged.

2 Eric Williams, *Capitalism and Slavery* (Chapel Hill, 1944).

3 Seymour Drescher, *Econocide: British Slavery in the Era of Abolition* (Pittsburgh, 1977).

4 Roger Anstey, *The Atlantic Slave Trade and British Abolition, 1760–1810* (London, 1975).

5 See in particular David Brion Davis, *The Problem of Slavery in the Age of Revolution, 1770–1823* (Ithaca, 1975).

6 Philip D. Curtin, *Economic Change in Precolonial Africa: Senegambia in the Era of the Slave Trade*, 2 vols. (Madison, 1975).

7 Stiv Jakobsson, *Am I Not a Man and a Brother? British Missions and the Abolition of the Slave Trade and Slavery in West Africa and the West Indies, 1786–1838* (Lund, 1972).

8 See Herbert S. Klein and Stanley L. Engerman, "Fertility Differentials between Slaves in the United States and the British West Indies: A Note on Lactation Practices and Their Possible Implications," *William and Mary Quarterly*, 3d. ser., 35 (April 1978): 357–74; Robert W. Fogel and Stanley L. Engerman, "Recent Findings in the Study of Slave Demography and Family Structure," *Sociology and Social Research* 63 (April 1979): 566–89. See also Herbert S. Klein, *The Middle Passage: Comparative Studies in the Atlantic Slave Trade* (Princeton, 1978).

9 See in particular Michael Craton, *Searching for the Invisible Man: Slaves and Plantation Life in Jamaica* (Cambridge, Mass., 1978); B. W. Higman, *Slave Population and Economy in Jamaica, 1807–1834* (Cambridge, 1976).

PART I

Abolition and the European

Metropolis

CHAPTER 2: **The Ideology of Antislavery**

Howard Temperley

The problem is easily stated: What was it, in the late eighteenth and early nineteenth centuries, that made men turn against an institution which, in one form or another, had existed since time immemorial? Why was slavery attacked *then*? Why not in the seventeenth century, or the sixteenth? Why, indeed, was it attacked at all?

Traditionally, the answers given to this question have taken two forms.

One is to describe how ideas, initially expressed by a handful of thinkers, were taken up, elaborated, added to, and ultimately incorporated into the beliefs of the population at large. This was essentially the approach of Thomas Clarkson, whose *History of Abolition* (1808) is notable both as the first attempt to provide a comprehensive account of the origins of the antislavery movement and as a model for later writers. In a foldout map which appears at the end of the introductory section of his work he shows how, beginning far back in the sixteenth century as tiny springs and rivulets, each marked with the name of some prominent thinker or statesman, the waters converge to become rivers, eventually "swelling the torrent which swept away the slave-trade."[1] As Clarkson saw it, the victory of the abolitionists represented the triumph of right thinking over error, of the forces of light over the forces of darkness. It had been a long struggle, extending over centuries, but in the end truth had prevailed.

Until a generation ago few historians felt disposed to dissent from this view. Although less overtly Manichean in their approach, they were prepared to accept Clarkson's analysis, at least to the extent that they saw the ideas which eventually came together and energized the antislavery crusade as having originated in the distant past, in most cases with identifiable individuals or groups. Few later commentators would have chosen, as Clarkson did, to include Pope Leo X or Queen Elizabeth in their list of precursors, nor would they have cared to invoke, as Clarkson also did, the hand of Providence as a guiding force; but at bottom the processes they described were much the same. This, for example, is the approach adopted in the early chapters of Frank Klingberg's *The Anti-Slavery Movement in England* (1926), and in one form or another it informs the work of most early twentieth century writers and many later writers, a notable recent example being David Brion Davis's *The Problem of Slavery in Western Culture* (1966).[2]

The principle challenge to this view has come from those historians who have seen the abolition of the slave trade and slavery as having been the result, not of moral, but of economic pressures. The classic statement of this case was Eric Williams's *Capitalism and Slavery* (1944). Williams, it is true, did not entirely discount the influence of moral teaching, to the extent that he saw the abolitionists as a "spearhead." They spoke "a language the masses could understand" and thereby "were successful in raising anti-slavery sentiments almost to the status of a religion in England." In this sense they helped the process along. But at bottom it was the forces of economic rather than moral change that mattered. It was "mercantilism" that created the slave system and "mature capitalism" that destroyed it. He states his case forcefully: "The attack falls into three phases: the attack on the slave trade, the attack on slavery, the attack on the preferential sugar duties. The slave trade was abolished in 1807, slavery in 1833, the sugar preference in 1846. These three events are inseparable."[3]

Leaving aside for the moment the question of whether the evidence will actually support this view, we may simply note that what we have here are two fundamentally contradictory explanations as to why abolition occurred at the time it did. In the one case it is seen as the product of a long process of intellectual inquiry. The antislavery argument that was presented to Parliament and the British public in the 1780s and 1790s was not, and given its complexity could not conceivably have been, the achievement of one group or even of one generation. Inevitably it was the work of many hands extending back over many generations. In the same way, the economic explanation is also dependent on the notion of gradual maturation which initially fostered slavery but ultimately created a conjunction of interests which destroyed it. In each case abolition is seen as the result of an extended chain of events which by the late eighteenth and early nineteenth centuries had created a situation in which the slave trade, and later slavery itself, could no longer be regarded as acceptable.

Comparing these two explanations, it may be noted that in one respect at least the economic view scores over what, for want of a better term, we may call the intellectual diffusionist account in that it is more firmly rooted in what are commonly regarded as the major developments of the period. Much of the plausibility of Williams's account, indeed, derives from the fact that Britain, the first nation to industrialize, also took the lead in the campaigns to abolish the slave trade and slavery. This is a development which the intellectual diffusionist account virtually ignores. Moreover, there is something patently unsatisfactory about any explanation of a historical event, particularly a historical event as important as the abolition of the slave trade and slavery, which is based on developments in the realm of ideas and which fails, at least in any detailed way, to relate those ideas to the actual lives of people of the period. Most ideas, as we know, have long pedigrees. Often, too, they are capable of acquiring a momentum of their own and can develop, almost regardless of changes in the material world, according to an inner logic of their own. But equally plainly ideas are shaped by circumstance, and the longer the time span the greater the likelihood of this happening. Thus in accounting for the attack on slavery we need to know not simply when ideas originated and who first formulated them, but what it was at a certain point in time that made man choose, out of all the ideas available, those particular ideas, and furthermore to act on them. To assume, as the abolitionists frequently did, that their ideas were right and that virtue requires no explanation is inadequate, since plainly not everyone agreed with them. We still need to be shown why what seemed right to the abolitionists—and, more to the point, to an increasingly large proportion of their contemporaries—had not seemed right to their predecessors.

Yet, if the intellectual diffusionist account has its pitfalls, so also does the economic explanation, the principal one being that it is exceedingly difficult to show that the overthrow of either the slave trade or slavery would actually have influenced the material interests of those who pressed for it, except, in some cases, adversely. So far as the attack on the British slave trade is concerned, as Seymour Drescher has recently argued in *Econocide: British Slavery in the Era of*

Abolition (1977), the whole theory of West Indian decline upon which Williams bases his thesis is without foundation. West Indian decline was the result, rather than the cause, of abolition.[4] Much the same may be said of the abolition of slavery itself, which further accelerated the decline process. As I attempted to show in an appendix to *British Antislavery, 1833–1870* (1972), the attack on West Indian slavery could not have been an attack on monopoly, since before 1833 a large proportion of the West Indian sugar crop was sold on the world market, which determined the price.[5] Rather, it was the abolition of slavery, which reduced production below that necessary to supply British needs, that created a monopoly, thus driving up prices and creating a demand for an end to differential tariffs. Nor is it easy to fall back on the alternative argument, often used in such cases, and say that what mattered were not economic realities but how men perceived them, since in each instance the results that ensued were widely predicted. Plausible though it might appear at first sight, and attractive though it might remain in theory, the truth is that the economic explanation fails to take account of the fact that slavery was itself very much a capitalist institution, that in general it offered a good return on investment, that it provided a plentiful supply of cheap raw materials, and that the usual effect of emancipation was to drive up the price of the products upon which the burgeoning industries of Europe and America depended.[6]

But if neither the economic nor the intellectual diffusionist accounts provide a satisfactory explanation, what alternatives are there? One obvious tactic, of course, is to try to link the two together. The problem here is that simple mixing does nothing to improve the quality of the initial ingredients. If both are defective, the same will inevitably be true of the final mixture. In the present instance, however, there is a special difficulty in that the two accounts are based not only on different but largely on diametrically opposing views of human nature. The intellectual diffusionists, in their explanation, place a high premium on disinterested benevolence and on the instinctive desire of those who were not themselves victims of, or indeed in any way implicated in, the practice of slaveholding to alleviate the sufferings of others. Williams, for his part, does not entirely discount this element. The abolitionists were "a brilliant band" and they, or at all events some of them, were genuine idealists. Nevertheless, their role has been "seriously misunderstood and grossly exaggerated," for what really destroyed the slave system was not altruism but greed, self-interest, and the lust for power—in other words, the same motives which had built it up in the first place. So unless we suppose, as

Williams does, that there were two quite separate groups involved, it is hard to see how the two views can be reconciled. That there *were* two groups is a theoretical possibility, but this is a view which, on the basis of the available evidence, it has so far proved impossible to substantiate, and in any case it is hard to see where the profit motive lay.

One possible way of getting out of this impasse, however, is to look again at the conceptual framework which historians have used. And here we may begin by noting that there is something essentially artificial about the way in which altruism and self-interest have been juxtaposed, as if they were the only motives from which the participants acted. Williams is plainly guilty of this, but so also are the traditionalists in their emphasis on those elements of right thinking and self-dedication which led W. E. H. Lecky in his *History of European Morals* (1884) to describe the crusade against slavery as "among the three or four perfectly virtuous pages comprised in the history of nations."[7] Large numbers of people, and certainly groups as large and variegated as those responsible for the overthrow of the slave trade and slavery, which of course included not only the abolitionists but all those who voted against these practices in Parliament and Congress, together with those who supported them in their efforts, are simply not moved, or at least not entirely moved, by abstract benevolence. Nor, for that matter, is economics, Adam Smith notwithstanding, merely the pursuit of individual self-interest. Adam Smith himself, significantly enough, disapproved of slavery for reasons which turn out on examination to have nothing to do with its immediate cost-effectiveness.[8] Thus even in his system, and no less strikingly in those of his successors, economics in this broader sense is seen as being concerned not merely, or even primarily, with how best to pursue short-term individual gains, but with the way in which societies actually do, or in theory should, order their affairs. Viewed in this way economics and benevolence no longer appear as opposing principles. As the Victorians in particular were well aware, the two could not only be reconciled but were often mutually supportive. Thus, whether we look at economic thought or at the possible range of motives which led large numbers of individuals, the great majority of whom were not abolitionists in the narrow sense, to turn against the slave trade and slavery, we find ourselves dealing with large-scale, and in many respects overlapping, systems of belief which are far too complex to be categorized in terms of either self-interest or benevolence.

To call these systems ideologies is, perhaps, to invite misunderstanding, although it is not clear what other word will suffice. Certainly it is not intended here to postulate a rigid set of assumptions which everyone opposed to slavery shared. Perhaps the word could be used in that sense with regard to some antislavery groups which expected a strict orthodoxy of belief on the part of their members, although even then there are distinctions that would need to be recognized. But if we take ideology to mean an assortment of beliefs and values shared by the members of a society and used by them to explain and guide social action, no such rigidity need be assumed. Such an ideology would be expected to change along with the society that produced it, and whose aspirations and beliefs it reflected. Nor should we expect that it would be logically consistent. Much of the impulse for change would come, in fact, from attempts to reconcile internal contradictions. Not surprisingly, many within the society would claim that their beliefs were not simply personal, or for that matter social, but represented universal truths. But whether they did or not is a question which might appropriately be left to philosophers or theologians; for present purposes they should be regarded as social products.

So how might such a concept be used to explain the development of the antislavery movement? One way to begin is to examine the character of the two societies, Britain and the northern United States, which found themselves in the forefront of the struggle. And here we may start by noting that both had experienced remarkable rates of economic growth in the course of the eighteenth century. Probably nowhere else in the world was the relative increase in wealth and population more striking than in the thirteen colonies. This, as we all know, was one of the factors which persuaded the British government to attempt to tighten its hold on the colonists, and so helped to precipitate the break with the mother country. Yet Britain's own rate of growth during these years, although less marked in relative terms, was also impressive, whether we compare it with what had happened in previous centuries or with the experiences of her political rivals. This was, as economic historians continually remind us, a period of crucial importance for the Western world. Instead of the rhythmic expansion and contraction of populations and their products which had taken place over the previous millennium, the gains of the eighteenth century represented the departure point from which began the sustained growth that has characterized the modern world. Britain and her ex-colonies were in the forefront of this development. Materially speaking, they had reason to feel proud of their achievement.[9]

A second characteristic that Britain and the northern states (as opposed to the South) shared was the fact that they had achieved this prosperity without direct recourse to slave labor, at least on any significant scale. To be sure, there was slavery in Britain right up to the end of the eighteenth century (the Somerset decision notwithstanding), and it lingered on in the northern states even longer. As late as 1820 there were still eighteen thousand slaves in the northeastern United States, and at the time of the first census in 1790 the figure was more than double that; but compared with the situation south of the Mason-Dixon line this represented a relatively modest stake in the institution. It must also be remembered that both Britain and the northern states had profited, and were continuing to profit on an ever-increasing scale, from the employment of slaves elsewhere. Nevertheless, the fact remains that, so far as their domestic arrangements were concerned, both were committed to an essentially free-labor system.

These points are too obvious to dwell on. Yet they are worth emphasizing if only because they help to explain why men in these two societies were so ready to accept ideas of progress, and in particular ideas of progress which linked individual freedom to material prosperity. The two, needless to say, are not necessarily connected. More often than not they have been seen as opposing principles, the assumption being that the pursuit of the one must necessarily entail the sacrifice of the other. Implicit in the whole idea of government is the belief that individual freedom must be given up to secure the benefits of an ordered society, among which must be included a measure of material satisfaction. How much freedom needs to be sacrificed is a matter of opinion, but history is not wanting in examples of societies welcoming tyrants because the alternatives of anarchy and lawlessness were regarded as even less acceptable. So the commonly expressed eighteenth century view that freedom and prosperity were not only reconcilable but mutually supportive, and that the more you had of the one the more you could expect of the other, is something that needs explaining. The explanation, I suggest, is to be found not in the ideas of the philosophers, still less in theories about the general progress of the human mind, but in the immediate lives of people of the period.

This, then, is one way of relating material and intellectual developments, and one that throws a good deal of light on the thinking of such figures as Adam Smith and the exponents of the secular antislavery argument generally. For what is striking about the secular case against slavery is the *assumption* that slavery was an economic anachronism. Smith's own attitudes are particulary revealing, because of all

eighteenth century commentators he was probably the one best qual-
ified to argue the case against it on strictly economic grounds. Yet, as
already noted, the case he actually presents is not based on economics
at all, at least not in any cost-accounting sense, but on the general
proposition that greater freedom would lead to greater prosperity.
Like other eighteenth century thinkers he expresses himself in terms
of universal principles, but at bottom it is a historical argument, derived from his own beliefs about the nature of the historical process.
Whatever the objective truths of Smith's arguments, the fact remains
that they are very much the product of one kind of society, and indeed of one particular class within that society.

An obvious objection to this argument is that, while it may very well
be true that Adam Smith rejected slavery for the reasons suggested,
it is by no means clear that other people did. Very few, after all, were
Smithians. The point that is being made here, however, is not that
Smith was important for his teachings (although Clarkson was happy
to cite him)[10] so much as for what he reflected about the continuing
processes that characterized the age in which he lived. Of course, not
even Smith himself realized that the Western world was entering a
new economic era. Nevertheless, it is evident that substantial increases in trade and improvements in agriculture had begun to be
made long before Smith's time and so were readily observable by his
contemporaries. Furthermore, if what is at issue here is the origin of
the Western idea of progress, it should be borne in mind that this
owed at least as much to developments in the field of knowledge as
to material changes. Certainly by the end of the seventeenth century
men not only knew more than their predecessors but knew that they
knew more.

Yet even if we grant that these developments go some way toward
explaining the secular case against slavery, it by no means follows that
they motivated the early leaders of the antislavery movement, most
of whom, if we may judge by the arguments they used, believed that
they were acting out of religious principles. This is a tricky problem
because by and large these principles stem directly from the Christian
tradition. But if, instead of following the Clarkson method of attempting to trace them back to their origins, we ask simply what it
was that brought them to the fore at this particular point in time, we
can perhaps make a start by observing that what was fundamental to
the whole attack on slavery was the belief that it was removable. Politics, we are continually reminded, is the art of the practical, but so
also are ethics practical in the sense that what is irremovable may be
deplorable, inconvenient, or embarrassing, but can scarcely be uneth-

ical. Ethics, in other words, implies optionality. Moralists may be more stringent in their views than politicians, but in this respect at least the underlying considerations are the same.

In a sense, of course, slavery always was removable to the extent that institutions men establish they can, given an adequate stimulus, usually get around to disestablishing. But until the eighteenth century that stimulus was generally lacking, with the result that slavery was accepted with that fatalism which men commonly reserve for aspects of nature which, whether they are to be celebrated or deplored, have to be borne. To argue against slavery was to argue against the facts of life. Before slavery could become a political issue—or even, in the proper sense, a moral issue—what needed to be shown was that the world could get along without it. And what better demonstration could there be than the development, within the heartland of Western civilization, of societies which not only did without slavery but which did very well without it, and which furthermore appeared to owe their quite remarkable dynamism to the acceptance of principles which represented the direct negation of the assumptions upon which slavery was founded.

This was not, of course, a development particularly likely to impress the inhabitants of those societies which relied directly on slave labor. They knew perfectly well how much they owed to their slaves, not only in a strictly economic sense, but for the maintenance of their whole way of life. They also knew that they were contributing in no small way to the prosperity of the free-labor societies by providing them with cheap raw materials and foodstuffs. And, by virtue of their position, they were well placed to judge the revolutionary nature of the abolitionists' demands—what a rapid shift from slave to free labor would mean in terms of political and social power. Often what they said in this regard was a great deal more realistic than anything said by their opponents. Yet the fact remains that as societies they were overshadowed by cultures whose values, deriving from a quite different set of historical experiences, were in the process of changing in ways that made the justification of slavery, even on hardheaded economic grounds, increasingly difficult.

What I am suggesting, in other words, is that the attack on slavery can be seen as an attempt by a dominant metropolitan ideology to impose its values on the societies of the economic periphery. And what I am also suggesting is that this attack was the product of a widening ideological gap occasioned by the extraordinary success, not least in material terms, of those societies which practiced a free-labor system, among which Britain and the northern United States were outstanding examples. For if we suppose that the manner in which societies gain their existence helps to form the ideas of their members as to how people in general should live, we must also, I think, concede that there were very powerful reasons why men in these two societies (and one could add France as a third) should have come to regard slavery as not only immoral but anachronistic.

This, of course, is a very different thing from saying that the promotion of their own economic interests *required* the abolition of slavery, because in most cases it did not. Nor is it necessary to argue that relative to the slaveholding societies the free-labor societies were becoming more powerful, although sometimes this was so. It was much easier for Britain to attack slavery after the departure of the American colonies. But by the same token it became correspondingly more perilous for the Americans themselves to do anything about it, and in the event little was done to remove the institution until war made action possible. Thus any general account which attributes the rise of the antislavery movement to considerations of economic necessity is open to serious objections.

Such objections can be avoided, however, if we think of the widening gap between the slaveholding and the nonslaveholding societies in ideological terms, always allowing that men tend to generalize from their own experiences, and that in the eighteenth century they took these sufficiently seriously to enunciate universal laws on the basis of them. It also seems to me that this approach has advantages over the intellectual diffusionist argument in that it does, from the outset, take account of the fact that ideas are rooted in the material conditions of life. The intellectual diffusionists do not, of course, ignore this fact, but their recognition of it is too often reluctant and belated, as when they argue that general trends in Protestant religious thought were antagonistic to slavery, and then admit that actually, in the slaveholding societies, precisely the opposite tendencies are evident. Southern clergymen, far from being critics of slavery, were among its principal defenders. Altogether it makes much more sense to admit from the start that the thrust for abolition emanated from the nonslaveholding societies and reflected their increasing buoyancy and self-confidence.

Yet even when this is taken into account it does not fully explain why, having decided that slavery was an anachronism, reformers in the metropolitan societies should have invested so much energy in securing its removal. After all, the perception of ideological differences, even differences affecting fundamental beliefs, does not necessarily or even usually lead to action. If slavery was indeed an anach-

ronism, why not simply let it wither away? Even in the case of the
slave trade, disapproval did not necessarily require that anything be
done about it, still less that Britain, having herself withdrawn from the
traffic, should go to such lengths to ensure that other nations did the
same. Nor are historical parallels of much help. In the fourteenth
and fifteenth centuries, the Italian commercial city-states experienced a tremendous acceleration in wealth and power which pushed
them ahead of most of the Mediterranean world economically, with
an accompanying cultural gap as well. Commercial labor was free labor, although slave labor continued to be used for agricultural and
domestic purposes. Yet there is no evidence that these dominant metropolitan centers tried to impose antislavery values derived from
their experience with free labor, even though one might have supposed that domestic slavery would have been easier to remove than
plantation slavery. Why, then, did the metropolitan powers of the late
eighteenth and early nineteenth centuries feel such a compelling
need to reach out and remake the world in their own image?

  To explain this phenomenon three further points must be noted.
The first is that the achievements of the Italian states, impressive
though they were, were confined to one small section of the globe,
beyond which lay a vast and unknown world. It was, moreover, a section of the globe which had seen the rise and fall of empires going
back over millennia. It is not without relevance that the flowering of
these states is known as the Renaissance. By contrast, there was no
precedent for the achievements of the dominant powers of the eighteenth and nineteenth centuries. In terms of scientific knowledge and
its application in the form of technology they were breaking new
ground. Their colonies and trading networks spanned the entire
globe. For the first time in history it had become possible—one might
almost say necessary—to believe in universal human progress.

  The second point to be noted concerns the impact of these developments on religion. The idea that individuals stood in need of improvement lay, of course, at the heart of the whole Christian system
of belief. So also did the notion that societies should be ordered in
such a way as to bring about such improvement. In theory, at any
rate, this was the source from which most European rulers derived
their authority. But in practice there had always been room for differences of opinion as to the precise form which improvement should
take. In large part this was because of the way in which religious belief and practice reflected social needs and aspirations. Thus in some
cases what passed for Christian behavior might have little to do with
belief as such, as when the early explorers of Africa, Asia, and

America described themselves as Christians and the native peoples they encountered as either heathens or savages.

Few would nowadays regard Europe's rise to dominance as a specifically Christian achievement. Nevertheless, contemporaries could not but be impressed by the fact that it was the Christian nations which had created the new world order. One consequence of Europe's expansion was to open up vast new areas to missionary activity. And, as with other missionary enterprises in the past, it is clear that what was being conveyed was much more than simply Christianity. More to the point, however, is the way in which these developments cast doubt on Christianity as conceived of in a purely spiritual or otherworldly sense. Eric Williams, as already noted, credited the abolitionists with "raising anti-slavery sentiments almost to the status of a religion in England."[11] Some years earlier Gilbert Hobbes Barnes in *The Antislavery Impulse* (1933) noted how, in the United States, changes in Calvinist thinking transformed the Great Revival of the 1820s into the antislavery crusade of the 1830s.[12] More recently, Ronald G. Walters in *The Antislavery Appeal* (1977) has gone a step further by arguing that in its later stages in the United States antislavery actually *was* "a highly generalized, all-encompassing religion of humanity."[13]

Yet if this was the case, and what we know of the history of the American movement in those years suggests that in large part it was, we may wonder whether in some measure the same might not also be true of antislavery generally. What I am suggesting, in other words, is that antislavery can be seen as a secularized or semi-secularized form of Christian evangelism, the secular components of which reflected the ideological set of the dominant metropolitan cultures. Broadly viewed, it was part of that process, observable in relation to other issues too, which led to evangelical beliefs becoming more secular and secular beliefs becoming more evangelical. In this sense, one might say, it represented a halfway house between the religious ideologies of earlier times and the more strictly secular ideologies of the modern era.

The third point that needs to be noted concerns the relationship between these events and the advent of modern nationalism. In his *Caution and Warning* (1767) Anthony Benezet quotes a West Indian visitor's observation that "it is a Matter of Astonishment, how a People who, as a Nation, are looked upon as generous and humane, and so much value themselves for their uncommon Sense of the Benefit of Liberty, can live in the Practice of such extreme Oppression and Inhumanity, without seeing the Inconsistency of such Conduct, and without feeling great Remorse."[14] He himself goes on to comment,

"How the *British* Nation [his italics] first came to be concerned in a Practice, by which the Rights and Liberties of Mankind are so violently infringed . . . is indeed surprising."[15] In the same year Nathaniel Appleton, a member of the Boston Committee of Correspondence, in his *Considerations on Slavery* castigated his fellow Bostonians by declaring "Oh! ye sons of liberty, pause a moment, give me your ear. Is your conduct consistent? Can you review our late struggles for liberty, and think of the slave-trade at the same time and not blush?"[16] Thus what concerned even these early critics of the slave trade and slavery—and their message was taken up and repeated endlessly in the debates in Parliament and Congress—was not simply that these practices were wrong, but that it was their own nations that endorsed them. Of course, this was an obvious tactic to adopt, since Parliament and Congress had the power to redress some—in the case of Parliament, all—of their grievances. But it is plain that what the abolitionists were appealing to was also an already widely held belief that their nations were the custodians of certain values which distinguished them from other nations, and which it was the duty of their respective governments to uphold.

It may be argued, of course, that there was nothing essentially new in this. There had been a time, after all, when oaths of allegiance and assent to the Thirty-nine Articles had been regarded as tests of who did and who did not belong to the body politic. But what was new, or largely new anyway, was the way in which, particularly in the case of Britain and the United States, this sense of nationhood was now seen as being linked to values associated with growth and progress. This was perhaps most evident in the case of the United States, which saw itself as representing a new departure in human government, one which, as its virtues became apparent, would serve as an inspiration to the rest of mankind. The British, for their part, although less naively optimistic, took a not dissimilar view of themselves, at least to the extent that they saw their nation as leading the world not merely in a political sense but in a technological and economic sense too.

No doubt similar trends, although perhaps less marked, can be identified in the case of other Western powers. Certainly, so far as Britain and the northern United States were concerned, slavery had come to seem not only an anachronism but a challenge to their progressive ideals. For that reason it could not simply be left to disappear of its own accord, which might take a very long time. Indeed, given the political influence and determination of the slaveholding interests, there was no assurance that it would happen at all. Thus the abolition of slavery and, as a first step, the abolition of its most objectionable and vulnerable feature, the slave trade, was something that had to be fought for. Fighting for it, moveover, meant not simply liberating slaves in distant colonies and states, but upholding ideals which would eventually find expression in countless other causes from criminal law reform to women's rights.

That the slave trade and slavery were the principal concerns of early humanitarian reformers is understandable enough. They symbolized in a peculiarly graphic way man's inhumanity to man and the total denial of human liberty. Yet their choice as objects of attack is not without irony. Over the years slavery had contributed significantly to the material prosperity of the metropolitan powers; to a considerable degree it was still doing so. Yet that material prosperity, by opening men's eyes to the potentialities of the new world order, had created an ideology in terms of which neither the slave trade nor slavery could be regarded as either necessary or morally acceptable.

NOTES

1 Thomas Clarkson, *The History of the Rise, Progress and Accomplishment of the African Slave Trade by the British Parliament*, 2 vols. (London, 1808), 1:259.

2 Frank Klingberg, *The Anti-Slavery Movement in England* (New Haven, 1926). David Brion Davis, *The Problem of Slavery in Western Culture* (Ithaca, 1966).

3 Eric Williams, *Capitalism and Slavery* (Chapel Hill, N.C., 1944), pp. 136, 178, 181.

4 Seymour Drescher, *Econocide: British Slavery in the Era of Abolition* (Pittsburgh, 1977).

5 Howard Temperley, *British Antislavery, 1833–1870* (London, 1972), pp. 273–76.

6 Howard Temperley, "Capitalism, Slavery and Ideology," *Past and Present*, no. 75 (May, 1977), pp. 94–118.

7 W. E. H. Lecky, *A History of European Morals*, 6th ed., 2 vols. (London, 1884), 2:153.

8 Adam Smith, *An Inquiry into the Nature and Causes of the Wealth of Nations*, ed. Edwin Cannan, 2 vols. in 1 (1904; reprint ed., Chicago, 1977), 1:411–13.

9 Howard Temperley, "Anti-Slavery as a Form of Cultural Imperialism," in Christine Bolt and Seymour Drescher, eds., *Anti-Slavery, Religion, and Reform: Essays in Memory of Roger Anstey* (Folkestone, England, 1980), pp. 335–50.

10 Clarkson, *History of Abolition*, 1:85–86.

11 Williams, *Capitalism and Slavery*, p. 181.

12 Gilbert Hobbes Barnes, *The Antislavery Impulse* (Washington, D.C., 1933), pp. 3–16.

13 Ronald G. Walters, *The Antislavery Appeal: American Abolitionism after 1830* (Baltimore, 1977), p. 51.

14 Anthony Benezet, *A Caution and Warning* (1767), in *Am I Not a Man and a Brother: The Antislavery Crusade of Revolutionary America, 1688–1788*, ed. Roger Bruns (New York, 1977), p. 114.

15 Ibid., p. 124.

16 Nathaniel Appleton, *Considerations on Slavery* (1767), in Bruns, ed., p. 136.

CHAPTER 3: **Religion and British Slave Emancipation**

Roger Anstey

In our study of British antislavery in an earlier period, *The Atlantic Slave Trade and British Abolition, 1760–1810*,[1] we attached special importance to intellectual and theological change, to religious dynamism, to the political weight of ministers of the Talents Ministry of 1806–7, to the brilliant stroke of taking advantage of a fortuitous politico-economic conjuncture in 1806 to abolish two-thirds of the British slave trade, and to the final 1807 abolition measure as manifestly against the national interest.

For sixteen years after 1807 the British antislavery movement was dominated by a concern to end the continued participation of foreigners in the slave trade, as this was confidently expected to lead to the speedy amelioration of slave conditions.[2] The only significant variation from this approach, apart from protests at cruelties inflicted on slaves, was to urge slave registration, formally a device for preventing the illicit importation of slaves, but which also enshrined the principle of statutory intervention in slave conditions.[3]

It was in 1821–22 that a concern to act against slavery itself emerged. Probably it was James Cropper, a Liverpool Quaker, who initiated action. Along with William Roscoe, William Rathbone IV, and William Rathbone V, Cropper was a member of a small liberal-radical, nonconformist group which had been important in Liverpool's earlier exertions against the British slave trade. Now in 1821, whether consciously or not, Cropper showed himself in an earlier tradition by concentrating on the impolicy of slavery. In a series of letters to Wilberforce, published in the *Liverpool Mercury*, he took for granted the inhumanity of slavery and argued that the key to the abolition of slavery lay in the equalization of duties on East and West Indian sugar, for once free-grown East India sugar competed on equal terms, the old West India system would be doomed and the way paved for slave emancipation.[4] Cropper also urged this course on Zachary Macaulay, and it was probably due to one or both of them that that polymath of benevolence, the London Quaker William Allen, obtained from the Yearly Meeting of 1822 authorization for the Meeting for Sufferings "to take any measures for the gradual abolition of slavery" pending the next Yearly Meeting.[5]

At this same time the aging Wilberforce was in the process of handing over the parliamentary leadership of the abolitionist party to T. F. Buxton, a fellow Evangelical, and it was as a result of discussions between Buxton, Wilberforce, Macaulay, Stephen, Cropper, Allen, Dr. Lushington (a lawyer and M.P.), Samuel Hoare (a London Quaker), and Lord Suffield (an Evangelical) and probably others that the Society for the Mitigation and Gradual Abolition of Slavery throughout the British Dominions was founded in January 1823.[6] In mid-May Buxton moved in the Commons that "the state of slavery is repugnant to the principles of the British Constitution and of the Christian Religion; and that it ought to be gradually abolished throughout the British Colonies with as much expedition as may be found consistent with a due regard to the wellbeing of the parties concerned." Hardly a radical proposal, yet only a much watered down version expressed in three resolutions was acceptable to Canning and the ministry. The essence of government policy was now amelioration with a view to eventual freedom—though the word itself was carefully eschewed. The government would leave the colonies themselves to enact the necessary measures, save in the Crown colonies where it could act by order-in-council, but the imperial Parliament would step in if the colonial response was insufficient.[7]

In the next ten years little effective action was in fact taken. How do we explain this? It is, firstly, the case that the West Indian representation in the Commons was significantly stronger in the three parliaments of the 1820s than it had been on the eve of the 1806–7 abolition. Barry Higman, using G. P. Judd's figures and supplementary evidence, finds, on a restrained definition of "West Indian," nineteen West Indians in the 1806 parliament, thirty-nine in 1820, forty in 1826, and thirty-six in 1830. Lushington, who had family connections in the West Indies, using an extended definition, arrived at a figure of fifty-six in 1825, which is also broadly supported by P. F. Dixon. This is certainly to be preferred to the wild figure of about 200 cited by Buxton and Stephen—though that figure is significant as suggesting that the abolitionist leadership may have been unnecessarily overawed. We have no figure for peers with West Indian connections in 1806, but Dixon has identified thirty-three in that house between 1821 and 1833.[8]

If the West Indians in the Commons were more numerous than at the beginning of the century, it would appear that committed abolitionists were fewer. Dixon's researches, together with supplementary enquiry, suggest a maximum of thirty-one and a minimum of fifteen.[9] In the Lords there just was no visible abolitionist group. There is also an interesting qualitative contrast with the situation three decades earlier. Whereas Tories constituted the largest single faction in the abolitionist group in 1796, only five (plus two more possibly) out of the maximum size group of thirty-one were not liberals in the 1820s.[10] The abolitionist party, especially after Wilberforce's retirement in 1825, had become predominantly liberal, and in this connection it is of some significance that the Whigs were out of office until 1830.

We may also invoke as a cause of failure the inability to harness free trade to the cause of emancipation, as Cropper had urged and as the Antislavery Society had accepted. Essentially this was because the East India merchants did not see on which side, in the Cropperian dispensation, their bread was buttered, and because the mercantile community generally could not be brought to link the cause of emancipation to that of free trade. "Our E. I. merchants have many of them opposing Interests and will not contribute [to Anti-Slavery Society funds]," lamented Cropper, himself an East Indian, in 1822; "I wish," sighed Macaulay six years later, "I could . . . see our commercial and manufacturing bodies duly affected with the evil effects of monopoly, and with a sense of the extensive benefits which cannot fail to result from its complete extinction."[11] To lend statistical support, Dixon has conclusively demonstrated that the 130 East Indians in the Commons between 1823 and 1830 provided a mere 19 of the 198 speakers or voters on the abolition side in the period.[12]

Finally, public opinion, though fully seized of the horrors of the slave trade, was seemingly not aware of the actual evils of plantation slavery. As Burn has shown, the abolitionist newspapers and periodicals were counterbalanced by others with more cautious views, and the former were too often of limited circulation, or featured emancipation only infrequently.[13]

The abolition campaign in the years 1823–30 had, then, achieved nothing significant; yet there was a longer term significance in the abolitionist activity of the period. The Anti-Slavery Society had not only come into being, but was quite efficiently organized; the tried devices of the provincial tour and of petitioning Parliament were again resorted to, and with more effect in terms of the number of petitions instigated and local associations formed. More use was made of the large public meeting, and one important departure made (not without fears that it would involve the fair sex in a unwomanly role)—the foundation of numerous ladies' antislavery associations.[14]

More important, the antislavery movement had already formed an important connection with religious dissent, and from 1829–30 onwards this was to blossom into a major force. This connection must be studied at three levels, the first of which is the theological.

To begin with, Evangelicalism—and dissent was by now largely Evangelical—had a substantial inheritance which, we have argued in our earlier work, had an important relevance to a dynamic of action against slavery. Evangelicals believed in the centrality in religious faith and experience of salvation through the redemptive work of Christ. They had a heightened sense of Providence as the sustaining power in the moral order, with the necessary implication of a coherent, if disturbing, philosophy of history. Equally, their lively sense of a particular Providence directing their own lives was an inescapable summons to mold the world to a righteousness which would avert national catastrophe, relieve the earthly sufferings of men, and pave the way for the salvation of men's eternal souls. For the Evangelical, slavery stood particularly condemned. This was because he apprehended salvation not least through the concept of redemption, and when he related the role of redemption, in its existential, individual application, to God's great redemptive purpose as made known in the Old Testament, he saw that, historically, redemption was release from physical bondage as well as from sin. Moreover, either because the influential Granville Sharp, in particular, had discussed the limited nature of the situational factors which, in the pages of Scripture, might seem to justify slavery, or because slavery must be subject to the total demands of the Law of love, virtually all forms of contemporary slavery stood condemned.[15]

Early nineteenth century dissent added to this heritage by a theological shift in emphasis which accommodated antislavery in a more conscious way than formerly. This can be seen in the writings of the Reverend Richard Watson, the most notable Methodist theologian in the four decades after John Wesley's death and one of Methodism's most influential preachers. In its fundamentals Watson's theology differed little both from that of Methodism's founder and from that of the Anglican evangelical luminaries of that same generation. The great themes of the Majesty of God, the depravity of man, and the salvation available through the redemptive work of Christ dominate his 123 published sermons and his *Theological Institutes* alike.[16] The tone throughout is concern for the spiritual, with the affairs of "the world" referred to only as frequently as is necessary to stress their subordination. Of course, the affairs of the world are linked to the world of the spirit in the frame of Providence. Watson, like a Stephen or a Wilberforce before him, saw the fall of France in 1814, for instance, as an assertion of God's honor and justice, Napoleon having "arrived at that point of arrogance which always by a law of Providence touches upon disaster." Britain, on the other hand, had escaped the sword because of the "diffusion of vital godliness."[17] There is an interesting contrast, however, in the ways Watson and Wesley conceived the growth of the Kingdom of God. For Wesley "The General Spread of the Gospel," to use the title of a key sermon on the subject, began with "a few young men in the University of Oxford"; thereafter, in his own metaphor, the leaven was conceived as spreading first through Britain, thence into America and to other Protestant countries. Thereafter countries where Protestantism and Catholicism coexisted would be the bridgehead to "those countries that were merely papish." Penultimately, the regenerate quality of Christian lives would bring in the savage and the heathen, while finally Israel herself would be saved and "the day of the Lord Jesus" would come. At another level, the extension of the bounds of the Kingdom would simply be from the least to the greatest, with kings and princes belatedly entering in with a tardiness exceeded only by "the wise and learned, the men of genius [and] the philosophers."[18] One cannot say that Wesley had no interest in the future temporal state of the world: it is just that he saw its fallen state as remediable only in terms of salvation and eschatology.

Watson, for his part, echoed Wesley's central assertion that the Gospel should be preached to all nations and that then the end would come.[19] But he was more prepared to allow temporal events along the way some significance. Commerce, for instance, was an "important instrument . . . of civil and religious improvement," a handmaid of the Gospel. Almost conversely, religion "was the most efficient instrument of civilization," and that role was worthy in itself, for religion was "the parent of morality, industry, and public spirit, the foundation and the topstone, the strength and the sinews, of all well-ordered society."[20]

A more schematic view of the purposes of Christ for humankind is contained in the second sermon on Ezekiel's vision. We know, says Watson, what is the design of God:

> His design is, that truth, the truth of the Gospel, shall be freely and universally proclaimed; that Christ shall be universally believed in and adored; that the purity, and justice, and kindness of his religion shall influence all the institutions of society; that all public vice shall be suppressed; that all public oppression and wrong shall be removed; that all nations, in a word, shall be blessed in Christ, that is, be brought into an enlightened, a holy, and a happy condition by the influence, of the Gospel.

To this end error must be banished and "its Papal and Mohammaden advocates must be put down"; there must be revolutionary change "in the low as well as in the high ranks" and "if all oppression and wrong are to be put down, what must become," Watson significantly adds, "of those combinations of men who would rivet for ever the fetters of the slave?" Not all of these changes, however, are to be "violent and tumultuous"; peaceful changes are

> more beneficial than those resulting from any alteration in the external form and condition of society, from the change of dynasties, and the different adjustment of the balance of power among nations: there are the mild and beneficial changes produced by the arts, by science, by education, by commerce, by civilization, and, above all, by the revival of the religion of Christ in old countries, and its introduction into new. . . . I see greater changes produced by the late revival of religion in England, infinitely more beneficial and permanent, than if there had been a political revolution every month.[21]

This last sentence reminds us of both Watson's traditional Wesleyan political conservatism and his quietism, and puts into perspective the function and significance of moral progress. It is not part of our contention to exaggerate the importance of temporal affairs in Watson's view of the future. But it is highly significant that a positive sense of the ancillary role of the extension of civilization and commerce and a concern for the end of abuses and the refinement of manners are woven in with Watson's theology, for it is into such a view that a growing conviction that slavery is a major evil so aptly fits. We must, indeed, reckon with the paradox that a basically spiritual view of the world was the dynamic for dealing with "mere" temporal evils.

Watson epitomized Wesleyan theology in his generation, as well as being its most comprehensive exponent. We know, moreover, that not only Quakerism but Congregationalism and the Baptist sects had become "evangelicalized" by about the turn of the eighteenth and nineteenth centuries, and from this may conclude that their theologies had much in common.[22] Of course, each dissenting sect had its varying emphasis, but these are barely relevant in our context.

The second level of the connection between dissent and antislavery stemmed from the missionary activity in the West Indies which the Methodists most extensively, but the Baptists and Congregationalists as well, had pioneered. From 1784 the Reverend Dr. Thomas Coke, Wesley's right-hand man, had in a highly personal way coordinated a work which had been started spontaneously by Methodist lay people—resident whites or émigré British—and which thereafter received a trickle of missionaries. Coke himself was an ordained clergyman of the established church, but had been driven from the curacy of South Peterton on account of his evangelical preaching. When, following his expulsion, Coke asked Wesley what he should then do, Wesley is said to have replied, in a classically evangelical formulation: "Brother, go out, go out and preach the Gospel to all the world!" It was Coke who in 1783 drew up his "Plan of the Society for the Establishment of Missions among the Heathens," and who was henceforth to devote his life to that cause.[23] For many years the fundraising to finance the dispatch of missionaries was in Coke's hands, but from 1813 onward formalization of this haphazard approach was begun with the establishment of district missionary societies within the Methodist connection, a labor in which Bunting and Watson played the leading roles.[24] In 1816 a central secretariat for the whole Methodist body was established, with Watson as the first, part-time secretary, and by the time of slave emancipation, missions were established in Antigua, the Bahamas, Barbados, the Bermudas, British Guiana, British Honduras, Dominica, Grenada, Jamaica, Saint Christopher, Saint Eustatius, Saint Kitts, Saint Vincent, Tortola, and Trinidad, not to mention independent Haiti.

Despite the fact that the beginnings of dissenting missionary endeavor in the West Indies coincided with the inception of the British antislavery movement, none of the missions saw their role as including antislavery propaganda. Coke himself modified his initial condemnation of "the evil of keeping them [Negroes] in slavery" in the harsh light of the prevalence of a slave-based economy in the Caribbean and the southern United States.[25] In the West Indies particularly the missionaries were dependent on planter tolerance for their very ability to preach and to reside. Instructions to missionaries in 1818 or

1819 said specifically that "your only business is to promote the moral and religious improvement of the slaves . . . without in the least degree, in public or in private, interfering with their civil condition."[26] Indeed, in 1824 it half seemed that Wesleyan missionaries in Jamaica had not only learned to live with slavery but positively to tolerate it, for in that year four of the ten on the island, including the chairman of the district, signed a resolution asserting that slave emancipation would do harm.[27]

In fact, such compromising was not to be. The many attacks on missionaries, physical or verbal, had already inspired Watson, secretary of the Missionary Society since 1816, to publish *A Defence of the Wesleyan Methodist Missions in the West Indies* in 1817, and his biographer, the Methodist historian Thomas Jackson, believed that the disclosures made therein by the missionaries of the brutal ignorance of the slave and "the state of oppression under which he groaned" began to influence religious opinion, as did the restrictions on the liberty of preaching which the planters attempted to impose.[28] Then in 1823 Rev. William Shrewsbury's chapel in Bridgetown, Barbados, had been sacked by resident whites. Although the Missionary Society was strangely backward in having the matter raised in Parliament—it could call on the services of two Methodist M.P.s, Thomas Thompson and Joseph Butterworth, but the protest was made by Buxton acting on his own initiative[29]—one feels that such an action, coming after numerous other acts of violence, intimidation, and obstruction, could only render hostility to slavery more positive.[30]

There were further reasons why the mid-twenties were a minor watershed in the evolution of Wesleyan opinion. The still young but increasingly influential Jabez Bunting—soon to be termed the Methodist Pope—having joined Watson as a mission secretary for the period 1818–20, returned to that post in 1821 and remained in it until 1824. Also a member of the recently formed Anti-Slavery Society's Corresponding Committee, he was one of the Society's most active leaders at this time. With Watson a mission secretary until 1826, it is not difficult to credit that the two leading men in Wesleyan Methodism should exert themselves to give the same positive quality to Methodism's antislavery witness as Bunting already had given, and Watson was to give, to the activities of the Anti-Slavery Society.[31] This, indeed, is the third level of the connection between dissent and antislavery.

A difference in Wesleyan attitudes was soon evident. Whereas the influential *Wesleyan Methodist Magazine* had stated in mid-1824 that "by what particular steps the removal of the evil [slavery] may be brought about, it is not our immediate province to enquire,"[32] now the action of the Jamaica missionaries was specifically disavowed. Not only were some of the offending missionaries recalled, but the Wesleyan London Committee put on record that "the Wesleyan Body . . . hold it to be the duty of every Christian Government to bring the practice of slavery to an end as soon as can be done prudently, safely, and with a just consideration of the interests of all parties concerned; and that the degradation of men merely on account of their colour, and the holding of human beings in interminable bondage, are wholly inconsistent with Christianity."[33] Next, Watson, probably the author of this statement, certainly drew up and steered through the July 1825 Wesleyan Conference a resolution which, though it affirmed the Christian slaves' duty of obedience, asserted "the *equally Christian* duty of the religious public *at home*, on the other hand, to promote by legislative measures the ultimate extinction of the system of slavery."[34] By early the next year this stance had blossomed into the editorial hope of the *Wesleyan Methodist Magazine* that the eulogized initiative of the Anti-Slavery Society would be rewarded by "numerous petitions to Parliament"—and we know that Watson had a good deal of influence in what went into the *Magazine*.[35]

During most of 1826 and through 1827, 1828, and the first half of 1829, there are few references to antislavery in the *Wesleyan Magazine*. This merely reflected the passivity of the Anti-Slavery Society in the same period, but, interestingly, whereas the latter came to life at the turn of 1829 and 1830, the Wesleyan Conference in July 1829 had already urged Wesleyans to join with their fellow Christians in petitions for the mitigation and ultimate abolition of slavery.[36] This initiative could have been due to Watson or to Richard Matthews, or to both. During 1830 the Wesleyan Methodist organization took further action against slavery. At the traditional May meeting of the Wesleyan Missionary Society (it was already the custom for various evangelical societies to hold public meetings in London annually in May, and it was evidently for this reason that the committee of the Anti-Slavery Society wrote a May public meeting into its standing orders at this time) Watson listed the Wesleyan missionaries who had suffered imprisonment in Jamaica: Campbell, Williams, Wiggins, Grimsdall, Whitehouse, and Orton, of whom Grimsdall subsequently died—an impressive roll call.[37] Their sufferings were elaborated upon in an appendix to the Missionary Society's report for 1829, together with accounts of the persecution of two slaves, Henry Williams and a black simply called George, for attending Methodist chapels in Jamaica.[38]

Despite the absence of any specific linking of emancipation and religious persecution, the most obtuse hearer would have made the appropriate connection.

Then at the conference in July 1830 the connection was specifically made. The call for petitions was repeated and particularly enjoined upon Methodists because of the church's missionary labors in the West Indies. Another departure was the summons, not merely to join in petitioning, but for the petitions to be "from each congregation, to be signed at its own chapel."[39] There is no indication of how many specifically Wesleyan petitions there were by April 1831, but even by 17 November, 370 had been entrusted to the Anti-Slavery Committee, while 1,578 out of a total of 1,626 were presented in the Lords on the previous day.[40] Nor was this the full extent of Wesleyan activity, for the same Leeds Conference that put petitioning on a confessional basis unequivocally enjoined upon Methodists the step of securing pledges from candidates in the July general election, of urging them to "give their influence and votes only to those candidates who pledge themselves to support in Parliament the most effectual measures for the entire abolition of slavery throughout the colonies of the British Empire."[41] Again we are told, as is entirely credible, that it was under Watson's guidance that the radical step of securing pledges, together with other antislavery resolutions, was taken by the governing body of a church which had traditionally been firmly conservative.[42]

What is true of the Methodists and the antislavery movement is true in varying measure of the other (Protestant) dissenting sects. All had been affected by persecution of their missionaries, and the death of the Congregational missionary John Smith when in jail under sentence of death seems to have had a particular effect.[43] They had also been brought closer to each other by the Evangelicalism which, save for the Unitarians, they had come to hold in common since the beginning of the century. Much involved in antislavery were a leading Baptist divine, Rev. Joseph Ivimey, and a Congregationalist and the vice president of the Protestant Dissenting Deputies, the Reverend Henry Waymouth.[44] In a number of ways, too, pains were taken to enlist and encourage the support of dissent for antislavery.[45] But whatever the contribution of the Society of Friends to the councils and the coffers of the Anti-Slavery Society, with a membership of about 16,000 the Quakers could not constitute a potentially important body of support in the country, while significant as was the numerical strength of Anglican evangelicals in the country, there was no organization for mobilizing it comparable to that of the Methodists.[46] Certainly on the Anti-Slavery Committee Quakers and Anglicans of the evangelical

Buxton stamp were more numerous than any other sect, but in anti-slavery as a whole the Methodists appeared to contemporaries to have been of primary importance. As early as August 1830 the diarist Greville observed that "it is astonishing the interest the people generally take in the slavery question, which is the work of the Methodists, and shows the enormous influence they have in the country."[47] At the April 1831 General Meeting of the Anti-Slavery Society, Sir James Mackintosh observed that "the Wesleyans were at present most conspicuous in the cause," a claim which another speaker, Daniel O'Connell, who had had his conflicts with them, endorsed.[48]

But if it is legitimate to cite evidence from early in 1831 for a pressure we are so far only concerned to trace up to the second half of 1830, we would make clear that from mid-1830 onward it is convenient again to study the antislavery movement as a whole rather than to single out religious and other threads separately. Much of what it is important thus far to grasp about the significance of the missionary involvement for antislavery is subsumed in Thomas Jackson's comment: "The establishment of Missionary Societies [i.e., the local societies within the Wesleyan body] and the holding of public Meetings in connexion with them, formed the commencement of a new era among the Wesleyan Methodists. . . . The generality of the Methodist societies, in all parts of the United Kingdom, feel themselves allied to converted negroes in the West Indies, to the pious Hottentots and Caffers in South Africa, the Hindoos and Ceylonese, and the inhabitants of the South Sea Islands."[49] Not less important was the way in which Watson attested the evolution of a theological position regarding missionary enterprise and slavery. In such a progression he cannot have been alone. Addressing the annual meeting of the Wesleyan Missionary Society in May 1830, he observed: "It struck me while the Report was in reading, that all our Missionary enterprises, all our attempts to spread Christianity abroad, do, in point of fact, tend to increase our sympathies with the external circumstances of the oppressed and miserable of all lands. It is impossible for men to care for the souls of others without caring for their bodies also. . . . We cannot care for the salvation of the negro, without caring for his emancipation from bondage."[50]

The very ingenuousness of the realization that evangelism could generate concern for the temporal condition of its beneficiaries is sufficient indication that major temporal triumphs may follow from purely spiritual concerns.

In October 1829 an editorial in the *Anti-Slavery Monthly Reporter* referred to the "torpor" on the slavery question which had "seized, with a few rare exceptions, on all classes."[51] In the following February, however, largely as a result of an interview with the colonial secretary in the Duke of Wellington's government, the Anti-Slavery Society committee, at least, had been brought to a sense that more urgent action was needed than the government had in contemplation if slavery was not to continue "for ages yet to come."[52] The next three and a half years saw a rising tempo of antislavery agitation with five main characteristics.

Firstly, traditional tactics were pressed forward with more vigor and success, especially the large public meeting and petitioning. The meeting convened by the Anti-Slavery Society committee in the Freemasons' Hall in May 1830, for instance, attracted an audience of 3,000, with several hundred more unable to gain admission.[53] Petitioning, too, reached new heights, with no less than 5,020 petitions against slavery presented to the first reformed Parliament in the opening months of 1833, and with the total number of antislavery petitions in this period far outstripping the number urging political reform.[54] Secondly, provincial support was canvassed by novel methods. The inspiration behind this departure was a group of radical abolitionists gathered around George Stephen, a younger son of James Stephen the elder. They conceived the idea of appointing paid antislavery agents, or lecturers, who would the more effectively arouse antislavery feeling in the country. Originally, if somewhat guardedly, accepted by the Anti-Slavery Society committee, the more radically inclined group around Stephen broke away in 1832 to form the Agency Anti-Slavery Society. The new approach was most effective, leading to the formation of up to 1,300 provincial antislavery associations.[55] Thirdly, and constituting an important inspiration of this last development, was the growth of immediatism in the British (as in the American) antislavery movement. David Davis has traced the origins of immediatism with particular reference to the pamphlet of the Quakeress Mrs. Elizabeth Heyrick, *Immediate not Gradual Abolition* (1824), which asserted that since antislavery was a war against the powers of darkness there could be no delay and no compromise—no gradualism. The opening paragraph of the instructions to the stipendiary agents makes the point with total clarity: "The system of colonial slavery is a crime in the sight of God, and ought to be immediately and for ever abolished."[56] Fourthly, because of the initiatives particularly of Lushington in the Anti-Slavery Society, and of Watson both in the Society and in the Wesleyan Methodist Conference, voters in parliamentary elections were urged to pledge their votes only to candidates who would agree to support immediate abolition if returned.[57] Although used as an electioneering device on previous occasions, it seems not previously to have been used on the scale it was used in the December 1832 elections. Moreover, it was regarded as a politically radical device, and it is interesting that the most conservative of all nonconformist denominations, the Wesleyans, should actively promote this technique. A fifth development was the forging of still closer ties between the two antislavery societies and nonconformity, especially the Wesleyan and Baptists, in the very particular political atmosphere of mid-1832 to mid-1833.

Not only from mid-1832 to mid-1833 but from 1830 onward, the political atmosphere of Britain had been dominated by the reform question.[58] That question had complex interactions with the achievement of emancipation. One clear effect of the preoccupation with reform was to inhibit antislavery activity. It is clear that during the reform crisis even ardent antislavery men soft-pedalled emancipation.[59] This was in part because, as the reformers that most of them were, they feared that to pursue both objects simultaneously would prejudice reform, and, as abolitionists, they believed that emancipation was most likely to be attained on the flood tide of achieved political reform. This holding back, however, did not prevent the building up of antislavery organization and sentiment—just the inception of a full-blooded Westminster campaign.

As for the ministry, its role was indeed modest; Howick, undersecretary in the Colonial Office, made very clear in private letters to his father, the prime minister, that no serious thought was given to a policy on slavery either by the ineffective colonial secretary, Goderich, or by a cabinet distracted by reform and many other pressing problems. With the virtual completion of the Reform Bill in June 1832, however, the political situation for emancipation changed greatly, especially as a dissolution of Parliament soon followed, and because nonconformist antislavery feeling reached a new pitch of intensity in the aftermath of the Jamaica slave rising of December 1831. This rising was the result of injudicious planter conduct, of some slaves seeing in the idea of Christian freedom a physical dimension, and of frustrated slave expectations resulting from demographic "imbalance" caused by the cessation of slave imports since 1807. One characteristic of its altogether vicious aftermath was the persecution of missionaries and slave converts alike. Buxton believed that nothing did more to arouse the religious public, and so did Macaulay. "The religious persecutions in Jamaica," the latter wrote to Brougham, "however have aroused them [the Methodists and dissenters] to a feeling of intense interest in the matter and they have not only caught

fire themselves but have succeeded in igniting the whole country."[60]
So strong was the feeling that the abolitionist leaders, in May 1832,
were alarmed at the militancy of their cohorts,[61] but a dissolution of
Parliament in August shifted attention to influencing the forthcoming elections—the first under the reformed franchise.

The striking feature of abolitionist exertions here—and it was the
Agency Anti-Slavery Society that did most by publishing nationally
lists of "pledged" and "irredeemable" candidates in a popular anti-
slavery journal, *The Tourist*—was their success in gaining pledges.[62] In
the event, a bloc of some 140–200 pledged candidates was actually
returned, and of the 134 precisely identified all save 8 were liberals,
thus stressing the liberal basis of abolition support.[63] It may therefore
seem surprising, when one recalls both the return of a Whig government with an increased majority and the sharp drop in West Indian
representation in the Commons,[64] that the swift passage of emancipation was not a foregone conclusion.

At first, and even before Parliament met, the framing of an emancipation bill by a cabinet committee made good progress, but by the
end of March Grey was persuaded that the Colonial Office (in fact,
his son's) plan of emancipation was impracticable and would harm
the West Indies and the mother country, and he would not approve
it.[65] Buxton's pressure in the Commons, however, compelled Althorp,
the leader of government business in the Commons, to name a day
when the government would bring forward a scheme—at which
point further confusion supervened on Goderich's enforced resigna-
tion and the succession to the seals of the Colonial Department of
Edward Stanley.[66] Stanley immediately began work on an emancipation scheme, and what for some weeks had been increasingly evident
now became crystal clear—that it was with the West Indians that the
real haggling, essentially over the amount and form of compensation
and over the terms of apprenticeship—would have to take place.[67]

Here was a paradox. Feeling in the country was strongly in favor
of emancipation, and in the Commons there was a very large bloc of
support. Yet the Lords, in the aftermath of the humiliation of the
diehards over the Reform Bill, were now determining the limits
within which the government might act. Time and time again ministers attested the need to secure West Indian cooperation in emancipation,[68] and it soon became clear that the government felt abolitionist pressure to be such that a measure *must* be enacted, but that there
was even more danger in affronting the West Indians' view of their
minimum requirements than there was in presenting to the abolitionists an insufficiently thoroughgoing measure. Why? Both because the

West Indians were a powerful and undiminished group in the Lords—some 30 strong, in what was effectively quite a small house—and because the Duke of Wellington and the party that he led were prepared to oppose any measure of emancipation which the West Indians, as an important interest group, would not accept. It is highly significant that Grey would only take up to the Lords the six resolutions on emancipation, passed by the Commons, when the Duke had written to the Earl of Harewood saying that he would offer no substantive opposition because the Commons had passed the resolutions *and* because the West Indians were satisfied.[69]

Eventually the act drawn by James Stephen the younger on the bases of the resolutions—his most important contribution to emancipation—was passed and the issue was decided by the end of July. The emancipation campaign had clear affinities with the earlier campaign for the abolition of the slave trade, but became more of a popular movement and used more popular, even radical methods. In the emancipation movement the role of Quakers paralleled that of their fathers a quarter of a century earlier, but on this later occasion the Anglican evangelicals in the ranks of active abolitionist sympathizers were overshadowed by nonconformists, especially Wesleyans and Baptists.

Some crude quantification of the nonconformist impact is now, in fact, possible. At the level of petitioning, which reached a new height in 1833, the *Methodist Magazine* reveals that nonconformists produced nearly three-fifths of the 5,020 petitions received—Wesleyans 1,953, and other nonconformists 873. The number of signatories to the Wesleyan petitions was, significantly, 229,426 at a time when membership stood at about 233,000.[70] A conclusive estimate of the extent of nonconformist influence in the 1832 general election could only come from the correlation of membership lists—which in the case of the Wesleyans, at least, do not exist in any number[71]—with poll books, but it is possible to make a rough calculation. Nonconformist membership in England (i.e., not Britain) for the nearest year to 1832 for which figures are readily available was:

Wesleyan Methodist	1831	232,883
Other Methodist	1831	55,299
Congregational	1838	127,000
Particular Baptist	1838	86,000
General Baptist and		
New Connexion	1830	10,869
Quakers	1840	16,277
Unitarians	1851	40,000
		568,328[72]

Next, it can be argued that evangelical nonconformity and old dissent were quite strongly represented among the categories of people who had come to enjoy the franchise by December 1832. A. D. Gilbert has recently calculated, from a sample of nonparochial registers, the occupational structure of evangelical nonconformity. The key conclusions for us are:

Occupation	All Nonconformists		Wesleyans	
	Total	Percent	Total	Percent
1. Merchants and manufacturers	245	2.2	76	1.7
2. Shopkeepers	796	7.1	253	5.8
3. Farmers	579	5.3	239	5.5
4. Artisans	6,531	59.4	2,750	62.7
5. Laborers	1,192	10.8	415	9.5
6. Colliers, miners, etc.	726	6.6	334	7.6
7. Other	928	8.5	318	7.2
	10,997	100.0	4,385	100.0[73]

Let us now proceed to some bold assumptions. We will assume that by the time of the 1832 election nonconformists in categories 1, 2, and 3 would have been likely to have enjoyed the vote; nonconformists in categories 5 and 6 would not. The difficulty comes with the most numerous category, artisans, but it may be justifiable to say that after the grant of the £10 household franchise one-half of this category would be enfranchised.[74] On these assumptions, 44.3 percent of all nonconformists would have had the vote. Reverting to the nonconformist membership figures, we will assume that only adults were church members, and that one-half, namely 284,164, were men; 44.3 percent of this figure is 125,885. The English electorate in 1832 has been computed at 609,772 and so the suggestion is that nonconformists constituted 20.7 percent of all voters.[75] Such a result says something about the likely political significance of gaining nonconformity over to emancipation—though one must remember that most of these would probably already have been gained to liberalism as the party of reform.

When one applies the same procedure and assumptions to the Wesleyan Methodists, it transpires that they constituted 8.4 percent of the electorate. On the face of it this is tantamount to asserting that the Wesleyan Methodist vote had considerable importance in the 1832 election, and not only because 8.4 is a significant percentage in itself,[76] or because the Wesleyan vote would have gone to the antislavery candidate who was normally a liberal. Equally important is the implication that the impact of the Wesleyan vote was magnified by virtue of being a swing vote, given the previously prevailing conservative stance of Wesleyan Methodism.[77]

It must be conceded that there is room for error in these calculations of the share of the suffrage held by nonconformists in general and by Wesleyans in particular. They are, for instance, at first sight incompatible with the figures J. R. Vincent prints on "The Political Sentiments of Wesleyans."[78] When we take the twenty-nine constituencies that it is directly possible to correlate with constituency size, we find that Wesleyan voters totalled a mere 3.6 percent of the electorate.[79] However, only three of the twenty-nine constituencies were in areas of Wesleyan strength—where the percentages were 3.1 (Bury, Lancs.), 9.0 (Halifax), and 12.7 (Rochdale), respectively. If we take this low figure and project from it the percentage of all nonconformists, we reach the not insignificant figure of 8.8 percent. Moreover, there is evidence that the number attending Wesleyan chapels was about double those in membership; it seems reasonable to suppose this was also true of the rest of evangelical nonconformity. W. R. Ward goes as far as to say that in an area of Wesleyan strength, Manchester, the population was divided into three roughly equal "constituencies"—Roman Catholic, Anglican, and Dissenter.[80] Of course, regional differences were important—with Wesleyans having most strength in Lancashire, Yorkshire, and the Potteries and the most political leverage in the borough[81]—and we must simply say that the nonconformist vote ranged from little more than zero to one-third of the electorate. With this qualification, a national nonconformist vote clearly in the higher part of the range between 8.8 and 20.7 percent is a significant political force and must have weighed greatly with politicians.

Popular pressure, largely coming from the religious public, was, then, crucial in 1832–33.[82] Its role is one of several interesting comparisons that the campaign for the abolition of slavery offers with the movement for the end of the slave trade. The earlier episode was still the era of what George Stephen called "sagacious manoeuvring within," whereas in 1833 only a massive, organized "pressure from without," exerted through Buxton in Parliament, brought the ministry to a commitment which then had to be honored. As in 1806–7, the Lords still played a key part, but whereas in these years Fox and Grenville had used all the political leverage they possessed to induce compliance in measures that they were determined to further, Grey and his colleagues in 1833 merely acted as brokers, though they did prevent a fatal junction between West Indians and Tory opposition peers. The West Indians in Parliament—paradoxically because the importance of the Caribbean in the imperial economy was declining—had more weight and were more effective in checking antislavery in 1823–33 than twenty-five years earlier. In the earlier case they had been spared abolition for two decades because of the conviction of independent men of the importance of the West Indies; in the later case their politically stronger position ensured for them terms of compensation which the Tory party believed such an established interest deserved.

We have seen that in 1806–7 the adroit use of the politico-economic conjuncture was of great importance in the passage of abolition. In the case of emancipation politico-economic considerations had only a negative influence. There is a most illuminating minute by the younger Stephen on this; in March 1832, in reference to a recent West Indian deputation, he observed that it was remarkable that the Secretary of State, in his proposed answer, had adverted so little to the effect of an emancipation measure upon the commerce of Britain. "It can however be scarcely necessary to deny that the bearings of the proposed law on the commercial interest of Great Britain have been really unheeded." Nor is there any need "for embarking on such a discussion." Suffice it to say that no lasting harm would have been done to the industry and trade of this country if sugar had been obtained from other parts of the world.[83]

There was another negative sense in which the politico-economic situation in 1833 was propitious for emancipation. Such was the depression in West Indian agriculture that the proprietors were prepared to grasp at an emancipation measure which included generous compensation. Rather as the Balkan peasant in a bad year must eat his seed corn, so the West Indian proprietor saw the lure of escaping from present insolvency by yielding up a long-term asset. Of economic forces positively demanding abolition there are none. Just as the East Indians, right through from the 1790s to the 1830s, failed to act as an interest group using antislavery as the cloak for free trade, so any group of emerging capitalists has left, in the mountains of literature and documentation, not a trace of its activities.

S. F. Woolley long ago substantially endorsed Halévy's view that the Reform Bill made no immediate difference to the size of the business interest in Parliament—indeed Woolley shows that it was less in the 1833 Parliament than in that of 1831.[84] Any case for the emerging capitalists having been responsible for emancipation must, therefore, presumably rest on some form of conspiracy theory. And when all depends on that, the case is lost indeed.

NOTES

Roger Anstey died before he had an opportunity to revise this essay. The editors have decided to reproduce it as far as possible in its original form.

1 London, 1975.

2 See, for example, Great Britain, *Hansard Parliamentary Debates* (hereafter cited as *Hansard*), 1st ser., 28 (1814): 803; also quoted in B. W. Higman, *Slave Population and Economy in Jamaica, 1807–1834* (Cambridge, 1976), p. 231.

3 For a summary of the registration campaign, see Sir George Stephen, *Anti-Slavery Recollections* (London, 1854; 2d ed., 1971), pp. 20–38. A government-sponsored slave registry bill was eventually enacted in 1817 with an ease that prefigured its subsequent ineffectiveness.

4 K. Charlton, "James Cropper and Liverpool's Contribution to the Anti-Slavery Movement," *Transactions of the Historic Society of Lancashire and Cheshire* 113 (1971): 57, 59. It was subsequently the view of the Antislavery Society that the initiative was Cropper's (see the quotation from the *British and Foreign Anti-Slavery Reporter* 2 [Mar. 1840], in G. R. Mellor, *British Imperial Trusteeship, 1783–1850* [1951], p. 125 n.).

5 Cropper to Z. Macaulay, 2 May and 8 May 1822, Clarkson Mss., Mss. 41267A, ff. 102–06, British Museum Additional Manuscripts (hereafter cited as BM Add. Mss.); diary of William Allen, 27 May 1822, quoted in William Allen, *Life with Selections from his Correspondence*, 2 vols. (Philadelphia 1847), 2:230; Friends House, London Yearly Meeting, Minute Book Vol. 22, 27 May 1822, p. 382. For testimony to Quaker initiative in the matter, see also Wilberforce to Lord Holland, 25 Feb. 1823, Holland House Mss., Mss. 51820, BM Add. Mss.

6 Sir Thomas Fowell Buxton, *The Memoirs of Sir Thomas Fowell Buxton*, ed. Charles Buxton (London, 1849), pp. 108–111; diary of William Allen, 5 Sept. 1822, 13 Jan. and 28 Jan. 1823, in Allen, *Life*, 2: 245, 326; Robert I. and Samuel Wilberforce, *The Life of William Wilberforce*, 5 vols. (London, 1838), 5: 160–67; Friends House, Meeting for Sufferings, Minute Book Vol. 42, 3 Jan. 1823, p. 628. The Society for the Mitigation and Gradual Abolition of Slavery throughout the British Dominions is hereafter cited as the Antislavery Society in both the text and the notes.

7 *Hansard*, 2d ser. 9 (1823): 275–87; Buxton, *Memoirs*, pp. 112–118; W. L. Burn, *Emancipation and Apprenticeship in the British West Indies* (London, 1937), pp. 80–81.

8 B. W. Higman, "The West India 'Interest' in Parliament, 1807–1833," *Historical Studies* 13 (1967): 1–5 (note Higman's definition of three levels of West Indian support); P. F. Dixon, "The Politics of Emancipation: the Movement for the Abolition of Slavery in the British West Indies, 1807–1833" (D. Phil. diss., University of Oxford, 1970), pp. 41–42 and app. B.

9 Dixon, "Politics of Emancipation," pp. 234, 336–74.

10 Anstey, *Atlantic Slave Trade*, pp. 283, 343–402 passim.

11 Cropper to Macaulay, 5 Aug. 1822, BM Add. Mss., 41267A, ff. 112–13; Z. Macaulay to "My dear Friend," 16 Feb. 1828, Brougham Mss., 10275, University College, London. See also Ian Rennie, "Evangelicalism and English Public Life, 1823–1850" (Ph. D. diss., University of Toronto, 1962), p. 178.

12 Dixon, "Politics of Emancipation," pp. 61–62 and app. C. Cf. Anstey, *Atlantic Slave Trade*, p. 307. As Dixon says, the figures almost suggest an inverse correlation between East Indians and abolitionists.

13 Burn, *Emancipation and Apprenticeship*, p. 84 and n. See also Stephen, *Recollections*, especially pp. 17, 43, and 69.

14 For the Antislavery Society's work, see *Anti-Slavery Monthly Reporter* (hereafter cited as *Reporter*), passim; Rhodes House, Oxford, Anti-Slavery Mss., E2/I–3, Minute Books, passim. For the importance of ladies' associations, see Macaulay to "My dear Friend," 16 Feb. 1828, Brougham Mss. 10275.

15 Anstey, *Atlantic Slave Trade*, chaps. 7 and 8.

16 Richard Watson, *The Works of the Reverend Richard Watson*, 12 vols. (London, 1834–37). The sermons are in vols. 2 and 4, and the *Theological Institutes* in vols. 10 and 12. An indication of Watson's influence and reputation is that the *Institutes* were in their fifth edition by the time they appeared in the *Works*.

17 Watson, *Works*, 4: 251, Sermon 101, "The Reign of God."

18 John Wesley, *The Works of John Wesley*, 14 vols. (Grand Rapids, n.d., re-issue of 1872 ed.), 6: 281–88, Sermon 63, "The General Spread of the Gospel"; ibid., 5: 37–52, Sermon 4, "Scriptural Christianity."

19 Watson, *Works*, 3: 239, Sermon 49, "The Gospel of the Kingdom." Watson, like Methodists in general, avoided the intricacies, not to say fantasies, of millennial projection. For a condemnation of such fantasies, see the influential Wesleyan divine Adam Clarke, *Christian Theology* (London, 1835), pp. 487–88.

20 Watson, *Works*, 2: 30–31, Sermon 2, "Thanksgiving for Peace"; ibid., p. 10, Sermon 1, "Ezekiel's Vision."

21 Watson, *Works*, 4: 181, Sermon 102, "Ezekiel's Vision" (second sermon on this subject). See also ibid., pp. 138–39, Sermon 93, "The Glory of God in the Face of Christ."

22 R. G. Cowherd, *The Politics of Dissent* (London, 1959), p. 18; Anstey, *Atlantic Slave Trade*, pp. 233–35; Frank Baker, *The Relations between the Society of Friends and Early Methodism* (London, 1949, reprinted from the *London Quarterly and Holborn Review*), p. 23.

23 John Ashley Vickers, *Thomas Coke: Apostle of Methodism* (London, 1959), pp. 33 n., 131 ff; G. G. Findlay and W. W. Holdsworth, *The History of the Wesleyan Methodist Missionary Society*, 5 vols. (London, 1921), 2: 11 ff. Note Findlay and Holdsworth's comment on the first age of Methodist missionary activity: "The Wesleyan Revival was a reaction against narrowing conceptions of the Gospel and the Church of Christ, whether Calvinistic,

sacerdotal, nationalist or particularist, of whatever kind. 'Universal Redemption' was the watchword of the Methodist preachers. The logic of Free Grace admitted of no limits to its application within the human family" (ibid., 1: 31). For a good overall study of missions in the West Indies, especially in relation to antislavery, see S. Jakobsson, *Am I Not a Man and Brother* (Lund, 1972), pt. 2, "The Missions and the Emancipation of the Slaves, 1823–1838."

24 R. Jackson, "Memoirs of the Life and Writings of the Reverend Richard Watson," in Watson, *Works*, 1: 134 ff., 164.

25 Vickers, *Coke*, pp. 169–72.

26 Instructions, probably by Watson, quoted in Watson, *Works*, 1: 280. See also R. Watson, "A Defence of the Wesleyan-Methodist Missions in the West Indies" (1817), in Watson, *Works*, 6: 494. That such was the actual missionary attitude is confirmed by missionary testimony (ibid., passim).

27 *Wesleyan Methodist Magazine*, 3d ser., 4 (Feb. 1825): 115–19; Findlay and Holdsworth, *History*, 2: 86–88. For a similar attitude on the part of Wesleyan Demerara missionaries, see Jakobsson, *Am I Not a Man*, p. 373 ff.

28 Watson, *Works*, 1: 213–14.

29 *Wesleyan Methodist Magazine*, 3d ser., 2 (Jan. 1824): 49–53; ibid., 4 (Nov. 1825): 628–43; *Hansard*, 2d ser, 13 (1825): 1285–1347; Buxton, *Memoirs*, p. 134; Findlay and Holdsworth, *History*, 2: 198–204; Jakobsson, *Am I Not a Man*, p. 373 ff.

30 Findlay and Holdsworth, *History*, vol. 2 passim, lists a dozen instances of persecution, and others, not mentioned, had taken place. It is all the more striking that the Missionary Committee's 1823 report dismissed the Shrewsbury affair as "the ebullition of the moment" (Watson, *Works*, 1: 383).

31 Rhodes House, Anti-Slavery Mss., E2/I, Minutes, 31 Jan. 1823, 9 Apr. 1823, 13 and 20 Jan. 1824, and passim; Watson, *Works*, 1: 598.

32 Review of vol. 1, *Slavery of the British West India Colonies Delineated* by James Stephen, *Wesleyan Methodist Magazine*, 3d ser., 2 (June 1824): 386–89.

33 Findlay and Holdsworth, *History*, 2: 86–88 and notes. For the effect of the Jamaica missionaries' actions on the development of the Wesleyan antislavery position, see Mary Turner, *Slaves and Missionaries* (University of Chicago Press, forthcoming).

34 *Minutes of the Wesleyan Methodist Conference*, 19 vols. (London, 1812–1877), 6: 52; Maldwyn Edwards, *After Wesley*, 2d ed. (London, 1948), p. 71; Watson, *Works*, 1: 411. A distinction insisted upon by Watson was that the Missionary Committee and missionary supporters would not *qua* supporters of missions formally propose (gradual) emancipation (R. Watson, "The Religious Instincts of the Slaves in the West India Colonies Advocated and Defended," sermon reviewed in *Wesleyan Methodist Magazine*, 3d ser., 3 [Oct. 1824]: 687–92). The question of what the Conference should do was also raised with Bunting by the Reverend William Morley in a letter of 14 July 1825 (Jabez Bunting, *The Early Correspondence of Jabez Bunting,*

1820–1829, ed. W. R. Ward, [London, 1972], p. 118). R. Jackson says that
it was Bunting who "first called upon the Methodist body to assert the
negro's right to liberty" (Watson, *Works*, 1: 598).

35 *Wesleyan Methodist Magazine*, 3d ser., 5 (Feb. 1826): 121–25 (note that the
editorial stopped short of a call to Wesleyans as such to organize and to
sign petitions); ibid., 3 (Sept. 1824): 618. See also Rhodes House, Anti-
Slavery Mss., E2/3, Minutes, 18 Jan. 1826, in which it was noted that a
letter from Watson was read stating that "He most heartily concurred in
the objects of the [Anti-Slavery] Society."

36 *Minutes of the Wesleyan Conference*, 6: 514–15.

37 *Wesleyan Methodist Magazine*, 3d ser., 9 (June 1830): 435.

38 Wesleyan Missions Report, appendix, cited in *Reporter* 3 (20 Aug. 1830):
349 ff.

39 *Minutes of the Wesleyan Conference*, vol. 6 (n.p. in author's notes); *Reporter* 3
(20 Aug. 1830): 349 ff; *Wesleyan Methodist Magazine*, 3d ser., 9 (Sept. 1830):
608–10.

40 Rhodes House, Anti-Slavery Mss., E2/3, Minutes, 17 Nov. 1830; Jakobsson, *Am I Not a Man*, p. 498.

41 See note 26.

42 B. Gregory, *Sidelights on the Conflicts of Methodism, 1827–52* (London,
1898), pp. 94–95. Gregory described Watson as "the master spirit of the
Conference" of 1830, and as "at the full height of his intellectual powers."
See also Edwards, *After Wesley*, p. 71.

43 R. Tudor Jones, *Congregationalism in England, 1662–1962* (London, 1962),
pp. 200–1001.

44 *Reporter* 3 (June 1830): 268.

45 For example, a letter from the Antislavery Society to the *Evangelical Magazine* (Oct. 1830, p. 440) calling for petitions; and in the "very great satisfaction" with which the Antislavery Committee received an assurance of
support from the Protestant Dissenting Deputies (Rhodes House, Anti-
Slavery Mss., E2/3, Minutes, 1 June 1830).

46 Between February 1826 and November 1832 the Society of Friends contributed £7,300 to the Antislavery Society, including £1,800 to the Agency
Committee (Meeting for Sufferings, Minutes, vol. 43, 3 Feb, 9 June, and
1 Sept. 1826, 7 Aug. 1829, and 21 July 1830: ibid., vol. 44, 3 Dec. 1831,
4 May, 18 May, 3 Aug., and 17 Nov. 1832).

47 Charles Cavendish Fulke Greville, *Greville Diary*, ed. F. W. Wilson, 2 vols.
(New York, 1927), 2: 59–60.

48 *Reporter* 4 (9 May 1831): 263, 271.

49 Watson, *Works*, 1:165–66.

50 Watson, *Works*, 1: 502.

51 *Reporter* 3 (Oct. 1829): 103. See also Burn, *Emancipation and Apprenticeship*,
p. 84 n., quotation from *Eclectic Review*, 3d ser., 3 (April 1830): 352.

52 Rhodes House, Anti-Slavery Mss., E/2/3, Minutes, 9 Feb. 1830. See also
ibid., Minutes, 13 Feb. and 2 Mar. 1830.

53 For a report of Brougham's speech, see *Reporter* 3 (June 1830): 253–56; Stephen, *Recollections*, p. 120.

54 Petition totals for the Reformed Parliament are given in *Wesleyan Methodist Magazine*, 3d ser., 13 (1834): 229. Compare the 5,484 antislavery petitions between October 1830 and April 1831 with the 3,000 reform petitions in the same period (Rhodes House, Anti-Slavery Mss., E2/3, Minutes, 1 Sept., 16 Sept., 17 Nov., and 1 Dec. 1830; *Reporter* 4 [5 Jan. 1831]: 25–75, and 4 [9 May 1831]: 252 n.; John Cannon, *Parliamentary Reform, 1640–1832* [Cambridge, 1973], p. 252 n.).

55 Stephen, *Recollections*, pp. 127–31, 143–53, 158. For the split, see Rhodes House, Anti-Slavery Mss., E2/3, Minutes, 1 June, 25 June 1831, 22 Feb., 7 Mar., 6 June, and 4 July 1832; *Report of the Agency Committee of the Anti-Slavery Society* (London, 1832); *The Tourist* 1 (26 Nov. 1832): 94; David B. Davis, "The Emergence of Immediatism in British and American Anti-Slavery Thought," *Mississippi Valley Historical Review* 94 (1962–62): 222n.

56 Davis, "Immediatism," pp. 219–21; Stephen, *Recollections*, p. 136; *Report of the Agency Committee*, 1832. See also the analysis of George Thompson's Agency lecture at Dover in Dixon, "Politics of Emancipation," p. 286.

57 Report of May meeting, *Reporter* 3 (June 1830): 265; *Minutes of the Wesleyan Methodist Conference* 6 (n.p. given); *Wesleyan Methodist Magazine*, 3d ser., 9 (Sept. 1830): 608–10; Gregory, *Sidelights on Methodism*, p. 550.

58 See especially Cannon, *Parliamentary Reform*, and Michael Brock, *The Great Reform Act* (London, 1973).

59 For the views of Cropper and Sturge, see H. Richard, *Memoirs of Joseph Sturge* (London, 1864), p. 33; for views of Allen, see diary of William Allen, May 1832, in Allen, *Life*, 3: 36.

60 Howick to Earl Grey, 29 May and 1 Dec. 1832, Grey Papers, 2d Earl, Box 24, University of Durham, England; Mary Reckord, "The Jamaica Slave Rebellion of 1831," *Past and Present* 60 (1969): 108–25; Higman, *Slave Population*, pp. 231–32; Buxton, *Memoirs*, p. 306; Macaulay to Brougham, 13 May 1833. Brougham Mss., 10544, private, and reprinted in Viscountess Knutsford, *The Life and Times of Zachary Macaulay* (London, 1900), p. 470, in which it is wrongly attributed to 1832.

61 Lushington memo, n.d. (between 17 Apr. and 12 May 1832), Brougham Mss., 10376, University College, London.

62 *The Tourist*, vol. 1, Sept. to Dec. 1832, especially 24 Sept., p. 10, 10 Dec., p. 104, and 17 Dec., p. 126.

63 For party affiliation and electoral information, see F. W. S. Craig, *British Parliamentary Elections Results, 1832–1885*, 3d ed. (London, 1976); Charles R. Dod, *Electoral Facts, 1832–1853, Impartially Stated*, ed. H. J. Hanham (Brighton, 1972). *The Parliamentary Pocket Companion, 1833* (London, 1833) gives biographical and political information about most candidates, and it may be significant that the clearly well informed compiler could find no more than eight pledged Scottish and Irish members. On the other hand, the Agency Committee list is in general likely to be more

accurate as regards English and Welsh members, and is therefore to be preferred.

64 Reduced to 19; see Higman, "West India 'Interest,'" p. 3. Note George Stephen's conclusion that "an Anti-Slavery House was for the first time returned by an Anti-Slavery public" (Stephen, *Recollections*, p. 168).

65 Howick, minute of discussions on slavery, 1833, Slavery Papers, no. 66, Grey Papers, 3d Earl; John C. Hobhouse diary, 12 Jan. 1833, quoted in Lord Broughton, *Recollections of a Long Life*, 6 vols. (London, 1909) 4: 268–69; Howick journal ms., 16 Mar. 1833 ff., Grey Papers, 3d Earl.

66 *Hansard*, 3d ser., 16 (1833): 826–27; Buxton, *Memoirs*, pp. 260–61. See also Rhodes House, Anti-Slavery Mss., E2/4, Minutes, 6 Mar. and 9 Mar. 1833.

67 For a voluminous file on the discussions between the government and the West Indies, January to September 1833, see Colonial Office, series 318, vol. 116, Public Record Office, London (hereafter cited as CO/PRO). The file is partly duplicated and complemented in printed minutes of proceedings between the government and West Indians, 16 January to 2 May 1833, in Grey Papers, 3d Earl, Box 147, item 53.

68 See, for example, Howick memo, 1 Dec. 1832, Slavery Papers, no. 56, and Howick journal ms., Grey Papers, 3d Earl; Stanley to West Indians, copy, 29 Apr. 1833, CO/PRO 318/116; *Hansard*, 3d ser., 16 (1833): 1188–89; ibid., 18 (1833): 547–50, 1201–11; diary of Lord Holland, 27 May, 29 May 1833, in E. D. Kriegel, ed., *Holland House Papers* (London, 1976), pp. 212–13.

69 Diary of Lord Ellenborough, 23 June 1833, in A. Aspinall, ed., *Three Early Nineteenth Century Diaries* (London, 1952), pp. 340–41. See also the Duke of Wellington's speech on 25 June 1833, in *Hansard*, 3d ser., 18 (1833): 1180–94.

70 *Wesleyan Methodist Magazine*, 3d ser., 13 (1834): 229. I have not come across this analysis elsewhere. The heading says that the list is as "just printed for the House of Commons," but I can find no trace of it in the Sessional Papers; the petitions, of course, are listed in the *Journal of the House of Commons*. The analysis totals the number of petitions and attached signatures in each of twenty-two dissenting denominations, and gives the crude total of petitions and signatures from all other sources.

71 This appears to be the case with Wesleyan Methodism, and it is less likely that such lists have survived in other denominations because of their much looser organizations. I am grateful to Dr. Clive Field for information regarding Wesleyan membership lists.

72 A. D. Gilbert, *Religion and Society in Industrial England: Church, Chapel and Social Change, 1740–1914* (London, 1976), pp. 31, 37.

73 Ibid., p. 63. Dr. Thompson of Fitzwilliam College, Cambridge, in a personal communication for which I am grateful, made the point that this sample is insufficiently random, in that nonparochial registers would not have included "high" Methodists who, in the tradition of John Wesley, would have been registered in their parishes. Thus the sample is skewed

in favor of the more radical Wesleyan members. If this means that the given sample includes more of the lower than the higher socio-economic categories, then the effect of the skewing is to underestimate the percentage of Wesleyans who would have had the vote, and thus to strengthen my argument for the electoral significance of the Wesleyan vote.

74 Gash is not as (rashly) specific, but quotes approvingly Brougham's description of the kind of person who occupied a £10 house in the boroughs: "Occupiers of such houses, in some country towns, fill the station of inferior shopkeepers; in some of the better kind of tradesmen [meaning, Gash makes clear, mechanics, artisans, and skilled workmen]—here they are foremen of workshops—there, artisans earning good wages—sometimes, but seldom, labourers in full work." Gash adds, "in a few boroughs it [the £10 household franchise] included the majority of householders; in some it excluded entirely the manual labourer. The £10 qualification was a middle-class franchise in so far as it gave the vote to the majority of the middle classes [*sic*] in the boroughs; but at many points it dipped below that class to take in a substantial element of the working class" (Norman Gash, *Politics in the Age of Peel* (London, 1953), p. 100 and n.).

75 Craig, *Elections Results*, p. 623.

76 Note in this connection that Bunting was frequently asked by parliamentary candidates to use his influence with Wesleyans (D. A. Gowland, "Methodist Secessions and Social Conflict in South Lancashire, 1830–1857" [Ph.D. diss., University of Manchester, 1966] p. 559).

77 Gash, *Age of Peel*, p. 111; series of articles by Humphrey Sandwich in *Wesleyan Methodist Magazine*, 3d ser., 8 (1829), especially pp. 314, 815–16. One must not overlook, however, the tendency of rank and file Wesleyans to question the conservatism of the leadership (Gowland, "Methodist Secessions," passim; *Wesleyan Methodist Magazine*, 3d ser., 10 [June 1831]: 422–25; ibid., 11 [Oct. 1832]: 741–44; ibid., 13 [Oct. 1834]: 767; W. R. Ward, *Religion and Society in England, 1790–1850* (London, 1972), passim).

78 Extract from the *Wesleyan Chronicle* (n.d.), in J. R. Vincent, *Pollbooks: How Victorians Voted* (Cambridge, 1967), pp. 69–70.

79 See Craig, *Election Results*, passim.

80 Ward, *Religion and Society*, pp. 126–28.

81 Private communications from Professor Ward and Dr. Thompson, which I gratefully acknowledge.

82 See Vincent, *Pollbooks*, p. 5: "The voting of clerical personnel and contemporary literature all suggest the immense importance of religious denomination for political and indeed every kind of behaviour." See also S. F. Woolley, "The Personnel of the Parliament of 1833," *English Historical Review* 53 (1938): 244: "It has been estimated that in every borough election of 1832 the nonconformists formed the backbone of the majority."

83 Stephen, draft of an answer, Mar. 1832, pp. 105–6, in Colonial Papers, Slavery, item 6, Grey Papers, 3d Earl.

84 Woolley, "Personnel of the Parliament of 1833," pp. 240–62, and especially pp. 244–46, 262.

CHAPTER 4: **The Public Campaign in England**

against Slavery, 1787–1834

James Walvin

Since the publication of Eric Williams's *Capitalism and Slavery* (1944) it
has proved difficult to offer an explanation of British abolitionism
without at least paying lip service to the central and determining role
of economics. For three decades the role of economics has dominated
the attention of historians of abolition. Without wishing to deny the
centrality of the economics of Caribbean slavery, it might be argued
that one main consequence of Seymour Drescher's recent work *Econocide* (and that of Roger Anstey and David Davis) has been to redirect
our attention to the complex *political* chemistry which contributed to
abolition and emancipation. This paper is a modest attempt in that
direction through a discussion of some of the themes that characterized public abolitionist politics and an examination of abolitionist tactics outside Parliament.

In the three main phases of abolition (1787–1807, 1814, and
1822–1834) perhaps the most striking feature was the transmutation
of abolitionist sentiment from the preserve of a handful of men of
sensibility into the widely accepted vocabulary of a massive political
constituency. It is hard to deny that the cause of the West Indian
slaves became a popular issue, both in the 1790s and in the mid-
1820s, more popular indeed than many other issues which have attracted historians' attention. In May 1792 Sir Samuel Romilly wrote
that "the cause of the negro slaves is at present taken up with much
warmth in almost every part of the kingdom as could be found in any

matter in which the people were personally and immediately interested. Innumberable petitions for the abolition have been presented
to Parliament and (what proves mens' zeal more strongly than petitions) great numbers have entirely discontinued the use of sugar. All
persons, and even the West India planters and merchants, seem to
agree that it is impossible the trade should last many years longer." [1]
Yet what a transformation this represented in a mere five years, for
when, in 1787, Thomas Clarkson had set out to spread the abolitionist gospel, he expressed himself surprised to discover "the spirit
which was then beginning to show itself among the people of Manchester and other places, on the subject of the slave trade and which
would unquestionably manifest itself further by breaking out into petitions to parliament for its abolition." [2] Urged on by the advice and
example of the Manchester abolitionists led by Thomas Walker (the
initial Manchester petition was signed by 10,639 people), the London
Abolition Society and its sympathizers throughout the country opted
for the petition to Parliament as the main form of expression and
political persuasion.

The petitioning of either House in order to remedy complaints or
seek redress was a traditional and accepted constitutional practice.
But it was the Association movement of 1779–1780 that confirmed
petitioning as the main means of channeling pressure onto Parliament from outside Parliament. Powerful and widespread as the Association movement was (pressing for limited parliamentary reform),
its use of the petition was soon made to appear small-scale by the
more prodigious efforts of antislavery. The abolitionist cause not only
transformed petitioning into a major and qualitatively new political
phenomenon, but it established petitioning (and the local activity
needed to raise a petition) as *the* central tactic of extra-parliamentary
politics in subsequent decades. After the success of the abolitionists
in 1787–1792 in rallying what contemporaries took to be "public
opinion," all subsequent reforming and radical movements used the
petition as their local rallying point, as an expression for their grievances, and as a way of impressing the size of their followings on Parliament. The campaigns for reform of Parliament, for repeal of the
Test and Corporation Acts, for a free press and for factory reform,
and against the Combination Acts and the poor law—these and many
other reform agitations of the years 1787–1848 used the petition extensively. Men of property and education who sought redress could
normally call upon their friends, colleagues, associates, or representatives for direct access to Parliament itself. But for those people,

growing in numbers all the time, who were beyond the political pale, the petition offered one of the few ways of being heard by the political world. Thus the petitions of the years 1787–1848 can be seen as the political voice of the dispossessed. Moreover, it was the abolitionists who first established both the legitimacy and the political effectiveness of the petition.

The method of petitioning was simple. A petition, the wording agreed to by a small committee or a group of sympathizers, was attached to blank sheets and deposited at various places around a town. The local organizers advertised the fact locally—and sometimes nationally—in the press or in handbills, and invited people to attach their names to the petition. Eventually the completed sheets were collected, stuck together, and rolled into one or several bundles for delivery. The petition was then presented to the Commons by an M.P. or to the Lords by a peer. Among the weaknesses of the scheme, however, was the fact that the place of deposit and signature could be subject to political threats and violence from opponents. In Manchester in the early 1790s for example, local magistrates effectively curtailed the collecting of radical petitions by threatening to refuse licenses to or to withdraw licenses from landlords who allowed their premises to be used for petitioning.[3]

Abolitionists, unlike the political radicals of the 1790s, had the advantage of not having to rely upon the tavern, pub, or public place for their meetings. So rapidly did abolitionism gain a respectable political foothold throughout the cities of England that all forms of religious, private, municipal, and civic meeting places were made available to the cause. It is striking that from an early date the campaigns against the slave trade recruited not only the support of sectional political interests but also the corporate support of cities and towns, churches and vestries, and a wide range of private and public organizations. Naturally, these bodies placed their properties and meeting places at the disposal of the abolitionist or petitioning cause. In the city of York, for instance, the abolitionist petition of 1788 came from the lord mayor and the community and as an officially sponsored document, it was available for signature at the local guildhall.[4] Indeed, it has never been stressed that in this, the first phase of abolitionism, the main advantage was, arguably, not merely the enormously popular base it rapidly established, but the degree to which it won over the formal structure of local government and seduced a wide range of corporate institutions. At its simplest, this meant that abolitionists did not face the tremendous difficulties of meeting in public and exposing themselves to the fluctuations in the political climate. At the local level abolitionists could always rely upon having a roof over their heads and on having influential local friends.

These advantages were important in the 1790s when the emergence of popular radicalism (English Jacobinism to its enemies), in conjunction with the lengthening shadow from France, transformed the political climate in England. War with France in 1793, and the disintegration in Haiti (with the loss of thousands of British troops in a forlorn campaign against former slaves in that island),[5] did nothing to help the abolitionist cause. The change in abolitionist fortunes in 1792–1793 is instructive. In spring 1792 an unprecedented 508 abolitionist petitions were delivered to Parliament; in Manchester alone 20,000 names from a population of 60,000 were attached to the petition.[6] By then, however, the English lower-class radicals, in a reprise of abolitionist tactics, had organized themselves into corresponding societies and had begun to publish cheap tracts, to organize massive public meetings, and to raise petitions for reform. The societies were spurred on by Tom Paine's *Rights of Man.* Moreover they believed that such rights "are not confined solely to this small island but are extended to the whole human race, black and white, high or low, rich or poor"[7] ; these societies consisted of men who had not been seen in English politics since the Wilkes' affair in the 1760s—and even then not in such numbers. The English radicals reminded their enemies (whose ideologue was Edmund Burke) of the sequence of events in France which, to their minds had produced such disasters. Popular associations, petitions, cheap publications, public lectures, large public meetings, pressure on Parliament: these, the lifeblood of abolitionism, were now adopted by the radicals. And in the process both came to be resisted as a potentially disastrous repeat of events in France. In the political confusion and fear of 1792–1793 abolitionists and radicals were transformed, in the eyes of their opponents, into one and the same specie, and it was one, moreoever, which used the same insidious political tactics. It was absurd, but symptomatic, that one writer spoke of "the JACOBINS of England, the Wilberforces, the Coopers, the Paines, the Clarksons."[8] The result was, at the public level, disastrous for abolitionism. "People connect democratical principles with the Abolition of the Slave Trade [complained Wilberforce] and will not hear mention of it."[9] One regretable consequence was a reluctance by the public to step forward. "I do not imagine that we could meet with 20 persons in Hull at present who would sign a petition, that are not republicans."[10]

While the radical societies helped to spread even further the *popu-*

lar commitment to abolition, they had the simultaneous and negative effect of undercutting the public political support of abolitionism.[11] It seems ironic that the societies which were responsible for furthering democratic and humane sensibility should ultimately (in the responses they provoked from the government and its friends) have proved harmful for all public forms of reforming politics. It is significant, for instance, that the great public pressure for abolition of the years 1787–1792 was not to be matched until the Vienna Congress threatened a renewal of slave trading in 1814. Of course, by the mid-1790s the central problem facing abolition, as Roger Anstey has shown, was not so much the need to raise public feeling as the logistical difficulty of aligning support in the Commons and Lords. In general, however, public abolitionism was driven underground by an entrenched opposition—headed by the reforming and abolitionist Pitt—which had come to fear all forms of public expression.

It would be wrong to claim that the subsequent history of English abolitionism merely followed the tactical patterns established in the first, explosive phase, but there seems little doubt that, in tactical terms, the old, well-trained methods were once more resurrected, though in a changed social and political climate and to a degree which far surpassed the earlier efforts. It was slow in developing, however, for the abolition of the slave trade in 1807 was followed by a period of uncertainty in which both sides awaited the results of abolition. It was soon clear that a tightening-up of anti-slave-trading legislation was needed, and in January 1812 Romilly recorded that he (along with Stephen, Brougham, Wilberforce, and Babington) decided that "the most effectual measure appeared to all of us to be in the establishing a registry of slaves in all the islands, and a law that every negro not registered should go free . . . "[12] The first British census taken in 1801, may have encouraged abolitionists to think of slave registration, but the prime motive seems to have been the importance of knowing more about the demographic facts of West Indian slavery and any alterations produced by illegal importations. Yet before registration was agreed to there was, at the Vienna Congress of 1814, the prospect of a French resumption of slave trading. An outcry followed the announcement of the slave-trade clauses of the Vienna treaty. Within a week the abolitionists had mustered support, called public meetings, lobbied the influential, and set in train the sequence of events so familiar in the years 1787–1792. The result was little less than staggering.

According to Romilly, the original meeting "produced a good effect. The example was followed in most of the great towns in England; and more than 800 petitions were, in little more than a month from this time, presented to Parliament against the slave trade, signed by 700,000 persons."[13] The petition presented by Wilberforce contained 39,000 names; that by the Duke of Gloucester, 25,000.[14] These figures surprised both friend and foe alike, for what they showed was that a substantial proportion of the total population (perhaps 1.5 million out of 12 million)[15] aligned themselves behind abolitionism—and this in the first wave of political agitation since the repressive legislation of twenty years before.[16] Whitbread recorded a fitting comment: "The country never has, and I fear, never will, express a feeling so general as they have done about the slave trade".[17] Moreover, so powerful was this feeling thought to be that it was assumed it would force the government's hand. According to the Ambassador to Spain, "the nation is bent on the subject. I believe there is hardly a village that has not met and petitioned upon it; both Houses of Parliament are pledged to press it; and the ministers must make it the basis of their policy." [18] Clarkson, intimately involved in negotiations with ministers, was convinced that the petitions were instrumental in changing government policy: "I cannot but think, that we have to thank the petitions for this Energy. No other satisfactory Reason can be given why Administration was so apparently indifferent to the Subject when the Treaty was made, and why so interesting since."[19] Whatever disappointments abolitionists met in the tortuous world of Congress diplomacy, they had shown—much to their own surprise— the speed, degree, and power of their political relexes. The problem they subsequently faced was how to use and shape the popular antipathy to slavery and the trade to improve the lot of, and later to liberate, the slaves in the West Indies.

The struggle for slave registration was very much an internal parliamentary affair, raised in 1815 by Wilberforce and Stephen, and given an added boost in 1816 by the Barbados slave revolt and its savage repression. While the planters and their friends blamed abolitionists for the revolt[20] (as they were to do again after the revolts of Demerara in 1823 and Jamaica in 1831), the debate about registration marked a qualitative shift in the domestic political argument. In the debate about the slave trade, the political attention of both sides was focussed primarily upon conditions on the slave ships, in West Africa, and only incidentally on slave societies. Registration, however, was concerned above all else with slave societies. Thus the Caribbean itself, particularly its demography and, later, its economics, gradually came to the fore of abolitionist and national politics. And the Registration Act—not finally enacted until 1819—provided an abundance of hard statistical evidence upon which to base political arguments. In the earlier phase of abolitionism, even, for example, after the report from the Privy Council in 1788, evidence generally took the form of personal testimony which, even when reliable, was subject to the inevitable distortion of memory and recollection. Registration and the resulting slave statistics imposed upon the abolitionist debate a degree of factual evidence which altered the very tone of the ensuing debate.

In the years after the war, as in 1791–1792, the abolitionist cause was helped by being carried along by the wider political debate about rights. These were, after all, the years when the politics of Catholic emancipation, electoral reform, poor relief, unionization, and industrial legislation were at their height. Yet slavery was seen to subsume many of the other political arguments about rights; it was, in fact, the most extreme form of a denial of rights. Throughout these years there was a growing awareness of the facts of slavery; the work of the Caribbean missionaries (and the evidence they fed back to their communities in Britain), the details (available after 1820) from slave registration, and the renewed vigor of the abolitionists all cumulatively spread the national appreciation both of the details and the problems of West Indian bondage. At every level black slavery formed a stark contrast to the very rights demanded by so many groups in Britain. And, in a nation which was itself permeated by the advance of large nonconformist communities (particularly in working-class areas) and by evangelicalism within the established church, slavery seemed to ever more people to be morally offensive.

Prominent abolitionists slowly came to the view that the ending of the slave trade would not, in itself, solve the problems of slavery. The earlier view that abolition would inevitably force the planters to ameliorate slave conditions and bring about gradual freedom was shown to be false (though we now know that abolition did indeed have profound effects on the slaves).[21] Available evidence, however, did not point to amelioration; missionaries did *not* write home about slave improvements and slave revolts and rumbling discontent were hardly evidence of a slow withering of slavery. Moreover, the continuing brutalities of the planters, their dogged commitment to slavery, and the persistence of their London spokesmen forced the abolitionists to only one conclusion—that emancipation must be forced upon the West Indies. To bring this about Parliament and the government, once again, would have to be subjected to the full weight of popular feeling. Throughout 1822 James Cropper badgered abolitionists with the need to step forward for emancipation, stressing a new economic argument—that should East Indian sugar be admitted duty free into Britain, it would destroy the economic position of the West Indian sugar producers. But, Cropper insisted, the first task was to shower the public with the facts of slavery, through newspapers and the activities of local societies.[22] Strengthened by the accession of new men, the humanitarians regrouped to press for emancipation. The campaigns which they set in train, similar in kind to their earlier efforts, were marked by unprecedented support. As in 1814, the nation seemed ready to come to their help in growing numbers. Leading emancipationists agreed that public support was vital to their efforts. Cropper wrote that "public opinion is necessary to some extent to the successful prosecution of our inquiries."[23] Macaulay was of a similar mind. "It is highly important to raise the public mind. . . ."[24] As a result, Clarkson set out on a national lecture tour, which produced 225 petitions and 200 local societies. A year later his tour had yielded 600 petitions.[25] Even Wilberforce was surprised. "The country takes up our cause surprisingly, the petitions, considering the little effort, very numerous."[26] Discussions with ministers, though disappointing, had secured the long-term commitment to emancipation (expressed in Canning's 1823 resolutions). What the abolitionists therefore felt they needed was massive and sustained public pressure, both to pin down reluctant ministers and to overcome the plantocratic opposition. Clarkson was convinced of "the Necessity *of going on with your Petitions. . . .* Will not an uninterrupted Chain of Petitions coming on during the whole of the present Session *show* Ministers that they will not be forsaken . . . will not the voice of the Nation, thus displayed, show the Planters the impossibility of a successful resistance, and will they not therefore be more inclined to submit?"[27]

The West Indian planters unwittingly came to the aid of the abolitionists when, in 1823, a slave revolt in Demerara was followed by excessive white responses and, in 1824, by the death in jail of a white missionary, John Smith, who was accused of fermenting trouble. White planters believed that the abolitionists stirred up the slaves by talking about black freedom; abolitionists, for their part, regarded such incidents as symptomatic of the iniquities of the slave system. Emancipation seemed to be the only answer.

By the mid-1820s a commitment to emancipation was not merely a popular feeling, but had been embraced by powerful sections of British society. As before, the structure of local government was recruited to the side of black freedom.[28] And to secure a stronger voice in Parliament itself, abolitionists began to oblige parliamentary candidates, as early as 1826, to declare themselves on slavery. In fact, few spoke up for slavery. One candidate in Yorkshire declared in 1826, "On the gradual abolition of Colonial Slavery, I am happy to believe there are not two opinions in the country." All his opponents agreed. One stated, "On the subject of slavery, I am happy to think there is here no difference of opinion." Another made the same point. "Gentlemen, with regard to the Slave Trade, I believe there is only one opinion." A candidate in Leeds was introduced with the remarks, "Mr. Willson is a Christian, he is a Protestant, he is a member of the Church of England: therefore he hates slavery both of mind and body."[29] Elections in which candidates were thought to be sympathetic to slavery provided opponents with a license for scurrilous attacks.

> Freeman of York! Be firm to your great Cause of Liberty and Justice! Never let it be said that you have been Represented by
>
> A Slave Dealer!
>
> Remember!—They who, for filthy lucre, can be induced to Chain, to DRIVE LIKE CATTLE, and even Sell their Fellow Beings BY AUCTION, may possibly not scruple to barter their votes or betray your interests in the *House of Commons, whenever a favourable opportunity may offer.*[30]

By the mid-1820s support for slavery had clearly become an electoral liability for parliamentary candidates. Conversely, it was assumed that right-thinking candidates would favour gradual emancipation.

By that time abolitionism had also taken on a new perspective, and one which was to gain in stridency in subsequent years. The question of the economics of slavery became ever more prominent in political argument. Early in 1822 Cropper had privately raised the question of East Indian sugar and the artificial protection which kept West Indian sugar viable and costly to the British consumer.[31] By October 1822 this issue had broken into print.[32] Within four years, open support for freely imported East Indian sugar had become a major political objection to slave-grown sugar, as one parliamentary candidate noted: "The difference in the duty on East and West India sugars operates as a bounty on slavery, and as a tax on the people of England, which they may reasonably require to be removed."[33] Elsewhere it was argued that slavery was "supported by an annual donation from this country, of *nearly four million sterling*, given in the way of exclusions, bounties, and prohibitory duties. . . ."[34] The message was clear; the British consumer of sugar was maintaining the slave system.[35] As the 1820s advanced, this argument, so consonant with

growing contemporary economic idealogy, could be found with growing frequency and stridency in abolitionist meetings and literature
and in Parliament. Indeed, the economic critique of slavery soon became a plea for free trade, and by April 1827 "the Chambers of Commerce of Manchester and Birmingham and the merchants and
manufacturers of Leeds and other places" were demanding both free
trade and an end to the sugar duties. The new industrial nation had
come to see that slavery was inimical to its wider economic interests.[36]

The pattern of agitation went on much as before, with the by-now
familiar and expected spate of petitions descending on Parliament at
regular intervals. Between February 1824 and June 1825, 204 petitions were delivered; in 1826, 363 arrived between February and
May. The total for that session was calculated at 674.[37] And the number of names attached to the petitions was enormous. It was not true,
as their opponents claimed, that abolitionist petitions were merely
copied from a model from the Abolition Committee. There seems
little doubt, however, that the abolitionist responses and petitions did
indeed become more uniform after the launching of the *Anti-Slavery
Monthly Reporter* in 1825. Yet even more important was the fact that
the abolitionists were able to claim that their meetings "were sub-
scribed by persons of every class."[38]

It was in the slaveholders' interests to undermine the credibility of
antislavery and to denounce abolitionist tactics; they belittled the petitions, suggesting that they were rigged, copied, or the result of in-
temperate excitement. Yet abolitionists never doubted that all the evidence pointed to genuine and massive popular support.[39] And from
June 1825 we are able to trace this support in greater detail through
the columns of the *Anti-Slavery Monthly Reporter*, which ran until 1836.
Founded by Macaulay, the *Reporter* provided a superb mirror of the
world of abolitionism, particularly in the provinces. Indeed, this publication itself became a main focus for activity, for, widely distributed
throughout the country, it gave information, guidance, and direction
to the national cause.[40]

The most striking contribution of the *Reporter* was the prodigious
volume of information about slave society that it fed to the reading
public. One issue after another regaled its swelling readership with
the minutiae of slave life; the nature of slave work, leisure, housing,
family patterns, punishments, and religions—any and all facets of
slave society passed through the pages of the *Reporter*. Moreover, this
journal provided the invaluable service of distinguishing *between* the
slave societies of the different islands. The result was that a much
more sophisticated analysis of Caribbean slavery began to emerge in

the political debate.[41] Perhaps it is this feature which makes the later phase of the abolitionist struggle so appealing to a modern historian. One finds, for example, exemplary analyses of slave populations (from registration returns), with telling comparisons with slavery in the United States.[42] Any plantocratic claim was immediately followed by a detailed and documented abolitionist answer. Equally important was the *Reporter's* regular resumé of official government evidence. Government pronouncements, publications, colonial laws, and ministerial missives were reported, analysed, and challenged.[43] The *Reporter* made accessible to the public information which would otherwise have been embalmed in official publications. This was particularly true of correspondence between ministers and the colonies.[44] The sum total of these efforts was to make public what had previously been a private and secretive world of politics. This inevitably made life difficult for the men concerned—but it made for excellent pressure group politics, and it illustrated, to anyone interested, just what could be achieved through such pressures. In the process, the role of the minister began to change, for he was now subjected to pressures from without as well as from within.

The abolitionist argument about rights shows how far the wider political debate had advanced since the 1790s. At that earlier period belief in the "rights of man" had tended to be the preserve of the popular radicals, but by the 1820s this term—given an even wider meaning—had become a central abolitionist belief. Emancipationists in Norwich in 1825 thought slavery "to be utterly inconsistent with the inalienable natural rights of men."[45] Of course, the arguments about slavery were inevitably about the slaves' "Civil and Religious Liberties,"[46] Methodists in Yorkshire considered slavery "directly contrary to the natural Rights of Man,"[47] and it is striking that the abolitionist petitions which flooded Parliament—upward of 3,500 by 1832[48]—were steeped in a political vocabulary which, in the 1790s, had been the preserve of artisan radicals. Indeed, in the 1790s men were jailed and transported for seeking such rights for themselves; thirty years later, many thousands of Englishmen demanded these same rights—for black slaves. Some spoke of the slaves' "inalienable Rights of liberty of which they have been barbarously robbed"; others of the need to restore their "Constitutional Freedom."[49]

Abolitionists assumed that slaves should enjoy the rights of Englishmen. They even argued that the slaves were in fact Englishmen 5,000 miles away from England, speaking at times of "black Englishmen."[50] A petition of 1830 spoke of the slaves as "British-born Subjects."[51] Another wanted to see slaves raised "to the Enjoyment of all the Civil and Religious Rights and Immunities which are the birthright of every British Subject."[52] Furthermore, it was assumed that these rights were divinely ordained—"sacred Rights which belong to all the Family of Man."[53] Abolition thus transmuted the concept of social rights from the Paineite, secular model into one which was divinely ordained. As such, of course, it was more difficult to challenge.

Tactically, the abolitionists pressed on with their well-tried methods, convinced all the time that the key to success was public pressure in conjunction with careful and sustained lobbying within Parliament. In 1828 the Duke of Gloucester commented: "Thank God we live in a country where public opinion is of immense power. Our Constitution I may say, is founded on public opinion; and it is the happiness of this country that we live under a constitution where public opinion can have its proper and due weight. It is to that public opinion I now look."[54] Gradually, their efforts began to yield results. One new dimension to this "public opinion" was the rapid proliferation of female abolition associations—a major innovation not merely in abolition circles but in British politics at large. From an early date it was appreciated that women abolitionists could exercise a unique influence over their own entourage, and they were requested "to endeavour to awaken in the minds of their families, and all those over whom they have influence, a lively sense of the injustice, inhumanity and impiety of Negro Slavery."[55] By 1828 female associations were reported to be increasing by leaps and bounds and it is quite clear that they sometimes exercised enormous influence in their localities.[56] Two women alone, for instance, raised 187,000 names for abolitionist petitions.[57] Moreover, abolitionism penetrated even deeper into the previously nonpolitical world, for children, through their literature of the 1820s and 1830s, were persuaded of the iniquities of slavery.[58] Of course, such books were written for the children of the middle and upper classes—the very groups within the immediate reach of the ladies' abolition associations.

The peak (or rather the series of peaks) of popular antislavery feeling came in the years between 1830 and the calling of the reformed Parliament after 1832. Throughout that period abolition was carried along by the wider agitation for "The Bill" for parliamentary reform. Furthermore, the reform of Parliament, at one stroke, brought emancipation much nearer. The West India lobby was crippled by the Act, just as the emancipation of the Catholics had added a sizeable group to the abolitionist side. Even staunchly pro-planter publications began to retreat and to side with black freedom.[59] By 1830 the prospects of the slavery lobby were bleak and politically unenviable.

The West Indians and their supporters were beleaguered. Lectures, sermons, public meetings, all in addition to the swelling body of abolitionist literature in tracts and newspapers, continued to spread abolitionism even further. Using the language of the age—an age dazzled by the reality and the potential of mechanical progress—Parliament was compared to "the steam engine which required only *the steam of public opinion*, strongly expressed, to enable it to annihilate Colonial Slavery at one majestic stroke."[60] Moreover, after 1830 that public feeling had become so powerful that the sole restraint on the size of antislavery meetings was the capacity of the meeting place. The General Meeting of the Anti-Slavery Society in 1830 attracted 2,000 people—with 1,000 locked outside.[61]

By 1830 abolitionists had abandoned the idea of gradual emancipation, demanding instead immediate freedom.[62] And much of this shift in feeling was due to the efforts of the Agency Committee of the Anti-Slavery Society, whose lecturers and publications proved extraordinarily effective.[63] Dividing the country into different lecture circuits, the Agency Committee sent out peripatetic lecturers who, like Clarkson earlier, attracted large crowds and encouraged local associations and publications. Wherever they lectured they faced packed crowds; droves of people—of both sexes—poured into the towns to hear them speak. Time and again crowds were turned away from packed halls; lecturers often obliged by giving a second lecture to the disappointed (despite the fact that their lectures often lasted more than two and one-half hours!).[64] In 1830–1831, in towns throughout the country, meetings in assembly rooms, chapels, courts, town halls, county halls, guildhalls, taverns, and even music halls were better attended than any in living memory. And by any standard these meetings were often of amazing duration. The General Meeting in Exeter Hall in May 1832 (3,000 inside, plus an overflow) lasted from 12:00 noon until 7:00 P.M.[65] Timing was often crucial in capturing the popular vote. A meeting called for 10:00 A.M. in Hexham was clearly a mistake; "the hour being very inconvenient to the shopkeepers and workmen of all kinds, the meeting, though respectable, was by no means numerous. . . ."[66]

In the face of such encroaching and vigorous opposition it was difficult to recruit support for slavery. Most religious organizations now supported emancipation. Quakers, nonconformists, the Church of England, and the Church of Ireland were joined by the Catholics in denouncing what they saw as an affront to the Almighty. The Church of Scotland placed its 300 congregations at the abolitionists' disposal.[67] Not surprisingly, by 1830–1834 many hundreds of the abolitionist petitions came from church organizations and congregations. Whatever political and economic criticisms were leveled at slavery, there is little doubt that, on the eve of black freedom, slavery was univerally seen to be irreligious; "highly offensive in the sight of God, disgraceful to us as a free and a Christian people. . . ."[68]

If there is one single theme which stands out in the thousands of petitions in the years after 1830 it is the complaint that slavery was offensive to English religious sensibilities—of all persuasions. It was, in the words of Methodists from Barnsley, "repugnant to our Religion."[69] Others thought slavery an "Anti-Christian system."[70] It was, in the words of women from Hereford, "a System alike revolting to the feelings of Mankind as inconsistent with the Counsels of Heaven."[71] To a degree this may have reflected the influence of the Agency Committee, whose lecturers were pledged to avoid political controversy and to abide by the view that "the system of Colonial Slavery is a crime in the sight of God, and ought to be immediately and for ever abolished."[72]

In this, its last phase, abolitionism was self-confident, incomparably supported, and convinced that emancipation was but a matter of time. Moreover, in these years one is more aware of active guidance exercised over the national movement, notably by the *Reporter*—a guidance which gave coherence to the massive upsurge in public feeling. It is difficult to see how it could have been otherwise, for so widespread had the agitation become that it clearly needed central direction unless it were to become too diffuse and fragmented.[73] The work of the Anti-Slavery Society and of the *Reporter* was clearly crucial. The bare facts of the publications record of the Society make amazing reading. In 1823, it published 201,750 copies of twenty tracts (at the time Clarkson was on a 6,000-mile tour lasting fifteen months). The year after, it spread 145,671 pamphlets across the nation; in 1825, the number went up to 236,250. Each year similar figures indicate the massive efforts put into the campaign. By 1830, more than a half-million pamphlets issued from the Anti-Slavery Society.[74] And all this in addition to the enormously impressive efforts of local societies—measured in the thousands—which both followed the lead from London and gave it their own local flavor and strength.[75]

What seems to have proved crucial in these turbulent, radical years was the news of the Jamaican slave revolt of Christmas 1831—the biggest such revolt in living memory. Its violence and destruction and the inevitable reprisals provided abundant evidence, if any more was needed, that slavery was damned. But the scheme for emancipation, preceded by apprenticeship, which was eventually agreed to by the

British government was not to the abolitionists' liking, and a new campaign was launched to improve the terms and conditions of the apprenticeship schemes.[76] Apprenticeship died, however, from its own shortcomings. Yet it has to be remembered that it did so to the accompanying campaign of the abolitionists who, for the last time, stirred up the nation to defend the interests of the blacks in the Caribbean. Then, as before, there was no doubt in the minds of all concerned that the abolitionist cause had come to dominate "the attention of every class of the community."[77] And as the dominant concern, this sentiment played a powerful role in undermining and ending both the slave trade and slavery.

NOTES

1 Samuel Romilly, *Memoirs of the Life of Sir Samuel Romilly, Written by Himself*, 2d ed., 3 vols. (London, 1840), 2: 2–3.

2 Thomas Clarkson, *The History of the Rise, Progress and Accomplishment of the Abolition of the African Slave Trade by the British Parliament*, 2 vols. (London, 1808), 1: 415–16.

3 James Walvin, "English Democratic Societies and Popular Radicalism, 1791–1800" (D. Phil. thesis, University of York, 1970), chap. 13.

4 City of York, "House Book, 1780–1790," vol. 45, York City Archives; K. A. Macmahon, ed., *The Beverley Corporation Minute Book, 1707–1835*, Yorkshire Archaeological Society, Record Series (1956), pp. 71, 75.

5 David Geggus, "The British Occupation of Haiti" (D. Phil. thesis, University of York, 1979).

6 *The Times* (London), 12, 20, and 31 March, 1792; Thomas Walker, *A review of the political events which have occured in Manchester during the last five years* (Manchester, 1794).

7 The words are those of Thomas Hardy, Secretary of the London Corresponding Society, in British Library, Additional Manuscripts (hereafter cited as Add. Ms.) 27, 811, fs. 4, 9.

8 *A Very New Pamphlet Indeed!* (London, 1793), pp. 3–5.

9 Robert Isaac Wilberforce and Samuel Wilberforce, *The Life of William Wilberforce*, 5 vols. (London, 1839), 2: 18.

10 Quoted in E. M. Howse, *Saints in Politics* (London, 1973), p. 44.

11 See James Walvin, "The Impact of Slavery on British Radical Politics, 1787–1838," in *Annals of the New York Academy of Sciences*, vol. 292 (1977).

12 Romilly, *Memoirs*, 3: 1.

13 Ibid., pp. 139–40; *Index to the Journal of the House of Lords, 1780–1819*, 49: 846–51.

14 Romilly, *Memoirs*, 3: 141.

15 *Gentleman's Magazine*, 1816, pp. 26–27; Chester New, *The Life of Henry*

Brougham to 1830 (London, 1961), p. 138. See also the petition from Guiseley in the Hailstone Bequest, York Minster Library, York.

16 Lord Cockburn, *Memorials of His Time* (London and Edinburgh, 1909), p. 271.

17 Frances Dorothy Cartwright, ed., *The Life and Correspondence of Major Cartwright*, 2 vols. (London, 1826), 2: 84.

18 Quoted in New, *Life of Henry Brougham*, p. 138.

19 Clarkson to unknown correspondent, September 1814, in Add. Ms. 41, 267A, f. 60.

20 Romilly, *Memoirs*, 3: 253–54.

21 See in particular Barry Higman, *Slave Population and Economy in Jamaica, 1807–1834* (Cambridge, 1976).

22 Cropper to Zachary Macauley, March 1822, in Add. Ms. 41, 267A, fs. 106, 108, 110, 112, 126.

23 Cropper to Clarkson, Add. Ms. 41, 276A f. 113.

24 Macauley to Clarkson, Add. Ms. 41, 267A, f. 125.

25 R. Coupland, *The British Anti-Slavery Movement* (London, 1933), pp. 121, 131–32; Howse, *Saints in Politics*, p. 155, n. 55.

26 Wilberforce, *Life*, 5: 177.

27 Clarkson, undated 1823 letter, in Add. Ms. 41, 267A, f. 126.

28 See undated letter, March 1824, Y. 326, York City Archives; letter of 23 May 1828, *Memorials to the Corporation, 1827–1833*, K. 109, York City Archives.

29 *Speeches and Addresses of the Candidates for the Representation of the County of York in the Year 1826* (Leeds, 1826), pp. 26, 52, 55, 92–93, 125.

30 *Representation of the City of York* (York, 1826), in the York Reference Library.

31 Cropper to Macauley, 1822 (n.d.), Add. Ms. 41, 267A, fs. 106, 108.

32 See pamphlet, *Society for the Amelioration and Gradual Abolition of Slavery*, 12 October 1822, in Add. Ms. 41, 267A, f. 126.

33 *Speeches and Addresses of the Candidates*, p. 26.

34 *Address to the Public on the Present State of the Question Relative to Negro Slavery in the British Colonies* (York, 1828), p. 14.

35 *Negro Slavery; or a view of some of the more prominent features of that state of slavery as it exists in the U.S.A. and in the colonies of the West Indies* (London, 1823), p. 117.

36 *Anti-Slavery Monthly Reporter* (hereafter cited as *Reporter*), no. 17 (31 October 1826), no. 22 (31 March 1827), and no. 23 (30 April 1827).

37 *Index to the Journal of the House of Lords, 1820–1833*, vol. 50; *Reporter*, no. 8 (31 January 1826), p. 73.

38 *Reporter*, no. 14 (31 July 1826), p. 197.

39 See Wilberforce in *Reporter*, no. 8 (31 January 1826), p. 73.

40 *Reporter*, no. 1 (30 June 1825), p. 1.

41 *Reporter*, no. 7 (31 December 1825), pp. 61–70.

42 *Reporter*, no. 26 (July 1827), pp. 1–16.

43 *Reporter*, no. 28 (September 1827), passim.

44 *Reporter*, no. 29 (October 1827), p. 102.

45 *Reporter*, no. 6 (November 1825), p. 57.

46 *Journal of the House of Lords*, 63: 53.

47 Ibid., p. 101.

48 Computed from returns in the *Index to the Journal of the House of Lords, 1820–1833*, vol. 50, passim.

49 *Journal of the House of Lords*, 63: 24.

50 *Reporter*, no. 29 (October 1827), p. 141.

51 *Journal of the House of Lords*, 63: 22.

52 Ibid., p. 31.

53 Ibid., p. 24.

54 *Reporter*, no. 36 (May 1828), p. 236.

55 *Reporter*, no. 4 (September 1825), p. 32.

56 *Reporter*, no. 37 (June 1828), p. 252.

57 Coupland, *British Anti-Slavery*, p. 137.

58 A. Opie, *The Black Man's Lament* (London, 1826). This book, and many others, can be found in the Osborne Collection of children's literature in the Toronto Public Library.

59 *Reporter*, no. 53 (October 1829), p. 101.

60 *Reporter*, no. 60 (May 1830), p. 225.

61 *Reporter*, no. 61 (June 1830), p. 229.

62 T. C. Granger, *Speech of T. C. Granger, Esq., at a Meeting of the Inhabitants of the City of Durham for the Purpose of Petitioning Parliament for the Abolition of Colonial Slavery* (Durham, England, 1830), pp. 3–4.

63 *Report of the Agency Committee of the Anti-Slavery Society* (London, 1831), pp. 6–7.

64 Ibid., pp. 6–22.

65 *Reporter*, no. 96 (May 1832), p. 137.

66 James Losh, *The Diaries and Correspondence of James Losh*, ed. E. Hughes, 2 vols., Publication of the Surtees Society, vols. 171, 172 (Durham, England, 1962–63), 2: 97–98.

67 *Reporter*, no. 61 (June 1830), p. 266.

68 *Reporter*, no. 62 (July 1830), p. 300.

69 *Journal of the House of Lords*, 63: 24.

70 Ibid.

71 *Journal of the House of Lords*, 63: 33.

72 *Report of the Agency Committee* (1831), pp. 2–3.

73 See "The Framing of Petitions," *Reporter*, no. 65 (October 1830), pp. 451–52.

74 *Accounts of the Receipts and Disbursements of the Anti-Slavery Society, 1823–1831* (London, 1831), in Goldsmith's Library, University of London.

75 See, for instance, *First Report of the Suffolk Auxiliary Society* ... (Ipswich, 1825); *First Annual Report of the Swansea and Neath Auxiliary Anti-Slavery Association* (Swansea, 1826).

76 *Reporter*, no. 108 (May 1833), pp. 145–148.

77 J. Philips, *The West India Question* ... (London, 1823), p. iii.

PART II The Impact of Abolition

on Africa

CHAPTER 5: **The Abolition of the Slave Trade**

from Senegambia

Philip D. Curtin

It would be convenient if Senegambia could serve as a case study, representative of regions supplying the Atlantic slave trade; but Senegambia was not typical. It was unique among such regions in having a "shore" facing the Sahara as well as the Atlantic. Senegambian ports on the desert and the ocean were points of departure for the Maghrib as well as for the Americas. It was also atypical in the timing of its contribution to the slave trade. For Africa as a whole, the curve of maritime exports rose gradually from the sixteenth century to a peak in the 1780s, then declined slightly before coming to a second peak centered about the 1840s.[1] Senegambia, on the other hand, began as one of the chief contributors to the sixteenth century trade, but it never again became a major supplier. Instead, its slave exports reached a kind of plateau from the 1710s through the 1760s, then declined steadily, with one exceptional spurt of activity in the 1780s. By the 1790s, the level of exports had sunk to barely half that of the peak decades (see table 5.1).[2]

Accurate information about the slave trade across the Sahara is much harder to come by, but it appears to have reached a peak in the first half of the eighteenth century. In the 1770s the religious revolution of the *torodbé* faction against the Denianke rulers of Fuuta Tooro was at least partly a revolt against Moroccan and Saharan influence in the Senegal Valley, a northern intervention that had helped to feed the trans-Saharan slave trade. That trade no doubt continued,

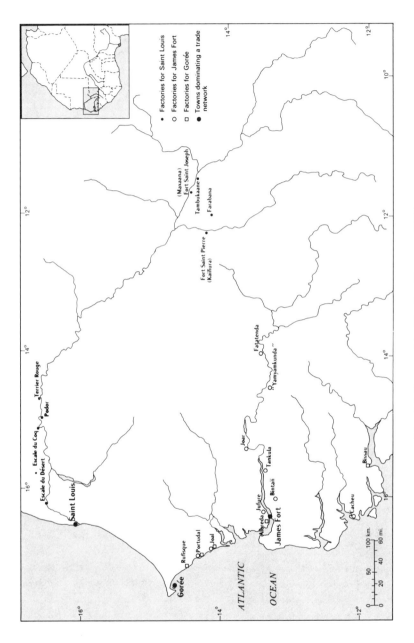

Map 5.1 Senegambian Trading Towns ca. 1820.

but it appears to have been comparatively small in the early nine-teenth century, when the maritime trade was passing out of existence.

Saharan influences, however, were important to Senegambia in more fundamental ways that gave Senegambian history in the nine-teenth century a different pattern from that of the Guinea coast. Sen-egambia alone of slave-supply regions for the Atlantic trade was largely Muslim in religion. It therefore participated more fully and directly than the others in the vast sweep of Muslim religious revolu-tions that remade the political map of the savanna belt from Cape Verde to the Red Sea.

In spite of these complicating factors, the superficial result of the legal abolition of the Atlantic slave trade by Britain in 1808 and the effective enforcement of abolition by France in 1831 can be stated quite categorically and simply: it was negligible. As the estimates in table 5.1 indicate, the total number of slaves shipped and the total value of slave exports declined steadily over the half-century from the 1790s to the 1840s, with no indication of a sharp discontinuity from *any* cause, though the slaves were sometimes given a new legal status. In the 1820s, for example, perhaps 500 were legally slaves and exported as such, but the Senegalese government also purchased slaves to serve in the army, and about 140 a year were *engagé à temps*—purchased as slaves but destined to serve under a disguised form of slavery in the French coastal sphere.[3] Some semilegal slave trade of this kind was to continue into the 1850s and later.

The gross measurement of regional exports disguised a much greater complexity. The Gambia, for example, could be closed to slave ships by the British batteries at the mouth of the river. This did not end the trade down the Gambia, but it imposed an overland march either to the coast opposite Gorée or to the navigable rivers in present-day Guinea-Bissau. But the numbers exported by these routes was not great in the 1830s and later, largely because of price factors. For reasons that are not well understood, the local price of slaves remained at a high level on the upper Senegal and in its vicin-ity, while slaves were up to 40 percent cheaper on the coast of Guinea-Bissau.[4]

Even though the immediate and direct impact of legal abolition was negligible, indirect consequences may have been more impor-tant—particularly consequences of the long and gradual decline in slave exports. This change in the export economy may well have been related to other detectable secular trends over the period from the mid-eighteenth to the mid-nineteenth centuries.

Two such trends are clear, and a third has been alleged. The first and most obvious is the rise of nonslave exports—what commentators at the time called "legitimate trade." This was not necessarily either a cause or a result of the declining slave trade, but the combination may well have brought major shifts in income within Senegambia, especially a diversion of income from those who profited from the slave trade to others who could profit from the new production for export.

This redistribution of income has been associated with an alleged increase in the use of unbridled military force by the secular aristocracy and their slave-soldiers, the *ceddo*, against the peasantry. Some historians have associated the power of the ceddo with the export of slaves and have seen this power growing steadily from the early eighteenth century, since the ceddo apparently profited from the sale of their captives. Then, as the export of slaves diminished, the ceddo and their masters, the kings, found their incomes declining. The ceddo therefore redoubled their efforts to take more captives, sometimes within the boundaries of the kingdom itself.[5] Such raids *did* sometimes take place, and anarchy seems to have increased in some parts of Senegambia, but this apparent increase may be the result of better evidence from European sources after about the 1770s. In any event, we still lack even the crudest index for measuring a rise in anarchy and oppression.

If there were such a rise, however, it could have been associated, and has been associated by historians, with the far more important set of political and religious changes that swept the western Sudan in the nineteenth century.[6] Senegambia had been largely Muslim since at least the sixteenth century, and the first king to be converted to Islam is reported for the eleventh century; but a very old and deep social and political tension had existed for centuries between the kings and the secular leadership on one hand and the Muslim clerics on the other. The clerics were often concerned in commerce as well as Islamic learning. They were often of foreign origin, which set them somewhat aside from the web of local kinship ties. Their mobility as merchants and wandering scholars brought them into contact with an ecumenical society far wider than the score or so of small states into which Senegambia was divided. By a very long tradition, they had asked for and often received from the secular rulers the right to administer particular towns and villages with full autonomy, so that the individual states were often pockmarked by scattered spots of clerical autonomy, linked in networks of religious and commercial interest. Within their own spheres, they commanded minor but significant military forces, and armed men went along with caravans to protect the goods and people in transit. What was to take place throughout Senegambia in the nineteenth century was the collapse of the secular rulers, the old aristocracy, and of the ceddo as a military force; and the substitution of political leadership, if not political control, in the hands of clerics who organized the masses through the agency of Muslim religious fraternities. One interpretation of these political and religious changes is to emphasize the demand for religious reform and purification. Another is to emphasize the oppression of the ceddo, on one hand, and an increase in the power of the peasantry on the other—the one caused by the declining slave trade and the other by the progressive shift to cash crops that put European goods, and especially guns, into the hands of the peasants. The peasants in turn rallied behind the Muslim clerics as the only available alternative to the discredited kings.

Although no single historian has put the case so simplistically, it is possible to reduce this pattern to a schematic set of causes and effects that began with the decline of the slave trade, making way for "legitimate" trade. This double shift in the economic sphere made for the rise of oppression and the reaction of the peasantry, led by clerics. To the extent that this pattern conforms to reality, slave-trade abolition could be assessed, not as negligible, but as all-important in forming Senegambian history in the nineteenth century.

Like many hypothetical relationships in history, this set poses some problems of cause and effect. Rather than seeing the decline of the slave trade as the cause of rising legitimate trade, it might be argued that merchants left the slave trade only when new "legitimate" opportunities appeared. The secular rulers and the ceddo might or might not have responded to the declining slave trade with more enslavement and oppression. The clerical rebels may have represented the peasant cause, but their explicit statements say nothing about the plight of the peasants and everything about the need for purity in Muslim belief and practice. For that matter, the religious revolts may well have been a protest against military oppression, but the religiously motivated armies of Shaykh Umar Taal and Samori Ture enslaved their enemies on an even larger scale than their secular predecessors had done. In this sense, it could be argued that they led to still more oppression of the kind that some had hoped they would remedy.

The problem here is to sort out these and associated relationships, to find which variables may be independent. Unfortunately, a complete answer is not possible, but recent research on Senegambian economic history allows the tracing of some of the *possible* connections—

particularly those that result from income redistribution in the wake of changes in Senegambian international trade.

The possible results of abolition begin with the nature of the slave trade itself, and here the peculiarity of the Senegambian slave trade comes into account. Where the supply of slaves from Africa as a whole rose with rising prices through the late seventeenth and eighteenth centuries (with a price elasticity of supply close to unity),[7] the elasticity of supply from Senegambia after 1730 or so was negative. Against an overall and quite steady increase in prices offered at the mouth of the Senegal from 1730 to 1830, the number of slaves supplied declined. And the rate of decline, at 1.5 percent per year, was even sharper than the price rise of 0.9 percent per year over the same period.[8]

This negative elasticity had one advantage for the suppliers of slaves. Prices rose as the number exported declined, so that the net income from the sale of slaves fell much less steeply than the quantity of exports did (see table 5.1). But the crucial question is, who within

Table 5.1
Senegambian Slave Exports, 1740s through 1840s
(decennial annual average)

Date	Number of Slaves Exported	Price per Slave: Invoice Sterling f.o.b.	Total Value at Current Prices	Total Value Adjusted for Ocean Freights & Import Prices, 1730s £ Sterling
1741–50	2,500	£ 10.05	£ 25,000	24,000
1751–60	2,250	12.80	29,000	26,400
1761–70	1,410	14.10	20,000	17,600
1771–80	1,210	17.90	22,000	18,400
1781–90	2,230	27.14	60,500	49,600
1791–1800	1,320	27.52	36,000	31,000
1801–1810	900	29.28	26,000	23,700
1811–20	—	—	—	—
1821–30	680	32.79	22,000	14,000
1831–40	400	34.33	13,700	14,500
1841–50	400	22.32	8,900	9,700

Source: Data from Curtin, *Senegambia*, 1:164, 166, 195, 336; 2:52–53.

Note: Invoice pounds sterling are the invoice values of goods traded in Senegambia by European merchants. This was the common eighteenth century way of reckoning, but to obtain constant values over time these European prices have to be adjusted to take account of decreasing ocean freight rates as described in the source. The second adjustment is for inflation and deflation of the European prices of imported commodities.

Senegambia enjoyed income or profits from this trade? What groups were losing as time passed? Foreign trade was not as significant at the eighteenth century level of Senegambian technology as it was to become at the nineteenth or twentieth century levels but slaves exported by sea in the peak decade of the 1780s were 87 percent of Senegambian exports.[9] Even though we cannot compare this figure with domestic production, it was a significant source of foreign exchange.

But slaves were not a costless export, even though slave raiding can be compared in some ways to the economics of burglary. Most slaves exported from Senegambia (as elsewhere in West Africa) had been kidnapped or captured in warfare. A smaller number had been political prisoners, the product of judicial condemnation, debt pawns sold off by creditors, or the like. Very few were domestic slaves sold by their masters to meet a momentary need for cash. This means that the original enslaver was not concerned with the "cost of production"—the cost of rearing a child until it was old enough to be sold into the trade. His only concern was the opportunity cost—the value of alternative uses for a captured person who was *not* to be sold into the slave trade. This is a significant fact in trying to understand how the gross sum paid for a slave on the coast, the f.o.b. price, came to be shared among the individuals and groups who were involved in the trade, right back to the ultimate captor, or the judicial authority that condemned a person to be sold into the trade.

The slave trade within Africa involved very high costs for guarding slaves, transporting them, and feeding them until the slavers from Europe turned up at the port. Even in regions immediately adjacent to the ports, holding and transaction costs and the merchants' profit ate up 40 to 50 percent of the f.o.b. price paid for a slave, and this percentage increased with distance from the port or with holding time till the actual date of sale. Such costs were especially high in the case of slaves who came from the far interior, beyond the head of navigation on the Gambia and Senegal rivers; and these slaves were a large proportion of the total exported from Senegambian ports—between about 45 and 85 percent of the total, the overall proportion through the eighteenth century being about two-thirds of the total. For the majority of the Senegambian slave trade, then, whatever payments were made to the original enslavers went to rulers and warriors further east—not to local kings and ceddo.

But that share was also very small. The cost of transportation was so great that the original sellers on the upper Gambia or Senegal rarely received as much as 5 percent of the f.o.b. price paid on the

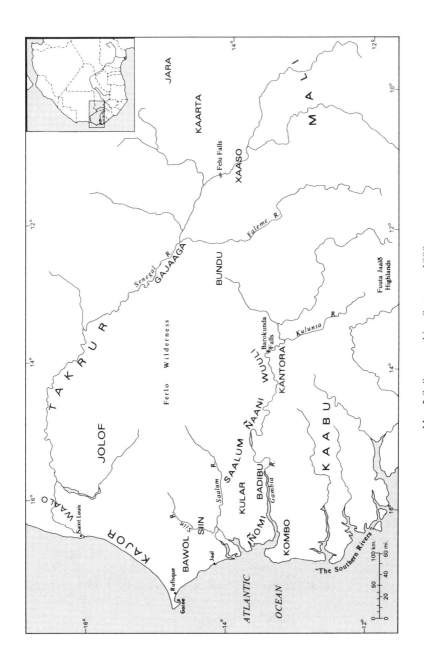

Map 5.2 Senegambian States ca. 1800.

coast.[10] This might have been high enough to encourage the sale of young male enemies—whose opportunity cost must have been very low, if not negative—but it was hardly enough to justify the costs of systematic slave raiding, at least for the sake of the Atlantic trade. The fact that the slaves from the far interior were overwhelmingly male supports this hypothesis. Women had a higher opportunity cost at the point of origin; the margin between the interior price and the coastal price was too small to justify the cost of transportation over this route of more than 400 miles.

But the political authorities along the trade routes profited from the slave trade in quite another way. They collected tolls from passing boats and caravans, usually, in the eighteenth century, at the rate of about 10 to 20 percent for each African jurisdiction. The total payout for a long trip from the upper Niger to the lower Gambia could therefore be considerable, and it was certainly more than the original enslaver might have received. For the Senegal water route from Maxaana to the coast some estimated cost accounts have survived from about 1785; they indicate that 32 percent of the delivered price on the coast went for tolls. As of that time and place, the payoff to the riverine rulers was about ten times the value paid to the original captors.[11]

On this basis, it is possible to make a rough comparison of the income from the slave trade enjoyed by various groups in Senegambian society. The enslavers in the far interior got very little indeed, at least from the Atlantic trade. Enslavers in the coastal and river kingdoms like Waalo, Bawol, Kajor, Ñomi, Ñaani, or Saalum could have received more, but they supplied only about one-third of the slaves entering overseas trade. Their take per slave was no more than half of the f.o.b. value, so that their maximum total income would have come to about 22 percent of the total value exported. Needless to say, these calculations are very rough, but they illustrate a point that will hold up even with a generous margin for error: historians of the slave trade who have assumed that enslavers received most of the income from the slave trade were wrong. Merchants' costs were certainly the largest share of the total cost, probably followed by tolls paid to political authorities.

It follows that the decline of the slave trade brought an irretrievable loss of income only for the enslaving authorities. (And, indeed, they might well have been able to compensate by selling more slaves into the local or North African slave trade.) Toll collections could be sustained as long as any commerce at all flowed down the trade routes, and these authorities collected the same percentages for all kinds of goods. The gradual replacement of the slave trade by "legitimate" trade could hardly have made much difference in the short run, since the incomes earned by moving goods to the coast would have gone to approximately the same people. But, as we shall see, it was to make a very important difference in the long run because the Europeans returned to the coast after 1815 with a policy of systematic gunboat diplomacy to force a reduction of tolls.

But this new use of force need not have deprived the African *juula*, or merchants, or even the kings and other authorities, of a net "take" from toll collections, because they collected at lower rates but from a larger volume of goods. During the half-century from the 1780s to the 1830s, gum, gold, ivory, hides, beeswax, and peanuts had all passed the former total value of slaves exported—and in real terms, not merely money rates (see table 5.2). Over that half-century, the

Table 5.2
Value of Principal Senegambian Exports, 1730s to 1830s

| Commodity | Annual Average Value in Sterling Values of 1731–40 | | |
	1731–40	1781–90	1831–40
Gold	£ 2,100	£ 150	£ 10,800
Gum	2,600	8,000	258,700
Hides	10	7	29,000
Ivory	1,100	160	10,100
Slaves	17,500	49,600	14,500
Beeswax	3,900	700	15,200
Peanuts	—	—	9,300
Total	27,210	58,617	347,600

Sources: Curtin, *Senegambia*, 2:98, 101; table 5.1.

Note: The reduction to 1730s prices and the allowance for freight rate changes have been carried out as described in note to table 5.1.

real value of exports rose nearly fivefold, an annual rate of increase of 3.5 percent. By the 1830s, the value of the slave trade had sunk to less than 2 percent of total exports. But this leaves the possibility that a sustained "abolition crisis" might have taken place in the intervening decades. Unfortunately, it is not possible to trace the flow of all significant commodities over this half-century, though it *is* possible to trace gum, with some allowance for a margin of error because of weak price date (see table 5.3). The result is so striking that a clear pattern emerges carrying broad credibility, even if the details are weak. Between the 1780s and the 1790s the price of gum rose without provoking increased production. In the next decade production be-

Table 5.3
Senegambian Gum Exports, 1780s through 1830s

Date	Annual Average Quantity in Metric Tons	Price per Ton in Current Invoice £ Sterling	Annual Average Value Adjusted for Ocean Freights and Changing Value of Imports, in 1730s £ Sterling
1781–90	321[a]	30.36[a]	7,990
1791–1800	381[b]	60.00	19,500
1801–20	725[b]	55.00[c]	36,600
1821–30	1,264[b]	61.00[d]	48,500
1831–40	3,390[a]	72.49[a]	258,700

Sources:
[a] Curtin, *Senegambia*, 2:98–101.
[b] Curtin, *Senegambia*, 2:64–65.
[c] Customs returns, dated 15 January 1818, for the first half of 1817, in Archives Nationales, Paris, section Outre-mer, Sénégal XIII 72.
[d] Ministère des colonies, France, *Statistiques coloniales*, annual series (Paris, 1822–).

gan to rise as well—and so rapidly that gum carried the greatest increase in exports over the entire half-century. Gum already came to half of the value of slave exports in the 1790s, and by about 1800 it was equal in value; the great Senegambian gum boom reached a peak in the 1830s, 1840s, and 1850s.

But the gum forests were not evenly distributed through the region. Most of them, indeed, were in the dry steppe country to the north of the Senegal River. The first accretion of income therefore flowed to the tribal authorities among the Moors of the steppe, whose slaves actually collected the gum and prepared it for sale. But even more income soon began to flow into the hands of the Saint Louis merchants and the sedentary rulers along the river—at least until the warfare between France and Britain came to an end and freed each power to act more forcefully in its African diplomacy.

The rapid increase of gum income may therefore have brought increased prosperity to the northern gum-trading and gum-producing region, while the region toward the Gambia and the Casamance stagnated. If so, the situation ended before 1820. Even though Gambian exports in that period cannot be disaggregated, their value by 1823 had reached nearly the same value as the combined exports of Gorée and Saint Louis.[12] By that time, Gambian exports in hides and beeswax had more than replaced the value of slave exports. The northern advantage was to weaken even more with the rise of Senegambian peanut production. By the 1840s, the exported peanut crop was worth £79,370 in 1730s pounds sterling. And this was only the beginning of a much longer trend that was to result in the one-crop export economy of Senegambia today.

With an outline of these alterations in foreign trade in hand, it may be possible to return with more security to the hypothesis relating these changes to the causes of the great jihads. Some points should become clear; others should become more probable in the light of major economic trends; and some hypotheses may be dismissed.

The decline of the slave trade was comparatively slow, and its value was small compared to the rapid rise of "legitimate" exports. If there was an abolition crisis for the secular nobility and the ceddo, it must have been slight. The local military received too small a part of the total export value of slaves to be deeply affected. This says nothing at all about the possible increase in oppression. It may have taken place, but the fact that slave prices remained high in the inter-African slave trade suggests that the ceddo raids may well have been designed to feed that outlet, not the Atlantic trade. If so, these represent a continuation of the anarchy, raiding, and civil war that prevailed in Fuuta Tooro and other desert-edge states under Moorish influence during much of the eighteenth century. And the Futaanke jihad of the 1770s was a reaction to the desert raiders, not to Europeans; though the early Almamate profited greatly from the new political unity of the Senegal Valley to collect tolls more effectively than ever before.[13]

The next significant stage in the religious revolution struck Waalo and Kajor in 1827–30. Unlike the Futaanke revolt a half-century earlier, this one, under the leadership of a cleric, the Serlin Koki, and a goldsmith, Diile Kumba Jombos Cam, had an element of social protest. It was unsuccessful in Kajor, won an initial victory in Waalo, but was then suppressed by French troops from Saint Louis.[14] Its initial success suggests political weakness in the Waalo aristocracy, but the date is well into the period of revived "legitimate" trade, and is therefore hard to associate with a declining slave trade. And it was much too early to be associated with new peasant strength built on peanut production. Peanuts were to come in Waalo, but not yet.

The most serious religious warfare in Senegambia appeared later—with the rise of Shaykh Umar Taal in Fuuta Tooro in the 1850s and with jihad of Ma Ba Jaxu (Diakhou) in Badibu or Rip in 1860. Shaykh Umar's movement gained power in Fuuta by peaceful religious adhesion, not through extensive military action, much less through peasant rebellions. Its military adventure took it eastward as a war of conquest by Muslim Futaanke over non-Muslim or partly Muslim populations. Economic historians have not tried to associate this movement with economic changes growing out of the export trade. That case could be made much more strongly, however, in regard to Ma Ba and other leaders in states bordering the Gambia. This was one of the first regions to move into really extensive peanut production for export, and a new flow of imported goods into the hands of juula and peasantry may well have helped them to build a movement to resist the secular rulers. If so, the date is too late to be a consequence of abolition, but well placed to indicate a possible consequence of the new legitimate trade alone.[15]

The rise in new exports can also be seen as an important cause of a new kind of European activity after the Napoleonic wars. In 1816 the British established a new colony on Banjul Island, christening the new town Bathurst. This was the first official British post on the Gambia since the evacuation of James Fort in 1779, and the known motives for the move reflected both abolition and the rise of nonslave exports. Abolition and the need for a post from which to suppress the slave trade were the official reasons, but the more pressing needs were those of the British merchants settled on the island of Gorée, which had been returned to France with the peace. They needed a new center for their commercial activities up and down the coast, and their initial interests turned mainly to the gum trade off the Mauritanian coast, and only secondly to the hides, gold, or wax of the Gambia hinterland. In the following year the French returned to Saint Louis (under British occupation in the last years of the war) with a principal interest in the gum trade of the Senegal River.

Neither reoccupied colony was overtly different from the kind of European post that had existed in the era of the slave trade. But the extent of the new trade soon attracted greater European investment, especially in trade goods loaned out to African or Afro-European traders who went up the rivers to do the actual trading. Along with new investment came new tools turned out by European industrial technology. The Senegal was a very hard river to use with human power and sail alone; the current was very strong in the season of high water, the only time of the year it could be navigated at all; and the prevailing wind also blew downstream. In 1819, the French began to operate the first steamboat on the river, which brought cheaper freight rates and, even more important, put every village near the river within range of water-borne artillery. Both powers established fortified posts upriver as well, and both began to use gunboat diplomacy to reduce the tolls that stood in the way of greater profits for their own traders in Bathurst and Saint Louis. Both, at various times, used the device of a legal monopoly granted to a local corporation to improve their bargaining position against the African suppliers. Tolls on the Senegal, which had been more than 30 percent by value in the 1780s, dropped by the period 1836–40 to an average of 4 percent. As trade became more complex, access to credit, insurance, and other functions of nineteenth century business organization came to be concentrated more and more in Saint Louis and Bathurst. European conquest was still a half-century away, but by the 1830s Europeans dominated Senegambian trade more firmly than they had ever done in the era of the slave trade.

But all of these changes were not a direct result of the increasing "legitimate" trade; both the rising prices in Europe, expressing new demands of an industrializing society, and the new way of maximizing the profit from that trade were reflexes of European industrialization. It has been argued that the abolition of the slave trade was also a result of industrialization, but the abolition of that trade seems to have had only a small impact on the Senegambian economy, compared to the new "legitimate" trade. As for the religious revolutions, the new spurt of foreign trade may have been a factor in the case of Ma Ba in Badibu and, somewhat later, in the disturbances in Kajor and elsewhere in coastal or riverine Senegal. But the reach of the new commerce hardly extended beyond the heads of navigation on the two rivers until late in the nineteenth century. Given the fact that the great movements of militant Islam in the nineteenth century took place clear across the western Sudan, their fundamental roots must be sought in influences with a similar geographical spread.

In conclusion, then, the end of the slave trade was not very important. It did not *cause* the rise of "legitimate trade," which happened simultaneously and independently; and the slave trade within Africa flourished long after the export trade had ended. It did not cause a very wide diversion of incomes within Senegambian society, which might have had important social and political consequences. Neither the rise of nonslave trade nor the decline of the slave trade had a really important influence on the great jihads, though the rise in the value of exports may have influenced the Senegambian part of that movement. But the very fact that the ends of the Atlantic slave trade had such modest consequences in this region is of some importance in itself. It helps to remind us that the course of African history before the industrial age was not nearly so subordinate to European influences as an older and more ethnocentric school of European historians of Africa used to believe, even though this conclusion will not necessarily hold for all of the supply regions of the Atlantic slave trade. The impact of abolition, like the impact of the slave export economy itself, was very different in different parts of the continent.

NOTES

1 Philip D. Curtin, *The Atlantic Slave Trade: A Census* (Madison, 1969); David Eltis, "The Export of Slaves from Africa, 1821–43," *Journal of Economic History* 37 (1977): 409–33.

2 Philip D. Curtin, *Economic Change in Pre-Colonial Africa: Senegambia in the Era of the Slave Trade*, 2 vols. (Madison, 1975).

3 Serge Daget, "L'abolition de la traite des noirs en France de 1814 a 1831," *Cahiers d'études africaines* 11 (1971): 14–58; Curtin, *Senegambia*, 1:189 n.

4 Curtin, *Senegambia*, 1:168.

5 Martin Klein, "Social and Economic Factors in the Muslim Revolution in Senegambia," *Journal of African History* 13 (1972): 419–41, p. 423; Claude Meillassoux, ed., *The Development of Indigenous Trade and Markets in West Africa* (London, 1971), p. 56.

6 See, for example, Martin Klein, *Islam and Imperialism in Senegal: Sine-Saloum, 1847–1914* (Stanford, 1968).

7 E. Philip LeVeen, "The African Slave Supply Response," *African Studies Review* 18 (April 1975): 19–28.

8 Curtin, 1:164, 189, 194–95.

9 Ibid., 1:187–99; 2:98.

10 Ibid., 2:44–47.

11 Ibid., 1:279–86.

12 Ibid., 2:100.

13 James B. Johnson, "The Almamate of Futa Toro, 1770–1836: A Political History" (Ph.D. diss., University of Wisconsin, 1974), pp. 24–104; David Robinson, "Abdul Qader and Shaykh Umar: A Continuing Tradition of Islamic Leadership in Futa Toro," *International Journal of African Historical Studies* 6 (1973): 286–303.

14 Lucie Colvin, "Kajor and Its Diplomatic Relations with Saint-Louis du Senegal" (Ph.D. diss., Columbia University, 1971), pp. 213–52; Boubacar Barry, *Le royaume du Waalo* (Paris, 1972), pp. 267–74.

15 Amar Samb, "L'Islam et l'histoire du Senegal," *Bulletin de l'IFAN*, ser. B, 33 (1971): 461–507; Charlotte A. Quinn, *Mandingo Kingdoms of the Senegambia: Traditionalism, Islam, and European Expansion* (London, 1972); Klein, *Islam and Imperialism*. For another interpretation of the balance between religious ideology and material interests in the jihads as a group, see Robin Horton, "The Rationality of Conversion," pt. 2, *Africa* 45 (1975): 373–99.

CHAPTER 6: **Abolition and Its Impact on Monies Imported to West Africa**

Jan S. Hogendorn and Henry A. Gemery

One of the least remarked effects of the abolition of the Atlantic slave trade is its monetary impact on West Africa. For a region which acquired a sizable portion of its domestic money supply through export earnings, the shift away from slave exports slowed monetary growth but, of more significance, produced a profound reduction in human costs, and thus a decided reduction in the real opportunity cost of money. Since much of West African monetary history tells of the rising social cost of money, the initial break in that pattern—perhaps temporary—is notable. The sections that follow discuss the social costs or savings associated with commodity, fiat, and imported monies; survey the imported monies current in West Africa during the era of the slave trade; and conclude by assessing the evidence for inferring a drop in both money supply growth and the social cost of money as the overseas slave trade ended.

THE COSTS OF MONIES

Whatever form a commodity money takes—cloth strips, iron bars, gold—it is obtained and used at some real cost to society. A direct production cost is incurred as well as the opportunity cost of maintaining a stock of the commodity in its monetary use (thus foregoing

99

the alternative commodity use[s]). With economic development, societies in the North Atlantic basin have moved toward money forms
which have minimal acquisition costs and near-zero opportunity
costs, i.e., fiat or bank monies whose scarcity value is maintained by
(or, too often, depreciated by) the actions of government bodies. As
the transfer from a commodity money to a fiat money occurs, a one-
time social saving accrues to society. H. G. Johnson has defined the
straightforward case: "Now consider the replacement of a commodity
money—the use of which is assumed for simplicity not to be subject
to seigniorage—by a purely paper money, assumed to be non-inter-
est-bearing and to cost nothing to print. The replacement frees the
resources embodied in the stock of commodity money for other more
productive uses and yields a social saving equal to the value of these
resources."[1] In the simplest circumstance, the argument is illustrated
by figure 6.1. The shift to a costless fiat money (S_1, identical with the
Q axis), when the commodity money (S) is supplied at constant cost,
generates the social saving $OPMQ_m$. The fact that the new money is
resource-costless does not reduce its price to zero, for the government restricts money creation to OQ_m, thus providing an identical
replacement for the commodity money stock previously available. All
is the same, except that the resources embodied in the old commodity
money are now free to move into their next best alternative use, and

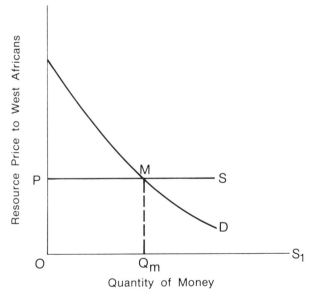

Figure 6.1 Social Saving Resulting from the Substitution of Fiat Money for Commodity
          Money.

additions to the money stock may now appear costlessly when the government decision-making body so decrees.

Or so a stylized monetary history of the West would have it. Monetary developments in West Africa, however, were far removed from the simple pattern of transfer from commodity to fiat money; yet, for all the complexity of those developments, the concept of social saving or social cost remains valid and relevant to the changing money forms. Two cases will serve to illustrate the point, the adoption of the cowrie and the abolition of the slave trade.

The growth of the cowrie zone in West Africa provides a perverse example of H. G. Johnson's point, in that indigenous commodity monies were supplemented and largely replaced by a currency analogous to a fiat money in all but the one crucial respect of being lower-cost. Like any fiat money, cowries possessed little intrinsic value and few nonmonetary uses. Like fiat money, they had the characteristic advantages of being small in size, durable, readily divisible, impossible to counterfeit, and in augmentable but not ready supply. Unlike fiat money, cowries were far from costless. The slave and commodity exports which financed their acquisition made them higher in cost than the African-produced indigenous monies (cloth strips, metal rods and bars) that they displaced. Rather than achieving a social saving, the adoption of the cowrie imposed a social cost on West Africa—a reversal of the Johnson lesson.

With abolition, however, the lesson returns to one of social saving. Instead of exporting a slave/commodity "bundle" in exchange for imported monies—cowries, iron bars, manillas—Africans now would export a commodity "bundle." There is a prima facie case for inferring a lower value to a commodity export than a human one, dramatically so on social cost grounds; but even on narrower valuation grounds the case remains strong. Human agents, like capital but unlike commodities, derive their lump sum value from the discounted value of their future marginal products. The real compensation to a society losing labor would be that value. However, since the market returns from slaving within West Africa were earned by a group different from that bearing the actual losses, slave sellers had no incentive to recognize the foregone discounted value of future marginal products in the price they would accept for their captives. The coercive nature of slave gathering thus insured that slaves were supplied at less than their full value to the losing society, social costs aside.

If slave markets as they functioned failed to recognize the direct economic costs of slavery, they failed even further in assessing the social costs. Social costs incorporated third-party effects (or externalities, in economists' terminology) resulting from slave-trading activities. These would include social, political, and psychological disruptions, and specifically the costs of organized defense, of armed patrols of scouts, and of the retreat from better farmland to poorer land as safety was sought in hilltop sanctuaries, as well as the climate of fear. When the imposed social costs are added to the economic costs, it becomes impossible to conceive of an alternative export which might have carried a higher real cost than slaves. Any commodity export appears lower-cost by a sizable margin. The fact that in the long-term coerced labor continued to play a part in the production and export of commodities, especially palm oil, does not upset that conclusion. Only in the event that slave acquisition to enhance indigenous production of such commodity exports continued at a volume equal to that carried on for the slave exports themselves would it be possible to question the reduction in real cost. To our knowledge no writer suggests such a possibility.

The diagrammatic argument for a social saving in West African money acquisition stemming from abolition is illustrated in figure 6.2. Before abolition, imported increments to the money stock (OQ_m) were acquired by trading slaves and commodities at a market value of OP_m.[2] But OP_m was a far from complete measure of the resource costs borne by all of West Africa. Had market prices recognized the

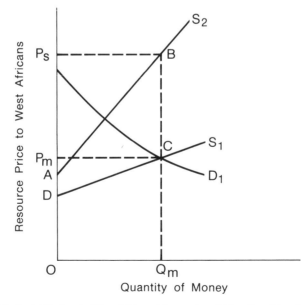

Figure 6.2 Social Saving in West African Money Acquisition Resulting from the Abolition of the Slave Trade.

external costs imposed by the coercive nature of slaving, the S_2 supply curve would have been relevant and the true price OPs would have been so high as to induce little or no effectual demand for imported money, and thus little slaving for that purpose, though, of course, at some lower price slaving might have occurred even with the full social costs incorporated. At the perceived price OP_m, however, OQ_m continued to be imported since the marginal social costs, BC, went unrecognized. The vertical distance between the two supply curves may be taken as a measure of the social costs of slaving throughout the OQ_m range; thus the total social costs imposed on the society were DABC. The total resource cost or opportunity cost of imported money was then $OABQ_m$.

Post-abolition, the social cost quadrilateral disappeared as slaves were no longer exported as payment for money imports. In the long term, there was further adjustment to an equilibrium defined by the original demand for imported money and a supply curve, S_1, now devoid of social costs. OQ_m could again be imported at the same market price OP_m—a price which now reflected the lower incurred resource costs of $ODCQ_m$.[3] What was before a social cost, DABC, now became a social saving. No measure of that saving can be made, since the social costs cannot be estimated; nonetheless, the evidence which does exist can be scrutinized to see whether money imports moved in the fashion consistent with the social savings analysis. To that end, a short survey of eighteenth and early nineteenth century imported monies is necessary.

WEST AFRICA'S MONEY IMPORTS

During the eighteenth century West Africa acquired imported monies in numerous forms. Normally, a portion of these money imports was financed through the export of slaves. The imported monies of most importance included cowries and copper in the form of bars, rods, wires, and manillas. Imported on a smaller scale were iron bars, guinée cloth, gold, and various coined money of overseas provenance.[4]

Cowries

The most important of the imported currencies was the cowrie shell. Possessing little intrinsic value and few nonmonetary uses, the shell money had all the requisite characteristics. Cowries (*Cypraea moneta*) were an import from the Maldive Islands in the Indian Ocean. Widely adopted as money on the coasts of that ocean, especially in Bengal, they were first imported to West Africa overland from North Africa after a long transit through the Middle East. No later than the eleventh century, they were already in use in the major markets of the middle Niger River. Some were even transshipped at Venice before crossing the Sahara. Long before the Atlantic slave trade began, their use had spread westward to Mauritania (before 1400) and southeast and southwest along the Niger.[5]

As an alternative or supplement to the indigenous commodity monies of West Africa, cowries had undeniable advantages. The "useful" commodity currencies such as cloth strips and iron bars were continually susceptible to leakage into their commodity uses. Slaves functioned as a currency only for transactions in very high denominations. The traditionally used metallic monies of Europe—gold, silver, copper, bronze—were always too limited in supply to serve as widely functioning currencies.

With the very large growth in the overseas slave trade in the eighteenth century there came very much larger imports of cowries. The shells spread east from the original area of use to Hausaland early in that century. Even before the growth of the slave trade, they had already moved "south to the forest between the Ivory Coast and the Niger Delta, where they merged with cowries imported by European traders by sea from the sixteenth century onwards."[6] Cowrie imports during the eighteenth century far exceeded those of any other currency; Marion Johnson has estimated that the annual average figure was about 160 metric tons per year during that time, with the imports coming largely from the Maldives via Ceylon to the chief European entrepôt, Amsterdam, and thence back to West Africa in the slavers' ships.[7]

The intimate connection between the imported cowrie currency and the export of slaves is clear. O. Dapper's *Description de l'Afrique*, published in 1686, states that "dan tous les achats, la troisième partie du payement se fait en boesjes [cowries], et les deux autres en marchandises."[8]

In William Bosman's *Description of Guinea*, 1705, we find him writing of the slave coast, "The disputes which we generally have with the owners of these slaves are, that we will not give them such goods as they ask for them, especially the boesies [cowries] . . . of which they are very fond. . . ."[9] Bosman notes that extra care was taken of the slaves exchanged against cowries in comparison with those exchanged against other goods, this presumably representing careful use of monetary policy by government officials.[10]

The Royal African Company found the shells "almost a *sine qua non*" for trading at Whydah, Ardra, and in the Bight of Benin.[11] It was common to find that Africans would exchange slaves only for some fixed ratio of the money import—sometimes one-quarter of the value, sometimes one-third, and sometimes as much as one-half.[12]

Even the roughest estimate of the money cost of cowrie imports to West Africa in the eighteenth century represents an heroic exercise in guesswork. It is possible, however, to use the ratio of one-quarter to one-third of slave exports paid for by cowrie imports. If the assumption is adopted that approximately half of the slaves exported during that century came from ports where the cowrie was ordinarily part of the transaction, then the coastal value of cowrie imports would have been on the order of 25 percent to 33 percent of £40 million, or about £10 million to £13 million.[13] Though such an estimate may be too high, this is not very likely, because no increment is included for cowries paid for by commodity exports or any other imported currency (copper, cloth, etc.) obtained through exports.

In the eighteenth century the use of cowries spread extensively north from the coast into the interior. Documentation is best for the central savanna, through the work of Paul Lovejoy. Lovejoy recounts eighteenth century movements of shell into Hausaland and Nupe, noting the north-south exchange through Oyo, the government of which was an exporter of slaves southward; the cowries received from the trade were reexported northward for slaves and other products of the savanna. Slave-cowrie transactions also figured in Niger River trade, with the Igbo shipping shell northward in exchange for slaves and other products. Eventually cowries shipped east-west by Muslim merchants reached the Volta markets, marking an enlargement of the trade in currency.[14] The evidence corresponds with economic logic in suggesting considerably higher prices for cowries in the interior, reflecting transport costs from the coasts. This of course meant more slave exports per unit of money import, and thus reflected an even higher real cost for money in the savanna than was true of the coast.

Copper

Money was also imported in the form of copper and copper alloys, shipped largely from Western Europe. In some areas (for example, the Cross River region of Nigeria) the copper took the form of rods, usually long, narrow, and bent double. For transactions in small denominations, copper wire was used. Along the Niger River delta a conventionalized brass bracelet called the manilla (from the Portuguese *manilha*, bracelet) was in use by the sixteenth century. John Barbot's *Description of the Coast of North and South Guinea*, published in 1746, describes the care needed in European copper fabrication, as Africans would refuse imperfect examples. Curtin guesses that total copper and alloy imports in the era of the slave trade were about 100 metric tons per year, with little probability that such imports ever exceeded 500 tons per year. The use of imported copper, like the cowrie, had spread inland during the slave trade, for example to Borno. But the world market price of copper rose significantly late in the eighteenth century, cutting back the area where this currency was in circulation.[15]

Iron

Though iron was imported primarily for its commodity uses, it too served as currency, particularly on the upper Guinea coast. The iron bars of Senegambia's international trade were, however, units of account, corresponding to the "ounce trade" along the coast to the south and east, and the iron bars did not circulate domestically as currency.[16] The use of iron as currency was thus presumably small by the scale of the cowrie or copper monies.

Cloth

Most cloth currencies of West Africa were of domestic manufacture. But in one important case the cloth currency was an import. This was the guinée cloth money of the Senegal area. Guinée cloth, called blue baft by the British, was a product of the looms of southeast India, in the region of Madras and Pondichéry. Dyed a dark indigo blue, this cloth displaced an earlier cloth currency of local manufacture in the later eighteenth century. Guinée cloth was not as intimately connected to the export of slaves as were the cowrie and the copper currencies, as the cloth was largely put into circulation among the Moors to the north, who were exporters much more of gum than of slaves.[17]

Gold

West Africa was, of course, a producer of gold, most of it mined in the Akan goldfield of the Gold Coast (now Ghana), the Bambuk goldfield in what became Mali, and the Boure goldfield of the present-day Republic of Guinea. Where gold circulated as a currency—as it did in a few areas such as Akan—it usually had been mined within West Africa. During the eighteenth century, however, in the heyday of the slave trade, considerable quantities of gold came to be smuggled from Brazil to pay for slaves. Brazilians could legally export only tobacco to Africa; gold could legally be shipped only to Lisbon. But Brazilian gold from the new strikes in Minas Gerais flowed in quantity, both (ironically) to the Gold Coast and to Whydah. With double irony, the slaves purchased for gold were often destined to mine that very metal in Brazil. For a time some gold actually flowed from Europe to West Africa, "since Gold Coast traders had begun to demand gold for their slaves."[18]

Curtin (whose paper "Monetary World" covers the subject thoroughly) gives some estimates on the quantity imported from Brazil. Records for 1718 to 1723 imply that some 40 kgs. of gold were exchanged annually for slaves at Dutch trading stations. Brazilian data give reason to believe that the shipments may have been much higher—as much as 478 kgs. for the year 1721.[19]

Coins

Coins minted in Europe and the Americas had some use as a circulating medium in the eighteenth century. Spanish or South American dollars (originally thalers) were introduced by slave traders, and had some circulation along the coasts. Their use is especially well documented by Curtin for Senegambia, where dollars were a medium of exchange from about 1720. Imports of Spanish dollars were sometimes made directly from Spain. Dutch 28-stuiver pieces were also important at first, but were eventually superseded by the Spanish dollar.[20] By and large these importations were small, and many silver coins ended in their commodity form, melted down for re-use as jewellry.

Meanwhile, across the Sahara gold mithquals (dinars), silver Maria Theresa dollars, and other coins were imported in part payment for slave exports, though again such imports appear to have been relatively small before the nineteenth century.[21]

In summary, a variety of imported currencies flowed to West Africa during the era of the slave trade. These currencies were acquired in large part through the export of slaves. J. D. Fage's estimate is that no more than one-quarter of the eighteenth century exports from coastal West Africa were items other than slaves.[22] For the most significant currencies, cowries and copper, slaves were even more im-

portant as payment for the money supply, for it was these two currencies that predominated in the most active slaving area from Dahomey
to the Cross River. Remaining in domestic circulation, these monies
formed a large part of the West African money supply. Rarely has
such a supply been acquired at so enormous a cost.

THE DECLINE IN MONEY IMPORTS

The decline in money imports to West Africa was an immediate result
of the abolition movement. This was seen first in the reduction in
slave exports following the British abolition of the seaborne trade in
1807 (with criminal penalties attached to trading in 1811), and the
French prohibition on trade which became effective in the late
1820s.[23] Curtin's latest estimates of exports by the British, French,
Portuguese, and Dutch from 1801 to 1810 show 207,000 slaves
shipped, less than half of the 429,000 shipped from 1761 to 1770.[24]
The slave trade eventually recovered to some extent, but the Brazilian and Spanish trade, plus the clandestine operations of the merchants of other countries, never shipped the volume reached in the
eighteenth century. The recent work of David Eltis shows a decadal
average of about 310,000 for each of the decades 1821–30 and
1831–40.[25]

Initially there was no export to replace the lost value of slave shipments. There were no cocoa exports until the 1890s, no cotton until
the 1850s (and that was a failure), no groundnuts from the Gambia
until 1834, from Senegal until 1840, and from northern Nigeria until
1912. The palm oil trade came to be the main replacement for slave
exports, and shipments grew to very high levels by mid-century. But
shortly after the ending of the slave trade palm oil exports were still
small, with only 873 long tons shipped to Britain in 1820 as compared
to the 22,000 tons of 1850.[26] (Most of the palm oil went to Britain; in
the first years of trade shipments to France were only about 5 percent
of the British total.)[27] Nor did timber exports fill the gap. West African teak shipments to Britain, though large at 23,251 loads in 1837,
were only 1 percent of that (297 loads) in 1817. Less dramatically, in
1817 barwood, camwood, ebony, and mahogany shipments together
were only 1,700 tons, one-third their combined 1837 figure. There
was neither growth nor decline in the standard staples—ivory, gum,
and indigo—during this period.[28]

Finally, the Saharan slave trade did not take up the slack. Ralph

Austen's recent census of the desert traffic shows Egyptian imports from 1810 to 1820 no higher than they had been in the eighteenth century, Libyan imports higher by a few thousand per year, Tunisian imports up by some 500 slaves per year, Algerian imports up by half that, and Moroccan imports up by some 2,500 per year.[29] Even if these figures had been higher, it must be recalled that a portion of these slaves came from outside West Africa (Darfur, the Nilotic Sudan, etc.), and that in any case most of the imported currencies were too heavy per unit of value to stand the desert crossing—especially the cowrie and the copper currencies. The only important money import in the desert trade was coinage.

Probably of more importance than these effects on the demand for money was the effect on the supply side. The slave trade was now in the hands of new traders—Brazilians, Spanish, and the clandestine illegal slavers of other nations. They had little or no access to the old sources of imported money, especially the cowrie. The cowrie trade had covered many thousands of miles and had used Amsterdam as its entrepôt; this was no longer possible. The slavers could neither visit the Maldives themselves nor (presumably) buy at Amsterdam, even had that been possible, because of the risk. That a system of middlemen dealing in money did not spring up to circumvent these problems leads to several questions as yet unanswered. First, it may be that West African demand for money was significantly elastic. Rather than pay much higher prices for imported money, Africans would use domestic substitutes and "make do" with the stocks that were available. Second, it is possible that the cowrie trade was not marked by economic profits as high as those pertaining to manufactured goods. It may not have paid traders to engage in the cowrie trade because transport costs were so high. Finally, there may be in these events a sign that constraints were developing in the Maldive Islands, some indications of which have recently been placed on our research agenda.

Whatever the reason—a decreased demand for money as an effect of abolition (slave exports significantly lower, commodity exports not yet having expanded to take their place) or a supply effect as just discussed—West African imports of currency declined greatly from their level in the eighteenth century. Quantitative evidence for this decline is strongest for the most important of the monies, the cowrie. Says Marion Johnson, "the abolition of the slave-trade by the very nations that were importing most of the cowries . . . though it did not put an end to the slave-trade, did greatly reduce the imports of cowries."[30] Whereas the English had been shipping some hundred tons of shell per year to Africa at the start of the nineteenth century, this figure had fallen to only six tons per year between 1810 and 1815.[31] Imports of cowries did recover, of course, but only with the growth of new exports in the 1830s. The effect of abolition was to halt the import of West Africa's most important money.

Less information is available on the metallic currencies. No complete set of figures for copper and iron imports exists. Here we must depend for our conclusion on the demonstrated decline in value of West African exports following abolition. Only if the demand for money had been so great that the mix of imported goods had shifted heavily to manillas, etc., could money imports have stayed high. We are aware of no evidence whatsoever that such a switch in the mix of imports occurred. With gold, the case is more clear. There is no mention made of significant gold imports in the decades after abolition.[32] The guinée cloth of Senegambia was apparently the first of the currency imports to recover, as "by 1820, gum exports had greater value than slaves had ever had, and gum was paid for in guinées. . . ."[33] [But by the eighteenth century, Senegambia was only a minor exporter of slaves, so that the guinée currency was not in any case a good example of the trade in slaves for currency.] Of all the currency imports, only those from the Saharan trade appear to have continued unabated. Where abolition had no effect, the money imports continued to come in the form of dollars and other silver coins high enough in value (by comparison with the cowrie, the manilla, etc.) to stand the cost of the desert crossing.[34]

CONCLUSION

With abolition, then, it is apparent that money imports fell drastically. This stage of slow monetary growth occurred as West African slavers, largely deprived of their major export market, found their incomes falling rapidly and with that fall their effectual demand for money. The shift from D_1 to D_2 in figure 6.3 illustrates that fall. The lesser quantity of money now imported, OQ_{m2}, was acquired at the lower real cost OP_{m2}. It is probable that even this short-run equilibrium position resulted in gains to West Africa as a whole, since the income losses suffered by West African slave traders were offset by the gains of those segments of the society that had suffered from depredations.

As commodity exports expanded, incomes, and accordingly the effectual demand for imported money, rose. This progressive right-

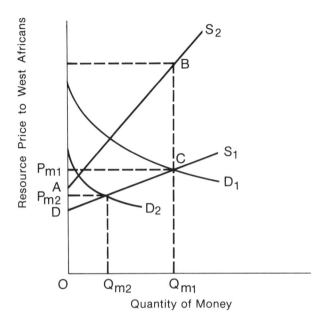

Figure 6.3 Social Saving in West African Money Acquisition Resulting from the Substitution of Commodity Trade for the Slave Trade.

ward shift of the demand curve meant that the pre-abolition position was recovered within decades, and that subsequently demand was well in excess of the pre-abolition level.[35] A static measure, taken at the point where the demand curve had recovered fully, would indicate that $P_{m1}Q_{m1}$ was re-attained. Increments to the imported money stock were then acquired with the social saving observed previously, DABC.

The magnitude of that saving cannot be known, nor is it possible to estimate the extent to which the saving was diminished by the persistence of illegal slaving and the continuation of forms of domestic slavery within West Africa. Both activities, to the extent that they occurred, could have continued to finance the importation of money.[36] The overall effect is nonetheless clear. As the Atlantic slave trade slowed and eventually ceased, there was a marked reduction in the opportunity cost of imported monies. West Africa gained a social saving akin to that derived from moving from a commodity to a fiat money. Apart from its humanity, abolition conferred on West Africa a real economic benefit. The durability of that benefit is a further question that only can be answered by an extended discussion of subsequent nineteenth century monetary developments.

NOTES

1 H. G. Johnson, *Further Essays in Monetary Economics* (Cambridge, Mass., 1973), p. 264. For a discussion and critique of the social saving concept and its application to historical research, see G. A. Gunderson, "The Nature of Social Saving," *Economic History Review*, 2d ser., 23 (1970): 207–19. In the present paper a social saving is defined as the difference in total resource costs incurred in obtaining the same quantity of money under two alternative export "bundles" of different composition.

2 These supply curves require care in their interpretation. S_1 is a normal supply curve in that it reflects the private costs, including profit, of imported monies delivered at the African coasts. S_2, however, is unorthodox. In including social costs, it focuses not on those which may have been directly involved in the collection and distribution of the monies, but rather on the social cost of the slaving conducted in order to pay for the imported monies. Such a construction would only be justified, of course, to the extent that slaves were captured and exported directly in exchange for money imports. This was indeed the case. The steeper slope (lower elasticity) of S_2 compared to S_1 occurs because imported monies were probably reasonably elastic in supply given only private costs, there being no particular observable constraint on increasing shipments at some higher price; whereas with S_2 the costs of social disruption increase rapidly as slaving intensifies.

3 Two points should be noted: (a) This analysis assumes that social costs flowed from slaving only; that none accompanied commodity production; and that slaves ceased to be exported for money. As a result, the post-abolition supply curve has no social costs attached. This simplification would be unwarranted to the extent that slaving to provide labor for commodity exports approached in quantitative terms slaving for export. (b) To reflect the historical case accurately, figure 6.2 should indicate an interim stage which occurred when abolition produced a fall in the effectual demand for money and a search for suitable commodity exports to substitute for slave exports. Figure 6.3 and the subsequent discussion attempt that task.

4 A. G. Hopkins, *An Economic History of West Africa* (New York, 1973), p. 111; Marion Johnson, "The Atlantic Slave Trade and the Economy of West Africa," in Roger Anstey and P. E. H. Hair, eds., *Liverpool, the African Slave Trade and Abolition* (Liverpool, 1976), p. 15.

5 See the two classic articles by Marion Johnson, "The Cowrie Currencies of West Africa," pts. 1 and 2, *Journal of African History* 11 (1970): 17–49, 331–53; see also Philip D. Curtin, "Africa and the Wider Monetary World, 1250–1850," in a forthcoming study of intercontinental monetary flows, edited by Maureen Mazzouai and John Richards; and Hopkins, *Economic History*, p. 68. Other accounts of the cowrie are to be found in Paul Einzig, *Primitive Money* (London, 1949); J. Wilfrid Jackson, *Shells as Evidence of the*

Migration of Early Culture (Manchester, England, 1917); Paul E. Lovejoy, "Interregional Monetary Flows in the Precolonial Trade of Nigeria," *Journal of African History* 15 (1974): 563–85; Dr. E. V. Martens, "Ueber verschiedene Verwendungen von Conchylien," *Zeitschrift für Ethnologie* (Berlin, 1872), 4: 65–87; and A. H. Quiggin, *A Survey of Primitive Money* (New York, 1970).

6 Hopkins, *Economic History*, p. 68.

7 M. Johnson, "Cowrie Currencies," pt. 2, p. 348; M. Johnson, "Atlantic Slave Trade," p. 20; Curtin, "Monetary World," p. 18.

8 O. Dapper, *Description de l'Afrique* (Amsterdam, 1686), p. 305. This passage first came to our attention through the article by G. I. Jones, "Native and Trade Currencies in Southern Nigeria during the Eighteenth and Nineteenth Centuries," *Africa* 28 (1958): 50.

9 William Bosman, *A New and Accurate Description of the Coast of Guinea . . .* (London, 1705), p. 364a.

10 Ibid., p. 362.

11 K. G. Davies, *The Royal African Company* (New York, 1970), p. 234.

12 M. Johnson, "Cowrie Currencies," pt. 1, p. 21 and pt. 2, p. 348; M. Johnson, "Atlantic Slave Trade," p. 20.

13 The estimate of 50 percent is calculated roughly, even impressionistically, from table 66 of Philip D. Curtin, *The Atlantic Slave Trade: A Census* (Madison, 1969), p. 221. Money value is taken from Henry A. Gemery and Jan S. Hogendorn, "The Economic Costs of West African Participation in the Atlantic Slave Trade: A Preliminary Sampling for the Eighteenth Century," in Gemery and Hogendorn, eds., *The Uncommon Market: Essays in the Economic History of the Atlantic Slave Trade* (New York, 1979), p. 156.

14 Paul E. Lovejoy, "Interregional Monetary Flows in the Precolonial Trade of Nigeria," pp. 563–85.

15 A. J. H. Latham, "Currency, Credit and Capitalism on the Cross River in the Pre-Colonial Era," *Journal of African History* 12 (1971): 599–605; Jones, "Native and Trade Currencies," pp. 44–46; Hopkins, *Economic History*, p. 69; Curtin, "Monetary World," pp. 20–22; M. Johnson, "Atlantic Slave Trade," p. 20; Eugenia W. Herbert, "Aspects of the Use of Copper in Pre-Colonial West Africa," *Journal of African History* 14 (1973): 179–94; John Barbot, *A Description of the Coast of North and South Guinea* (London, 1746), p. 382; Marion Johnson, "Cloth Strip Currencies" (paper delivered at the Annual Meeting of the African Studies Association, Houston, Texas, November 1977), p. 3.

16 Hopkins, *Economic History*, p. 68; Philip D. Curtin, *Economic Change in Pre-Colonial Africa: Senegambia in the Era of the Slave Trade* (Madison, 1975), pp. 234, 239, 244.

17 Curtin, *Economic Change*, pp. 259–61; M. Johnson, "Atlantic Slave Trade," p. 20.

18 Curtin, "Monetary World," pp. 8, 16; M. Johnson, "Atlantic Slave Trade," pp. 19–20.

19 Curtin, "Monetary World," p. 16.

20 A. G. Hopkins, "The Currency Revolution in South-West Nigeria in the Late Nineteenth Century," *Journal of the Historical Society of Nigeria* 3 (1966): 473; Curtin, *Economic Change*, pp. 264–65.

21 Lovejoy, "Interregional Monetary Flows," p. 563; Marion Johnson, "The Nineteenth Century Gold 'Mithqual' in West and North Africa," *Journal of African History* 9 (1968): 547–70.

22 J. D. Fage, *A History of Africa* (New York, 1978), p. 273.

23 Hopkins, *Economic History*, pp. 112–14.

24 Philip D. Curtin, "Measuring the Atlantic Slave Trade," in Stanley L. Engerman and Eugene D. Genovese, eds., *Race and Slavery in the Western Hemisphere: Quantitative Studies* (Princeton, 1975), p. 112. These are figures from Curtin's *Census* as corrected by Roger Anstey and Johannes Postma.

25 David Eltis, "The Export of Slaves from Africa, 1821–1843," *Journal of Economic History* 37 (1977): 429; personal communication from David Eltis.

26 Colin W. Newbury, "Prices and Profitability in Early Nineteenth Century West African Trade," in Claude Meillassoux, ed., *The Development of Indigenous Trade and Markets in West Africa* (London, 1971), p. 92.

27 Jan S. Hogendorn, "Economic Initiative and African Cash Farming: Pre-Colonial Origins and Early Colonial Developments," in *Colonialism in Africa 1870–1960*, vol. 4, *The Economics of Colonialism*, ed. L. H. Gann and Peter Duignan (Cambridge, 1975), p. 310.

28 Newbury, "Prices and Profitability," p. 92.

29 Ralph A. Austen, "The Trans-Saharan Slave Trade: A Tentative Census," in Gemery and Hogendorn, eds., *The Uncommon Market*, pp. 35, 39, 41.

30 M. Johnson, "Cowrie Currencies," pt. 2, p. 349.

31 M. Johnson, "Cowrie Currencies," pt. 1, p. 22. No doubt the fall in cowrie imports was partly due to wartime shipping shortages as well as to the decline in slave exports.

32 See the discussion of gold in Curtin, "Monetary World," pp. 16–17; see also M. Johnson, "Atlantic Slave Trade," pp. 19–20.

33 Curtin, *Economic Change*, p. 268.

34 On the coasts the slave exports that continued after abolition resulted in a large-scale importation of silver coin also, but this coinage was ordinarily not put into domestic circulation. David Eltis, "The British Contribution to the Nineteenth-Century Transatlantic Slave Trade," *Economic History Review*, 2d ser. 32 (1979): 215–19.

35 Evidence for a rightward-shifting demand curve may be found in Marion Johnson's description of the cowrie trade's recovery: "With the development of the palm-oil trade, however, the cowrie trade recovered; by the 1830s, between 60 and 100 tons went annually to the Gold Coast alone, and from 1835 at least 50 tons a year to the coast east of the Volta. By 1850 the Gold Coast was importing at the rate of some 150 tons a year. Most of these cowries were still coming from the Maldives and other East

Indian islands (60 tons were reported to have come to Liverpool from Manila in 1848), but at Whydah the first experimental shipments of Zanzibar cowries were received in 1845." M. Johnson, "Cowrie Currencies," pt 1, p. 22. Note that the introduction of the Zanzibar cowrie from the 1840s represents the beginning of supply curve shifts.

36 There are a number of recent accounts and analyses of slave use within Africa. See especially Martin Klein and Paul E. Lovejoy, "Slavery in West Africa," in Gemery and Hogendorn, eds., *The Uncommon Market;* S. Miers and I. Kopytoff, eds., *Slavery in Africa: Historical and Anthropological Perspectives* (Madison, 1977); C. Meillassoux, ed., *L'esclavage en Afrique precoloniale* (Paris, 1975); and the overview by Martin Klein, "The Study of Slavery in Africa: A Review Article," *Journal of African History*, vol. 19, no. 4 (1978).

CHAPTER 7: **From the Atlantic to the Indian Ocean: European Abolition, the African Slave Trade, and Asian Economic Structures**

Ralph A. Austen

Abolition began in the Atlantic as a European effort directed against a European institution. Even the conflict between the zeal of Britain and the hesitation of other powers in combating the slave trade does not mar this symmetry; Britain, after all, had been the number one slaving power in the previous era. Arguments about the historical meaning of Atlantic abolition must thus center around transformations of a European and European-dominated economic system.[1]

The case of the Indian Ocean is more complicated. The slave trade here, and the larger economic system into which it fed, were primarily Asian. Nonetheless, in the period of most intensive slaving that immediately preceded abolition, Europeans had become politically dominant and economically very active in the Indian Ocean sphere. Abolition was thus a blow by a European power (again, and now exclusively, Britain) against a specific trade in which it had never been seriously involved, but within a system over which it exercised some control. Moreover, in East Africa the transition from effective suppression of the oceanic slave trade to the imposition of colonial rule was more rapid and closely linked than in West Africa.

The arguments about Indian Ocean abolition are thus bedeviled by more irreconcilable ranges of perception than those centered on western Africa. East Africa is the original base of Coupland's classic view of abolition as a moral crusade, and contemporary historians

117

can still present the British effort there as a selfless endeavor against a massive Asiatic evil.[2] The most serious counters to this interpretation present the Indian Ocean slave trade as insignificant in the periods prior to European domination of the area, flourishing only as a peripheral feature of the Atlantic-centered Western capitalist system, and abolished in response to the logic of transformation within that system.[3]

This paper will confront the issues raised in the debate over changes in the Indian Ocean system brought about by the shifts from autonomy, through European domination, to abolition and colonialism. The paper's four broadly chronological sections will thus focus on three geographical arenas of political economy: East Africa as a source of slaves and an object of colonialism; the Arabian, Iranian, and Indian regions bordering the Red Sea and the Persian Gulf which functioned as the Asian metropoles of East African trade; and the European global system which eventually dictated the conditions of East African trade and development in general. Throughout the essay the major questions asked will be: At what point did East Africa shift from an Asian to a European economic hegemony? Why was abolition a part of this process? And how were the internal development and external dependency of East Africa affected by this shift?[4]

THE EAST AFRICAN SLAVE TRADE AND THE INDIAN OCEAN ECONOMY BEFORE DA GAMA

From some time early in the first millennium A.D., East Africa was integrated into an economic system that spanned the entire Indian Ocean. The major centers of mercantile organization, shipping, and commercial handicraft production within this system were located at its northern corners, in Egypt as well as in the Persian Gulf. While Egyptian traders made the first known voyages to East Africa, and remained powerful throughout the Middle Ages in the commerce between India and the Red Sea, it was Iranian and, especially, Arabian and Indian merchants who came to dominate the East African trade.

East Africa's role in this system always remained peripheral, both in the general sense that it was less important than other areas and in structural terms as a supplier of raw materials with limited development of its internal economy. Among the goods exported from medieval East Africa gold and ivory always appear to have been of greater value than slaves. Nonetheless, it can be argued that the East African slave trade played a vital role in the total Indian Ocean economy.

The debate about the importance of the pre-modern East African slave trade is first of all a dispute about numbers. Despite concurrence among a wide range of scholars that the quantity of slaves taken from this area before 1750 was low, I have contended elsewhere that it was considerable, amounting, in the period between 650 and 1500, to over five million individuals, of which slightly over half came from the Swahili coast and the rest from the Red Sea area.[5]

The numbers themselves are important for the present discussion mainly because they indicate that East African slaves would have made a major impact upon whatever sectors of the receiving society employed them. In the case of the Mediterranean Islamic world, most of whose slaves came from the Saharan trade, the Caucasus, or Southern and Eastern Europe, the principal areas of servile employment were urban domestic service and the military.[6] For this region, then, we can consider the extensive slave imports as mainly supporting high levels of elite household consumption and a large, elaborate state apparatus (which Wallerstein and others have associated with archaic "political empires" rather than the modern "world systems").[7]

In the medieval Indian Ocean system African slaves also played important domestic and military roles, but in addition they constituted an essential part of the commercial labor force in the Persian Gulf. These *Zenji* slaves are best known for their participation in the drainage of the Basra salt flats during the ninth century. This episode led to a sensational revolt, and is thus indisputably interpreted by modern historians as atypical, although by itself it must have involved considerable numbers of people. What is usually ignored in such dismissals of the *Zenji* uprising is that it signaled a drastic stage in a more continuous development of commercial date production along the entire Persian Gulf coast. For most areas and periods, the units of production were smaller than the estates being formed in ninth century Basra, and the labor demands were certainly less intensive. Nonetheless, investment in this agricultural system required a regular East African slave trade, and dates in turn provided a major bulk commodity in the shipping commerce coming out of the Persian Gulf.

For this key metropole of Indian Ocean commerce, therefore, slaving helped to build a capitalistic world system in the sense that Wall-

erstein attributes exclusively to the Atlantic-centered European hegemony.[8] Once looked on in this way, the Indian Ocean system must
be recognized as far less dynamic than its European counterpart.
First, the Indian Ocean slave traffic of this period proceeded at only
one-fifth the pace of the later Atlantic trade.[9] Moreover, the Persian
Gulf, while ideally located for commercial purposes, suffers from severe limitations of rainfall, a lack of arable soil, and climatic conditions that are not conducive to maximum human effort. Finally,
throughout its medieval and most of its modern history this region
experienced a high level of instability which hampered economic enterprise.[10] It is thus not surprising that the commercial agriculture of
the Persian Gulf never expanded (and periodically contracted) between its ninth century spurt and 1500.

During this period some improvements were made in the technology of the shipping which linked the Indian Ocean as a whole, but
there were also declines in gold production and in the commercial-
agricultural complex of Egypt which lend an air of depression to the
last autonomous phase of the regional economy.[11] Nevertheless, what
is important about the medieval Indian Ocean system for this discussion is its structure; later European intervention would affect the
rates of growth in trade and production, but what impact would such
changes have on the underlying patterns of development?

EUROPEANS IN THE INDIAN OCEAN:
THE PRE-ABOLITIONIST PHASE

The entry of the Portuguese explorer Vasco da Gama into the Indian
Ocean in 1498 is conventionally seen as a major watershed in world
history, marking the first step in the subjugation of the Asian world
to Europe. The only immediate major effect of this event on the Indian Ocean economy, however, was to divert that portion of the region's trade which was destined for Europe from overland routes
across the Levant to an all-sea passage around the Cape of Good
Hope. This traffic initially consisted mainly of transit goods (largely
spices) from Southeast Asia, although it would later extend to commodities (including slaves) produced within the region. But until the
serious abolitionist measures of the late nineteenth century, the European presence seems to have aided the development of those Asian
economic structures which encompassed the main East African slave

trade. The trade, and with it the commercial productivity of the Persian Gulf (and now also of the Red Sea), probably reached their greatest levels during this phase of European hegemony. What, then, is the link between these two factors?

First, if we examine the political and economic goals of the European powers in the Indian Ocean, it becomes clear that none except the Portuguese saw themselves in serious competition with the existing Asian economic system. The Portuguese, in the sixteenth century, did attempt to control the entire perimeter of the Indian Ocean so as to limit, or at least levy taxes on, Asian trade. Within a little over one hundred years, however, it was clear that Portugal could hold on to only Mozambique and a few ports of western India. Even to develop these the collaboration of Indian merchants was needed and when, during the latter eighteenth century, this arrangement began to break down, Indian trade shifted its East African focus northward to Zanzibar, where Omani Arabs had established a rival commercial base.[12]

The major French bid for a role in the Indian Ocean economy began in the mid-eighteenth century and was centered on the Mascarene Islands just east of Madagascar. The attempt to build up slave plantations on these islands, and also to use them as a base for control of India, brought France into wide-ranging conflict with Portugal and Britain. Asians, especially the Omani Arabs of Zanzibar, were always France's allies in these efforts and, as will be seen, the French contributed positively to the extension of Arab commercial agriculture from the Persian Gulf to the East African coast.

Britain, the power which ultimately achieved the most extensive control over the Indian Ocean, had the least specific economic aims. Politically, Britain had gained mastery over the Indian subcontinent by the early nineteenth century, and was generally concerned to maintain relations throughout the region on terms which would provide security at a minimal cost of further administration. Britain thus established an "informal" empire in the Persian Gulf, the Red Sea (including the formal Aden colony), and on the Swahili coast. British agents in these places were backed by naval power, but British economic enterprise was not predominant and the official policy of free trade did, in fact, respect the activities of Asians as well as of other European nationalities.

The fact that Portugal and France themselves traded in East African slaves did not appear to have much effect on Asian trade from the region. The Portuguese initially took Mozambique slaves only to India, and thus duplicated (or sometimes directly supported by resale

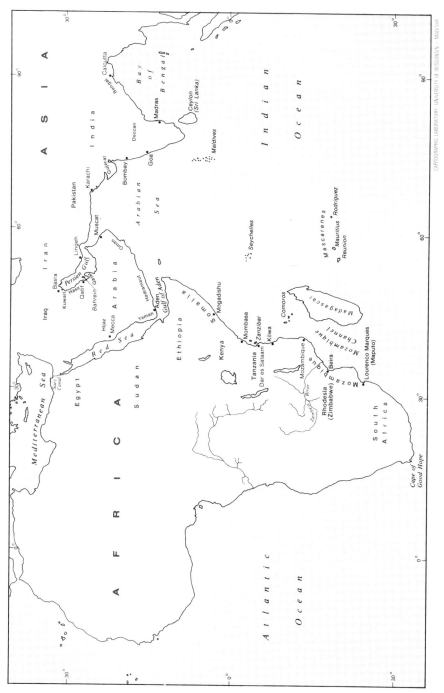

Map 7.1 The Western Indian Ocean in the Nineteenth Century.

to Asians) the traditional commerce of the region. Trade to Brazil did not become significant until after 1810, when it developed as a result of an expanding coffee-growing sector; but by this time the Portuguese sphere of operations at both the coast and the interior of East Africa was fairly well delineated from that of the Arab-Swahilis operating via Tanzania.[13]

The French slave trade to the Mascarenes was significant only from the 1750s through the first decades of the nineteenth century. Some of these slaves were purchased from Omàni and Swahili merchants in Kilwa and Zanzibar, so there would appear to have been problems in allocating supplies between this area of demand and Asia. However, the very reliable evidence on the rate of slave trading in the subsequent period suggests that during both the eighteenth and nineteenth centuries the net rate of slave trading from East Africa vastly increased.

Calculations of the Islamic slave trade out of the Swahili coast and the Red Sea in the period between 1500 and abolition indicate that the rate rose more than 25 percent over the previous period, and that at its height during the nineteenth century the traffic more than doubled. This trade is associated with some degree of decline in the demand for slaves in the military sectors of the receiving areas (particularly India), accompanied by a major rise in the commercial deployment of servile Africans. In the Persian Gulf this period witnessed new expansion in date planting and growth in the pearl-fishing industry to the point where the region became a significant consumer of black slaves. Similarly, the Arabian coast of the Red Sea appears to have used more slaves for agriculture and pearl fishing. The greatest expansion of all took place on the Swahili coast—including the northern Tanzanian mainland, the two islands of Zanzibar, and the Kenya coast—where major plantations were established to produce cloves, cereals, and coconuts.[14]

The fact that such an expansion of a slave-based economy was taking place in a European-dominated zone at a time when Europe was abolishing slavery and the slave trade may appear as a paradox. It can be explained in three possible ways: the Asian system was an anachronism thriving despite European advances; Asian expansion was a function of European capitalism and would eventually confront the contradiction between such a process and slavery; or Asian slave-based capitalism and European capitalism were compatible. In the remainder of this section I will explore the first two explanations and demonstrate why they are inadequate. If the third explanation is valid, then abolition becomes a paradox; it will thus be dealt with separately in the next section.

European abolitionists themselves often liked to think of Asian slavery as an autonomous system that they should not tolerate in areas under their influence. However, it was precisely the more progressive aspects of the European economic presence, including the British, which encouraged the growth of the East African slave trade. The law and order that the British established in the Persian Gulf accounts directly for the expansion of agriculture and pearl fishing, and the consequently increased demand for slaves.[15] On the Swahili coast the French had introduced clove and sugar planting which, with varying success, the Omanis subsequently pursued in Zanzibar. Finally, Europeans purchased a number of the goods produced in this slave system, including Zanzibari cloves and Red Sea coffee, while European ships carried other products between Indian Ocean markets.

If it is impossible to separate the European presence from the expanded Asian economic system, can one see that system, in the centuries immediately preceding abolition and formal colonialism, as already structurally dependent upon Europe? Dependency in international economic relations is notoriously difficult to define, but for present purposes it can be assumed to mean some combination of the following: (1) a process of change within the dependent/peripheral sector which is either determined or blocked by the dominant/central sector, to the latter's own advantage; (2) assumption by the dominant/central sector of control over those functions within the joint system which provide the highest level of return, in terms of either simple distribution or opportunities for the further development of productive capacities.[16] In both these dimensions the slave economy of the post-1500 Indian Ocean displays only a limited degree of dependency.

The process of change by which slave-using industries grew and spread during this period is essentially continuous with the structure of the regional economy before the arrival of Europeans, and thus cannot be attributed to their presence. The most European-linked and sensationally expansive of these enterprises, the Zanzibari clove plantations, did suffer by the mid-nineteenth century from the effects of over-commitment to a commodity with a limited world market. However, the fall in clove prices was not a function of European development, nor did it significantly benefit Europeans. Moreover, the Arab-Swahili planters struck by this conjuncture were able to protect themselves, in part by falling back upon autoconsumption rather than export production, and in part by diversifying their exports to include more cereals, oil seeds, and coconut goods, for which there still was a growing market.[17]

The European impact was more pervasive in certain critical sectors of the Indian Ocean economy than in the structure of the system as a whole. Thus the very ability of the Portuguese and their Atlantic successors to reach this region by an all-sea route represented an advance over indigenous navigation. Despite some efforts in the nineteenth century, Arabian and Indian shippers could never compete with Europeans in transoceanic carriage; but they did fairly quickly adapt many aspects of Western construction and armament to their own vessels, which could then function on a par with Europeans inside the Indian Ocean. Only the introduction of steam vessels during the latter nineteenth century brought Europeans back to a superior position on most, but not all, local routes (particularly not those linking the Persian Gulf with East Africa).[18]

European factory-manufactured commodities also entered Indian Ocean markets, and by the late nineteenth century some metal goods, and particularly cheap white cotton cloth, began to replace the products of indigenous handicraft industries. However, a large demand for regionally produced goods, including imported foods and specialized artisanal items, survived this onslaught. Moreover, the slave trade remained almost entirely self-contained, as the exports from the East African interior depended upon minimal investments of European munitions, textiles, and copper, while payments from Red Sea and Persian Gulf buyers consisted of local agricultural and fishing products.

Finally, the financial management of the Indian Ocean trade at all its key points—Arabia, Ethiopia, and the Swahili coast—remained throughout the nineteenth century a virtual monopoly of Indian merchants and bankers. Most of the Europeans operating in this area were nothing more than shippers who depended, like their Arabian or African counterparts, on the well-capitalized Indians for brokerage, credit, and a variety of other services.[19]

The slave economy of the Indian Ocean thus seems compatible with the European presence in the area on terms of parity, if not total equality. There is nothing paradoxical about this if one recognizes that commercial slavery itself is a logical extension of European or any other capitalism into underpopulated areas, rather than assuming that it represents a separate "mode of production."[20] It is thus not

surprising that Europeans stimulated the development of slavery in
the Indian Ocean; why, on the other hand, did they eventually make
such strenuous efforts to suppress it?

ABOLITION

Even more than in the Atlantic case, the abolition of Indian Ocean
slaving must be seen as a British rather than a European policy. The
two other Western powers in the region, Portugal and France, had
engaged in the local slave trade before the first abolitionist measures
were passed in Europe and India, and both continued, after 1806, to
carry on such commerce through whatever legal or illegal avenues
were open to them.[21] The suppression of European slave trading in
the Indian Ocean took almost as long as the abolition of the Asian
trade; however, since it does not present issues really distinct from
those of the Atlantic, this effort will not be analyzed here.

While the effort to end the Asian trade in East African slaves involved Britain in a virtually solo confrontation with local participants,
the ensuing political process remained quite complicated.[22] Regulations, treaties, and means of their enforcement had to be arranged in
British India (which included both directly administered areas and
princely states), the Persian Gulf, and the Red Sea (containing a wel-
ter of Arabian, Persian, Somali, and Ottoman jurisdictions), as well as
in the Sultanate of Zanzibar on the Swahili coast. Between 1805 and
1842 responsibility for such measures lay with the British authorities
in India who, for reasons discussed below, proceeded very cautiously.
After 1842 the Foreign Office took charge from London and initiated
bolder policies; even so, the decisive treaty with Zanzibar was not
signed until 1873, and slave trading in the Red Sea did not slow down
drastically until formal European occupation of the Somali, Eritrean,
and Sudanese coasts in the 1880s.

From an Indian Ocean perspective it is easier to explain why abolition took so long than why it happened at all. The explanation of
their own actions by the British actors was essentially ideological.
They felt that slave trading was morally reprehensible and must
eventually be eliminated no matter what the cost. In the long run
most of them believed that a more productive local economy could
only arise after slavery was abolished. The task for historical analysis
of this effort is to determine how such motivations are objectively
linked to both short- and long-run economic changes in the region.

The costs of abolition as perceived by British decision makers were essentially political. The British position in the Indian Ocean centered around the control of India itself, and was buttressed by alliances with weaker but still autonomous states in the rest of the region, particularly in the Persian Gulf and on the East African coast. Slave trading was first abolished in Indian ports under direct British rule, since these had to conform to the laws of the empire as a whole. However, even in the indirectly ruled portions of India British officials had to take careful steps to establish proper legal procedures for banning slave trading, which was very much in the economic interests of the local merchant and ruling groups. Outside of India the British encountered the core of the slave-manned sectors of the regional economy and consequently met severe resistance to abolition. Faced with a choice between extending the zone where the slave trade was forbidden and supporting a major political ally, the British Indian authorities usually favored the latter. Thus in 1826 Britain refused to establish a protectorate over Mombasa so as not to antagonize Zanzibar.[23]

When the Foreign Office took over Indian Ocean antislavery efforts after 1842, ideological commitments unrelated to any regional interests obviously gained strength in the determination of policy. The economic and social basis for these commitments is therefore better sought elsewhere in this volume, in chapters dealing more directly with the Atlantic system.

In the Indian Ocean itself, the role of ethnically British private sector interests was relatively small both in the total commerce of East Africa and in the formulation of antislavery policy. The individuals who took consular roles in the Persian Gulf, the Red Sea, and Zanzibar were all recruited from the public sector, unlike the representatives of Germany and the United States, who were often local merchants.[24] The one British entrepreneur who did play an important role in British antislavery and colonizing policy in East Africa was Sir William Mackinnon, a man who had earned a considerable fortune running a merchant house and steamship line in the Indian Ocean. But Mackinnon's entry into the political arena appears to have been based upon the influence of already-committed figures in the regional abolitionist establishment. Moreover, his ventures into imperialist and proto-imperialist undertakings eroded rather than increased his fortune, making it necessary for his most recent biographer to expend more effort defending his rationality than his morality.[25]

The real embodiment of British imperial economic commitments to the Indian Ocean system as a whole and to East Africa in particular

was the Indian merchants, who played such a central role in trade
and finance at all major ports. Antislavery policy, however, was not
promoted from this social group, which had neither ideological nor
economic interest in its accomplishment. Instead the Indians became
victims of abolitionism, although in a relatively minor way, through
restrictions on the trade itself, which was mainly carried on by Ara-
bians with various credit links to the Indian community. More dam-
aging to the Indian position and to the general growth of the Indian
Ocean system was the insistence by British officials in Zanzibar and
Oman that Indians residing there were British subjects, and thus legally prohibited from both dealing in and owning slaves. This policy
not only imposed considerable immediate losses upon the local Indian communities, but also restricted their entire role in the Swahili
coast and Persian Gulf economy since they, as the principal creditors
of insolvent Arab or Swahili planters, could no longer foreclose on
their debtors and shift their own capital and skills from commerce or
finance into production.[26]

Antislavery policies therefore cut against not only the structure of
the Indian Ocean economy as established by Asians, but also against
the most serious British imperial stake in this system as it existed or
could be expected to develop. The confinement of Indians to a kind
of comprador position within that economy even contributed to its
underdevelopment insofar as Arabs or Swahili planters were thereby
encouraged to respond to falling commodity prices, drought, or civil
disorder by resorting to autoconsumption rather than commercial innovation, since their plantations would survive even if they produced
nothing to offset accumulated debts.

Some Marxist historians have suggested (without any documentation) that such attacks on local capitalism were intended to prepare
the way for the replacement of Asian entrepreneurs by Western capitalists.[27] If this is true, it was a rationale not apparent to the European
promoters of abolition, since they were not in competition with the
existing Indian Ocean economy. They did, however, believe that the
establishment of a moral order according to their precepts would
spontaneously lead to advances in local economic development
through a linkage of institutions and psychology, which both liberal
and Marxist theorists recognize as modernization (see chapter 2). To
understand both the motivation and the consequences of such
changes in East Africa it is necessary to look briefly beyond the period
of the major abolitionist campaigns and to examine the system which,
under mainly British and German colonial rule, replaced the slave
economy.

FROM ABOLITION TO COLONIALISM

The European scramble for East African colonies in the 1880s and 1890s was linked to antislavery efforts in a complex, somewhat ambiguous manner. The push for control of African territory was clearly aided by commitments to abolition, which accounted for the British fleet being stationed in the area, and provided the German government with a vehicle for raising moral and financial support at home to aid its conquest of the Tanzanian mainland.[28] Nonetheless, Britain had earlier recognized a conflict between its political goals in the Indian Ocean region and radical action against the slave trade; moreover, neither Germany (nor France and Italy in the Red Sea area) launched their new colonial ventures primarily on abolitionist grounds or even pretexts.

It has been argued by a number of contemporary historians that antislavery efforts, whatever their intended political goals, created social crises in peripheral areas such as the Swahili coast which then tended to pull in European powers concerned with the stability of these areas. While the treaties limiting the slave trade did cause friction between the Sultan of Zanzibar and elite groups under his suzerainty, there is no evidence that the entire regime was in danger of collapse, or that British efforts to support the ruler incited German bids for a local protectorate.[29]

The establishment of formal colonial systems in East Africa cannot be understood as predominantly an expression or a result of abolition; nonetheless, in their development through the first decades of the twentieth century, colonial regimes did complete the task of suppressing both the slave trade and slavery in this area. They did so by creating an infrastructure which directly attacked the institution of slavery, and an economy which no longer required slave labor. In neither of these tasks, however, did the European powers overcome the contradictions between their larger views of an optimal transformation of the local system and the immediate need to maximize their own advantages within that system.

This contradiction became obvious during the earliest phases of colonial occupation when local administrators hesitated to use the legal and military forces at their disposal to effect a complete suppression of slavery. Such an undertaking would have increased vastly the costs—through both increased government activity and decreased revenues—of an establishment whose main task was to maintain minimal control over territories with a dubious ultimate value.[30] A bolder initiative against the existing structure was represented by the construction of major rail lines through both British and German East Africa. While there can be little doubt that the initial and primary goal of both of these transport links was strategic, they were also expected to liberate African labor from the onerous chore of head porterage, and to provide a positive basis for market mobility within the areas served.[31]

However liberating these infrastructural innovations may have been in terms of internal labor relations, they bound the local economies as a whole to dependent ties with the exterior. Not only was the explicit orientation of both administrative thinking and railroad routing focused upon closer ties to the metropolitan economies; but the very form in which these imported elements had to be financed— through payments in metropolitan currency, ultimately disbursed abroad—meant that the internal economy had to concentrate heavily upon raw material exports. In this sense colonial efforts against slavery contributed to dependency and underdevelopment. The guiding rationale in the choice of these policies, however, was not maximization of linkages with the metropoles (which objectively gained little wealth from East Africa), but rather the establishment of a new system of local order which, it was assumed, would bring mutual benefits.

This same pattern of thought pervaded the determination of productive strategies. Raw material production in colonial East Africa meant essentially agriculture, and the European regimes were faced with two possible models of commercial farming: expatriate plantations or indigenous smallholdings. The first was closest to the system developed in the previous Asian slave economy; the second was closer to the abolitionist ideal.

Plantation systems flourished throughout colonial East Africa, but for present purposes we can only look briefly at the cases of Zanzibar and Kenya. In Zanzibar the British government maintained the structure they had inherited from the later nineteenth century: mainland migrant (although now voluntary) labor; Arab owners now protected from expropriation by Indian debt-holders through explicit legislation to this effect; and boom-bust cycles in clove growing which, under the conditions of such hobbled local enterprize, produced general stagnation.[32]

The Kenyan system was more dynamic, but also more costly. Control over land, labor, and markets by white planters required coercion of the indigenous population and a skewing of government services (paid for mainly by African taxes) in favor of Europeans. The planters, on the other hand, did risk large amounts of their own capital in developing a variety of commercial crops for both export and local consumption. Moreover, they extended both their investments and their influence on government policy so as to move beyond raw material production into limited industrialization, an undertaking in which they were joined by local Indian capitalists. The Kenya planter class was eventually removed from power by a metropolitan government which did not want to continue bearing either the financial or the ideological-political costs of such a regime. Although the present economy of Kenya still reflects much of the dynamism and many of the gross inequalities of its plantation heritage, the agricultural sectors have shifted in the direction of peasant production.[33]

Peasant systems used the colonial infrastructure to shift the base of export production from nodal areas, which drew their labor from the hinterland, to the hinterland itself. Given the existing investment in administrative personnel and transport networks, such a system appeared cheaper, more stable, and much more consistent with the colonial officials' abolitionist-derived image of their own mission than any form of plantation development.[34]

Yet in a broader, structural sense the peasant economies of Uganda, Tanzania, and, for that matter, most of colonial West Africa, do not represent a radical transformation of the slave-based systems that characterized precolonial Indian Ocean commercial agriculture. There is still a great disparity in modes of production and consumption between the nodal institutions (in this case infrastructural rather than productive) and the sources of labor (now exporting low-cost commodities rather than factors of production). Moreover, in the long run such systems have not proved to be as stable or efficient as they once seemed. For not only could an educated elite of Africans lay claim to the European positions of authority within the commanding infrastructure, now vastly expanded at considerable expense, but once a shift was made further demands for redistribution of a limited set of rewards could culminate in various forms of corruption, disorder, and brutal authoritarianism, as evidenced by the most recent history of East Africa.

Antislavery and its realization through the peasant-bureaucrat colonial state did not, then, "modernize" Africa by providing the conditions for a total social transformation on the Western model. If the aim of European intervention in the Indian Ocean economy was not modernization but dependency, it might have been more rational to support some form of plantation system, which would have centered

on a local elite more committed to capitalism and better able to finance its own development than the regimes which have prevailed in
the area.

CONCLUSION

Abolition in the Indian Ocean cannot be understood as either a moral
movement separate from European economic interests or the instrument and inevitable result of the extension of those interests overseas. Abolition here (and I would be willing to make the same argument in somewhat different terms for the Atlantic base) was essentially
an expression of the ideology that accompanied Western expansion
into the Indian Ocean. The mixture of economic and political motives and sheer technological capacity, which explain this expansion
itself, have not been analyzed in this essay because that is obviously a
separate and very complex question.[35] What is important here is the
evidence that the ideological commitments of the expansionists often
conflicted with their political and economic goals, as well as with the
impact of their technology.

Yet, in one form or another, the ideology persisted. From a moral
point of view it does appear desirable that slavery should have been
abolished in the region, and that European planters failed to gain
control over Kenya and its neighboring territories. The problem (as
in the closely related contemporary debate over South African white
regimes) lies in reconciling a negative application of "human rights"
values to overseas areas with the realization that the positive alternatives are unlikely to meet the expectations of those demanding
change. The nineteenth century abolitionists and their immediate
successors knew that they might have to sacrifice some not very vital
economic advantages to achieve their ends, but were still convinced
that through a combination of inspiration, tutelage, and the inevitable (if slow-working) laws of unilinear evolution they could make
over the benighted areas of the world in their own progressive image.
Today we know better, but it is not clear how we can act better.

APPENDIX

Appendix Table 7.1
General African Slave Population of Arabia and the Persian Gulf

	Observation	Original Source
A. 1700–19	1,700 slaves owned by Omani Sultan Saif ibn-Sultan with 20,000 date, 61,000 coconut trees	Omani chronicles[a]
B. 1824	Muscat suburbs contain mainly Abyssinian slaves	Keppel, British traveler[b]
C. 1831	Bahrein population 50% slave or slave-descended	Wilson, British resident, Persian Gulf[c]
D. 1835	Oman more than ⅓ African	No source given[d]
E. 1862/63	Nejd (central Arabia) ¼–⅓ African	Palgrave, British traveler[e]
F. 1870s	15,000–50,000 Africans in Oman	Various British, French sources[f]
G. ca. 1904	Survey of Persian Gulf	Eyewitness and various British reports[g]

Bahrein	6,000 slaves, 5,000 free blacks; plus others uncounted; total population, 100,000[h]
Basra	Blacks "fairly numerous"; total population, 58,000[i]
Hasa	Blacks "fairly numerous"; total population, 67,000[j]
Kuwait	4,000 blacks; total population, 35,000[k]
Lingeh Town	1,500 blacks; total population, 12,000[l]
Oman	"Large" black population; total population, 471,000[m]
Qatar	4,000 slaves, 1,500 free blacks, plus others uncounted; total population, 27,000[n]
Qatif	"Some" blacks; total population, 26,000[o]
Trucial Oman	Blacks "exceptionally numerous" on coast; total population, 72,000[p]

Total population of areas mentioned, 868,000
Black/slave population at 10% of total, 86,000, plus minimal population in areas not mentioned = 90,000–100,000

Source: Adapted from Ralph A. Austen, "The Islamic Red Sea Slave Trade: An Effort at Quantification," *Proceedings of the Fifth International Conference on Ethiopian Studies*, sec. B (Chicago, 1979), pp. 455–56.

[a] R. D. Bathhurst, "Maritime Trade and Imamate Goverment: The Principal Themes in the History of Oman to 1728," in Derek Hopwood, ed., *The Arabian Peninsula* (London, 1972), p. 103.

[b] George Keppel, *Personal Narrative of a Journey from India to England* (London, 1827), p. 23.

[c] Great Britain, *Parliamentary Papers* (hereafter cited as PP), vol. 51 (1837/38), "Slave Trade (East India)—Slavery in Ceylon," (no. 697), p. 10.

[d] Reginald Coupland, *East Africa and its Invaders* (Oxford, 1938), p. 31.

[e] William Gifford Palgrave, *Narrative of a Year's Journey through Central and Eastern Arabia (1862–63)*, 2 vols. (London, 1865), 1:452.

[f] Robert Geran Landen, *Oman Since 1856* (Princeton, 1967), p. 151.

[g] J. G. Lorimer, *A Gazeteer of the Persian Gulf, Oman and Central Arabia*, vol. 2, *Geographical* (Calcutta, 1908), apps. A, B, passim.

[h] Ibid., p. 241.　　　　　[k] Ibid., p. 1051.　　　　　[n] Ibid., p. 1531.

[i] Ibid., p. 276.　　　　　[l] Ibid., p. 1097.　　　　　[o] Ibid., p. 1536.

[j] Ibid., p. 645.　　　　　[m] Ibid., p. 1391.　　　　　[p] Ibid., p. 1537.

Appendix Table 7.2

Black Slaves in the Labor Force of Arabia, India, and the Persian Gulf

	Observation	Original Source
1. Seafaring		
A. 1300s	Abyssinians as guards on Indian Ocean-China ships	Ibn-Battuta, 1333–42 (travels on such a ship)[a]
B. 1580s	Abyssinian community in India specialized as sailors	Linschoten, Dutch traveler[b]
C. 1597	Blacks are sailors between Swahili coast and Red Sea	dos Santos, Portuguese traveler[c]
D. 1600s	Sidis as major naval power at Jinjira Island, off Deccan coast	Various sources[d]
E. 1860s	African "domestic slaves" as major element in dhow crews	Various Royal Navy reports[e]
2. Agriculture		
A. 860s	Zenj labor in Abbasid Basra drainage project, "tens of thousands"; 500–5,000 on individual estates;	Various chronicles[f]
	25,000 laborers required to achieve soil changes in area over time reported	Archaeological analysis of affected areas[g]
B. 1050	30,000 agricultural slaves held by Qarmatians on northeastern Arabian coast	Nasir-i-Khusraw, Persian traveler[h]
C. 1850s	Black slaves not used in cultivation, Iran	Polak, German physician serving in Teheran[i]
D. 1870–1904	Slaves brought to main agricultural areas of Oman	Various British, French reports[j]
E. 1876	Slaves in date, coffee cultivation of Hijaz, Yemen	Wylde, British consul, Jiddah[k]
3. Pearl Fishing		
A. 1200s	Bahrein fleet of 200 boats, 1,000–2,000 men; divers suffer embolisms	Idrisi (d. 1166)[l]

Appendix Table 7.2, *continued*

	Observation	Original Source
B. 1480s	Bahrein fleet of 1,000 boats	b. Majid, ca. 1490[m]
C. 1580	Bahrein fleet of 200 boats	Teixeira, Portuguese traveler[n]
D. 1831	Bahrein divers are ⅓ slaves plus freeborn Africans (mainly of Swahili origin)	Wilson, British resident, Persian Gulf[o]
E. 1830s	Total Persian Gulf fleet of 4,300 boats, ca. 30,000 men	Wellsted, British traveler, naval officer[p]
F. 1856	Same fleet: 3,000 boats, ca. 27,000 men	Bombay government report[q]
G. 1878	High slave mortality in Red Sea pearl fishing	Malcolm, British antislavery agent, Egypt[r]
H. 1882–83	Several Sudani pearl divers among slaves seeking protection	Moncrieff, British consul, Jiddah[s]
I. 1890s	High slave mortality in Persian Gulf pearl fishing	W. F. Prideaux, British resident, Persian Gulf[t]
J. 1905–07	Survey of Persian Gulf[u]	Various British reports[v]

Total Persian Gulf:	4,500 boats, 74,000 men	
Bahrein	917 boats, 17,633 men	
Kuwait	461 boats, 9,200 men	
Lingeh Town	72 boats, 1,306 men	
Qatar	815 boats, 12,890 men	
Trucial Oman	1,215 boats, 22,045 men	

Source: Adapted from Austen, "The Islamic Red Sea Slave Trade," pp. 455–56.

[a] Ibn-Batoutah, *Voyages*, trans. C. Defreney and B. R. Sanguinetti, 4 vols. (Paris, 1858), 4:59–60.

[b] Jan Huyghen van Linschoten, *Voyage to the East Indies*, trans. Arthur Coke Burnell, 2 vols. (London, 1885), 1:265 ff.

[c] Joao dos Santos, "Aethiopia Orientales," in Samuel Purchas, *Purchas, His Pilgrimes*, 20 vols. (Glasgow, 1905), 9: 252.

[d] Graham Irwin, *Africans in Asia* (New York, 1977), pp. 155–61.

[e] Christopher Lloyd, *The Navy and the Slave Trade* (London, 1949), p. 195.

[f] Alexandre Popovic, *La Revolte des esclaves en Iraq au III*[e]/*IX*[e] *siecle* (Paris, 1976), pp. 63–65.

[g] Howard S. Nelson, "An Abandoned Irrigation System in Southern Iraq," *Sumer* 18 (1962):67–72.

[h] Nassiri Khosrau, *Sefer Nameh*, trans. Charles Shefer (Paris, 1881), p. 227

[i] Jacob Edward Polak, *Persien* (Leipzig, 1865), p. 248.

[j] Landen, *Oman*, pp. 151–52.

[k] Foreign Office Confidential Prints, "Correspondence . . . Relating to the Slave Trade," Foreign Office 541 series (hereafter cited as FO 541), 21, p. 6, Public Record Office London.

[l] Edrisi Abou Abdallah, *Geographie*, trans. P. Amadée Jaubert (Paris, 1836), 1: 373.

[m] G. R. Tibbets, *Arab Navigation in the Indian Ocean before the Coming of the Portuguese* (London, 1971) p. 213.

[n] Piedro Teixeira, *Travels*, trans. William F. Sinclair (London, 1902), p. 176.

[o] PP, 51 (1837/38): 9.

[p] J. R. Wellsted, *Reisen in Arabien* (Halle, 1842), p. 182.

[q] John Fryer, *A New Account of East India and Persia* (London, 1909), p. 364.

[r] FO 541/22, "Correspondence," p. 48.

[s] FO 541/25, "Correspondence," pp. 79–85.

[t] Joseph E. Harris, *The African Presence in Asia* (Evanston, 1971), pp. 37–38.

[u] If these figures are compared with items listed under row G, appendix table 7.1, it will be evident that large, visible African populations correlate with extensive pearl fishing. The absence of Africans from earlier observations of pearl fleets suggests that slaves were not needed by this industry in significant numbers before its major nineteenth century expansion. The absence of specific counts of Africans from areas specialized in agriculture rather than pearl fishing suggests that slaves and their descendants were simply not as visible in this less concentrated occupation.

[v] J. G. Lorimer, *A Gazeteer of the Persian Gulf, Oman and Central Arabia*, vol. 1, *Historical* (Calcutta, 1915), pp. 2220–61.

Appendix Table 7.3
Global Slave Trade out of Africa

Route	Period (A.D.)	Size (millions)	Annual Rate (thousands)
Red Sea	650–1920	4.1	3.2 [a]
Swahili Coast	650–1920	3.9	3.1 [b]
Trans-Saharan	650–1910	9.0	7.1 [c]
Total Islamic		17.0	13.4
Atlantic	1450–1870	11.5	27.4 [d]

Source: Adapted from Austen, "The Islamic Red Sea Slave Trade," p. 464.

[a] Austen, "The Islamic Red Sea Slave Trade," table 4, p. 461.

[b] Ralph A. Austen, "The Islamic Slave Trade out of Africa (Red Sea and Indian Ocean): An Effort at Quantification" (Paper presented at the Conference on Islamic Africa: Slavery and Related Institutions, Princeton University, June 1977).

[c] Ralph A. Austen, "The Trans-Saharan Slave Trade: A Tentative Census," in Henry A. Gemery and Jan S. Hogendorn, eds., *The Uncommon Market: Essays on the Economic History of the Atlantic Slave Trade* (New York, 1979).

[d] Philip D. Curtin, *The Atlantic Slave Trade: A Census* (Madison, 1969). Curtin's figures have been adjusted upward on the basis of the work, among others, of David Eltis, "The Direction and Fluctuation of the Transatlantic Slave Trade, 1821–1843," and Serge Daget, "British Repression of the Illegal French Slave Trade," both in Gemery and Hogendorn, eds., *The Uncommon Market*, esp. pp. 291, 419; and Seymour Drescher, *Econocide: British Slavery in the Era of Abolition* (Pittsburgh, 1977), pp. 205–13.

NOTES

1 I do not mean to imply that the West African economy was simply a reflection of the European one in this period. See Ralph A. Austen, "The Abolition of the Overseas Slave Trade: A Distorted Theme in West African History," *Journal of the Historical Society of Nigeria* 5 (1970): 257–74.

2 The classic works are Reginald Coupland, *East Africa and its Invaders* (Oxford, 1938), and Coupland, *The Exploitation of East Africa* (London, 1939). Cf. R. W. Beachey, *The Slave Trade of East Africa* (New York, 1976).

3 Edward A. Alpers, *Ivory and Slaves in East Africa* (Berkeley, 1975); A. H. M. Sheriff, "The Slave Mode of Production along the East African Coast, 1810–1873" (paper presented at the Conference on Islamic Africa: Slavery and Related Institutions, Princeton University, June 1977).

4 All evidence in the subsequent sections that is not otherwise accounted for has been taken from Ralph A. Austen, "The Islamic Slave Trade out of Africa (Red Sea and Indian Ocean): An Effort at Quantification" (paper presented at the Conference on Islamic Africa, Princeton University, June 1977); Austen, "The Islamic Red Sea Slave Trade: An Effort at Quantification," *Proceedings of the Fifth International Conference on Ethopian Studies*, sec. B (Chicago, 1979); and Austen, "Commercial Frontiers: the Indian Ocean," in *An Economic History of Africa*, a work in progress.

5 Apart from Alpers and Sheriff, the principal proponents of this view are Neville Chittick, "East African Trade with the Orient," in D. S. Richards, ed., *Islam and the Trade of Asia* (Oxford, 1970); and Ghada Hashem Talhami, "The Zanj Rebellion Reconsidered," *International Journal of African Historical Studies* 10 (1977): pp. 443–61.

6 Ralph A. Austen, "The Trans-Saharan Slave Trade: A Tentative Census," in Henry A. Gemery and Jan S. Hogendorn, eds., *The Uncommon Market: Essays on the Economic History of the Atlantic Slave Trade* (New York, 1979). Even in the Mediterranean major exceptions to this nonproductive deployment of slaves can be found; see M. Talbi, "Droit et Economie en Ifriqiya au IIIe/IXe siecle: le paysage agricole et le rôle des esclaves dans l'economie du pays" (paper presented at the Conference on Islamic Economic History, Princeton University, 1976); Halil Inalcik, "Service Labor in the Ottoman Empire," in Abraham Ascher et al., *The Mutual Effects of the Islamic and Judaeo-Christian Worlds* (New York, 1979).

7 Immanuel Wallerstein, *The Modern World System: Capitalist Agriculture and the Origins of the European World-Economy in the Sixteenth Century* (New York, 1974), pp. 15–16, 60, and passim; see also Nels Steensgaard, *The Asian Trade Revolution of the Seventeenth Century* (Chicago, 1975).

8 I use the term *capitalistic* here without much concern for Marxist debates about modes of production, which are discussed briefly in note 20 below. For data on the slave-labor force in Indian Ocean agriculture, see appendix table 7.2.

9 See appendix table 7.3.

10 For an excellent general account of the historical development of the Persian Gulf, see John Barrett Kelly, *Britain and the Persian Gulf, 1795–1880* (Oxford, 1968), pp. 1–61.

11 See the chapters dealing with this period in M. A. Cook, *Studies in the Economic History of the Middle East* (London, 1969).

12 Alpers, *Ivory and Slaves*, pp. 172–85; Michael N. Pearson, *Merchants and*

Rulers in Gujurat: The Response to the Portuguese in the Sixteenth Century (London, 1976), passim.

13 Alpers, *Ivory and Slaves*, pp. 223–53; Allen F. Isaacman, *Mozambique: The Africanization of a European Institution: The Zambezi Prazos, 1750–1902* (Madison, 1972), pp. 89–91.

14 See appendix table 7.2; Robert Geran Landen, *Oman Since 1856* (Princeton, 1967), pp. 60–66, 146–52; Frederick Cooper, *Plantation Slavery on the East Coast of Africa* (New Haven, 1977).

15 Kelly, *Britain and the Persian Gulf*, pp. 366, 834.

16 For an introduction to the concept of dependency as applied to African history (but not as used here), see Peter Gutkind and Immanuel Wallerstein, *The Political Economy of Contemporary Africa* (Beverly Hills, 1976).

17 Cooper, *Plantation Slavery*, stresses the use of slaves for autoconsumption and social status, and argues that the system was essentially stagnant by the late nineteenth century.

18 Landen, *Oman*, pp. 115–22.

19 Ibid., pp. 131–44; Sheriff, "Slave Mode"; Richard Pankhurst, "Indian Trade with Ethiopia, the Gulf of Aden, and the Horn of Africa in the Nineteenth and Early Twentieth Centuries," *Cahiers d'Etudes Africaines* 14 (1974): 453–97.

20 Sheriff, "Slave Mode," holds to the belief that slavery was ultimately incompatible with capitalism, while Barry Hindess and Paul Hirst, *Pre-Capitalist Modes of Production* (London, 1975), view it as potentially a subordinate form of the capitalist mode of production. For more empirically based and (in my opinion) theoretically useful attempts to relate slavery to broader categories of development, see the contributions to *Comparative Perspectives on Slavery in the New World*, pts. 1 and 2, *Annals of the New York Academy of Sciences* 292 (1977): 3–144; and Frederic L. Pryor, "A Comparative Study of Slave Societies," *Journal of Comparative Economics* 1 (1977): 25–49. The only study of Islamic slavery to employ anything like this kind of comparative apparatus is Cooper, *Plantation Slavery*—a very stimulating work, but one which arrives at conclusions I find untenable; see Ralph A. Austen, review of *Plantation Slavery on the East Coast of Africa* by Frederick Cooper, *Journal of African History* 19, no. 3 (1978): 464–65.

21 The post-1815 Portuguese and French East African slave trades and "emigration" schemes are elaborately documented in Foreign Office Confidential Prints, series 541, *Correspondence . . . Relating to the Slave Trade*, Public Record Office, London. See also chapter 11 of this volume.

22 The best summary of this process is in Kelly, *Britain and the Persian Gulf*.

23 Ibid., pp. 426–29; J. M. Gray, *The British in Mombasa, 1824–1826* (London, 1957), passim.

24 These officials were either on active duty in the Indian military and civil services, or employed through the Foreign Office post-mercantile consular organization described in D. C. M. Platt, *The Cinderella Service* (Hamden, Conn., 1971).

25 John S. Galbraith, *Mackinnon and East Africa* (Cambridge, 1972), especially pp. 29–70.
26 A. H. M. Sheriff, "The Rise of a Commercial Empire: An Aspect of the Economic History of Zanzibar, 1770–1873" (Ph.D. diss., University of London, 1971), pp. 427 ff.; Landen, *Oman*, pp. 149–50.
27 Sheriff, "Slave Mode"; Richard Wolff, *The Economics of Colonialism: Britain and Kenya, 1870–1930* (New Haven, 1974), pp. 30–46.
28 Suzanne Miers, *Britain and the Ending of the Slave Trade* (New York, 1975); Franz Ferdinand Muller, *Deutschland-Zanzibar-Ostafrika; Geschichte eine deutsche Kolonialeroberung* (Berlin, 1959).
29 This "peripheralist" view of nineteenth century imperialism has been most fully developed by Ronald Robinson and David K. Fieldhouse; see in particular Ronald Robinson and J. A. Gallagher, *Africa and the Victorians* (London, 1961); and David K. Fieldhouse, *Economics and Empire, 1830–1914* (Ithaca, N.Y., 1973). For a more extensive bibliography and critique, see Ralph A. Austen,"Economic Imperialism Revisited: Late Nineteenth-Century Europe and Africa," *Journal of Modern History* 47 (1975): 519–29.
30 This hesitation forms a major point in the critical interpretations of British abolitionism by two African historians; see G. N. Uziogwe, *Britain and the Conquest of Africa* (Ann Arbor, 1974), pp. 155–71; Moses D. E. Nwulia, *Britain and Slavery in East Africa* (Washington, 1975), pp. 169–204.
31 A. M. O'Connor, *Railways and Development in Uganda* (Nairobi, 1965), pp. 1–50, 156–64; John Iliffe, *Tanganyika under German Rule, 1905–1912* (Cambridge, 1969), pp. 72 ff.
32 Michael F. Lofchie, *Zanzibar: Background to Revolution* (Princeton, 1965), pp. 140 ff.; John Middleton and Jane Campbell, *Zanzibar: Its Society and Politics* (London, 1965), pp. 20–21.
33 E. A. Brett, *Colonialism and Underdevelopment in East Africa* (New York, 1973), pp. 1–11, 165–216, 266–311; Colin Leys, *Underdevelopment in Kenya* (Berkeley, 1974).
34 Brett, *Colonialism*, pp. 217 ff.
35 See Austen,"Economic Imperialism Revisited," pp. 519–29; also Daniel Headrick, "The Tools of Imperialism: Technology and the Expansion of European Colonial Empires in the Nineteenth Century," *Journal of Modern History* 51 (1979): 231–63.

CHAPTER 8: **Abolition and Economic Change**

on the Gold Coast

Edward E. Reynolds

The end of the slave trade came earlier to the Gold Coast than to most other areas of Africa, yet the transition to a new economic base was not particularly rapid. Trade with the international exchange economy in a number of commodities existed before the end of the slave trade, but the expansion of the traffic in ivory, gold dust, and even palm oil was not very marked after abolition. Plantation agriculture on the Gold Coast, using slaves to produce coffee and cotton, was revived by several European nations in an attempt to find an alternative to the slave trade. After some initial success these efforts failed, partly because the relatively densely populated African societies in the area had traditional institutions which were inimical to easy integration with the international exchange economy. Communal land ownership and low levels of labor input were perhaps the most important of these institutions. Nevertheless, the efforts to establish alternatives to the slave trade helped to create conditions which were prerequisites to the success of the later cocoa economy, the originators of which were missionaries and their African agents. In this context, A. G. Hopkins' comment that "the structure of legitimate commerce marked an important break with the past and signified a new phase in the growth of the modern economic history of West Africa"[1] seems particularly pertinent.

This essay assesses economic change on the Gold Coast during the nineteenth century by examining agents and areas of change, and by exploring innovations as well as possible continuities with the slave trade era.[2] I intend to examine briefly Afro-Europeans and other merchants at Accra and Cape Coast, main cities which were bridges between the Gold Coast and the European world-economy; to consider the operations of these groups in commercial activities, as well as in other activities; to explore the alternatives open to each of these groups when commercial activities were closed to them; and to examine in some detail the results of the educational and agricultural activities of the Basel missionaries, who founded the Presbyterian Church of modern Ghana. I will then consider the pioneer efforts of African Basel Mission agents from Akropong in using family land as plantations for growing cocoa, and will show that the Basel Mission's agricultural and educational activities contributed to the emergence of cocoa as the country's most important export.

Elsewhere I have examined the rise and fall of African merchants in the nineteenth century, the details of which need not detain us here.[3] Briefly, the peace treaty following the defeat of the Asante people at the Battle of Katamansu, the governship of George Maclean, and the peace that Maclean was able to maintain ushered in a period of prosperity on the Gold Coast. The rise of the African merchants, some of whom were descendants of former English and Danish slave traders and others of whom were enterprising Africans often related to chiefs, depended on many factors. Among these factors were the ability to import and export goods independently, the availability of credit from European merchant houses, and the introduction of steamships, which shortened the transportation time between Europe and Africa and eliminated the seasonal problems involved with sailing vessels. The success of such merchants was reflected in their economic and political standing in society at a time when the power of the traditional rulers on the Gold Coast was waning.[4]

These merchants were also known and referred to as the educated Africans. A few of the educated Africans of European parentage had studied abroad. Many of the others, especially those in the Cape Coast area, had been educated in local Methodist schools. From the 1830s through the 1860s most of these educated men sought employment in trade or in the expanding British government on the Gold Coast. After the 1860s the better educated Africans turned to the practice of law instead of following their forefathers into commerce. By the 1860s the wealth, power, and influence of the African merchants had begun to decline. This decline can be attributed to the increasing presence of Great Britain on the Gold Coast, lack of credit, an overextension of the merchants' commercial activities, the over-charging of African merchants by British merchants, and the rise of oligopolistic European companies. The efforts of African merchants in gold mining and the rubber trade towards the end of the nine-teenth century may be seen as attempts by the group to stage a come-back.

A more important contributing factor to the region's economic transition was probably the invitation, in 1828, by the Danish Gover-nor Richelieu to the Basel missionaries to work in the Gold Coast. The basic outline of the history of the Basel missionaries is available elsewhere.[5] Here I intend to establish that there was a direct link between the African ministers of the Basel Mission and the cocoa plantations long before Teteh Quarshie, traditionally regarded as the founder of the cocoa economy, brought cocoa from Fernando Po in 1879. In fact, Teteh Quarshie was able to get a job in Fernando Po as a blacksmith because he had been trained as such by the Basel mis-sionaries, and he is better known as a blacksmith than as a farmer.

The initial efforts of the Basel missionaries from 1828 were con-centrated at Christiansborg; however, after repeated failures they moved to Akropong in 1835. Following the arrival of eight black families in 1843 to aid the missionaries, the work of the mission began to take root. This work took the form of evangelization and educa-tion, including industrial and agricultural education. The trading wing of the Basel Mission, the Basel Trading Company (founded in 1859, and the parent firm of the present Union Trading Company of Ghana), was an active participant in the commercial life of the coun-try. Akropong, in the state of Akuapem (often called Akropong-Akuapem) became the center of Basel Mission activities. In 1848 a seminary was founded for training ministers for the mission, and most of the early seminary students were from Akropong and Chris-tiansborg.

Students from Christiansborg were predominantly the children of Danish descendants, whose opportunities in both commercial and ag-ricultural pursuits were not very good. Not only were the plantation efforts of the Danes, which had begun in the 1780s, largely unsuc-cessful,[6] but the poll-tax disturbances that disrupted local trade in the 1850s and competition from the Basel Trading Company reduced the commercial alternatives. In the absence of viable economic alter-natives, many of these Danish descendants, whose parents had been engaged in commercial life, sought employment with the Basel Mis-sion as agents, teachers, evangelists, and ministers. However, they also availed themselves of new opportunities as these developed.

C. C. Reindorf, the Ghanaian historian, was typical. Reindorf entered the seminary at Akropong to train for the ministry, but he left in order to trade. When he was unsuccessful in trade, he returned to seminary. Even after becoming a cathechist, Reindorf retired temporarily to establish a coffee plantation near Aburi in Akuapem. Later in the nineteenth century other Danish descendants worked as clerks for the Basel Trading Company and other European concerns. The most educated went to work for the government, though the latter was to become increasingly dissatisfied with their nationalistic activities.

The activities of the Afro-Europeans and other African merchants illustrate the changing economic conditions of the country, and the beginnings of the cocoa economy. But if the cocoa seeds came from the Basel Mission and its African agents, the capital which generated the transition from the abolition era to the modern economy came from the palm oil trade in Akuapem. This capital was invested in purchasing additional land and in the initial cocoa farms cultivated early in the 1860s. As will become evident, Akropong-Akuapem, the capital of the Akuapem state, played a crucial role in the transition to a modern economy. Akuapem has had a long tradition in agriculture, and during the days of slave trade the principal occupation was known to be farming. The Akuapem people supplied the Accra and Adangbe area with food; in exchange they received salt, dried fish, gunpowder, guns, iron, and cotton manufactures.[7] That the Akuapems should have engaged in agriculture is not surprising. Unlike the people of the western region of the Gold Coast, the Akyem and the Asante, the Akuapems did not have any gold mines; and unlike the coastal people and the people of the Volta River, the Akuapems could not engage in the fish trade. But Akuapem, unlike Asante and Akyem, was known as a kola-producing region. Thus farming and the sale of agricultural produce was a natural occupation for the Akuapems.

In 1733, people from the state of Akyem in the region of Abuakwa, who had helped the Akuapems to fight the Akwamus, settled at Akropong to rule the state at the invitation of the inhabitants. Most of these invited settlers were soldiers; the land given to them was the property of the Larteh people and other Guan groups. The settlers could not continue with the gold-mining activities which had been their main occupation in Akyem before their move. They accordingly turned to farming and, like other people in Akuapem, they sold their agricultural goods to people on the coast.

Following the abolition of the slave trade during the nineteenth century, palm oil became a staple export from the Gold Coast. Most of the oil came from the eastern region, particularly from Akuapem and Krobo. Although the volume of the trade was not large and in no way compared with the oil exported from the Niger delta, the palm oil trade was significant in providing the capital for investments in land and the labor which made the transition to cocoa possible. Akuapem palm oil production was geared not only to the external export trade: some of it was sold in other internal regions. Furthermore, palm wine was distilled into gin (Akpateshi), which found markets in wide areas. When the question of the source of capital for cocoa is raised, the response is always "ngo ne nsa" (palm oil and gin).

The increasing palm oil trade in the nineteenth century was accompanied by two developments: the acquisition of more land and the acquisition of slaves.[8] The acquisition of more land was imperative for the people of Akropong. Their original land allocation was insufficient, and disputes with other Akuapems probably stimulated the need to acquire more. The Akropongs' acquisition of land for plantations in the direction of Akyem was probably facilitated by the fact that the people of Akropong had originally come from Akyem. In fact, the plantations of the Akropong clergy who pioneered the cocoa industry were located on land acquired from Akyem near and around Koforidua in the eastern region.[9] Labor requirements were met with slave purchases from the northern and Volta regions. Akuapem Christians of the Basel Mission churches lost their slaves in 1863 when the Basel Mission abolished the use of slavery among its membership. By the late 1860s, Akuapem was full of people who had taken refuge in the area in the wake of the Asante wars and the disturbances in the Volta region. Most of the refugees, and other slaves from the Volta region, remained in Akuapem after the cessation of hostilities and the emancipation of slaves in the colony in 1874, and, being landless, provided labor for both the palm oil and cocoa industries.

While the above developments were taking place, the activities of the Basel Mission in the areas of agriculture and evangelization also contributed to the transition to the modern economy. The earliest cocoa seeds were sent to Akropong in 1857 from Surinam;[10] however, these seeds did not survive.[11] In 1861 more cocoa trees were planted; these survived. Worms and beetles presented problems; from time to time, the Mission smeared the trees with chloride of lime mixed with hog fat as protection against the worms. All reports indicated that in 1863 the cocoa trees were growing beautifully.[12] By 1866, the trees planted at Akropong were bearing fruit, and seeds from ripe pods were being replanted.[13] In 1867, more cocoa plantations were established at Akropong,[14] and by 1869, in spite of strong fences built around the plantations, the cocoa trees reportedly were being stolen by the townspeople.[15] The Basel Mission tried to encourage its Christian followers and churches to cultivate cocoa; clearly its contribution to the evolution of the modern economy was substantial. The following case studies of some of the earliest cocoa farmers provide further illustrations of this contribution.

David Asante (1830–1892) was probably more instrumental than anyone else in the implementation of the systematic cultivation and spread of cocoa in Akuapem and beyond. Although Asante was the first African minister to be ordained by the Basel Mission, his name is not as well known in most Ghanaian and scholarly circles as the names of Theophilus Opoku and N. T. Clerk. Asante's father was Owusu Akyem, a nobleman who was decapitated in 1845 during riots at Christiansborg while on a trip with the paramount chief of Akuapem. Owusu Akyem owned one of the earliest farms at Bewase, near Konko on the road to Koforidua. Asante's mother was Nana Kome, who also owned a farm at Konko. Asante was converted and was subsequently baptized on Christmas Day in 1847, and was a member of the pioneer class of the Akropong seminary in 1848. He was sent to Basel with a cousin, Oforikae, in 1857; although Oforikae died, Asante was educated and ordained in Basel before returning to Akropong in 1864. Persons who have known Asante claim that he brought cocoa seeds when he returned from Basel. How Asante secured the seeds is not known, but the Mission in Basel may have imported them for him. The seeds were planted at Konko on the road to Koforidua on land owned by his mother. According to her descendants, the funds used by Nana Kome to obtain the land came from making and selling palm oil.[16]

In 1871, David Asante acquired more land to expand his plantation. His private journal gives a detailed description of how this expansion occurred. According to Asante, his mother had given him some gold and beads tied in a cloth when he left for Basel.[17] Asante gave the gold to the Basel Mission authorities in return for some expensive beads known as *Kokronoma*. The *Kokronoma* beads belonged to the Akuapem state, and one of the paramount chiefs had used them as collateral for a loan from the missionaries. The missionaries sent the beads to Basel when the money was not repaid. When Asante returned to the Gold Coast, he returned the beads to the paramount chief; in appreciation, in 1871 the chief gave Asante some land, on which Asante planted cocoa.

Asante redistributed the early cocoa yields from his farm among relatives and other Christians. The nephew of David Asante, Rev. Henry Ofusu (1864–1918), established a cocoa farm at Konko in 1885 when he was a teacher at the Presbyterian middle school at Akropong; and one of the early large cocoa plantations was that of the Reverend Simon Mfodwo Koranteng (1845–1916), the brother of Rev. Asante. Rev. Koranteng was the father of Nana Ofori Kuma, who was the paramount chief of Akuapem from 1914 to 1920 and from 1931 to 1941. Koranteng (ordained in 1873) established another cocoa farm at Konko, and in fact retired early from the ministry and lived on his plantation until his death in 1916. Abenaa Korantema, the sister of Asante and Koranteng, used money she had made from palm oil to buy land to establish cocoa farms; from the 1880s, Abenaa Korantema lent money to people, especially Guans, seeking funds to purchase land.

The labor for the cocoa farms of Asante, Koranteng, and Korantema was provided by Korantema's children. Probably for this reason, as well as for matrilineal inheritance considerations, Asante and Koranteng bequeathed their farms to their nephews. Asante originally had planned to leave his cocoa farms to his children, but later entries in his journal indicated a change in favor of his nephews. He did, however, bequeath to his children his house, originally built by his elder brother, Kwame Amanin, who had made a fortune in trading in palm oil and gin. It is still known as David Asante's house.

The Reverend Theophilus Opoku (1842–1913), a cousin of David Asante, also established a cocoa plantation, at Osuhyen near Koforidua. In Opoku's writings, including his autobiographical statement before his ordination, he indicated that he was the last of the six children of his father. A sickly child, he told his parents he would go to school since he felt that his physical condition would not allow him the energy needed for farming. Opoku was ordained in 1872 after his seminary training, and his cocoa-growing activities began some years later.

As in the case of David Asante, the capital for Opoku's plantation at Osuhyen came via his mother from the palm oil trade. Although the precise date for the establishment of the plantation is not known, it probably was in operation by the 1880s; Opoku had the cocoa plantation during the time of his ministry at Adukrom from 1884 to 1890. This farm was inherited by Rev. C. E. Opoku and his sisters, but has not been maintained since the death of the former in 1952.

Theophilus Opoku's elder brother, Ohene Kwaku, who died in 1896, had also invested in cocoa with money made in palm oil, palm wine, and gin. When Ohene Kwaku died, he had a prosperous cocoa plantation at Akropong.

The Reverend Philip Kwabi's (1835–1925) farming activities are probably better known than his work as an evangelist. Although seven years older than Theophilus Opoku, the two men were in seminary at the same time. Reports of Kwabi's performance as a student and as an evangelist were not flattering, and ordination came very late for him. Kwabi maintained a large cocoa plantation at Asuoya on land which had been acquired by his mother, who had also been involved in the palm oil trade. The seeds for the plantation had been secured from David Asante's farm at Konko in the 1880s.[18]

The Reverend Peter Hall (1851–1937) was the son of one of the original West Indian settlers who were brought to Akropong as the nucleus of the Christian community.[19] Although the West Indian families worked for the Basel Mission, they were given days off to work for themselves. Many of the West Indians were involved in farming as well as in church work. They were already used to the export economy, having participated in the palm oil trade. The land given to the West Indians was part of a grant, comprising about half of the town, made to the Mission by Nana Addo Dankwa.[20]

Peter Hall established a cocoa farm when he was the pastor of the Presbyterian Church at Akropong from 1882 to 1888; this farm still stands. During the same period he also started a plantation near the farm of David Asante in Konko. He later became the first moderator of the Presbyterian Church of the Gold Coast.

Besides these pioneers of the cocoa industry, other people from the Basel Mission churches turned to cocoa farming, beginning in the 1880s. One group included teachers and catechists of the churches. Another was made up of individuals who had been dismissed from the mission as teachers and evangelists for "moral" reasons, and for practices pertaining to "heathenism." "Moral" reasons meant having an affair, or fathering a child out of wedlock. Practices pertaining to "heathenism" included participating in traditional festivals and activities. People who were dismissed from employment by the church often could not get work elsewhere because of "bad testimonials"; these people often turned to cocoa farming. The plantation activities of agents dismissed from the Basel Mission provided them with a viable and profitable alternative, and perhaps explain why these agents did not become involved in the kind of nationalistic activities that engaged agents in the western region when their economic ambitions were frustrated.

Finally, it should be noted that while the initial purchases of land for the production of cocoa utilized profits from palm oil, the capital for most Akuapem land purchases after 1900 was acquired by soldiers who fought in the Asante war, or by construction workers on the Gold Coast railroads. Two nephews of Theophilus Opoku, who wanted their own land and did not want to farm on family land, provide examples: Kwadwo Bekoe, who died in 1969 at 96, fought in the Asante war and used the wages he received to finance his purchases; Darko Mensah, who died in 1973 at 88, secured his capital by working on the railroads.[21]

The economic activities on the Gold Coast during the nineteenth century did not represent a complete break with the past. While the period was an era of innovation, many economic activities were linked to the period before the slave trade. The palm oil trade, which provided capital for land purchases, represented both continuity and innovation insofar as it had connections with Akuapem's past trade in agricultural produce. Thus the success of the cocoa industry was based on attempts to find substitutes for the slave trade which, while not hugely successful in themselves, did at least bring about changes in the institutional framework of the local economy. Moreover, the leaders in the early development of the industry were missionaries, who obviously saw successful production for the international exchange economy, and the associated changes in local institutions, as entirely consistent with their Christian mission. Ironically, however, the Basel Mission and the early ministers were also the first to turn against cocoa plantations when they began to lose members of their congregations who were residing on plantations, or who had moved to acquire more land.[22] Post-abolition developments on the Gold Coast provide further illustrations of the African response to changes in the international economy, as well as of the difficulty in separating the moral from the economic strands in the abolitionist impulse.

NOTES

This article is based on a larger work in progress on the economic history of Ghana, and incorporates interviews conducted from 1972 to 1978. The taped interviews were conducted in the Akuapem dialect of the Twi language, and are available from the author at the University of California, San Diego.

1 A. G. Hopkins, *An Economic History of West Africa* (London, 1973), p. 124.
2 Internal and long-distance trade were becoming important during the pe-

riod following abolition. Ivor Wilks has pointed to the increase in the Asante kola trade to the north as a result of deliberate state policy. See Ivor Wilks, "Asante Policy towards the Hausa Trade in the 19th Century," in Claude Meillassoux, ed., *The Development of Indigenous Trade and Markets in West Africa* (London, 1971), pp. 124–41.

3 See Edward Reynolds, "The Rise and Fall of an African Merchant Class," *Cahiers d'Etudes Africaines* 54 (1974): 253–64; Edward Reynolds, *Trade and Economic Change on the Gold Coast, 1807–1874* (London, 1974).

4 See Edward Reynolds, "The Declining Political Power of Gold Coast Chiefs following Abolition," *Sankofa*, (Legon, Ghana), in press.

5 See E. T. Koramoa and Edward Reynolds, *Ghana Presbyteri Asafo: Mfe Oha ne Aduonum Adwuma, 1828–1978* (Accra, 1978); Noel Smith, *Presbyterian Church of Ghana* (London, 1965); Hans Debrunner, *A History of Christianity in Ghana* (Accra, 1967).

6 For information about Danish plantation activities, see H. Jeppeson, "Danske Plantageanlag po Guldkysten, 1788–1850," *Geografish Tidsskrift* 65 (1966): 48–88; Georg Norregard, *Danish Settlements in West Africa 1659–1850* (Boston, 1966).

7 H. Meredith, *An Account of the Gold Coast of Africa* (London, 1812), p. 227.

8 Early migrations and the acquisition of land in the nineteenth century are considered in Marion Johnson, "Migrants Progress," *Bulletin of the Ghana Geographers' Association* 9 (1964): 4–27; ibid., 10 (1965): 13–20.

9 Although the present paper concentrates on the role of the clergy from Akropong in the early development of the cocoa industry, the parts played by clergymen, catechists, and teachers from Larteh, Aburi, and Odumasi in Krobo will appear in a book on the economic history of Ghana, in progress.

10 In spite of the documentary evidence of the introduction of cocoa to the Gold Coast, a high official at the Ghanian Cocoa Board told me that no amount of research or evidence could take away from Teteh Quarshie the credit of introducing cocoa to the country in 1879. He conceded, however, that even in Teteh Quarshie's family the credit for bringing cocoa from Fernando Po is given to his brother.

11 Johannes Haas to the Honourable Evangelical Missions Committee in Basel, 22 Jan. 1858, in "Quarterly Report" for 1857 from the Akropong [Ghana] Station of the Basel Mission, p. 4, Basel Mission Archives, Basel, Switzerland (hereafter cited as BMA).

12 Johann Jacob Lang to Evangelical Missions Committee, 6 Nov. 1861, in report of the Akropong Station 1861, p. 4, BMA; enclosure to the "Annual Report" of Akropong Station for 1861 (Feb. 1862), p. 2, BMA; Lang to Evangelical Missions Committee, in enclosure to the "Annual Report" of Akropong Station for 1862 (Jan. 1863), p. 3, BMA.

13 Lang to Evangelical Missions Committee, 22 Jan. 1866, in "Annual Report" of Akropong Station for 1865, p. 4, BMA.

14 Lang to Evangelical Missions Committee, 25 Jan. 1867, in "Annual Report" of Akropong Station for 1866, p. 2, B.M.A.

15 Henry Marchaud to Evangelical Mission Committee, 31 Dec. 1869, in report from Akropong Station, pp. 1–2, BMA.

16 I recently discovered a private journal that Asante kept from 1864 until his death in 1892. One of his daughters, Ophelia Asante, born in 1880, is still alive as this publication goes to press. Madam Yaa Tweneboaa of Akropong and the late Rev. H. J. Keteku knew Asante, and have told the author much about him.

17 This practice was not uncommon; often when boys came of age they were given a certain amount of gold tied in a cloth, which they put around their waists. Such gold was often used for redemption if the boy was captured in war.

18 Interview with Nana Yaa Tweneboaa and Opayin Kwabena Awuku, 14 May 1978, Akropong, Ghana.

19 For an outline history of the West Indian settlement, see N. T. Clerk, *A History of the West Indians of the Basel Mission, 1843–1943* (Kumasi, Ghana, 1943). Verbatim copies of this document are in circulation under various authors' names, but they are all copied from Clerk.

20 Interview with H. J. Keteku, 15 Aug. 1972, at Akropong, Ghana, who explained to the author that the paramount chief had a selfish motive for granting the missionaries so much land. According to Keteku, the land that Chief Obuobi Atiemo had granted to the Danes at Amenapa was far removed from the town; when the Danes on the plantation died, the townspeople could not appropriate this improved land because it was so far from the town. The general belief was that the Basel missionaries would also die after improving their land, and since this property was in town, the people expected to take it over when the missionaries died. However, the Basel missionaries thrived.

21 Interview with Darko Mensah, 5 Dec. 1972, Akropong, Ghana.

22 See Theophilus Opoku, "San-Konu-w'abe," *Christian Messenger* (Akropong, Ghana), 31 Mar. 1911, pp. 29–31.

PART III The Illegal Slave Trade

CHAPTER 9: **The Impact of Abolition on the**

Atlantic Slave Trade

David Eltis

The long road to the final abolition of the Atlantic slave trade from
the Danish edict of March, 1792, to the full enforcement of the
American anti-slave-trade law and the movement toward abolition in
Cuba in the 1860s was marked by volumes of legislation and international treaties. The motives of the nations or groups which were
responsible for these moves have been subjected to rather more study
than has their impact on the slave trade itself. Potentially this impact
was profound. In the last sixty years ships were liable to capture, their
crews and, more rarely, their owners subject to imprisonment and
sometimes death, and nearly 200,000 members of slaver cargoes were
freed. Most major seafaring nations stationed cruisers off the African
coast at various times and some, in partnership with Britain, established international tribunals or courts of mixed commission at different locations around the Atlantic to adjudicate the prizes taken by
these cruisers. But these measures could not prevent the forcible
shipping of nearly two million Africans to the Americas under the
flags of nations which had officially abolished the slave trade, a number not far below the peaks reached in the last decades of the eighteenth century. How did this traffic differ from that of the previous
century, and to what extent was it affected by the various international attempts to suppress it? A comparison of recent work by a
number of scholars on the last phases of the legal slave trade on the
one hand and, on the other, data culled from British Foreign Office

records on nearly 2,500 slavers in the early years of the illicit trade
provide partial answers to these questions.[1]

For the major branches of the slave trade to the British and French
Caribbean and to Brazil and Cuba, formal abolition came in stages in
the quarter century after 1807. Most of the illegal trade was to Brazil
and Cuba. Slave imports to the latter became illegal in 1821, and to
Brazil, from Africa north of the equator in 1815, and from the rest
of Africa in 1830. Abolition in these areas meant simply that impediments to the trade appeared which were not there before. In the
importing area returning slave ships were denied access to regular
port facilities, and government officials at all levels expected payments in return for tolerating slave imports. While at sea the slave
ship in the post-abolition period had to contend with the British navy.
As a result of Anglo-Spanish and Anglo-Portuguese treaties of 1817,
the navy had the right to detain ships sailing under the Spanish, Portuguese, and (later) Brazilian flags which were found with slaves on
board, and take them before the courts of mixed commission set up
under the same treaties. In the later 1830s these impediments increased as further treaties and parliamentary acts broadened the conditions under which the navy could detain ships.

The available data allow us to compare trends before and after
abolition in certain key variables such as ship size, crew size, slaves
carried per ton, voyage time, and, less satisfactorily, mortality rates.
Such comparisons will provide a base for generalizations about the
illegal traffic and the impact of measures to suppress it beyond that
used by contemporaries like Thomas Fowell Buxton, David Turnbull,
Richard Madden, and a number of naval officers whose published
impressions have shaped many modern accounts of the illegal traffic.
The picture of small, overcrowded ships returning from a quick trip
to the coast and experiencing a high mortality rate in the process was
accepted even before the British parliamentary committees of the
1840s began their hearings and it has certainly endured since.

We turn first to the issue of ship size which, as in earlier times,
revolves largely around the question of the size of the unit used to
measure the ship. Not only were there differences between nations
on this point, but from time to time definitions changed within nations. Table 9.1 (A) presents samples of tonnages from the last years
of the legal trade, and (B) gives the equivalent data which are available for the illegal trade. The figures are all in British measured tons
of the years 1773 to 1835, as far as can be determined. The English
data for the 1790s must be used carefully for comparative purposes,
as there was a marked increase in the size of the British slave ship in

the years before 1807. This was due to a large extent to legislation which in 1788 and 1799 restricted the allowable number of slaves per ton, and perhaps also to the increased tendency of the British slave merchants to seek slaves south of the equator, where bigger ships were normally used. In addition there was the uncertain impact of the 1786 law, which required all British vessels to register in measured tons, and had the effect of increasing the registered tonnage of ships by one third.[2] The English data in table 9.1 (A) are for the period after this act went into effect but before the 1799 act further restricted the slave per ton ratio. Thus the average tonnage might be higher than would have been the case without Dolben's 1788 act.

A comparison of sections (A) and (B) of table 9.1 indicates that no radical change occurred in the size of the slave ship between the late eighteenth century and the 1820s and 1830s. Only the means of ship tonnages from Nantes, both calculated from very large samples, show a decrease between the two periods. However, as effective prosecution by French authorities did not begin until the late 1820s, and as French ships were largely protected from the British navy by their flag, the trend can scarcely be attributed to abolition. It is more likely the result of the shift of French slave traders to African supply zones north of the equator in the nineteenth century. British ships, on the other hand, drew from the same general areas as Cuban and Bahian slavers. Both Cuba- and Bahia-bound ships show decreases in the late 1830s, and there is a suggestion of a similar trend in the Rio de Janeiro figures after 1840. The Cuban trend is the most pronounced because southeast Africa became a significant source for slaves after 1835, and this required larger ships. But between 1841 and 1843 the mean rose once more, though again this was at a time when recourse to southern supply zones was increasing.[3]

There is some documentary evidence of smaller ships being used before the trend shows up in the tonnage data. In 1836 an anti-slave-trade bill that was brought before the Brazilian legislature set a minimum tonnage for ships clearing from Brazilian ports for Africa.[4] But this was at a time when the southeast Africa traffic, with its larger ships, was at a low ebb and the observed effect might be due simply to distributional changes unconnected with abolition. Unfortunately the tonnage figures for the early 1830s are too scarce to allow a testing of this hypothesis. Turnbull also commented on the small size of the Cuban slave ship in 1837,[5] but as his source was the *Balanza Mercantil*, the subject of his comments must have been ships clearing out of Havana. As these returned in 1838, what he was observing here was the beginning of the trend to smaller ships shown in table 9.1.

Table 9.1
Tonnages of Slave Ships in Selected Branches of the Trade, 1763–1843

	Mean	Standard Deviation	No. of Observations
A Pre-abolition			
Cleared from English ports, 1790–97[a]	190.6		512
Cleared from Nantes, 1763–77[b]	170.0	68	270
Loanda to Rio de Janeiro, 1795–1811[b]	152–212		n.a.
Arriving at Rio de Janeiro, 1821–30[c]			
(1) upper limit	223		13
(2) lower limit	152		
Cleared from U.S. ports, 1783–1807[d]	118.1		35
B Post-abolition			
Cleared for Cuba, 1821–30	183.5		69
1831–37	169.2		102
1838–40	132.1		84
1841–43	168.9		27
1821–43	161.6	100.4	Total 282
Cleared for Rio de Janeiro, 1831–40	189.7		264
1841–43	161.8	70.6	79
Cleared for Bahia, 1821–30			
(1) upper limit	166.6		51
(2) lower limit	104.1		
1831–38	164.8		20
1839–43	128.4		60
Cleared from Nantes, 1814–33[c]	145.0		337

Notes: Tonnages are in the British measured ton used in the period 1773 to 1835. Most of the above observations entered the historical record in tons different from this standard.

All data not specifically attributed below are from the data bank; see text.

[a] D. P. Lamb, "Volume and Tonnage of the Liverpool Slave Trade, 1772–1807," in Roger T. Anstey and P. E. H. Hair, eds., *Liverpool, the African Slave Trade and Abolition* (Liverpool, 1976), p. 101.

[b] Herbert S. Klein, *The Middle Passage* (Princeton, 1978), pp. 31, 181.

[c] Reported tonnages for Brazil-bound ships, 1821–30, could be biased upward because of the limitation of 5 slaves per ton placed on Portuguese ships by the 1817 Anglo-Portuguese treaty, as well as by Portuguese law. The British consul estimated that recorded tonnages were actual tonnages inflated by 60%. Thus the upper limit is the tonnage as recorded, and the lower limit is the recorded tonnage multiplied by 0.625.

[d] T. T. Hamm, "The American Slave Trade with Africa, 1620–1807" (Ph. D. diss., University of Indiana, 1975), pp. 384–444.

[c] Serge Daget, "Long cours et négriers nantais du trafic illegal, 1814–1833," *Revue française d'histoire d'outre-mer* 62 (1975): 113.

But did abolition prevent an upward trend in ship size from developing? Herbert Klein, after examining trends in tonnages of both English slave ships and Nantes slavers, has commented that by the end of the eighteenth century

> an optimal size ship had ... come to dominate the trade with 54 percent of the ships (landing slaves in Jamaica) being in the 100–199 ton range. It would thus appear that a much more specialized vessel had emerged than a century earlier. This would mean that a vessel in the 100–149 ton range made the ideal transport for slaves across the Atlantic. That the British could have employed larger tonnage is obvious when we look at both the Royal African Company ships of a century before and the contemporaneous West Indiamen, which averaged at least 100 tons more per vessel than the slavers. That the British did not employ this larger tonnage, at least prior to 1800, would seem to suggest that coastal and upriver African trading required the use of smaller ships. . . .[6]

Klein is writing here of pre-1786 tonnages, which according to Lamb should be increased by 54.2% for slave ships of this size for purposes of comparison with post-1786 tonnages.[7] Klein's optimal range thus emerges as 154 to 230 post-1786 tons, and the figures for the 1820s and 1830s in table 9.1 are comfortably within this range, with the exception of the Nantes data. Thus there is no need to look elsewhere for explanations of the relatively small ship used in the slave trade in this period. It has been suggested that a premium on the ability to use shallow creeks and bays for concealment from naval cruisers, as well as a need to spread the risk of capture, induced ship owners to use ships much below the average ocean-going tonnage of the period.[8] But it is more likely that the optimal size for slave trading was also close to the optimal size for escaping the navy's clutches, or alternatively, that without any attempt to suppress the trade tonnages would have been the same. As for risk aversion, the widespread use of joint stock companies in this period made the use of small ships for this purpose unnecessary.

It is hard to see any productivity-improving measure in the first half of the nineteenth century which, but for abolition, would have benefited the slave-shipping sector. The productivity gains in the shipping industry as a whole that North has depicted arose from lower manpower requirements attendant on a fall in the incidence of piracy, and to the development of markets which permitted fewer voyages in ballast.[9] Neither of these sources seem pertinent to a branch of the industry in which large crews were required simply to control the cargo, as well as to handle the more sophisticated rigging of the nineteenth century slaver.

Table 9.2 shows tons per crewman for selected samples of slave ships and nonslave ships. There are abundant data on crews in the Foreign Office records, but many are biased downward to an uncertain extent because British observers in the Americas normally reported the arrival of a slave ship at an American port after the ship had disembarked its cargo prior to entering the port.[10] The Sierra Leone data, based on ships captured (in the main) off Africa but bound for the Caribbean and Bahia, are free of this bias. Slave ships arriving at Jamaica in the eighteenth century tended to be larger than the average English slave ship,[11] and might well have had a higher crew per ton figure than average. Ratios for Jamaican ships, moreover, are for the end of the middle passage, after crew mortality had occurred, thus contributing further to an upward bias in the ratio. The nineteenth century Sierra Leone data, on the other hand, are for the start of the return voyage. Table 9.2 shows clearly that tons per crewman on slave ships did not change very much in the fifty years separating the two periods, but that the slave ship average fell further behind the general industry average. The point is illustrated by the comment of the Portuguese consul in Havana in 1838 that slave ships "were manned at a rate of fifteen men for every 100 tons as opposed to six for normal trading vessels."[12]

It is unlikely that abolition had much influence over the slave ship trend. Of course, had slave trading continued larger ships would eventually have come into use, but the employment of such ships depended on the advent of steam or the construction of harbor facilities, neither of which was a realistic proposition much before 1850. We can conclude, therefore, that before 1838 or 1839 the Cuban- and Brazilian-based slave traders were in fact using the optimal size slave ship, and that abolition had little effect on the size of the crew manning that ship. After these years there was a shift to smaller vessels, though these remained well within Klein's optimal range, and presumably some increase in crew size.

For the captive cargo the size of the ship was of secondary importance to the number of slaves it carried, and perhaps also to the design of the ship. The conviction that abolition induced the slave traders to shift to smaller, finer-lined ships, built for speed rather than for carrying capacity, was widely held at the time of the illegal traffic and has persisted since. If the slaver of the 1820s and 1830s was no smaller than its predecessors, was it designed differently? The closest the Foreign Officer records come to this subject is, data on rigging, at

Table 9.2
Tons per Crewman for Slave and General Shipping, 1700s and 1800s

	Tons per Crewman	No. of Ships
A Pre-abolition		
1. English slave ships arriving at Jamaica, 1782–86[a]	7.5	106
2. Slave ships leaving Nantes, 1763–77[a]	4.6	270
3. Ships from Jamaica entering London, 1766[b]	15.9	–
B Post-abolition		
4. Ships adjudicated at the Sierra Leone court of mixed commission, 1821–43[c]	5.8	230
5. Ships entering New York harbour, 1834[d]	21.0	–

[a] *Klein, Middle Passage*, p. 143. The Klein and Davis figures have both been adjusted by the amount suggested by French to allow for the 1786 change in registered tonnage. See Christopher J. French, "Eighteenth Century Shipping and Tonnage Measurements," *Journal of Economic History* 33 (1973): 440.

[b] R. Davis, *The Rise of the English Shipping Industry* (London, 1962), p. 71.

[c] Data bank; see text.

[d] Douglass C. North, "Sources of Productivity Change in Ocean Shipping, 1600–1850," *Journal of Political Economy* 76 (1968): 961.

best a partial proxy. Quantitative evidence on hull design is scarce, but naval reports suggest that the rounded, deep, slow-sailing British merchantman design encouraged by pre-1854 ship measurement rules was replaced by the finer lines of early clipper-type hull design. Even in the 1820s most ships in the Cuban traffic were being constructed specifically for the slave trade in the United States and the Iberian peninsula.[13]

While for general freight there was little change in sailing time between the seventeenth and mid-nineteenth centuries, for high value, perishable cargoes improved times were possible from the end of the eighteenth century.[14] In the slave trade mortality was strongly influenced by time spent at sea, and the Baltimore clipper, variously rigged but normally with at least one mast with a fore and aft sail, represented therefore a significant technological advance. Tables 9.3 and 9.4 show voyage times for ships sailing from Africa to the Americas before and after abolition.

The Rio de Janeiro traffic was legal before 1830 and illegal thereafter, but there is no statistically significant difference between the mean voyage time in the decade before and the thirteen years after 1830. A potentially more useful comparison is between more widely

Table 9.3
Middle Passage Voyage Times of Slave Ships, Selected Years, 1791–1843

	Mean Voyage Time in Days	Standard Deviation	No. of Ships
English ships arriving at Jamaica, 1791–98[a]	61	22	187
Ships arriving in the Caribbean, 1816–43[b]	48.4	15.3	14

[a] Klein, *Middle Passage*, p. 167.
[b] Data bank; see text.

Table 9.4
Middle Passage Voyage Times of Slave Ships Arriving at Rio de Janeiro, 1821–43

	Region of Embarkation					
	Cape Lopez to R. Congo		Angola		Southeast Africa	
	Days	No. ships	Days	No. ships	Days	No. ships
1821–30	34	90	34	138	63	61
1831–43	34	4	38	46	60	10

Source: Data bank; see text.

separated periods; table 9.3 compares a sample of fourteen ships that arrived in the Caribbean (all but one at Cuba and the Bahamas) between 1816 and 1843 with Klein's data on all ships that arrived at Jamaica from Africa between 1791 and 1798. The nineteenth century sample is tiny, but its distribution by African region of embarkation is similar to that of the Jamaican ships, and Cuba and the Bahamas are only slightly farther away from Africa than is Jamaica. The difference between the two means is significant at the .005 level, and even if we include three voyage times from southeast Africa to Cuba (no ship carried slaves to Jamaica from this region between 1791 and 1798) the difference is still significant at the 0.025 level.[15]

The point is illustrated and supported by the numerous complaints of naval officers from the beginnings of the patrol onward about the poor sailing qualities of their ships relative to the slavers. While Palmerston complained acidly in later years that the enthusiasm of the Admiralty for suppression was such that "if there was a particularly old, slow going tub in the navy, she was sure to be sent to the coast of Africa to try to catch the fast sailing American clippers . . .,"[16] the problem seems to have been a more general one. British naval ships were built along the lines of British merchant ships—rounded, long, and deep—with the intention of carrying a large armament in place of a large cargo. They were, in fact, probably not unlike the English slave ships that disembarked in Jamaica between 1791 and 1798, and the cries of the naval officers and their policy of buying up condemned slave ships as tenders to the squadron provides eloquent backing for the quantitative findings above.[17]

The packing of slaves, measured by the slave per ton ratio, is a more contentious topic. In 1842 a 36-foot sloop, the *Minerva*, bound from Ambriz to Bahia, was captured with 126 slaves on board. The slave hold was fourteen inches high, and half the cargo as well as all the crew were forced to remain on deck the whole time. Her burden was just under 25 British tons, giving a slave per ton ratio of 5 to 1.[18] In the same year the *Jeniviva*, 44 tons, had a ratio of nearly 6 slaves per ton. Similar cases preoccupied Buxton and the anticoercionist lobby in the British Parliament in the 1840s; they suspected that naval suppression increased slave loading rates. Table 9.5 shows that, at least for the Caribbean, the ratio remained in the same range in the 1820s as it had in the previous century, though it should be noted that the British ratio, allowing for the tonnage changes of 1786, was below two to one.[19] Once more the initial impact of abolition appears to have been rather slight. A sharp increase in the rate (significant at the 0.0001 level) appeared after 1830 in the Caribbean traffic, and a further significant increase in both the Brazilian and Cuban trade occurred in the late 1830s, although part of this was a function of the smaller ship which came into use at this time, and perhaps also of an increase in factor efficiency.[20] Whatever the cause, the mean rate as well as the variation around the mean probably reached historic highs in both major branches of the trade after 1837, though not such highs as LeVeen and some contemporaries estimated. It is obvious that the impact of attempts to suppress the trade must have been delayed, and there seems no reason, in view of the earlier discussion, why the ratio should have decreased in the absence of abolition.

Recent work has shown that conditions on board, as well as mortality, were more likely to be influenced by the time spent on the ship than by loading ratios. Sailing time, as we have seen, probably decreased, but of the three legs into which a slaving voyage from the Americas was divided the second, the stay on the coast of Africa, was the longest. In the illegal phase of the trade slaves did not normally go on board until just before the ship set out on the return journey, though the alternative of waiting in a cramped barracoon on shore

Table 9.5
Slaves per ton Embarked in Africa, Selected Branches of the Trade, 1711–1843

	Slaves per Ton	Standard Deviation	No. of Ships
Ships leaving			
Nantes, 1711–77[a]	2.20	0.70	764
Ships bound for			
the Caribbean			
1821–30	2.13	0.68	52
1831–36	2.51	0.98	44
1837–43	3.00	0.77	46
Ships bound for			
Brazil			
1821–30 upper[b]	2.90	1.18	74
lower	1.81		
1831–37	2.64	1.04	17
1838–43	3.49	1.36	34

Note: For comments on the measured ton used here, see note to table 9.1.

[a] Klein, *Middle Passage*, p. 186. All other data from data bank; see text.

[b] For an explanation of these limits, see reference c, table 9.1.

may not have been any more salubrious. Slave ship crews, however, continued to be exposed to the coastal disease environment as the ship, while awaiting her cargo, simply moved to another part of the coast or else remained at the trading point empty of both goods and slaves. As the Foreign Office observers recorded both ship departures from the Americas as well as their return with slaves, it is possible to examine some roundtrip voyage times as well as the return voyage times already referred to.

Table 9.6 shows round trip voyage times for selected branches of the traffic, except that the return journey from Jamaica to Europe is excluded for those ships clearing from English ports. English ships traded in approximately the same African regions as did Havana slavers, and after adjusting for the extra distance to Africa from England and the improved sailing performance of the nineteenth century vessel, the similarity of the time spent on the coast in the two periods is striking.

The Bahia figures are puzzling. The standard round trip from Bahia to the west coast of Africa in the eighteenth century was six to seven months,[21] and the 1821–1822 figures are consistent with this. The drop, beginning in 1829–1830 (before total abolition, it should be noted), was either unrepresentative or a result of suddenly improved supply conditions in Africa which allowed ships to spend less

Table 9.6
Round Trip Voyage Times for Slave Ships

Port of Clearing	No. of Days	No. of Ships
English Ports[a]		
1791–98[b]	260	187
Havana		
1821–25	210	33
1826–30	221	86
1831–34	210	83
1835–38	231	80
1839–43	166	30
Bahia		
1821–22[c]	231	30
1829–30	126	27
1841–42	110	6
Rio de Janeiro		
1837–38	212	37
1839–40	187	25
Pernambuco		
1840–42	213	10

[a] The time for ships leaving English ports is for the journey from England to Jamaica via the African coast.

[b] Klein, *Middle Passage*, p. 157.

[c] Pierre Verger, *Flux et reflux . . . de la traite des Nègres entre le Golfe de Benin et Bahia de Todos os Santos du 17ᵉ et 19ᵉ siècles* (The Hague, 1968), pp. 660–61. All other data from data bank; see text.

time gathering a cargo. Voyage time on the return trip from the Bight of Benin in the 1820s averaged 31 days (32 observations), so that if the figures in table 9.6 are accurate, the slave cargo must have been collected on average in less than two months in these years. This is certainly out of line with experiences in other periods and other regions.

The Rio de Janeiro figures, on the other hand, seems unusually high and presumably reflect in part the rapid expansion of trade with southeast Africa, where return voyage times were nearly two months longer than to other supply zones. In any event, as time spent on the coast made up between a third and a half of total trip time, and as sailing times decreased between the two periods, it would be hard to argue that time spent on the coast was lower in the nineteenth century than it had been before, the fragmentary Bahia figures notwithstanding. Perhaps abolition and the suppressive measures that followed added to the existing pressures of costs and crew mortality to keep the stay on the coast to a minimum, but the dominating constraint, ultimately demographic in origin, appears to have been the difficulty of assembling a cargo.

Table 9.6 adds further to the evidence of significant change occurring in the late 1830s. Starting in 1839 the round trip voyage from Havana fell below six months for the first time, despite the trend toward increased trade south of the equator. The figures for Rio de Janeiro in 1839–1840 are also significantly different from those for the previous two years. It is unlikely that conditions in Africa as a whole can explain this trend, though local variations in supply would certainly affect the time taken to assemble a cargo. Rather, the explanation seems to lie in the improved organization of the slave traders. Not only did the larger Cuban- and Brazilian-based traders begin to operate their own factories on the coast in the later 1830s, they also began to supply these establishments with trade goods freighted by ships other than slavers which often sailed under flags less susceptible to British interference. Of the 216 ships condemned at Sierra Leone between 1821 and 1843 for which information is available, 183 freighted out their own trading cargo and 23 sailed with nominal cargo or in ballast, but the whole of the latter group sailed in the years 1839 to 1843. Clearly some traders had developed sufficiently sophisticated operations to permit slave ships to leave the Americas only when the slave cargo was expected to be ready. The cost of transporting the trading cargo was of course increased enormously, but lower slave ship costs and reduced ship captures obviously outweighed this cost.

We may now face the mortality issue directly. The direct quantitative evidence of higher mortality rates in the post-abolition period is limited to before and after samples for three pairs of exporting and importing regions. The 346 ships arriving in Brazil from Angola between 1821 and 1830 with information about on board deaths had a mean mortality rate of 7.24 percent. Records of only 20 ships in the 1831–1843 period survive, and their mean mortality rate of 16.9 percent is apparently a considerable increase. The rate for southeast Africa to Brazil shows a similar jump. However, the high standard deviations, which plague all slave ship mortality data, mean that the difference is not statistically significant and, moreover, that there is an indeterminate amount of downward bias in the pre-1831 data, which we have noted elsewhere.[22] Finally, the disembarkation zone in the samples, namely Brazil, covers a wide range of sailing routes and voyage conditions. The third pairing, upper Guinea to the Caribbean, also saw an increase in mortality rates from 12.2% in 1711–1777 (175 Nantes-based ships) to 19.5% for 1821–1843 (24 ships based at various ports), but again the figures are not statistically significant.[23] Thus the quantitative evidence of the impact of abolition on slave mortality is more inconclusive than that for some other important variables in the trade.

The potential effect of abolition is no clearer. One of the key determinants of mortality was the embarkation region in Africa, with the Bight of Biafra and southeast Africa having mortality rates at least double those of other supply zones. Ultimately Cuban slavers did begin to trade east of the Cape of Good Hope, and attempts to suppress the traffic probably encouraged this pattern. But more than offsetting this upward pressure on mortality rates was the early closure of many Bight of Biafra ports to slave ships; in addition, from 1830 to 1835, for quite different reasons, southeast Africa was completely cut off from the transatlantic traffic.

Other potential explanations of mortality must also be set aside. The slave per ton ratio did rise during the 1830s, but mortality was already up from eighteenth century levels when this trend emerged, and the ratio has never correlated very closely with mortality in other branches of the traffic.[24] Both voyage time and time spent on the coast might similarly be rejected, as the former declined and the latter remained constant before declining in the late 1830s. It is also hard to see how treatment of the slaves could have worsened as a result of abolition. If suppression had any effect, it increased the spread between slave prices in Africa and those in the Americas. Slave property would thus become significantly more valuable to the shipper.

On a more empirical level there is the experience of the naval captors of slave cargoes in the bights, who found it almost impossible to bring down mortality rates on the voyage to the Sierra Leone court, despite the incentive of Admiralty bounties for slaves landed alive and their providing the slaves with extra food, more space where possible, and the admittedly dubious benefits of medical care.[25] The image of slaves sailing from the bights in British naval ships of the same basic design as the slave ships of the 1790s, in conditions less crowded and on shorter voyages than those of the 1790s, but nevertheless dying off at a rate perhaps 50% greater than their eighteenth century predecessors, is not a little improbable, but it is nevertheless not far from the truth. There were of course local effects. Coastal factors were occasionally forced to release slaves because months of blockade had reduced food supplies and had eliminated the possibility of embarking the slaves, and there must have been cargoes which left the coast in a weakened condition on account of the cruiser squadron, but it would be stretching credibility to generalize this effect. On balance, it seems likely that an increase in mortality did occur at this time, but that the influence of abolition on this phenomenon is unclear, at least before 1843.

There remain a number of other shipping costs which abolition could have affected. Ships in the Cuban traffic were frequently armed in the 1820s, and the connection between this and the activities of the cruiser squadron would seem to be obvious.[26] However, the practice died out by the mid-1830s, and at no point was a Bahian ship, as much within the navy's catchment area as Cuban ships, ever found armed. There seem to be two explanations, neither of them connected directly with abolition. Until at least 1827 Spanish ships in the Caribbean were subject to depredation by pirates who, until a few years earlier, had been loosely employed by the new governments of Spain's former Latin American colonies as part of their wars of independence.[27] Secondly, Spanish ships in Africa, unlike Portuguese, were known for their own piratical activities even before the Spanish trade became illegal.[28] Indeed, it has been suggested that when piracy was finally controlled in the Caribbean many of the corsairs switched to the slave trade.[29] Certainly the depredation of Portuguese slave ships continued into the early 1830s.[30]

This situation possibly affected the wages of crewmen also. The payrolls of six ships in the Cuban traffic between 1828 and 1839 list wages of $30 to $40 a month for able seamen, which with slight exaggeration was said by an English African merchant to be "higher than the pay of a master of a respectable British merchantman."[31] Brazilian wages were comparable if the *Emilia* operating out of Bahia in the early 1820s was typical.[32] Once more the obvious explanations is that there was an equalizing differential for carrying on an illegal occupation. Yet the risk involved for the seamen at the hands of Brazilian and Spanish authorities as well as the Royal Navy was minimal, except in those few cases where physical resistance took place. No British or mixed commission court had the power to punish crew members taken off British soil, and the most a captive could expect was a few days at Sierra Leone, a place with frequent connections with slave trading haunts.

Alternative explanations for the better wages of slaver crews are more plausible. Wages were always higher in the Americas than in Europe, but, more important, they were normally paid on condition that the cargo was landed successfully—a proviso which would elicit a premium; the only matricula where this stipulation is absent, for example, listed wages at $30 a month. Moreover, sailing a slave ship such as the one "with crowded canvas" which "glanced up the estuary at Sierra Leone like lightning"[33] in 1834 perhaps required skills beyond those required on a British merchantman. On most muster rolls examined there are two classes of seamen, with the second and smallest categorized as "ordinary" or "assistants" and paid up to a third below the "able seaman" rate. For both these reasons average wages were almost certainly below $30 per month, and a good part of the differential between this and Lebergott's range for able seamen of $11 to $17 in the general shipping industry is accounted for by the dangers of piracy and disease on the African and Caribbean coasts.[34] If a differential remained after adjusting for these differences it is hard to see how abolition could have contributed to it.

Most of the above arguments apply also to officer's pay, but senior officers had an additional emolument in the form of commissions calculated on the final selling price of the slaves. James Tobin's estimate of 6 percent as the standard commission rate paid to captains in the late eighteenth century[35] is similar to nineteenth century levels,[36] and where the latter were lower, as in the Brazilian trade, the master and other officers were allowed to carry slaves on their own account. We should note, however, that as slave prices went up any commission calculated as a fixed percentage would of course rise.

Finally, we turn to a shipping cost which could provide a particularly large clue on the impact of abolition. Insurance was normally available during the illegal slave trade, but costs varied enormously. In the Cuban traffic between 1821 and 1836 rates were normally 20 to 25 percent of total outset costs.[37] For the Brazilian traffic in the first decade or so after total abolition rates were lower—11 to 15 percent.[38] It would be wrong, however, to assume that the peacetime eighteenth century rate of 5 percent would have applied in the absence of abolition. In 1814, at the close of the European war, a new Spanish slaver obtained a 7½ percent rate from a London company on a contract which specifically excluded the eventuality of capture by a British cruiser,[39] and part of the difference between this and the 20 percent rates paid later must be accounted for by the piracy factor already mentioned. At the end of a better than average year of captures by the Royal Navy, a Cuban slave trader wrote that speculators had resolved to fit out no more vessels for the trade. Yet the navy was only one of four factors equally responsible for this; piracy (or "the spoliation they [the slave traders] have repeatedly experienced from such of their own fraternity as might be stronger . . . "),[40] high mortality rates, and low prices in Cuba were the others. Evidence on capture ratios indicates that no more than three-quarters of the insurance costs paid by Cuban-bound slavers and perhaps one-quarter in the case of Brazil-bound ships can be attributed to the impact of the navy in this period.[41] In the later 1830s, however, contracts began to include a variety of different clauses, and rates varied erratically. In some cases only a portion of the voyage could be insured, in others contracts were written on the ship but not on the cargo. For a time in the Cuban traffic only ships under the Portuguese flag could get insurance; in the Rio trade clauses indemnifying only 50 percent of the loss in the event of capture by a cruiser appeared.[42] Rates of up to 40 percent in Havana and 50 percent in Rio de Janeiro are cited, and at times no insurance was available at all.[43] It is consequently very hard to estimate an average insurance rate for the trade as a whole after 1836, but clearly rates rose substantially, adding yet a further indication of critical change in the business of slave trading in the late 1830s.

In summary, the major impact of abolition in both the Cuban and Brazilian trades, and British attempts to suppress them in particular, came in the late 1830s. Most of the indicators reviewed above, which taken together portray both conditions for the slave and costs for the slave trader, show signs of significant change only at this point. Conditions appear to have worsened and costs to have changed, though the net direction of the change is not altogether clear. It is hard to avoid the conclusion that two events were responsible for these changes. The first was the Anglo-Spanish treaty of 1835, which provided for the condemnation and break-up of ships equipped for the trade as well as those caught with slaves on board. The treaty was ratified on 30 August 1835, but the Act of Parliament creating a new commission for the mixed court did not pass until March 1836, and not until 28 June 1836 was the new court opened in Sierra Leone.[44] The slave trader response, the most obvious manifestation of which was the use of the Portuguese flag, was apparent by the end of the year. The counter of the Sierre Leone court to this ploy came in 1838 when, at the initiative of H. W. Macaulay, the national character of a vessel was taken as the owner's place of residence rather than the owner's nationality.[45] Thus the Cuban traffic was subjected to a double blow, broadly measured by large increases in court business in the last six months of 1836 and the latter part of 1838. In a lengthy despatch written in October 1836 Charles Tolmé, the British consul in Havana and, perhaps because of his business links with the slave traders, one of the most perceptive of the Foreign Office representatives, accurately predicted developments in the Cuban traffic. The slave traders, he wrote, intend

(1) to establish more factories on the Coast of Africa and there to have a constant supply of slaves and of articles for . . . equipment, (2) to send out all those articles and whatever may be required for bartering against slaves by foreign, in preference American ships, (3) to send their slave vessels in ballast . . . (4) to send much smaller vessels than heretofore . . . (5) to send three or more (ships) to load in the same place, (6) to avail themselves of the Portuguese flag. . . .[46]

Underwriters, he noted, were still not certain of the success of these devices.

The equivalent to the 1835 treaty for the traffic to Brazil was the 1839 Act of Parliament, which in effect applied the terms of the treaty to Brazilian-bound ships.[47] As a peacetime assault on the flag of an independent nation this act, as the Duke of Wellington noted at the time, was unprecedented. It allowed British cruisers to stop and search Portuguese ships, and if specified slave-trading equipment was found on board, to take the ships before any British Vice-Admiralty court, which was empowered to confiscate cargoes and to break up the ship. Here, however, we are concerned with the impact of the act rather than its standing before an emerging law of nations, and the trends discussed above are testimony enough to this impact. These events, it should be noted, were merely the first of a series of actions against the trade, a series which would include direct British attacks on the barracoons as well as action by both Cuban authorities and the Portuguese in Angola. The American cruiser squadron and joint British and French naval action of 1840s should also be noted.

Although the impact of the British initiatives shows up clearly in the measurement of what we might call the physical, as opposed to the financial, variables in the traffic, the British effect on the overall costs of the slave trader was much less pronounced. Thus while well over half of the 646 ships captured or wrecked by the navy between 1821 and 1843 met their fate in the last eight years of the period, less than two-thirds of these expeditions were a total loss to their owners. The remainder were ships captured empty of either slaves or trading cargoes, some after disembarking their slaves successfully in the Americas. Most of these empty ships were taken in the years 1836 to 1843. Thus the effectiveness of the British moves is to some extent illusory.

More important, many of the changes described above should be viewed not as cost-increasing consequences of naval action, but as cost-saving reactions to it. Insurance rates certainly increased mark- edly in the later 1830s, as we have seen, and in addition slave traders faced the higher costs of sending their outbound trading cargoes by separate ships, often under the American flag. But other costs were reduced substantially to the point where these higher charges, at least in the Cuban trade, were completely offset. The smaller ships, faster sailing times, and higher slave loading ratios apparent in the later years of the period are examples of such significant cost-saving developments. Hypothetical accounts, derived in part from the tables presented above and in part from captured slave trading correspondence, have been constructed for the period before and after the 1835 treaty and the 1839 Act, and they illustrate these phenomena clearly enough. They suggest that the major impact of the navy was on profits rather than costs, but that the overall effect was in any event rather small. Indeed, a preliminary reworking of LeVeen's analysis on this subject suggests that without the navy slave imports into the Americas would have been only 7.3 percent greater and exports from Africa perhaps only 3 percent more.[48]

Thus our questioning of the impact of formal abolition on the slave trade is not restricted to the 1820s and early 1830s. Cost trends for the later years support a broader devaluation of the effect of abolition in general and of the navy in particular. Any eighteenth century trader would have been at home in the traffic of the early years of abolition, and in the later years, at least to 1843, the adaptability of the trader was such as to allow him to meet every initiative with an effective countermove. Why, then, did the trade come to an end? Perhaps it is not going too far into the realm of speculation to suggest that the navy could only be successful when it had something approaching the full power of domestic law behind it. The British, French, and American slave trades were suppressed with relative ease once the governments concerned decided to act against them. In the struggle against the Brazilian and Cuban traffic the navy was at its most effective when it came closest to assuming those domestic powers (as it did under the 1839 Act and with the decision to invade Brazilian territorial waters in 1850), or when it acted with the partial cooperation of the country importing the slaves (as it did with Cuba in the 1860s). At no time in the campaign was a citizen of Spain, Portugal, or Brazil executed, imprisoned, or subject to any financial loss (beyond that of the value of his ship and its contents) at the hands of the British, for any slave trading offence committed on the high seas—indeed, without an unprecedented extension of British law, such actions could not have been taken by the British. Under these circumstances, to expect the navy to suppress or even seriously dent trade between one continent and another, when the governments and trading communities in both areas were fully committed to that trade, was unrealistic. It is surprising not that abolition and the navy had so little effect, but that they had so much—though bearing in mind the very high slave loading ratios of the later period, the net effect of their impact for the victims of the traffic must remain open to question.

NOTES

The research for this paper was carried out with the help of funds from Canada Council and the University of Rochester. I would also like to acknowledge the invaluable advice and encouragement given by Stanley L. Engerman.

1 The base of these data is Great Britain, *Parliamentary Papers* (hereafter cited as PP), vol. 49, 1845 session, "Return of the Number of Slave Vessels Arrived in the Trans-Atlantic States since 1814," pp. 593–633. Records of many other ships from the Foreign Office 84 series (hereafter cited as FO 84) at the Public Record Office, London, have been added, as well as supplementary information collected by Professors Serge Daget and Herbert S. Klein and kindly made available to the author. For a fuller description of the data bank, see David Eltis, "The Direction and Fluctuation of the Transatlantic Slave Trade, 1821–43: A Revision of the 1845 Parliamentary Paper," in Henry A. Gemery and Jan S. Hogendorn, eds., *The Uncommon Market: Essays on the Economic History of the Atlantic Slave Trade* (New York, 1979), pp. 273–98.

2 The impact of this is unclear. See Christopher J. French, "Eighteenth Century Shipping Tonnage Measurements," *Journal of Economic History* 33 (1973): 434–43; D. P. Lamb, "Volume and Tonnage of the Liverpool Slave Trade, 1772–1807," in Roger T. Anstey and P. E. H. Hair, eds., *Liverpool, the African Slave Trade and Abolition* (Liverpool, 1976), pp. 105–7; Herbert S. Klein and Stanley L. Engerman, "Slave Mortality on British Ships, 1791–1797," in Anstey and Hair, eds., *Liverpool,* pp. 120–21; Roger T. Anstey, "The Volume and Profitability of the Slave Trade," in Stanley L. Engerman and Eugene D. Genovese, eds., *Race and Slavery in the Western Hemisphere: Quantitative Studies* (Princeton, 1975), pp. 3–4.

3 This may be illusory, because after 1839 increasing numbers of American ships were employed, and in many cases it is the American tonnage that was reported even though the ship was under Spanish colors (the Spanish ton was 40 percent smaller than the British ton). The increase in tonnage may thus be the effect of multiplying an American ton by 1.6. A further consideration is the fact that table 9.1 makes no allowance for the shift south of the equator made by Cuban traders, which would have required bigger ships. Thus one could argue that, especially in the later 1830s when Cuban ships visited southeast Africa, a constant average tonnage disguises

a decrease in real tonnage. However, the proportion of Cuban slavers trading with Mozambique was never very large.

4 G. Jackson and F. Grigg to Palmerston, 30 September 1836, FO 84/199. See also the comments in Vice Admiral Colpoys to Admiralty, 22 May 1832, Admiralty 1 series (hereafter cited as Adm 1), vol. 288, Public Record Office, London; it should be noted, however, that Colpoys was commenting on the traffic between northern Brazil and Senegambia, where small ships had always been used.

5 David Turnbull, *Travels in the West: Cuba* (London, 1840), p. 118. This was probably the source for the average figure used in LeVeen's accounts for the whole period 1821–40 (E. Phillip LeVeen, *British Slave Trade Suppression Policies, 1821–1865* [New York, 1977], p. 165). As we can see, it was highly atypical.

6 Herbert S. Klein, *The Middle Passage* (Princeton, 1978), p. 159; for similar comments on the Nantes fleet, see p. 183.

7 Lamb, "Volume and Tonnage," pp. 105–6.

8 LeVeen, *Suppression Policies*, p. 91.

9 Douglass C. North, "Sources of Productivity Change in Ocean Shipping, 1600–1850," *Journal of Political Economy* 76 (1968): 960–64.

10 This explains the high ratios that LeVeen found for 1834–43 (LeVeen, *Suppression Policies*, p. 87, table A-1, row 3).

11 Lamb, "Volume and Tonnage," p. 101; Klein, *Middle Passage*, p. 143.

12 C. D. Tolmé to Palmerston, 4 August 1838, FO 84/247.

13 W. Macleay to Aberdeen, 24 June 1829, FO 84/91.

14 North, "Sources of Productivity Change," p. 962.

15 Middle passage times for Nantes ships sailing to St. Domingue, 1711–77, were significantly longer than those for Jamaican ships (Klein, *Middle Passage*, p. 192).

16 Palmerston to Russell, 13 August 1862, quoted in A. E. M. Ashley, *Life and Correspondence of Henry John Temple, Viscount Palmerston*, 2 vols. (London, 1879), 2: 227. For a comparison of the sailing capabilities of naval vessels and slave ships, see Commodore Collier to Admiralty, May 25, 1828, Adm 1/1683.

17 Surprisingly, improved speed was obtained without an increase in shipbuilding costs between the two periods. Costs in England were estimated at between $35 and $45 per ton for a 200-ton ship (R. Davis, *The Rise of the English Shipping Industry* [London, 1962], p. 375). In 1840 the indefatigable slave trade department of the Foreign Office instructed the Baltimore consul to investigate the supply of ships from his area to Cuba, and his estimate of the cost of a clipper was from $7,000 to $10,000, or $40 to $60 a ton (M. McTavish to Palmerston, 30 January 1840, FO 84/332). Though most slavers were built in the U. S., not all, even in the later 1830s, were Baltimore clippers, and costs in other parts of America were lower. Average costs were thus probably below this range, and in real terms there may well have been a decrease in costs between the two periods. It is important to note, however, that the costs here are for different

types of ships—the eighteenth century British merchantman and a nineteenth century clipper type. As the advantages of the latter, in view of the characteristics of the slave cargo already mentioned, were such that the switch to the faster ship would have occurred anyway, we can conclude that abolition had little or no impact on construction costs.

18 J. Barrow to Aberdeen, 19 September 1842 (enc.), FO 84/441.

19 Klein, *Middle Passage*, pp. 143–47; Lamb, "Volume and Tonnage," p. 103.

20 See David Eltis, "The Transatlantic Slave Trade, 1821–43" (Ph.D. diss., University of Rochester, 1979), pp. 114–65. See also LeVeen's discussion, *Suppression Policies*, pp. 101–2. The high ratio in the late 1830s was noted by at least one Foreign Office observer; see C. D. Tolmé to Palmerston, 17 September 1839, FO 84/280.

21 Pierre Verger, *Flux et reflux . . . de la traite des Nègres entre le Golfe de Benin et Bahia de Todos os Santos du 17ᶜ et 19ᶜ siècles* (The Hague, 1968), p. 660.

22 Eltis, "Direction and Fluctuation," pp. 291–95.

23 Klein, *Middle Passage*, p. 199. All other figures are from the data bank.

24 Klein and Engerman, "Slave Mortality," pp. 118–20; "Facteurs de mortalité dans le trafic français d'esclaves du XVIIIᶜ siècle," *Annales: Economies, sociétés, civilisations* 31 (1976): 1213–24; David Northrup, "African Mortality in the Suppression of the Slave Trade: The Case of the Bight of Biafra," *Journal of Interdisciplinary History* 9 (1978): 55–57. Regressions run with data on captured ships from both the Bight of Biafra and the Bight of Benin show that neither slaves per ton nor voyage times have significant explanatory power over mortality rates. This confirms Northrup's analysis based on Bight of Biafra ships only.

25 Northrup, "African Mortality," pp. 47–64.

26 For the fights between the two, see W. E. F. Ward, *The Royal Navy and the Slavers: the Suppression of the Atlantic Slave Trade* (London, 1969).

27 Kenneth F. Kiple, "The Cuban Slave Trade 1820–1867" (Ph.D. diss., University of Florida, 1970), p. 55; H. H. Lance to Canning, May 11, 1823 (enc.), FO 84/23.

28 S. Cock to Admiralty, 27 April 1818, Adm 1/4457; Captain Willis to Admiralty, 2 February 1819, Adm 1/2720.

29 José L. Franco, *Politica continental americana de España en Cuba, 1812–1830* (Havana, 1947).

30 W. Macleay to Aberdeen, 8 December 1828, FO 84/81; R. Hesketh to Palmerston, 31 August 1831, FO 84/122; Findley and Smith to Aberdeen, 29 May 1830, FO 84/104.

31 H. W. Macaulay to Palmerston, 18 November 1836 (enc.), FO 84/168. For payrolls, see W. Macleay to Palmerston, 21 July 1829 (enc.), FO 84/100, and 1 January 1829 (enc.), FO 84/91; H. W. Macaulay and W. W. Lewis to Palmerston, 15 April 1839, FO 84/269; W. Cole and H. W. Macaulay to Wellington, 5 June 1835 (enc.), FO 84/166.

32 H. Hayne to Castlereagh, 16 February 1822 (enc.), FO 84/17.

33 F. H. Rankin, *The White Man's Grave: A Visit to Sierra Leone in 1834*, 2 vols. (London, 1836), 2: 119.

34 Stanley Lebergott, *Manpower in Economic Growth* (New York, 1964), p. 537. Interestingly, Lebergott's observations for voyages to Africa and the Caribbean are higher than the mean, with wages for an 1847 voyage to Africa listed at $19.

35 PP, vol. 22 (1847/48), House of Commons Select Committee on the Slave Trade, Third Report, p. 3.

36 See nn. 31, 32.

37 W. Macleay and E. Schenley to Palmerston, 31 August 1835, FO 84/172; J. Brackenbury to Canning, 27 February 1826 (enc.), FO 84/54.

38 W. G. Ouseley to Palmerston, 19 May 1836, FO 84/204, and 7 July 1841, FO 84/365.

39 Rear Admiral Durham to Admiralty, 29 July 1814, Adm 1/335.

40 Extract of an unsigned letter from St. Iago de Cuba to Lord Aberdeen, 15 January 1830, FO 84/107.

41 Eltis, "The Transatlantic Slave Trade, 1821–1843," pp. 210–18.

42 E. Schenley to Palmerston, 31 January 1837, FO 84/216; W. Macleay to Palmerston, 15 October 1835, FO 84/170; H. Hamilton to Palmerston, 11 November 1836, FO 84/204; PP, vol. 22. (1847/48), House of Commons Select Committee on the Slave Trade, Third Report, p. 76.

43 W. G. Ouseley to Palmerston, 7 July 1841, FO 84/365; C. D. Tolmé to Palmerston, 17 September 1839, FO 84/280; Turnbull *Travels*, p. 142.

44 J. Campbell and W. W. Lewis to Palmerston, 5 July 1836, FO 84/191. For Palmerston's criticism of the delay, see his dispatch to Sierra Leone of 29 August 1836, FO 84/189.

45 H. W. Macaulay to J. Bandinel, 20 May 1839, FO 84/266. For Macaulay's subsequent explanation of this point to the 1842 select committee on West Africa, see PP, vol. 40 (1842), "Report of the Select Committee on the West African Possessions," p. 285.

46 C. D. Tolmé to Palmerston, 15 October 1836, FO 84/201.

47 Great Britain, *Statutes at Large*, 2 and 3 Vict., c. 73.

48 Eltis, "The Transatlantic Slave Trade, 1821–1843," pp. 228–32, 236–37, 254.

CHAPTER 10: **Abolition of the Abolished:**

The Illegal Dutch Slave Trade

and the Mixed Courts

Pieter C. Emmer

Did the Dutch participate in the illegal slave trade? Heinrich Heine was positive that they did, and in his poem "Das Sklavenschiff" (The Slaver) described the greedy calculations of the Dutch merchant "mijnheer van Koek" (Mr. van Koek).[1] More recently the historians van Dantzig, Mannix and Cowley, and Ward have suggested the same.[2]

This paper is written with the intention to show that the abolition of the Dutch slave trade was effective as far as the triangular trade between the Netherlands, Africa, and the West Indies was concerned, but that slave imports into the only remaining Dutch plantation colony, Surinam, continued after the Dutch slave trade had been abolished. The paper has been divided into four sections. The first deals with the legal abolition of the Dutch slave trade at home, as well as the reaction in the Netherlands to this legislation, or rather the lack of such a reaction. The second reviews the proceedings of the Anglo-Dutch mixed court at Freetown, Sierra Leone. The third focuses on the mixed court at Paramaribo, Surinam. The concluding section considers the factors that were of importance in stopping the illegal trade.

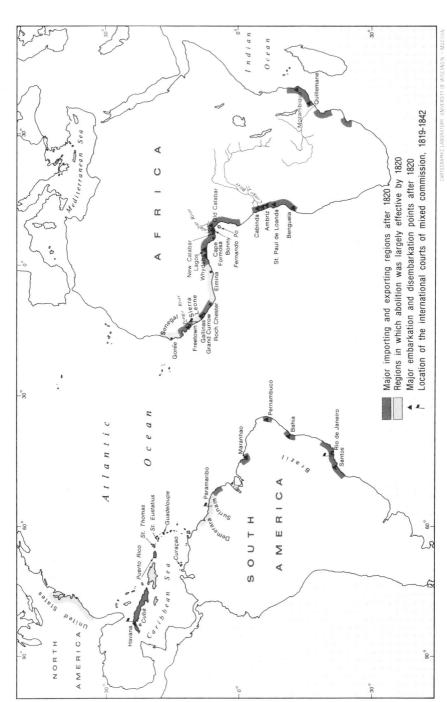

Map 10.1 Regions Involved in the Transatlantic Slave Trade after 1820.

Major importing and exporting regions after 1820
Regions in which abolition was largely effective by 1820
Major embarkation and disembarkation points after 1820
Location of the international courts of mixed commission, 1819–1842

CARTOGRAPHIC LABORATORY, UNIVERSITY OF WISCONSIN – MADISON

ABOLITION OF THE DUTCH SLAVE TRADE

It was in fact the English who put an end to the Dutch legal slave trade. Their occupation of the Dutch West Indian possessions during the course of the Napoleonic wars made Surinam, Berbice, Essequibo, and Demerara, as well as the Antillian islands, subject to that famous decision of the British parliament in 1806 which prohibited the slave trade in newly conquered West Indian possessions.[3] On 15 June 1814, right after the formation of the new Kingdom of the Netherlands, an order in council was issued that made illegal any slave trade originating in Dutch ports. The opening paragraph stated that the British minister in the Hague had specifically asked for this order. The treaty with the United Kingdom signed two months later, which restored most of the Dutch West Indian possessions to the Netherlands, included a special article abolishing the slave trade. Finally, on May 4 1818, the two countries signed a separate bilateral treaty abolishing the slave trade and providing for the establishment of two Anglo-Dutch (mixed) courts, as well as for special Dutch and English naval squadrons, to suppress the slave trade.[4]

The treaty of 1818 required a change of Dutch penal law to permit prosecution of Dutch slave traders. The subsequent debate over the proposed legislative act provided the Dutch parliament (which included representatives from Belgium) with an opportunity to discuss the slave trade issue. None of the members actually opposed abolition, but some found the proposed punishment for agents who had sold insurance to illegal slave traders too harsh. One of the members asked for more harmony between Dutch and British legislation on this issue. Under this new Dutch law it remained unclear whether a Surinam planter would be allowed to go to Africa himself to fetch slaves. Dutch crew members on slave-trade vessels could not be prosecuted if they had not been made aware of the illegal aim of the voyage. In general, however, the discussion was rather mild and members were well disposed toward the government's proposals. One even called the abolition of the trade "un des plus beaux triomphes de la philosophie chrétienne," and praised the Dutch king, William I, for being the first sovereign on the continent to abolish the trade. In the end the law was passed with only five votes against it.[5]

Outside Parliament there was almost no public reaction to the law ending the Dutch slave trade. In fact, nothing changed. The shipping firms that had been engaged in the trade had ceased to do so after the renewal of hostilities between England and France in 1803.[6] The planters in Surinam, Demerara, Berbice and Essequibo had not been able to buy imported slaves legally since 1806.[7]

The only record of a reaction which has survived is an internal memo, probably written to inform the King before the latter issued the first order in council in June 1814. The unknown author is rather pessimistic about the possibility of putting an end to the trade. There was an upsurge in the demand for slaves, and the slavers would do everything in their power to escape British suppression measures. France had been very clever in stalling abolition for another five years. This internal report acknowledges the fact that Christian principles and the trade in slaves were incompatible. However, slaves were for the most part prisoners of war and, in addition, the slave trade provided Africa with European goods and civilization. Of course, none of the slaves were actually asked whether they would like to go to the West Indies, but the same disregard was applied to soldiers, who were often sent to foreign parts against their will. The memo finished by suggesting that the "bigot Swedenborg" was behind the British zest for abolition because of his interest in founding a new Jerusalem in Africa.[8]

THE ANGLO-DUTCH COURT AT FREETOWN, 1819–1871

The Dutch judges who were sent to the Anglo-Dutch court at Freetown, Sierra Leone, were a very strange mixture. The first appointment was made in February 1819, when D. Van Sirtema was named judge; at the end of April E. G. P. Bonnouvrié was appointed commissioner of arbitration. Both had held administrative posts in the tropics before, and the Dutch government had rather high expectations of these two appointees.[9]

These high hopes were soon deflated: Van Sirtema appeared to be a troubleshooter who caused trouble rather than resolved it. Almost immediately he accused his fellow countryman, Bonnouvrié, of undermining his own authority. And he antagonized his English colleagues by refusing to admit proctors to trials because these representatives had no legal standing in Dutch law. The Dutch government solved this problem by instructing the Dutch judges to adjust to British legal customs. However, the attitude of the Dutch judge had upset the English, since it had given support to Spanish and Portuguese obstruction in matters of procedure in the other mixed courts for the suppression of the slave trade at Sierra Leone.

Van Sirtema's uncooperative attitude had more direct consequences in the cases of two illegal slave ships that were tried before the Anglo-Dutch court. In one instance, involving the *Eliza*, the Dutch judge refused to take the case since the ship had been captured with only one slave on board, all the others having been hastily disembarked. The Anglo-Dutch treaty only spoke of illegal slavers with slaves on board, so. . . . The second case involved the *Marie*, a ship with only black "passengers" on board, so the captain asserted. Van Sirtema refused to call those "passengers" to the witness-box. These ships were condemned as illegal slavers only after a vote among the two English and two Dutch members of the court had been taken in which the Dutch commissioner had supported his English colleagues.[10]

The English judges were outraged by Van Sirtema's behavior: "In the affair of the *Eliza* he [Van Sirtema] appears to be more the anxious advocate of these convicted dealers in slavery than the judge, and has not even hesitated to blame his colleague, Mr. Bonnouvrié, the Commissioner of Arbitration on the part of the Netherlands, for having decided agreeably to his own conscience." It seemed impossible "to cultivate a spirit of conciliation and harmony" with the Dutch judge.[11] The Dutch Colonial Office was very unhappy about the affair, and instructed Van Sirtema once again to comply with British juridical practice. However, without any notification, the Dutch judge had left Freetown for home.[12]

After Van Sirtema had left, the Dutch government did not appoint another second representative to the mixed court. From 1820 to 1822 Bonnouvrié remained in Freetown as the Dutch commissioner. From 1822 to 1824 J. A. de Marrée was the appointed judge while the Dutch commissioner was on leave, and in 1825 Bonnouvrié returned, this time as judge; he remained until his final departure in 1828.[13] After that year the Anglo-Dutch mixed court functioned without a Dutch representative until the court was dissolved in 1871.[14]

With the exception of Van Sirtema, there was little or no disharmony between the Dutch and English judges. In fact, except during the first year of the court, the English could always overrule their Dutch colleague, and after 1828 they could do as they pleased. Obviously, the Dutch government had full trust in the anti-slave-trade policy of the British government. This was not the case with the Portuguese, Spanish, and Brazilian governments, which all had established mixed courts with Britain at Sierra Leone, and whose judges in Freetown were suspicious of British suppression measures.[15]

The "Dutch" ships involved in the trials at Freetown explain why the Dutch government didn't really need to be concerned: none were

of Dutch origin (see appendix table 10.1). It would take more than
the available space to tell the details of each ship which was captured
flying the Dutch flag or with Dutch ships' papers on board. The majority of such ships were French, and had been made "Dutch" by
obtaining new papers. As a matter of fact, most ships had also obtained Danish or Spanish papers and most of them also had retained
their French nationality.

A typical example was the case of the *La Fortunée*, which was captured by an English naval vessel. During the chase the captain of the
La Fortunée had been standing on the bow of his ship with two tin
boxes in his hand. As soon as the man-of-war had shown the Union
Jack, the captain had dropped one of these boxes into the sea. The
ship was captured and the remaining box contained only French papers. The Anglo-Dutch court decided to try the case because one of
the crew members of the *La Fortunée* remembered that the captain
had ordered each crew member to learn a strange-sounding Christian
name by heart. Of course, it was a matter of convenience to assume
that the other tin box had contained Dutch papers, but the English
judges were reluctant to consider the *La Fortunée* as French and to
send her to a French court at Gorée or in Senegal. The Dutch judge
protested against the handling of the case, but in vain.[16]

On the other hand, during the years 1820 to 1826 most of the illegal slavers which were captured with Dutch papers on board had obtained their Dutch nationality at Saint Eustatius, one of the Dutch
Windward Islands. Both the English and Dutch judges were convinced that the governor of that island had been selling Dutch papers
to vessels employed in the trade. The Dutch government ordered a
thorough investigation, and after 1826 this practice was stopped, in
spite of the fact that the governor had not been removed.[17]

The ships which were captured after 1826 and were then subject
to lawsuits in the mixed Anglo-Dutch court were only assumed to be
Dutch, but were in reality of French origin. Usually the Dutch papers
had been thrown overboard and the court took the captain's affidavit
about them for granted. In one instance the captain as well as the
papers had disappeared.

All of these cases were taken on by the Anglo-Dutch court as a
matter of convenience. The absence of one of the Dutch judges and,
after 1828, of both Dutch judges made it easy for the British legal
authorities to use this particular mixed court in Freetown to condemn
illegal slavers of uncertain nationality. This was more difficult at the
other mixed courts in Freetown, in which the British judges had only
as many votes as their Spanish, Portuguese, and Brazilian counter-

parts. In addition, the French naval court in Sénégal was reluctant to accept cases of illegal slaving transferred from Sierra Leone, when there existed no definite proof of the French nationality of such ships.[18]

The cargoes of those ships which had been declared legal prizes by the Anglo-Dutch court did differ substantially from the cargoes carried by legal slavers during the eighteenth century. Some of the ships carried guns, powder, textiles, and liquor as usual, but most illegal slavers just bought the slaves for cash. Obviously, the "equipment clauses" in the treaties abolishing the slave trade made themselves felt. These clauses enabled the courts to condemn a ship suspected of illegal slaving which had slave irons and a removable deck on board, or too many victuals and too much kitchen equipment in relation to the number of crew.[19]

Finally, what happened to the crew of a captured slaver after a trial had declared their ship to be a legal prize? The rules laid down for the mixed court stipulated that the Dutch judges would look after the crews of ships which were captured flying the Dutch flag. The first judge, Van Sirtema, had no problems: all crew members of the ships confiscated during his time in office had left town within a few days. His successor, however, was faced with the crew members of the *Aurora*, all ex-soldiers of Napoleon, who only wanted to travel to the West Indies.[20]

There was considerable pressure from London to apply Dutch criminal law in cases involving the crews of illegal slavers captured as Dutch vessels. In fact, in 1824 the Dutch lower house passed new legislation to make penal sanctions in such cases more stringent.[21] The Dutch judge in Freetown observed that the new legislation was useless: none of the crews of the illegal "Dutch" slavers were Dutch nationals.[22] Only in one case did the Dutch authorities start a legal procedure. In 1862, when the illegal slaver *Jane* had been captured and declared a legal prize, the English mentioned that the first mate lived in Rotterdam. However, it soon became clear that this man had taken on his job in good faith, and the case was dismissed.[23]

THE ANGLO-DUTCH COURT AT PARAMARIBO, 1819–1845

The illegal slave trade to the Dutch West Indies was not directed to the Dutch Antilles. These six rather small islands did play an important part in the Dutch slave trade of the seventeenth and eighteenth centuries, but only as transit harbors. There seems to have been no reason for illegal slavers to have brought their slaves to Curaçao first, before selling them in a plantation colony.

In Surinam the situation was different. There was a demand for slaves, and in addition, there were long stretches of unpatrolled coastline and plenty of opportunities to mix the new Africans among the slaves already present in the colony. The Surinam planters, who might have hoped for a reopening of the slave trade after the Dutch had taken over from the English, were disappointed. Not only did the Dutch government comply with British wishes to insert an abolition clause in the treaty of 1814, under which Surinam was surrendered to the Dutch, but The Hague also chose Paramaribo as the seat of the second Anglo-Dutch mixed court for the suppression of the slave trade.

The official archive of this mixed court reveals that only one ship had been subject to an official trial and declared to be a legal prize—the *La Nueve of Snauw*, in 1823. The crew members were able to leave Surinam without going through any legal procedures; none of them were Dutch. One of the crew members, an Englishman, was sent to Barbados to be tried, and the 54 slaves taken aboard the *La Nueve of Snauw* were emancipated and placed under government supervision.[24] The fact that only one case of illegal slave trading was brought before the mixed court only showed that neither the Dutch nor the British flags were used in the slave trade to Surinam. However, it would be naive to assume that no illegal slave imports had taken place. The unofficial archive of the mixed court, the private notes and observations of the British judges, tells much more than the official one.

These records suggest that the British judges in Paramaribo were not to be envied. They were looked upon as intruders and as representatives of that victorious group in Europe which was after the destruction of the West Indian plantocracy. In spite of their isolated position, the British judges were able to win some remarkable battles in the long fight for abolition—at least, that was the way they looked upon it themselves. On the other hand, the emancipation of Surinam slaves did not take place until 1863, and the last British judge had left the colony in 1845. Thus it is also possible to consider the achievements of the British judges as the results of small concessions on the part of the Dutch government which were granted in order to silence those awkward informers.[25]

The British judges achieved at least three objectives during their sojourn in Surinam. In the first place, in April 1821 they put a complete stop to the importation of slaves from the French Caribbean.[26] Immediately after their arrival in 1819 the British judges had written to London about the importation of "New Africans," carried from the French Antilles mainly by French ships. Legally, there was little that could be done: the French slaves were supposed to have lived on French territory for some time and to be part of the legal intra-Caribbean slave trade. The papers of the slavers in this trade were probably "plausible," the British judges reported to their superior, but "if His Excellency would only personally inspect the Negroes or appoint any respectable gentleman to examine them and make a report to His Excellency, the Excellency would be immediately convinced that the admission of such Negroes in this colony for sale is a violation at once of the French, Dutch and British laws."[27] After some pressure from London, King William I himself decided to stop the intra-Caribbean slave trade from the French territories, against the advice of the Dutch Colonial Office. This ban on the French trade would end as soon as France had stopped all slave trading between the Caribbean and Africa.[28]

In the second place, in several instances the British judges gave information to the Dutch colonial authorities on slaves newly arrived from Africa. Of course, this was a very difficult job, obstructed by all the Surinam whites, and in several cases the governor refused to do anything with the information thus provided. Moreover, the British judges were not allowed to place an advertisement in the local newspaper asking for more information on the illegal slave trade.[29] In several cases the British judges managed to put some pressure (via London and The Hague) on the Dutch authorities, and during the governorship of De Veer (1822–1828) they were successful. Several illegal slave ships were captured and either tried before a Dutch court in Surinam or sent on to a French court.[30]

In the third place, several of the British judges tried to liberate some groups of slaves. Having tried to gain information on the status of the emancipated slaves of the La Nueve of Snauw, who had been placed under the supervision of the Dutch colonial government and were unable to leave the jobs assigned to them, they went on to press that government to liberate the "kidnapped Africans" of other illegal slave vessels. They cited in particular the slaves of the French vessel La Legère, most of whom had been able to escape before the vessel had been turned over to a French court. Finally, the British judges wanted the liberation of the "Barbados Negroes"—in general, those slaves who had come with (or without) their English masters to the Dutch colony just before the British parliament enacted emancipation in 1833.[31]

In most cases, the Dutch Colonial Office instructed the Surinam authorities to give in to the wishes of the British judges. In 1826 legislation was passed to set up a complete registration of all Surinam slaves. This measure put an end to the illegal slave trade in Surinam, except for a few isolated cases. In 1828 a British judge in Paramaribo reported to the British foreign minister in London, "I am happy to communicate to your Lordship the foregoing circumstance as it tends to confirmation of the hopes, which I have before ventured to express, that at length the slave trade in this colony for the present is overcome."[32] In 1843 the Dutch government freed the 29 slaves of the *La Nueve of Snauw* who were still alive, their 10 relatives (they had married since 1823), and 417 "kidnapped Africans" from other slave vessels adjudicated before the Dutch court in Surinam.[33]

Of course, British intervention did not change the Dutch attitude towards slavery itself. The actions of the British judges led to many violent reactions; the last judge, Edward Schenley, felt constantly in danger for his life and that of his family. When he started to complain openly about the mistreatment of the slaves in Surinam, he became dangerous to the safety of the planters. Some of them brought a lawsuit against Schenley accusing him of slander. In his correspondence with London, Schenley had denounced some members of the Surinam courts and councils as cruel slave owners. His letters to the Foreign Office were printed in the Parliamentary Papers, and this news (and the names he had mentioned) had traveled back to Surinam.

In 1845 Schenley left for England, and he was tried *in absentia* and found guilty of slander. The British government put pressure on The Hague to suspend the sentence, but the whole affair blew over, since Schenley did not return and London never appointed a successor.

After 1845 the mixed court ceased to function.[34]

FACTORS IN STOPPING THE TRADE

The abolition of the Dutch slave trade was not necessary. Long before the international apparatus to stop the slave trade had been set in motion, the Dutch slave trade had collapsed. Already in the last years before the French occupation of the Netherlands in 1795–1796, the Dutch slave trade had dwindled.[35] After the Napoleonic wars were over, the legal measures taken to stop the trade were obviously sufficient to direct former Dutch slave-trade firms into other branches of commerce; no trace has been found of an illegal slave ship originating from the Netherlands.

The only Dutch plantation colony in the West Indies, Surinam, was in need of new slaves from Africa after the long interruption in imports, following the British occupation. The bilateral measures to stop the trade did not suffice here. The mixed Anglo-Dutch courts could not stop these importations because the slave ships destined for Surinam were neither Dutch nor British. It was the abolitionist zeal of some of the British judges in Paramaribo that put pressure on the colonial authorities to stop the illegal slave imports. The Dutch government in The Hague usually complied with the British desire for the release of slaves captured on board the slavers. In addition, the Dutch government put an end to the sale of Dutch papers to illegal slave ships by a corrupt governor of Saint Eustatius.

The illegal slave imports into Surinam came to an end in 1826 after the introduction of slave registration in the colony. This raises a question about the impact of juridical measures to stop the trade. It should be remembered that no West Indian law could be applied unless it had the approval of the government in the Netherlands and unless it was accepted by the plantocracy. As for as the Dutch government was concerned, the bleak prospects of the Surinam plantation economy and the pressures from Britain, were sufficient stimuli to both stop the Dutch slave trade and to put an end to illegal slave imports into Surinam.

As for the plantocracy, no real effort was made to re-open the transatlantic trade. Only when slavery itself came under attack did the plantation financiers in the Netherlands combine forces with the plantation owners in Surinam in order to influence the decision-making process. The abolition of the slave trade was accepted without further ado, though the law was bent somewhat to allow for another decade of limited slave imports.

The final abolition in 1826, however, does indicate that the legal measures to stop slave imports into Surinam must have coincided with the diminishing of the buying power of the planters. On the Dutch home market Surinam had to face heavy competition from the two new sugar producers, Brazil and Cuba.[36] It seemed that, more than anything else, the open Dutch sugar market forced the slave trade to Surinam to come to an end. In 1841 an empty Portuguese slaver had called at Paramaribo and, according to the British judge, the crew had learned that the Surinam planters could no longer afford to buy slaves.[37]

APPENDIX

Appendix Table 10.1
Ships Declared Legal Prizes by the Anglo-Dutch Courts

Name and Nationality of Vessel	Date and Place of Capture (if known; see map)	Name and Nationality of Captain	No. Slaves Carried	Port of Departure (if known)	Destination (if known)
		Vessels Tried at Freetown			
Eliza English or French	9 Oct. 1819	John Discombe English	1 man	St. Thomas	
Virginie French	10 Oct. 1819 Trade Town	B. Canez French	7 men 8 women 13 boys 4 girls ──── 32 total	St. Eustatius	Guadeloupe
Marie or *Maria* French	30 Jan. 1820 Pongo River	Francesco Vigne Genoese	2 boys	St. Eustatius	
Aurora French	23 Oct. 1822	Libray French	None	St. Eustatius	
De Bey English or American	19 May 1825 Gallinas	William Woodside English or American	None	St. Eustatius	
Z French	3 July 1825 Andra (near New Calabar)	Dernis Kderne French	None	St. Thomas	
La Venus French	1 Sept. 1825 Cape Formosa	André Desbarbes French	None	St. Thomas	
Amable Claudina French	12 Sept. 1825 Elmina	Claudio Picaluga Genoese	34 no breakdown	Curaçao	
Charles French	19 Dec. 1825 Calabar River	Louis l'Oiseau French	128 men 23 women 37 boys 55 girls 22 dead ──── 265 total	St. Eustatius	
Hoop English	3 Jan. 1826 Gallinas	Jacob Walters English or American	None	St. Eustatius	
Vogel French	22 Jan. 1826 Grand Currow (near Cape Mount)	Jean Blaisse French	None	St. Thomas	Surinam

Appendix Table 10.1, *continued*

Name and Nationality of Vessel	Date and Place of Capture (if known; see map)	Name and Nationality of Captain	No. Slaves Carried	Port of Departure (if known)	Destination (if known)
		Vessels Tried at Freetown			
La Fortunée French	5 May 1826	Jean Jacques Gimberd French	52 men 30 women 18 boys 25 girls 120 dead 245 total	St. Thomas	Surinam or Cuba
Henriette French	11 Aug. 1826	L'Espoir Raouland French	128 men 89 women 36 boys 39 girls 75 dead 59 landed before trial 426 total		
De Snelheid French	28 Sept. 1826	Paul Lieutaud French	23 no breakdown	St. Eustatius	
Lynx French	9 Jan. 1827	Pierre Eugène Terasse French	124 men 59 women 26 boys 55 girls 13 dead 277 total	St. Thomas	
Fanny French	7 May 1828 Old Calabar	André LaLonde French	146 men 41 women 30 boys 35 girls 28 dead 280 total	Cuba	Cuba
Coquette French	6 Jan. 1829	Emile Vincent French	74 men 49 women 26 boys 36 girls 35 dead 220 total		
Jeune Eugenie French	6 Jan. 1829 Old Calabar	Neils Williams English or American	14 men 16 women 8 boys 8 girls 4 dead 50 total		

Appendix Table 10.1, *continued*

Name and Nationality of Vessel	Date and Place of Capture (if known; see map)	Name and Nationality of Captain	No. Slaves Carried	Port of Departure (if known)	Destination (if known)
		Vessels Tried at Freetown			
Jules French	6 Jan. 1829 Old Calabar	André Ferraud French	111 men 24 women 23 boys 49 girls 13 dead ——— 220 total		
Adeline French	9 Feb. 1829 Clarence Cove, Fernando Po	Sarassin French	None		
Hirondelle French	26 Feb. 1829 Old Calabar	José Carreto (unknown)	49 men 5 women 1 girl 23 dead 34 landed before trial ——— 112 total		
Jane American	12 Sept. 1862	A. Prince American	None	Rotterdam	Cuba
		Vessels Tried at Paramaribo			
La Nueve of Snauw Spanish (Cuban)	1 Mar. 1823	Conningham (unknown)	54 no breakdown 4 escaped ——— 58 total	Havana	Surinam

Sources: Archief van het Ministerie van Koloniën, 1813–1890, vols. 2309, 2310, 2326, Algemeen Rijksarchief, The Hague (hereafter cited as ARA); Archieven van de West-Indische Bezittingen en Suriname, 1828–1845, Supplement Suriname, stukken bij of overgebracht met de bestuursarchieven, vol. 13, item 6, ARA; Archief van het Ministerie van Buitenlandse Zaken, 1813–1870, vol. 3468, ARA; Foreign Office 315 series, vols. 20, 21, 55, 58, Public Record Office, London.

NOTES

This chapter is a shortened version of P. C. Emmer, "Engeland, Nederland, Afrika en de slavenhandel in de negentiende eeuw," *Economisch- en Sociaal-Historisch Jaarboek* 37 (1974): 44–144.

1 Heinrich Heine, *Heinrich Heine: Werke und Briefe*, ed. H. Kaufman (Berlin, 1961), 2: 201–7.

2 A. van Dantzig, *Het Nederlandse aandeel in de slavenhandel* (Bussum, The Netherlands, 1968), pp. 124–25; D. P. Mannix and M. Cowley, *Black Cargoes* (London, 1962), pp. 191–215; W. E. F. Ward, *The Royal Navy and the Slavers* (London, 1969), p. 120.

3 Roger Anstey, *The Atlantic Slave Trade and British Abolition, 1760–1810* (London, 1975), pp. 364–90.

4 Archief van het Ministerie van Koloniën, 1813–90, vol. 2316, Algemeen Rijksarchief, The Hague (hereafter cited as ARA); *Handelingen der Tweede Kamer der Staten Generaal*, 1818, apps., pp. 5–11.

5 *Handelingen der Tweede Kamer der Staten Generaal*, 1818, p. 18.

6 W. S. Unger, *Het archief van de Middelburgsche Commercie Compagnie* (The Hague, 1951), vol. 23, items for 6 Sept. 1814, and vol. 24., items for 24 Jan., 17 Feb. 1815.

7 Pieter C. Emmer, "Surinam and the Decline of the Dutch Slave Trade," *Revue française d'histoire d'outre-mer* 62 (1975): 245–51.

8 Archieven van de Algemene Staatssecretarie en van het Kabinet des Konings, vol. 6555, ARA. For Emanuel Swedenborg's ideas about Africa, see Philip D. Curtin, *The Image of Africa* (Madison, 1964), pp. 26–27, 115.

9 Ministerie van Koloniën, 1813–90, vol. 2316, 29 Apr., 20 June 1819.

10 Ibid., vol. 2316, 20 Jan. 1820, and vol. 2309, 9 Mar., 25 June 1820; *Slave Trade*, Irish University Press Series of British Parliamentary Papers (hereafter cited as I.U.P., *Slave Trade*), 63: 469.

11 Ministerie van Koloniën, 1813–90, vol. 2309, 9 Mar., 25 June 1820.

12 Ibid., vol. 2316.

13 Ministerie van Koloniën 1813–90, vol. 2316, and vol. 2309, 2 May 1823, 4 Jan. 1824.

14 L. Bethell, "The Mixed Commissions for the Suppression of the Transatlantic Slave Trade in the Nineteenth Century," *Journal of African History* 7 (1966): 90–93.

15 W. E. F. Ward, *Royal Navy*, p. 82; Bethell, "The Mixed Commissions," pp. 85–86.

16 I.U.P., *Slave Trade*, vol. 9, pt. 3, pp. 111–16; Ministerie van Koloniën, 1813–90, vol. 2310, 19 June 1827.

17 I.U.P., *Slave Trade*, vol. 9, pt. 1, pp. 81–82, 75–86; Archieven van de West-Indische Bezittingen en Suriname, 1828–45, Supplement Suriname, stukken bij of overgebracht met de bestuursarchieven, vol. 13, item 6, ARA.

18 I.U.P., *Slave Trade*, vol. 12, pt. 1, pp. 10–11, 85–86, 88–89, and pt. 3, pp. 73–74; Foreign Office 315 series (hereafter cited as FO 315), vols. 21, 58, Public Record Office, London.

19 See in particular data on the *Amable Claudina* and the *De Snelheid* in I.U.P., *Slave Trade*, vol. 9, pt. 1, pp. 77–78, and pt. 3, pp. 117–18; FO 315, vols. 21, 58.

20 Ministerie van Koloniën, 1813–90, vol. 2309, 2 May 1823, and vol. 2326.

21 I.U.P., *Slave Trade*, vol. 10, pt. 2, pp. 84, 88; *Handelingen der Tweede Kamer der Staten Generaal*, 1824, Dec. 18.

22 Ministerie van Koloniën, 1813–90, vol. 2310, 18 Feb. 1827.

23 Archief van het Ministerie van Buitenlandse Zaken, 1813–70, vol. 3468, ARA; Archief van het Ministerie van Justitie, 1813–70, vol. 4805, 13 Feb. 1863, ARA.

24 Archief van het gerechtshof inzake wering van de slavenhandel, vol. 2, item 36, 5 Feb. 1821, ARA.

25 I disagree with J. P. Siwpersad, *De Nederlandse regering en de afschaffing van de Surinaamse slavernij, 1833–1863* (Groningen/Castricum, The Netherlands, 1979), pp. 1–68, who attributes far too much influence to both the government of British Guyana and the presence of the British judges in Surinam.

26 Ministerie van Koloniën, 1813–90, vol. 2316, 16 Apr. 1821.

27 Gerechtshof inzake wering van de slavenhandel, vol. 2, item 36, 5 Feb. 1821.

28 Ministerie van Koloniën, 1813–90, vol. 2326, 18 May, 1821.

29 Ibid., 7 Sept. 1822; Gerechsthof inzake wering van de slavenhandel, vol. 2, item 36.

30 Siwpersad, *De Nederlandse regering*, p. 49, mentions the American vessel *Olive Branch*, with 500 Negroes aboard, and the *La Legère*, a French slaver carrying 253 slaves.

31 Gerechtshof inzake wering van de slavenhandel, vol. 2, item 37, 28 July 1843.

32 I.U.P., *Slave Trade*, vol. 12, pt. 1, p. 174.

33 Siwpersad, *De Nederlandse regering*, p. 57.

34 I.U.P., *Slave Trade*, 33: 306–33; 35: 324–26; 36: 193–94.

35 Johannes Postma, "The Dutch Slave Trade: A Quantitative Assessment," *Revue française d'histoire d'outre-mer* 62 (1975): 242.

36 J. J. Reese, *De suikerhandel van Amsterdam van 1813 tot 1894* (The Hague, 1911), app. G.

37 Gerechtshof inzake wering van de slavenhandel, vol. 2, item 39, 19 Sept. 1841.

CHAPTER 11: **France, Suppression of the Illegal Trade, and England, 1817–1850**

by Serge Daget

It is striking that the old English language historiography tends to reduce French participation in the suppression of the slave trade to something near insignificance. Historians such as Soulsby and Lloyd have accepted without challenge unsubstantiated assertions made by Captain Leeke in 1821 or by Commander Hotham thirty years later.[1] To leave the matter there, however, is to pervert our view of important aspects of French nineteenth century attitudes, as well as the history of the slave trade and international relations, particularly as they pertain to the West African coast. In addition, such attitudes perhaps camouflage a major phenomenon—namely, the reconstruction of a colonial ideology.

The present paper questions the French capacity to put a maritime force at the service of what we shall call an official abolitionist morality, and examines the obstacles to the campaign against "a scourge which for so long desolated Africa, degraded Europe and afflicted humanity," in the words of the plenipotentiaries at the Congress of Vienna.[2] This paper does not explore the reactions of the slave-owning colonists, and takes small account of those of the slave traders. Studies of slave trade suppression have already examined the role of law and the judicial system, and we have previously analyzed the reactions of the Nantes maritime administration to efforts to escape suppression to 1831.[3] Here, in contrast, we attempt to glimpse the individual or collective psychology of the sailors involved in suppression and to understand the changing attitudes of the French government in the course of a third of a century, as well as to compare the aim of suppression with the means employed. Such a process is difficult when little is known of the French sailors involved and their attitudes towards England.

THE FIRST YEARS OF THE FRENCH SQUADRON

After the allied victory of 1815, the abolitionist ideology had fewer popular adherents than ever in France, and its activists saw themselves relegated to the role of followers of official decisions. Revolutionary in origin (of heightened significance at a time of monarchical restoration), associated with the defeat and with the English, abolition was written into an additional article in the second treaty of Paris, a move which from the first was viewed as a Machiavellian maneuver executed by the principal victors, the English. The envied rival was using ostensibly humanitarian means to further its ambitions for political, commercial, and indeed military hegemony. Such an attitude was clearly in evidence and did not bode well for the implementation of abolition. Nonetheless, after three years of delays the first French abolition law was promulgated without discussion on April 15, 1818. Nine weeks later the royal ordinance of June 24 instituted a French naval squadron to suppress the slave trade on the coast of Africa.

Three warships arrived without delay, first at Saint Louis in Senegal, then at Gorée. The choice of ships was not accidental; *L'Argus* and *L'Ecureuil* were the former H.M.S. *Plumper* and *Bouncer* before being seized from the English, and *L'Iris* had just left the builder's yard. These vessels just counterbalanced the English squadron, which at this time consisted of the *Semiramis*, 245 tons, the *Cherub*, 115 tons, and the *Tartar*, 245 tons.[4] The mission of French men-of-war was to visit "all French ships" suspected of being slavers while on patrol in the seas off Senegal, from Portendick in the north, where the Trarzas freely traded gum with the English, to Joal in the south. But a second and equally important purpose was to reassert a French presence in the area after seven years of occupation by the English.

Such a squadron offered several political advantages. To the metropolitan abolitionists, it represented royal authority and could compensate for possible shortcomings in administration. The squadron was of even greater use from the point of view of foreign affairs. It helped to stem the incessant recriminations from London after Vienna, Castlereagh's reconvening of the new conference in 1816, and its final adjournment sine die in 1817.[5] It demonstrated that a weakened nation could escape from a commitment more or less forced on it by England—commitments that neither Portugal, Spain, nor Holland had been able to avoid. Above all, it established French independence in the face of the universality of English power, notably at sea.

All this makes it still more surprising that the French fleet proved itself incapable of results against the numerous French slave traders active on the coast. It was not a question of secret instructions not to interfere; on the contrary, the minister of the navy insisted repeatedly on the *political* necessity of stopping lawbreakers, and identical orders were addressed to the West Indian station. In fact, the efficiency of suppression depended as much on the willingness of the executors of policy on the coast as on the orders issued by Paris. On the coast, sailors defeated by England were being asked to follow orders from a Restoration government partly put in place by England, orders, moreover, on an aspect of the Negro question.

In the naval documents one does not often come across opinions like those of the captain of a frigate, Cornette de Vénancourt, before his departure for Senegal, where he stayed for a year. In 1816 he wrote that "there exists at Rochefort a large number of negroes, whose residence in this town has produced a disgusting mixture in the inhabitants' blood."[6] What is interesting is not the virtue of the people of Rochefort, but the racism of an eventual commander of the station responsible for the suppression of the slave trade. Vénancourt was descended from American plantation colonists and, indeed, we can see as much from his comments. But though such comments are infrequent, it is significant that the naval minister, Portal, had to remind his colleague at foreign affairs to use the official phrase "trade in blacks" when the latter continued to speak of the "negro trade".[7]

To this inhibiting force others were added, though of quite different kinds. The Restoration brought reprisals against sailors who had rallied to Napoleon in the Hundred Days; at the end of 1815 and in 1816 the officer class was purged. After the disastrous example of the shipwreck of the *Meduse*, captained by a former emigré who had not set foot on a vessel for a quarter of a century, the reintegration of the purged officers had been rapid: there remained 37 officers "eliminated" from the royal service from the 371 initially prosecuted.[8] These dismissals resulted in the quick enrollment of the former naval

men in the merchant marine with the automatic rank of *capitaine au
long cours* (master). Coupvent, Bouché, Camin, de Malfilâtre, Bouf-
fier, Danglade, and Sempreur were men expelled for political reasons
who became officers in the illegal trade, which presented a further
opportunity for resisting the regime.[9] Sempreur and Danglade directly confronted the French antislave trade squadron. The first,
summoned by the captain of H.M.S. *Thistle*, presented himself "in full
uniform of his rank"; he had previously revived his old friendship
with the commander of the French fleet—provocations which shocked
London. Danglade was in command of a slave vessel seized by Delas-
salle d'Harader, captain of the *Sapho* of the French West Indies station. D'Harader became an accomplice in the slave trade when he
accepted 600 dollars from his old comrade-in-arms before freeing
him in Puerto Rico with fourteen negroes to sell under the guise of
provisions.[10] Such an act added little to the honor of the French suppressive squadrons.

Looked at more closely, family ties, or better, esprit de corps, must
have proved important in the sailors' psychology. Fifteen cases show
brothers and other relatives distributed between the royal navy and
that branch of the merchant navy involved in the slave trade. Statistically these links may not be significant, and family solidarity did not
often reveal itself. Yet it is likely that the family spirit, or the esprit de
corps which perhaps regulated the behavior of the squadron, was
stronger than the attachment to the official abolitionist morality.

Finally, equivocal attitudes were nurtured by the political authorities in Paris. During the first twenty months of organized suppression, the commander of the squadron, Mauduit-Duplessix, did not
seize a single slave ship. The government of Senegal attempted to act,
but without success, since the court of Saint Louis released the slavers
seized by the administration. As if to reward his failure, the king con-
gratulated the inactive commandant along with the active governor,
and on his return to France Mauduit-Duplessix was promoted.[11] The
minister told his successor, Clémendot, to "show that the existence of
the African station is not . . . an empty demonstration."[12] But when,
three weeks after taking command on the coast, Clémendot chased
and captured a French slaver, the minister reminded him that the
fleet had a *double* mission—"the protection of French commerce and
the suppression of the slave trade."[13] These must have appeared incompatible.

"How far do we pursue investigations of suspected ships?" Admiral
Hamelin asked the new minister, Clermont-Tonnerre. The latter re-

plied by pointing to the impossibility of anticipating "all" possible circumstances, but specifying limits to naval activity. There were two intangible principles: first, the refusal of the right of visit sought by England, which was nothing but an attack on national sovereignty; second, the obligation to protect convoys of neutral ships (France was on the verge of intervening in Spain). Beyond that the government counted on the wisdom of its representatives at sea, with the ultimate wisdom being simply that the presence of the French squadron would in itself divert the slave ships into legitimate trade. The alternative to such an approach was unclear, and the instructions contained no comment on tactics. All actions resolutely taken with "zeal and prudence" would receive royal approbation.[14] Some months earlier, when the Spanish expedition was still just a possibility, Clémendot was ordered to oppose "even with force, if he has any need of it," all searches of French ships by foreign vessels "of those nations which are strong"—in effect, the United States and England.[15]

In 1823, after almost ten years of abstention from the international morality defined in Vienna, the government and the new officers in charge of suppression were at an impasse. England accused the French squadron of shirking its responsibilities, the ministers of dereliction of duty, and the royal household of complicity. As proof it cited its own suppressive measures against the French slave traders.[16] The policy adjustment made in 1823 answered a need which was principally political.

FRENCH AND BRITISH SQUADRONS, 1823–1831

The royal slave trade ordinance of January 1823 implicitly renewed the law of 1818. The conclusions of a broad inquiry, ordered by Clermont-Tonnerre, accentuated the gravity of the situation: "The choice is not in doubt, the trade must end: several reasons demand it." The principal reason was the eventuality of a conflict with England, an armed conflict in this context. Six weeks later the French navy was mobilized against the slave traders.[17] At the same time, it was recognized that there was a lack of sufficient warships, and an indirect pledge of cooperation was given to England. It remained, however, to rally the sailors to the cause. In 1821 baron Portal still felt that they would find it offensive to be offered bonus money for the slaves they captured. In the following year, however, Clémendot advocated precisely this policy and from June 30, 1825, crews were rewarded with a maximum of 100 francs per impounded Negro, a measure based on the long experience of the English.[18]

From these modifications we pass to other changes. A French law of 1825 dealt with "barratry" (the proper naval term), avoiding the word "piracy," because it referred to the internationally recognized crime specified in United States and British anti-slave-trade legislation passed in 1820 and 1824 respectively. In the same year the Cour de Cassation delivered, for the first time, a decree directly inspired by the official abolitionist morality when it ordered the pursuit of slave traders "in the sacred interest of humanity and of human rights, and as a result, the vindication of the public order." The decree was reinforced in January 1826, when fitting-out for slave trading was declared to be the same as the act of trading itself.[19]

At another level, 300 shipowners petitioned against the slave trade, but none were from Nantes or Bordeaux, the major French slave-trading ports at this period. Inspired by the abolitionist propaganda that had become so prevalent since 1822, they incorporated their humanitarian decision in the new economic thinking; the slave trade in itself would not put an end to the economic crisis, but their postwar experience of world trade convinced them that even without the slave trade French overseas commerce would soon return to the levels of the years before 1789.[20] As a result of all this, despite the incompetence of the new ministers, despite powerful slaving opposition, the second French slave trade abolition law was promulgated in 1827. Penalties included banishment for slave traders, who were officially designated as "criminals." This was a measure which would remain a dead letter.[21]

There were parallel changes on the African coast, partly because the English were well aware of French metropolitan developments. From this time political constraints were as important for the French government as for the sailors. The government now felt impelled to make the squadron more numerous. In fact, the French squadron was not far behind the English in numbers. Since 1822 the English squadron had stood at nine warships; the French squadron was comprised of four, then five, and finally six vessels.[22] With new men in command—Clémendot, then La Treyte, and above all Massieu de Clairval and Villaret de Joyeuse—the results appeared surprising and satisfying.

Between 1823 and June 30, 1825, the French squadron visited twenty-five slavers at Bourbon in the Indian Ocean, in the West Indies, and on the African coast. After court proceedings, fourteen were released on the grounds of being doubtful, or because of lack of evidence, and the other eleven were condemned. These numbers are in addition to those ships seized by the public prosecutor for voyages in 1821 and 1822. It is useful to compare these eleven condemned ships with those which appeared at Sierra Leone in the same period. There, the international mixed commission and the English Vice Admiralty courts condemned ten slavers—six Portuguese, two Brazilian, one African, and one of unknown nationality. The same courts considered thirteen other cases involving authentic French nationals (sometimes sailing under Dutch flags), Spaniards, Brazilians, and African stores of black chattels—the barracoons; in these cases the slaves were freed but the vessels were not condemned.[23] The Royal Navy at this time seized only one slaver off Cuba, and none at all off the coast of Brazil, whereas the French West Indies squadron took at least three French slavers from Nantes. Thus a comparison of the French and English attempts to suppress the slave trade indicates an equality: eleven slavers condemned by the French, ten by the English.[24]

On both sides the situation produced complex attitudes. Between 1826 and 1831 London increased pressure, insisting on the elimination of the remaining participants in the French slave trade, but at the same time the Admiralty ordered its naval commanders to act with greater caution towards French slavers. Since 1814 Britain had condemned sixty-five French ships, though some had been indemnified and others restored to the owners. Increasingly, the British, after freeing the slaves in Sierra Leone, handed over the slavers to the French squadron or escorted them to Gorée.[25] After having leveled the worst accusations against France, London finally recognized that the government in Paris and the new squadron were acting in good faith.

In the West Indies, at Bourbon, and on the African coast the French commanders showed that this was justified. Between 1826 and 1831, thirty-three slavers were arrested and condemned. As this constituted only 15 percent of all ships suspected of being in the illegal traffic at this period, it is not an impressive figure. The change of policy nevertheless generated a fusion of the sense of duty and morality in the squadron. One man, Massieu de Clairval, a descendant of well-known slavers, ordered his subordinates to treat the Africans transported to Cayenne with compassion. They were also to show themselves at Sierra Leone to make known the results of their activities: it was not a matter of settling accounts, but of confirming the English in their new respect for the French flag.[26] At Bourbon a gov-

ernor hitherto incapable of repressive actions suddenly began to employ abolitionist terminology; in Cuba the French consul advertised
the penalties for breaking the law, and his Rio de Janeiro counterpart
prepared himself for the next abolitionist initiative.[27]

This is not to say unanimity prevailed. Among the English, the Admiralty, the Crown law officers, Vice Admiral Fleming, and Commodore Hayes denounced the French trade continually. Among the
French, those responsible to the naval minister, Duperré in the West
Indies, and Admiral Roussin in Rio forever decried the treachery of
the English—"those gratuitously insulting islanders."[28]

Nevertheless, an entirely new mentality came to prevail along the
African coast. On January 29, 1829, Villaret de Joyeuse recom-
mended to the minister that France should agree to the right of
search. The experience of Brazil and other European nations suggested that national dignity would not be compromised by such a
step.[29] Though the suggestion had no immediate effect, it was in fact
put into practice thirty months later under the July monarchy. From
the end of August 1831 officials at the naval ministry were studying
possible methods of Franco-British cooperation, "so far as the personal disposition of the officers might allow . . . "; the formula is repeated word for word in the instructions given in the middle of September to Brou, the new commander of the French station.[30] After
three weeks of discussion, the bilateral convention of November 30
was signed, and ratification followed fifteen days later.

Since 1822 there had been some militant abolitionists in the government. One of the central figures in the period just beginning,
Louis-Edouard Bouët, the future Bouët-Willaumez, described the attitude on the coast towards the new agreement as follows: "We had
but one exclusively philanthropic goal, and who marched alongside
us in pursuit of it? England, the chief ally of France in July, 1830.
What did it matter to us then whether it was an English or French
officer who set foot on our merchant vessels?"[31] Did,then,the issue of
French suppression in this 1817–1831 period hinge on nothing but a
frame of mind?

To sum up, during the period up to 1831 two opposing policies
had been influencing suppression operations: the idea of supranationality advocated by England and put into practice with several nations; and, pulling in the opposite direction, the policy of national
sovereignty defended by the United States and by France. The effectiveness of British suppression had been greatly increased by the
right of visit conceded by the Dutch, Portuguese, and Spanish. Between 1817 and 1831 we know of 1,236 known or suspected slave

ships listed in the 1845 Parliamentary Paper,[32] to which must be added at least 482 French slavers, giving a total of 1,718 ships. The Royal Navy in effect condemned 171 of them, that is, 10 percent of the total international trade. French opportunities for suppressing the non-French trade scarcely existed (except for those ships trafficking in French colonial waters)—first, because the French refused to collaborate with England on account of the threat to national sovereignty implied by the right of search; and second, because as a logical extension of this position the French refused to enter suppression treaties with other nations. French repressive activities were thus restricted to French citizens. Of 482 proven French slavers, the French seized 65 and condemned 51 of them; that is, 13.5 percent and 10.6 percent respectively of the illegal French traffic.[33] The policy of French autonomy did not imply a negative balance sheet on the subject of the slave trade. On the contrary, it could be proved statistically superior to the results obtained by the politics of supranationality.

At the very least we must now abandon the old idea that France was not effective against its own slavers. Certainly, if we judge the absolute values, England was three times more effective than France, and the figures of Africans liberated by the two countries are scarcely comparable, but these obviously depend on the number of slaves that happened to be on board at the time of capture. More than 400 proven French slavers did slip through the suppression net, and these may well represent 80,000 slaves with a total value of 120 million francs. The new frame of mind was counterbalanced by solid material reality, and the latter was not something the harbor authorities or the central government could afford to ignore.

The question remains, however, did the right of visit convention give a new impetus to suppression, particularly French suppression, and if so, which slave ships were affected?

THE FRANCO-BRITISH IDYLL AND ITS DECLINE

Was there ever such an idyll? The convention of 1831, refined in 1833, was agreed to by the smaller European slaving nations. This seemed to justify the two Western powers and to show that French national sovereignty had not been infringed. After the French occupation of Algeria in 1830, two conventions signed by France and Great Britain with Sardinia and Tuscany gave the two former nations the right of visit over the slavers of both smaller powers. These reinforced France in her new network of influence in the Mediterranean. The convention with England enabled France to strengthen her position in the West Indies, an enduring source of false papers used in the illegal trade.[34] But in effect all these events confirmed the supranational abolitionist policy of the English. The Foreign Office exerted increasing pressure on Spain, Portugal, and Brazil, signed a mass of treaties with Latin American countries, and in 1836 began a huge new diplomatic offensive designed to activate the major Western powers on the suppression issue. A convention with Haiti, ratified in December, 1840, took on a symbolic value by conveying black condemnation of the slave trade on the very borders of Cuba and, even more important, close to the United States. The latter had refused in 1834 to participate in the new initiatives, and continually refused to countenance the idea of an international antislavery league. By tactical error or equivocal design, France rejected the British proposal that she assent to all new conventions signed. This had the dual effect of leaving the door open to the attitudes of earlier days, permitting the simple rejection of treaty terms, as well as of encouraging the activities of the remaining major slaving powers, the Iberians and the Brazilians.

At first the idyll was undisturbed. The combined effects of a third abolitionist law, promulgated by Louis Philippe in 1831, and the right of visit conventions with Great Britain, had eliminated the French trade from those maritime areas stipulated in the first clause of the 1831 convention. Articles 3 and 5 of this convention, which could have created problems, did not in fact do so. They recognized the numerical superiority of the English naval forces, providing as they did for double the number of warrants for English cruisers as for the French cruisers. (A warrant allowed a cruiser of one nation to visit those merchant ships of the other nation suspected of slave trading.) In principle the number of warrants limited the number of men of war authorized to repress slave traders, but this did not limit the overall number of the squadron. The English fleet might include a large number of cruisers which could not act against the French, but which were free to interfere with the slavers of other nationalities.[35]

There is no carefully kept record of such warrants in the French archives, but it seems that in 1832 fifteen French cruisers were licensed by the British Admiralty, and in 1833, twenty-one—while French warrants were issued to twenty-two English warships; in 1836 the numbers were sixteen and thirty-eight respectively, the latter being an unusually high number and suggesting that the convention was not being enforced. It is simpler to enumerate the French ships which made up the West African squadron between 1832 and 1841:

1832: 4	1834: 3	1836: 5	1838: 5	1840: 4
1833: 3	1835: 3	1837: 4	1839: 4	1841: 6

Following the 2:1 ratio of the conventions, one might conclude that the number of English cruisers on the coast of Africa with warrants issued by France was low. In fact, until 1840 the English squadron operating against French merchant ships was never as strong as it was at the time of the Restoration—before the right of visit conventions of 1831 and 1833. Until 1838 it did not appear certain that France had perceived the advantages which articles 3 and 5 provided; the benefit was not realized until 1842.[36] To limit the strength of the French squadron was to limit the effectiveness of the right of visit agreement by reducing the possibilities of official British naval action against French merchant ships. In any event, France did not concentrate her suppression efforts on the African coast: in 1833 she preferred to have seven cruisers with warrants off Brazil and nine in the West Indies, out of a total of twenty-one. In 1838 the five vessels listed above were on paper only; there were probably only two off Africa out of a total of twelve cruisers with warrants. The naval minister announced to Lemarié, commander of the African station and a man more interested in the protection of commerce than the suppression of the trade, that he was not able to strengthen the French squadron.[37]

This was the time of the Franco-Mexican affair. It was also the period when, on the coast, the idyll began to decline—long before the crisis burst in Europe. The French squadron had not been completely inactive. It had visited thirty-two ships between 1832 and 1838—five North American, one Brazilian, one Sardinian, four Spanish, ten English, and eleven Portuguese. In 1834, in the Salum River, the *Bayonnaise* arrested the *Aguila de Oro*, a Spanish vessel with no slaves on board but captained by the notorious Theodore Canot, who paid for his crime in a Brest prison.[38]

Two factors destroyed the era of cooperation: national feeling and commercial developments. In the first place, enforcement of suppression had not been without friction: the case of the *Africaine* had been settled by an ill-natured cabinet-level exchange; that of the *Sénégambie*, a ship equipped by the colony of Senegal to recruit sixty-three Africans destined for military service, produced a confrontation between colonial governments and, indirectly, the metropolitan authorities. This vessel was taken while sailing to Gorée, escorted to Sierra Leone, and condemned for slave trading in British waters. The affair marked the beginning of a long series of difficulties raised by methods of recruitment of *engagés libres*, in what both sides considered to be a disguised form of slave trading when it was practiced by their opponents. Such vexations and, at the end of September 1841, the affair of the *Marabout* added spark to the powder and generated sufficient pretext for a crisis on the issue of the right of visit.[39] In the second place, in the eyes of the English, French commercial development on the African coast was by now a powerful contributor to deteriorating relations. The *Malouine* expedition is well known, and had a double purpose: to repress the slave trade and to convert the coastal population to "legitimate" trade.[40]

These commercial developments fueled British fears that their own commercial supremacy might be affected by the intrusion of rivals now capable of producing cheap and reliable goods. At the same time, the French government was tempted to establish a political presence on the coast as part of a strategy which involved the colonization of Algeria and the extension of colonization in Senegal. Bouët had signed treaties ceding territory and sovereignty to Cap des Palmes and to Gabon.

By the end of 1841 there seemed nothing left of the idyll. The crisis was underway. But it was a crisis the historical significance of which it is important not to exaggerate.

THE CRISIS AND ITS RESULTS ON THE AFRICAN COAST

For France this crisis was a means of lancing the abscess created by reverses to French Middle Eastern policy. The double pretext was, first, the gradual build up of difficulties on the coast, and, second, the refusal of the legislature to involve France in a multiparty treaty of suppression incorporating the right of visit. This treaty was prepared by Palmerston, endorsed by Aberdeen, signed by the French government, and submitted to the legislature for ratification in December 1841. From the diplomatic viewpoint the refusal to ratify was rare and not in keeping with tradition. The affair personally compromised Guizot.[41]

As foreign affairs minister, though in effect head of the government, the Protestant Guizot had been committed to militant abolitionism for twenty years. He was well acquainted with English culture, and politically convinced that the future of Western Europe would depend on the close collaboration of the two principal powers. But he was little interested in the political moods within France, and he underestimated the dislike, the anglophobia, and the strength of national feeling aroused by the setback on the Eastern question. His situation was doubly compromised: threatened with political oblivion, he was forced to follow the wishes of both the upper and lower Chamber and to accept rejection of the treaty; but he also had to deal with a crisis in which his opponents moved from an attack on the proposed 1841 treaty to an attempt to repeal the conventions of 1831–33.

A crisis undoubtedly, but hardly a new one. It had already been acted out in almost identical terms a quarter of a century earlier. What in 1844 was called "a difficult affair" had been the "great affair" of 1821. The war fever was the same in 1843 and 1822. Many of the men were the same; Guizot, Broglie, and Mackau had already been concerned about the right of visit between 1820 and 1822. Billault, a principal in 1842, spoke the language that had been used by Fitz-James in 1827; a baron Dupin was equivalent to a comte de Kergolay. The *Journal du Havre* published the same attacks against the right of visit that it had published in 1827 and 1831, without a change of theme or vocabulary. Indeed, the difficulties of 1822 were perhaps harder to overcome in the face of an autonomous cruiser system bent on vengeance than when the problems were tempered by a convention which had operated for ten years without too much ill feeling. This crisis was a case of history repeating itself. If it proves anything, it is not the way in which the French perceived the Negro question in 1843, as a recent author has appeared to discover,[42] but more markedly the continuity of the French approach to the issue. All this would explain in part why Guizot was able to ride with the domestic reaction without too much difficulty and, by minimizing the diplomatic effects of an error, achieve an honourable settlement. Much more than in a Europe somewhat taken aback by the crisis, the elements of a solution lay in the direction of the African coast.

A solution lay, first, in the difference between the behavior of the French commercial sector on the coast and the abuse it poured on the English in the metropolis. On the coast, between 1837 and 1846 it delivered 68 percent of its exports to "English possessions"—that is, in the region of 52 million gold francs: the English possessions were very interested in merchandise, two-thirds of which consisted of English manufactured goods. In return, the French commercial sector took 25 million gold francs' worth of African products. That trade with black Africa, amounting to a derisory 0.65 percent of total

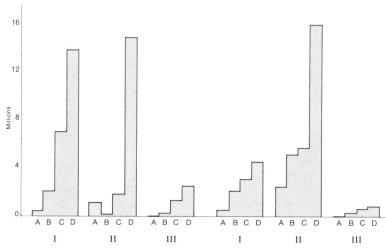

Figure 11.1 Annual Average Value of French Commerce with Africa.
Source: *Tableau décennal du commerce extérieur de la France*, Paris, 1869.

A: 1831–1836   I: West coast of Africa, excluding English possessions.
B: 1837–1846   II: English possessions in Africa
C: 1847–1856   III: Other
D: 1857–1866

French commerce,[43] does much to explain the lack of zeal among merchants toward the promise of the *Malouine* expedition; Bordeaux and the Régis brothers at Marseilles remembered these African commercial possibilities only at the outset of the crisis.[44] The detractors of the convention in the Chamber were motivated by a profitable nationalism, but not by serious economic interests.

Second, a solution was encouraged by a drive to increase public awareness of Africa, which opened as the crisis reached its height. The drive was begun with royal support for the creation of an Institut d'Afrique with clearly defined colonial ambitions. At the height of the anglophobe agitation in both chambers, the Institut brought together a membership which included many British subjects together with well-known legitimists and backers of the regime. The impact of the activities of this group was strengthened by the circulation in certain quarters of official propaganda on the establishment of French factories on the coast—results of the *Malouine* expedition. This made a discrete link between the *"mission de civilisation et d'humanité"* associated with the official abolitionist morality and the policy of augmenting the cruiser squadron.[45]

Guizot sought parity in the French and British squadrons. What the naval minister refused on November 5, 1842—arguing a shortage of funds and the uselessness of an increase in the face of the British ability to double their fleet without delay—he was obliged to agree to on November 6. The English had thirteen or fourteen ships, and on Aberdeen's advice the Admiralty was slowing down the expansion of the squadron. Nevertheless, in 1844 the squadron was increased from fourteen to twenty-one vessels, and in April 1845 the French issued twenty-five warrants to the British for the African coast, and fifty-four in all. On April 25 the French had forty-three English warrants: seventeen for the West Indies, nine for Brazil, four for Madagascar, and thirteen for the African station where the terms of the 3d and 5th articles were fully enforced.[46]

At the outset of the crisis, the number of warrants was increased by both sides, a move which was more shrewd than dangerous. The English appreciated it, as the increased strength served to make the right of visit conventions more effective at the very moment when the Anglo-American treaty was just going into force. At the same time, no objections could be raised in France because the increase restored the balance of force, and the sailors on the coast, where dignity was a compensation for numerical weakness, welcomed it and injected new spirit into the fleet's activities. Between October 1842 and March 1843 three French warships had visited one Hamburg, one Swedish, and twenty-three English ships, one of which, the *Saint Christopher* had been taken and escorted to Sierra Leone.[47]

Even at its height, therefore, the crisis had been always been under control. It seemed destined to serve as a safety valve for a political group within the French Assembly, sustained by lampoonists on the outside. Guizot was masterminding a clever game; in feeding the crisis he was trying to stifle it, and he was successful. His greatest success was the conference held in London in May 1845 between Lushington and de Broglie, in which practitioners of suppression, Denman and Bouët-Willaumez, were consulted as expert advisers, with harmonious results—including a new convention which satisfied the adversaries on the subject of the right of visit, and boosted French efforts to suppress the trade to an all time high.[48]

Article 10 of the new convention suspended for ten years the agreements of 1831 and 1833, and provided at the end of this term either for their reinstatement in stronger form, in order to satisfy the abolitionists in both camps, or for their abrogation. Article 8 compensated for the lack of French treaties with other nations by carefully spelling out the procedures to be used to verify the flags of suspected vessels. Article 7 suppressed the right of visit simply by requiring the return of all warrants. Articles 4 and 6 provided for the engagement of African chiefs in abolitionist treaties, and the use of force to ensure that such treaties would be respected. Articles 2 and 3 laid down the basis of naval cooperation between the twenty-six ships, half of them steamers and half sailing ships, which under article 1 both countries were to provide.[49]

In 1845, for the first time since 1817, the estimates for the French squadron (Division navale) appeared as a separate item in the national budget; the amount was six million gold francs. At the end of December 1845, nineteen ships were waiting at Gorée for the implementation of the agreement. On March 6, 1846, seven steamers (from 160 to 450 hp.), twenty sailing ships, one transport of 800 tons, and a hospital ship provided a force armed with 180 cannons, and manned by 2,840 sailors.[50] Twenty-three of these ships were active for the whole year on the coast. But from October 1846 the minister was thinking of reducing their number to twenty-two vessels, of which twenty were effectively present; this was in fact the situation up to August 1847. At the end of May 1848 the station was reduced by twelve or fourteen cruisers, including nine of the vessels on active service.[51] The agreement had been in full force on the French side for twelve months. It was a political game, however, for the new French republic to suppress slavery on the one hand but on the other to reduce the means of suppression. This game was not entirely satisfactory, but financial constraints must be borne in mind: the cost of the Division navale took up one-fifth of the naval budget, which had fallen to 30 million gold francs. On May 8, 1849 a Franco-British protocol reduced the French station to seven ships. But Bouët-Willaumez tried to save "his creation" from the disaster, and as late as April 1850, the time of his final departure from the African coast where he had worked for twelve years, he again sent seven to nine ships on suppression duties.[52] This naval force had not been inactive, even though its achievements were not comparable to those of the English. Between March 1846 and March 1847 captures rose to fourteen; one Sardinian, and one English vessel—the *Mary-Jane*—were arrested, but the bulk of the seizures were Brazilian. Among the latter was the *Ilizia*, the black cargo of which was the origin of the population of Libreville.[53] These ships were seized on the basis of the French law of 1825 against barratry. But the tribunal at Brest declared that the act of piracy was not sufficiently established and did not justify the seizures; this decision effectively eliminated all possibility of the fleet suppressing the trade. Only three of the foreign ships were recognized as valid prizes.

The question remains, where were the advantages for France in having twenty-seven cruisers on the coast (one more than the 1845 convention provided for)? The French negotiators in 1845 knew that such a force would be used rarely: apart from the lack of French slavers, it was virtually impossible to act against the indirect trade, or those supplying ships and trading goods; moreover, the cruisers were rarely used against the vessels of those nations with whom France had not signed conventions. While such a question does not pertain directly to an examination of the official abolitionist morality, it is nevertheless worth considering.

One advantage of the new Division navale was to counterbalance the effect of the Anglo-American treaty of 1842; in response to the claims of newcomers, with its 180 guns France was able to reaffirm on new ground its rank as the second most important world power. The second advantage was that a reinforced fleet provided a guarantee against conflicts large and small, and demonstrated the French ability to challenge English hegemony. French warships were at once a deterrent and an affirmation. Between 1836 and 1844 Le Havre sent six ships to the African coast, but between 1846 and 1850 it sent forty-four, and sailings from Nantes jumped from sixteen to twenty-five. Régis from Marseilles established a small Marseillais monopoly at Ouidah from 1841, and did not hesitate to rely on the official protection of the squadron. Finally, the warships fostered the establishment and growth of trade factories, which are the first sign of the rebirth of the colonial ideology, camouflaged for the moment behind other motives. Already commercial ends were served by punitive expeditions against black pilferers and debtors. Yet it was not primarily because of the French fleet that trade with the coast reached 200 million francs between 1847 and 1856, and more than 500 million in the following decade. During this period the English cruisers were more numerous than they had ever been, and it was the existence of an enforced order, whatever its national origins, rather than the presence of French strength that encouraged trade. The strength of English suppression was thus beneficial to French commerce. It is likely that the French authorities were themselves aware of this effect.

In Paris in 1850 a commission on the slave trade met to explore opportunities of reinforcing suppressive measures. Its central focus was the need to avoid entrapment in the *machiavélisme anglais*; its principal hope was that the Brazilian government would persist in its new policy of suppressing its own slavers, thus bringing the main branch of the traffic almost to a close. The commission adjourned indefinitely, without coming to any conclusions. The naval minister concluded his instructions to Bouët-Willaumez's replacement with the comment that "similar considerations were to govern the conduct of the squadron on the west coast of Africa."[54] The French government may have opened the door to an English monopoly of slave trade suppression, but such an attitude was now consciously dictated by political and commercial considerations.

CONCLUSION

This contribution has shown that, contrary to the belief propagated by Anglo-Saxon historiography, there existed a French fleet for the suppression of the slave trade. Its actions were not entirely negative.

It is true that, compared to the suppression activities of the Royal Navy cruisers, its results seem scanty. Several factors contributed to this ineffectiveness. Firstly, the fact that the resumption of the French slave trade was regarded as a part of the economic recovery of the ports. Secondly, the fact that the suppression of the trade was in the service of an international humanitarianism, and the French were never completely convinced that this suppression, in practice, was not designed to help British economic interests. Thirdly, the fact that the system of suppression, as an appeal to the sense of the duty of the sailors, took no account of their personal, political, and psychological feelings, which had been shaped by a century of collective good conscience about the slave trade.[55]

In other words, those responsible for suppression could see the trade as an economic necessity, consider the Negro as an irredeemable brute, and regard the English as the immediate and historical enemy. Morality was not a sufficiently strong motive for suppression: struggles on its behalf had never been glorious. Government policy found justification instead in national pride and commercial expansion—and the cruisers serving these interests produced some results, both immediately and for the future.

APPENDIX

Appendix Table 11.1
Squadron Strength, France and Great Britain, 1818–50
(ships with warrants)

| Date | Stations Other than the West Coast of Africa[a] | | West Coast of Africa | | Total | |
	France	Great Britain	France	Great Britain	F.	G.B.
1818			3	3		
1819			4	7		
1820			5	6		
1821			6	6		
1822			6	9		
1823			4	9		
1824			4	9		
1825			5	9		
1826			6	8		
1827			6	10		
1828			6	8		
1829			6	6		
1830			4	6		
1831			4	7		
1832[b]	11	13	4	6	15	19
1833	17	16	3	6	20	22
1834	15(?)		3	6	18	
1835	27		3(2)	6	30	
1836	21	39	4(5)	6(?)	25	
1837	19		4	6(?)	23	
1838	19		4(2)	6(?)	23	
1839	19		3	5(?)	22	
1840	13(?)		3	12	16	
1841	24	45	6	13	30	
1842[c]	34	36	14(6)	19	48	64
1843	34	37	13(14)	13	48	49
1844	34	29	13	19	47	56
1845	30		13	21	43	50
1846[d]	36		28	25	64	
1847	28		22	30	50	
1848			14(12)	27		
1849			7(10)	27		
1850			7(9)	24		

Note: The figures in parentheses represent the probable actual strength of the squadron.

[a] West Indies, Brazil, Madagascar-Bourbon.
[b] Conventions of 1831 and 1833.
[c] "Crisis."
[d] Convention of 1845.

(*continued*)

Appendix Table 11.1, *continued*

Sources for the list in the table are selected from two deposits: (1) ANSOM, Généralités; (2) PRO/FO. It is possible to check this list with other sources, in A.N. Marine, or PRO/Admiralty, for example; or Aff. étr. Afrique.

1. *French Archives*

From 1818 to 1829, see ANSOM, Généralités, 154/1286 (1820), 166/1347, correspondance avec le chef de la station; 154/1287 (1823). 162/1273, reports from Clémendot to naval minister, 1822–23. 172/1384, commander of station to minister. 166/1340, for the stations under command of Massieu de Clairval and then Villaret de Joyeuse, the same type of documents. For 1830 to 1850, see ANSOM, Généralités, 208/ 1518, 1519, 1520. These items are mainly warrants, changes of ships, discussions between French ministers of Marine et Aff. étr, or between these two and the Foreign Office. For matters internal to the ministry of Marine, see ANSOM, Généralités, 175/ 1405, since 1842. Idem, Généralités, 150/1246, croisières de la Division navale, 1846– 48. A.N. Marine, BB¹ 648, 653, 661, for the period 1847–50.

2. *British Archives*

Between 1816 and 1828, see *British Parliamentary Papers, Colonies*, Africa, nⁿ 50: West Africa General, Sessions 1812–74 (rpt. Shannon, Ireland), pp. 132–33 (pp. 94–95 of the original).

Between 1830 and 1850, see PRO/FO 84/181, Casimir Périer to Lord Granville, 6 Feb. 1832; FO/ 84/158, folio 27–28, 27 Feb. 1834; FO 84/181, Sébastiani to Granville, 3 May 1835, to Palmerston, 30 juin 1835. New list dated 29 Oct. 1835; FO 84/207, fⁿ 87–88, 29 Sept. 1836; fⁿ 147, 12 Jan. 1837; FO 84/224, fⁿ 11, 12 May 1837. FO 84/256, fⁿ 7, 11 May 1838; fⁿ 92, 18 Aug. 1838; fⁿ 100–102, 28 nov. 1838. FO 84/291, FO 84/ 328, notably for the *Sénégambie* affair; FO 84/370, fⁿ 179, 1 Mar. 1841; FO 84/414, fⁿ 187, 1841. After this bundle, the French sources and British seem to be in accord, minor errors and omissions excepted. The data from these sources may be compared with the list published by Christopher Lloyd, *The Navy and the Slave Trade* (London, 1949; rpt. F. Cass, 1968), pp. 279–82.

NOTES

This essay has been translated by James Walvin, *avec les grands remerciements de l'auteur*.

I would like to thank Roger Anstey, Ralph Austen, Philip Curtin, David Eltis, Pieter Emmer, and James Walvin, who commented on an earlier version of the essay.

1 H. S. Soulsby, *The Right of Search and the Slave Trade in Anglo-American Relations, 1814–1862* (Baltimore, 1933); C. Lloyd, *The Navy and the Slave Trade* (London, 1949; reprint ed., F. Cass, 1968), pp. 48–50.

2 Arch. ministère des Affaires étrangères, Paris (hereafter cited as Aff. étr.), *Mémoires et Documents*, ser. 685, *France et divers Etats*, vol. 312, July 1814– June 1815: Congrès de Vienne. See documents divers relatifs à la traite des nègres. *Annales Maritimes et Coloniales*, 1809–15 (hereafter cited as AMC) (Paris, 1816), 2, 369; Niels Rosenkrantz, *Journal du Congrès de Vienne, 1814–15*, mss ed. by G. Nørregård (Copenhagen, 1953).

3 J. Vidalenc, "La traite négrière en France sous la Restauration, 1814–1830,"

(*Proceedings of the 91ᵉ Congrès National des Sociétés Savantes*, Rennes, 1966) (Paris, 1969) 1: 197–229; Serge Daget, "Long cours et négriers nantais du trafic illégal," in J. Mettas, P. C. Emmer, and J. C. Nardin, eds., *La Traite des Noirs par l'Atlantique: Nouvelles approches* (Paris, 1976), pp. 90–134.

4 J. Vichot, *Répertoire des navires de guerre français* (Paris, 1967), p. 148. On the British cruisers, see Serge Daget, "British Repression of the Illegal French Slave Trade: Some Considerations," in Henry A. Gemery and Jan S. Hogendorn, eds., *The Uncommon Market: Essays in the Economic History of the Atlantic Slave Trade* (New York, 1979), pp. 415–438.

5 Aff. étr., Afrique 23, Traite des Noirs (hereafter cited as TdN, 1814–16), for the proceedings of this conference.

6 C. de Vénancourt to naval minister, 29 July 1817, Archives nationales, Paris Marine (hereafter cited as A.N. Marine), BB⁴ 394.

7 Portal to Pasquier, 30 Jan. 1820, Archives Nationales, Section d'Outre-Mer, Paris (hereafter cited as ANSOM), dossiers Généralités, 166/1347.

8 A.N. Marine, CC¹ 777, 1815–18.

9 See Daget, "Négriers nantais," p. 120, n. 57. To these seven names could be added twenty others, all purged officers and known slave traders, some of whom were convicted or died on the African coast.

10 For Sempreur, see ANSOM, Généralités, 154/1286, and contemporary British publications; for Danglade and Harader, see papers of the minister Clermont-Tonnerre, AM GG² 53–56. The minister kept everyone in the government fully informed of this affair.

11 Service Historique de la Marine, Paris, Dossiers personnels. The note of congratulations and promotion is in A.N. Marine GG² 37, 23 Aug. 1821. This may also be found in AMC 14 (1821): 938.

12 A.N. Marine, BB⁴ 417, Instructions "secrettes" (a register).

13 ANSOM, Généralités, 154/1287, Jan. 1823; for the remarks of 26 Dec. 1821, several days after the arrival of Clermont-Tonnerre at the ministry, see A.N. Marine GG² 53–55.

14 A.N. Marine, BB⁴ 414 bis, naval minister to Adm. Hamelin, 20 Dec. 1822.

15 ANSOM, Généralités, 154/1287, preliminary instructions from the minister, 18 Aug. 1821. The same source, Jan. 1823, ordered Clémendot "not to exaggerate his instructions."

16 Public Record Office, Foreign Office series (hereafter cited as PRO/FO), 83/2266, Law Officer's reports, folio 87, 17 Oct. 1821. Information comes from Sierra-Leone; see *Gazette of Sierra-Leone*, 26 Feb. 1822. The late Professor Roger Anstey provided us with a quote from Rothesay Papers, National Library of Scotland, 6228/531–32, 4 Jan. 1824, where Sir Charles Stuart sent to Chateaubriand, French minister of foreign affairs, a list of twenty-four French slavers from Nantes. See also, in PRO/FO 84/32 and 33, the information sent by Sir George Canning to Lord Granville, English Ambassador to Paris, 7 May and 26 June 1824. Ibid., folios 132–36, 20 Nov. 1824, Stuart to baron de Damas, and the response from Damas in which he denounces seven English slavers. For further information, see Serge Daget, "British Repression," pp. 425–34. See note 32 *infra*.

17 Le rapport du baron de la Mardelle, 30 June 1823, ANSOM, Généralités, 191/1472; AMC 18 (1823): 264. For the royal ordinance, see ANSOM, Généralités, 154/1287, 154/1285; FO/PRO 84/25.

18 ANSOM, Généralités, 162/1273, Clémendot to naval minister, reports at sea, 20 Mar. 1821, 20 Oct. 1821. Idem, Généralités, 172/1384, 2 Aug. 1825, for the text of ordinance.

19 *Recueil Sirey, 1825–1827* (Paris, 1843), p. 258, n. 5.

20 For references to *Tableau décennal*, see appendix table 11.1. The grand total of "commerce extérieur" reached 1,168 million gold francs. Separate returns for North and West Africa were not made until 1831, so it is not possible to discover the value of general commerce with the West African coast up to 1827. The value of this commerce, however, probably did not surpass 10 million gold francs, of which 3.8 million was with the "possessions anglaises d'Afrique," as cited in *Tableau décennal, passim*.

21 The debate around the question occupies more than one hundred printed pages; see AMC, 2nd ser., I (1827): 549–657.

22 A.N. Marine, BB⁴ 464 and 474. Between 1822 and 1829, sources on French cruisers are not very precise, since certain men-of-war are on temporary service on the West African coast for a few months each year. A.N. Marine BB⁴ 489 gives in a general file four cruisers for 1827, six for 1829, of which five were in active service for the whole of this year.

23 R. Meyer-Heiselberg, "Notes from Liberated African Department in the Archives at Fourah Bay College, Freetown, Sierra Leone," Scandinavian Institute of African Studies research report no. 1, mimeographed (Uppsala, 1967); Serge Daget, "Les archives de Sierra Leone et la traite illégale française," *Annales Université d'Abidjan*, ser. D (Lettres), 8 (1975): 288–97.

24 F. W. Knight, *Slave Society in Cuba during the Nineteenth Century* (Madison, 1970), app. 1, p. 197; L. Bethell, *The Abolition of the Brazilian Slave Trade* (Cambridge, 1970), pp. 132–34.

25 Daget, "British Repression," table 17.3, pp. 427–28.

26 Massieu de Clairval to Comm. of the *Alcibiade*, 15 Dec. 1826, A.N. Marine BB⁴ 485.

27 ANSOM, Généralités, 154/1287, report from Cheffontaines, governor at Bourbon to minister, 29 Aug. 1829; idem, Généralités 166/1342, Consul de France to naval minister, Rio de Janeiro, 10 July 1828.

28 PRO/FO 84/59, 83, 72, 123, covering the period between 1826 and 1831 contains numerous complaints against French merchant ships. On the French side, see Archives départementales Charente-Maritime, *Papiers Fleuriau*, La Rochelle, Mi(crofilms) 178 to 181, for the comments of Adm. Roussin, 10 may 1829, Rio de Janeiro, at sea, on board the *Duquesne*.

29 It was the opinion expressed by the French commander on the West African coast, Joyeuse to naval minister, 29 jan. 1829, ANSOM, Généralités, 166/1340. He adds: "Cette mesure qui ne compromet la dignité d'aucune nation, porterait le coup le plus sensible à la traite, et elle est d'une exécution facile puisque l'Espagne, le Portugal, le Brésil, la Hollande reconnaissent la compétence du tribunal établi à Sierra-Leone."

30 Granville to Sébastiani de la Porta, 19 Feb. 1831, Aff. étr., Afrique 27, TdN 1831–36; after being prompted by Palmerston (instructions to the Ambassador, 4 Féb. 1831, PRO/FO 84/123). See French instructions to Commander Brou, from naval minister, 14 Sept. 1831, A.N. Marine, BB⁴ 539.

31 Reprint of Bouët to *Courrier français Paris*, 30 June 1842, in *Journal officiel de la Martinique*, 20 Aug. 1842, ANSOM, Généralités, 166/1340.

32 Great Britain, Parliamentary Papers, 1845, vol. 49, *Return of the Number of Slave Vessels Arrived in the Transatlantic States since 1843*, pp. 593–633.

33 The full French data of French ships involved in illegal slave trading appear in my *Répertoire des expéditions négrières illégales françaises au XIXè siècle*, forthcoming as Appendix I and II of my thesis for Doctorat d'Etat at the Sorbonne. It is based on archives in France, Great Britain, Denmark, Portugal, Sénégal, and Sierra Leone. The late Prof. R. Anstey and Profs. H. S. Klein, S. Engerman, P. C. Emmer, Sv. Green-Pedersen, G. Debien, H. Brunschwig, and J. Ganiage have helped me very much with their useful comments on this. D. Eltis has published a shortened part of this work as an appendix to "The Directions and Fluctuations of the Transatlantic Slave Trade, 1821–43: A Revision of the 1845 Parliamentary Paper," in Gemery and Hogendorn, *The Uncommon Market*, pp. 273–301; see 299–301. In the same book, see my "British Repression," tables 17.2, p. 429, and 17.3, pp. 431–32, for further information.

34 S. Daget, "Le *Charles* à Old-Calabar, en 1825," forthcoming in Maison des Sciences de l'Homme, ed., *Mélanges en hommage à Henri Brunschwig* (Paris, Ecole des Hautes Etudes en Sciences Sociales).

35 See Louis Blanc, *Révolution Française: Histoire de Dix Ans, 1830–1840* (Paris, 1849): vol. 4, *Documents historiques*, no. 6, pp. 484–85; Idem, ibid., Convention supplémentaire du 22 mars 1833, pp. 486–90; and Annexe à la convention supplémentaire, undated (but of the same date), pp. 490–93.

36 Note to the minister, 31 Oct. 1842, ANSOM, Généralités, 208/1520. See appendix Table 11.1 for further information and sources.

37 Instructions to Lemarié, 11 Apr. 1835, AM, BB⁴ 575.

38 On Theodore Canot, see L. G. Bouge, "Théophile Conneau, alias Théodore Canot, négrier en Afrique, fonctionnaire en Nouvelle-Calédonie, 1804–1860," *Revue d'Histoire des Colonies*, vol. XL, 1953 (1), no. 138, pp. 249–63; Roger Pasquier, "A propos de Théodore Canot, négrier en Afrique," *Revue Française d'Histoire-Mer*, vol. LV, 1968, no. 200, pp. 352–54; Gabriel Debien, "Théodore Canot condamné comme négrier en 1834," idem, vol. LVIII, 1969, no. 207, pp. 214–24; G. Debien, "Encore mon ami Canot, 1842–1844," *Enquêtes et Documents, Centre de recherches sur l'Histoire de la France Atlantique*, vol. II, 1973, pp. 222–26. S. Daget, "Encore Théodore Canot: Quelques années de la vie d'un négrier et quelques questions," *Annales Université d'Abidjan*, ser. I (Histoire), vol. V, 1977, pp. 39–53; Svend E. Holsoe, "Theodore Canot at Cape Mount, 1841–1847," *Liberian Studies Journal*, 4 (1972): 163–81.

39 For the *Africaine*, see PRO/FO 84/256; for the *Sénégambie*, ibid. 84/328; for

the *Niger, Dorade,* and *Henri,* see reports from Doctor's Commons, PRO/ FO 83/2269, dated 22 June 1840. For files on the interference of cruisers with merchants ships, see ANSOM, Généralités, 166/1340. Idem, A.N. Marine, BB⁴ 602 and 614. See also 8 July 1841, Aberdeen to Bourquemy, French Ambassador to London, folios 117–19, referring to the "numerous complaints" of French masters against naval officers in command of the fifteen ships of the Royal Navy's African squadron.

40 Reports on the voyage of the *Malouine,* Bouët report folio, Archives nationales, Intérieur, Commerce F¹² 2588.

Certain observations in a report by Bouët to the minister and to the chambers of commerce are somewhat disturbing. The report assesses the strength of the slave trade, notably in the Gallinas area between Sierra Leone and Liberia. If its references to the psychology and behavior of Africans do not contain the violence of Vénancourt's comments, neither do they indicate any profound change in French attitudes toward the Negro. Bouët was explicitly concerned with the commercial possibilities of the region. French ships were able to sell French provisions to the slave traders, as well as other products from French entrepôts, though he regretted that the latter were "approvisionés par les manufactures britaniques." At this time, beginning his African career, Bouët was concerned only with the national economic interest when he supported what the ministers would soon call the "indirect trade." Six years later he would have a very different outlook. He was by then commanding officer of a squadron of twenty-six warships assigned specifically to the suppression of the slave trade. See the book written by Bouët-Willaumez, *Commerce et traite des Noirs à la côte occidentale d'Afrique* (Paris, 1848; reprinted 1979). See also Bernard Schnapper, *La Politique et le commerce français dans le golfe de Guinée* (Paris, 1961); Michèle Daget, "Le Carrière africaine de Bouët-Willaumez" (M.A. diss., Université Sorbonne, 1969).

41 Aberdeen to Cowley, 12 Feb. 1842, FO/PRO 84/414.

42 L. C. Jennings, "France, Great Britain, and the Repression of the Slave Trade 1841–1845," *French Historical Studies,* vol. 10, no. 1 (Spring 1977), pp. 101–25. It does not appear that the content of this essay corresponds with its title.

43 *Tableau décennal du commerce extérieur de la France . . . 1857–1866,* vol. 1 (Paris, 1869), pp. 56–61. (Figures in the *Tableau décennal* for "possessions anglaises" and for "autres régions" of Africa exclude all of North Africa and Senegal.)

44 28 Oct. 1842, naval minister to commerce minister, for the problems created by the tardy response of the merchants. The former wrote: "Nous serons devancés par les Anglais sur ces points et peut-être par les Etats-Unis"; see ANSOM, Généralités, Sénégal IV, 29.

45 On the *Institut d'Afrique,* see S. Daget, "A Model of the French Abolitionist Movement and Its Variations," in Christine Bolt and Seymour Drescher, eds., *Antislavery, Religion and Reform* (Folkestone, 1980), pp. 64–79. For commercial matters, see AMC, 1843, 2nd ser., vol. III, *Partie non officielle,*

pp. 566–72. These semiofficial releases are reprinted with minor changes by newspapers; see *Journal des Débats*, 30 Oct. 1843, pp. 1–2. After 1844, the ministry of Agriculture and Commerce distributed news information on the facilities and opportunities for trading on the West African coast. See A.N., Intérieur, F^{12} 7208, no. 269, June–July 1845, pp. 3–4; no. 432, Sept.–Oct. 1848, pp. 1–7, for samples.

46 Guizot to naval minister, 27 and 31 Oct. 1842, Aff. étr., Afrique 14, TdN 1837–42. See also ANSOM, Généralités, 208/1520 and 1521, April 1842 to April 1845, for correspondence between the two ministries as the crisis evolved, and their exchange on the numbers of vessels involved in the suppressive squadrons. See details on these numbers, below, in appendix table 11.1.

47 Folios 83–84, 224–225, FO/PRO 84/473. See also Meyer-Heiselberg, "Notes from Liberated African Department," p. 50.

48 Minutes of proceedings of conference between de Broglie and Lushington, held in London, March–May 1845, Aff. étr., Afrique 22, TdN 1842–45; and idem, Afrique 30, TdN 1845–46. On the English side, see PRO/FO 97/430. The text of the convention dated 29 May 1845 in Guizot, *Mémoires pour servir à l'Histoire de mon temps* (Paris, 1864), vol. VI, *Pièces historiques*, XIII, pp. 446–51.

49 Idem, Ibid.

50 A.N. Marine, BB^4 635 and 639; Aff. étr., Afrique 31, TdN 1845–50.

51 A.N. Marine, BB^4 648, 18 Aug. 1847. For détails of these ships and those that remained in service, see A.N. Marine BB^4 653 and 661. Cf. appendix table 11.1, below.

52 Reports from Bouët to naval minister, at sea, dated 28 July and 21 Oct. 1849; of 2 Jan. 1850, A.N. Marine, BB^4 661.

53 On the captures, see A.N. Marine, BB^4 639. On the *Ilizia*, see G. Lasserre, *Libreville et sa région* (Paris, 1958); H. Deschamps, *Quinze ans de Gabon* (Paris, 1965). There is no information on the *Mary Jane*.

54 Naval minister to Commander of the Station, 12 Dec. 1851, ANSOM Généralités, 143/1273; also, Aff. étr., Afrique 32, TdN 1850–51, fol. 93–107.

55 I. Sachs, *La Découverte du Tiers-Monde* (Paris, 1971), p. 55.

PART IV American Demographic and Cultural Responses

CHAPTER 12: **The Reality behind the Demographic Arguments to Abolish the Danish Slave Trade**

Hans Christian Johansen

When the Danish government decided in 1791 to start an investigation of the Danish slave trade, it set up a committee of high government officials which in December 1791 submitted a report of 102 pages. Since the decision in the Royal Council to issue the 1792 ordinance was based on this report, it is natural to study the arguments in the report to discover why the slave trade was abolished earlier in Denmark than in other European countries with economic interests in Africa and America. The report gives thorough treatment to humanitarian and international aspects of the slave trade, but the most careful study is reserved for the economic consequences of abolition.

The slave trade *per se* was given only slight attention. It was agreed that the trade was unprofitable to the country because of the low prices of slaves in the Danish West Indies and the great loss of lives among Danish sailors on the two to four ships which yearly took part in the trade. It was particularly unprofitable to the treasury, which supported the forts in Guinea and had given large subsidies to the privileged slave-trading companies in previous years, but had received little revenue in return. In a period of fiscal reconstruction after the large rearmament expenses in 1788, the latter argument had great political weight.

The most thorough examination of the economic consequences of abolition of the slave trade was instead concentrated on the possible effects on the sugar plantations in the Danish West Indies, on the

221

mercantile marine which transported sugar from the West Indies to Denmark and from Denmark to a number of European countries— between 40 and 100 Danish-Norwegian ships were engaged in the trade yearly—and on the sugar refineries in Copenhagen and a few other cities in the kingdom. In all these areas there were important employment and foreign exchange implications which could not be ignored by the late-mercantilistic statesmen in the government.

It was, however, the situation in the West Indies which was most important, because if—as the report concluded—the harm done by abolition to sugar production could be minimized, it would seem that there would be proportionally less damage caused to the economic system.

According to modern trade theory, the most important effect of an import ban on production goods (*in casu* slaves) would be increased domestic production (i.e., production of slaves by means of slaves) at prices exceeding world market prices, and therefore higher production costs for the final goods (sugar). The committee report does not use this approach in a consistent way. It only discusses whether it is possible to encourage a self-sustaining slave population, and makes no reference to the costs of such a policy relative to the importation of slaves. The implicit assumption is that there are no cost differences, and that the competitive position of the Danish plantations would not deteriorate if only domestically produced slaves were available. The crux of the report, therefore, is the analysis of slave demography. How is it possible to maintain a slave population on the islands without enforced immigration?

The report assumes that the crude birth rate among the slaves in the 1780s was 19 births per 1,000 slaves, and that the mortality rate was 35 deaths per 1,000 slaves, or, if three years with epidemics and famine were left out, 29 deaths per 1,000 slaves. This means that the yearly decrease in the population in normal years was about 1 percent, and that it would be necessary to increase the number of births or reduce mortality decisively, or both, if the slave population was to be maintained by its own reproduction.

Such a birth rate was—compared to contemporary European societies—very low. In Denmark in the late eighteenth century there were about 35 births per 1,000 inhabitants in spite of a smaller proportion of the population in the fertile age groups. The committee therefore regarded low fertility as the main problem, and it emphasized four causes: (1) the disproportion between the sexes as a result of importation (in Saint Croix, for instance, about 54 percent of the slaves were male); (2) unstable sexual relations because of the absence of formal marriages among the slaves; (3) too little care for pregnant slaves and slave babies because masters wanted to make the most use of the mothers' working capacity; (4) too many slaves employed in domestic work (it was not explained how this could influence fertility—was it because these female slaves were isolated from the field workers and therefore unlikely to become pregnant?) The committee found that it was possible for the masters to influence these four factors, especially if the ban on imports—as proposed in the report— did not come into force until after a transitional period which could be used to buy more female slaves. There was no reference to the fact that the changes might bring about higher costs for the master.

The level of slave mortality was more in accordance with contemporary European levels. Although the age distribution among the slaves should have favored a lower mortality rate, the report found mortality conditions less alarming than those influencing fertility, and admitted that it would be difficult for the masters to reduce mortality, since there was no cure for most of the epidemics and tropical diseases which caused many deaths. The report mentioned, however, that the death rate was higher among African-born Negroes than among creoles, and that abolition of the trade, for this reason alone, would reduce the mortality.

On the basis of these considerations, the 1792 ordinance provided that the Danish slave trade from Africa and imports to the West Indies should stop at the end of 1802, that in the intervening period there should be no duty on imported Negresses and, from 1795, no taxes on female *field* Negroes, and that exports of slaves from the islands should be prohibited. In its conclusion the report pleaded for better religious instruction of the slaves and for encouragement of formal marriages, but the ordinance took no steps to introduce such measures.

POPULATION GROWTH RATES AMONG THE SLAVES

The number of Negro slaves in the Danish West Indies is known from tax rolls; these figures are shown in table 12.1. The cultivation of sugar started on a large scale in about the middle of the eighteenth century, and the importation of slaves increased the working force on the plantations by about 3 percent yearly, in spite of low fertility and high mortality. The largest imports were made during European wars when the islands profited from Danish neutrality.

Table 12.1 shows that the planters during the transition period after 1792 built up a large stock of slaves, but that after 1802, contrary to the expectations of the committee, there did not develop a self-reproducing slave population. When the importation of slaves stopped, the slave population decreased by about 1 percent a year— i.e., at the rate that the committee in 1791 thought was normal with free importations.

Several explanations for this unfavorable development are possible. The committee may have been misinformed about the real situation in the islands, the mistakes being related either to slave demography or to plantation economics. It is also possible that the development should be explained primarily by factors beyond the government's control, such as the development of the international sugar economy.

Table 12.1
Number of Slaves in the Danish West Indies, 1761–1846

Year	St. Croix	St. Thomas	St. Jan	Total	Annual Growth Rate in Preceding Period (percent)
1761	13,489	3,632	2,020	19,141	
1765	15,699	3,734	2,024	21,457	2.9
1775	23,384	3,979	2,355	29,718	3.3
1786	22,539	4,703	2,322	29,564	− 0.0
1791	21,549	4,214	1,845	27,608	− 1.4
1792	22,240	4,279	1,917	28,436	3.0
1796	24,368				
1798	26,634				
1799	26,399				
1801	26,954				
1802	27,006	5,737	2,492	35,235	2.2
1815	24,339	4,848	2,445	31,632	− 0.8
1826	21,356	4,548	2,206	28,110	− 1.1
1835	19,876	5,032	1,971	26,879	− 0.5
1846	16,706	3,494	1,790	21,990	− 1.8

Sources: P. P. Svejstrup, *Bidrag til de tidligere dansk vestindiske øers økonmiske historie* (Copenhagen, 1942); Svend E. Green-Pedersen, "The History of the Danish Negro Slave Trade, 1733–1807," *Revue française d'histoire d'outre-mer* 62 (1975): 196–220; "Vestindisk Kopibog, 1804," National Archives, Copenhagen.

THE DEMOGRAPHIC SOURCES USED BY THE COMMITTEE

The members of the 1791 committee had never themselves visited the West Indian Islands, but their work in the departments of government made them well acquainted with the daily correspondence with the Danish officials on the islands. Furthermore, the most important person on the committee, Minister of Commerce and Finance Ernst H. Schimmelmann, had large plantation interests in the islands.

Nevertheless, the information about slave demography available to the committee was relatively scarce. Much was of a qualitative nature—partly taken from books describing the situation in other West Indian areas. The statistics found in the report cover only part of the islands. The birth and mortality rates are calculated from figures from Saint Croix, and their totals do not agree with figures of the tax rolls. The sex ratios are taken from plantations holding about 25 percent of the slaves; it later became evident that these plantations had a biased slave stock, so that the surplus of males was smaller than assumed. Similarly a list, the object of which was to demonstrate that well-run plantations had higher birth rates than those mentioned above, used evidence from an earlier period. This was probably not done deliberately to give a false impression of demographic trends; after all, the collection of vital statistics was everywhere in its infancy, and better information was simply not available. But it is doubtful whether we can accept the causes of the negative reproduction rate postulated in the report.

THE 1804 STATISTICS

When the transition period expired in 1803 many planters complained that the slave population was still too small, and though the government refused to prolong the transition period, it decided in 1804 to collect further data which might throw light on the living conditions of the slaves on plantations. A questionnaire was sent to the islands in July 1804; information about that year for each of the 302 plantations was returned late in 1805 and early in 1806.

The subjects examined by the questionnaire are indicated by table 12.2, which gives figures for the combined slave populations of all of the plantations; figures for each plantation are also kept in the Danish National Archives.[1] It is not possible to compare this information with other sources, and its reliability must therefore be evaluated from its internal consistency.[2]

The age and sex distributions appear to be probable for a population with a heavy immigration. The age-specific mortality rates are not unlikely, compared with contemporary European experience, although the number of stillborn children is more than double the rate known for Europe. The figures seem to indicate that these stillborn are not included in the number of births, since the sex ratio for births is more probable when the stillborn are added to the births. Most of the other information cannot be checked.

Table 12.2 shows a birth rate of 26 births per 1,000 slaves, or 29

Table 12.2
Census of Plantation Slaves, Danish West Indies, 1804
(combined figures for all three islands)

1. Total number of slaves				27,837	
2. Male slaves				14,606	(52.5% of all)
3. Female slaves				13,231	(47.5%)
4. West Indian-born				15,147	(54.4%)
5. African-born				12,690	(45.6%)
6. Christian slaves				18,080	(64.9%)
7. Heathens				9,756	(35.1%)
8. Occupations					
Field Negroes				21,461	(77.1%)
Domestic slaves				1,974	(7.1%)
Used in handicrafts				2,005	(7.2%)
Disabled Negroes				2,397	(8.6%)

9. Age distribution

Age	Male	Female (number)	Male	Female (percentage)
Below 5 years	1,345	1,363	9	10
5–10	1,192	1,070	8	8
10–20	2,317	1,841	16	14
20–30	3,394	3,208	23	24
30–40	2,833	2,326	19	18
40–50	1,829	1,576	13	12
50–60	1,025	1,100	7	8
60 or more	686	744	5	6

10. Mating	Married couples	Unmarried couples with permanent sexual relations	Total
Number of couples	579	3,316	3,895
Number of births in 1804	62	630	692
Births per couple	0.11	0.19	0.18

11. Births
Boys	342	(48% of all)
Girls	375	(52%)
Total	717	
Number of baptized children	286	(39.9% of new-born)

12. Married persons belonging to other plantations
Male	1,026
Female	1,173

13. Age distribution of deceased slaves in 1804

Age at death	Male	Female	Male	Female
			(percentage)	
Stillborn	72	30	12	7
Below 1 year	84	50	15	12
1–5	51	47	9	11
5–10	18	14	3	4
10–20	35	33	6	8
20–30	72	62	12	15
30 or more	248	177	43	43
Total	580	413	100	100

14. Children belonging to domestic Negresses
Boys	275
Girls	275

15. Negroes belonging to inhabitants on the plantations as their personal property
Men	428
Women	545
Children	251

16. Land use
Sugar production	28,391 acres	(37.5%)
Commons	6,218	(8.2%)
Provisions	3,929	(5.2%)
Uncultivated	35,488	(46.9%)
Laid out to Negro houses	1,626	(2.1%)

17. Position of slave houses
High sites	3,917 houses
Low sites	1,374
No information	5,194
Total number of houses	10,485

18. Use of field labor force
Guards	1,069 slaves
Distillery and boiler	2,602
Herds	1,005
In the infirmary	375
Common field workers	13,342

Source: Generaltoldkammeret, Dokumenter vedr. Slavehandelskommissionen 1783–1806, National Archives, Copenhagen.

Note: The original figures have been used in table 12.2, without corrections. Totals do not in all cases agree with individual plantation figures. Slaves in the cities are not included in the figures.

births per 1,000 if the stillborn are included, and a mortality rate of 36 deaths per 1,000 slaves. The rates are at a somewhat higher level than those mentioned in the 1791 report, but the difference between the fertility and mortality rates is the same in the two surveys. Part of the explanation for the higher fertility and mortality rates in 1804 may be that the urban slaves had different rates than the plantation slaves, and that the conditions on Saint Thomas and Saint Jan, where less sugar was grown, were different from those on Saint Croix.

In the 1804 statistics in the National Archives it is possible to study differences in the demographic variables on individual plantations, and some of the variables that indicate the general living conditions on these plantations. Such a study has been carried out, based on a 20 percent sample (60 plantations); every fifth plantation mentioned in the material was selected.[3] The sample plantations show wide variations in their demographic conditions—e.g., the birth rates vary between 0 and 80 per thousand, and the mortality rates between 0 and 91. This is, of course, partly a result of random variations caused by the small size of the individual plantations, but is it possible to find a pattern showing a correlation between demographic phenomena and other figures from the 1804 statistics?

The demographic and social variables derived from the sample include the ratio of male slaves to all slaves, the ratio of females in the fertile age group to all females, the incidence of marriage and baptism, the number of slaves per house, the proportion of field laborers in the total labor force, and the size of the plantation labor force. Correlations between each of these variables and the birth rate are weak and often produce a sign opposite to the one expected. In order to examine the combined effects of the independent variables a number of multiple regressions have been run, but with equally poor results.[4] While these are undoubtedly disappointing, they at least allow us to establish that the factors causing low fertility in the Danish possessions were not those specified in the 1791 report.

It is also possible to test some of the hypotheses about the factors influencing mortality. Independent variables, in addition to those already specified, include creoles as a percentage of all slaves, sugar area as a percentage of all plantation acreage, and various age ratios. Again, however, there is no close correlation between any of the aforementioned variables and mortality, and the only satisfactory multiple regression included such variables as the fraction of slaves below 5 years old and the birth rate, which only points to the truism that high mortality rates were prevalent on estates that had a high birth rate but few small children.[5] Clearly we cannot ascribe any large explanatory value to the equation. It must be concluded—as was the case with the birth rate—that the independent factors that could be influenced by the planters seem to have had an insignificant impact on the mortality level.

CONCLUSION

The analysis in the preceding section seems to indicate that the variation in birth and mortality rates among plantations in 1804 was a result primarily of chance, because of the small size of the plantations. This fact does not preclude as a possible explanation for the failure of the reproduction policy that the planters found it unprofitable—even when importation of slaves was prohibited—to invest in an improvement of the slaves' general living conditions. On the other hand, if it was a question of costs we should expect that the reproduction rate would be high when there were profitable years for the sugar plantations and that there would be a greater loss of slaves in lean years. This was not the case, however, even though the period after 1792 was characterized by large fluctuations in sugar prices. It is most likely that the planters were not able—whether they wanted to or not—to increase fertility or to reduce mortality to a level which secured a sufficient labor force for the plantations. The intentions of the 1792 ordinance were therefore never fulfilled.

NOTES

1 Generaltoldkammeret, Dokumenter vedr. Slavehandelskommissionen 1783–1806, National Archives, Copenhagen.
2 The governor of the Danish West Indies was ordered to have the information collected by the local government officials themselves, rather than by the planters; it was believed that the yearly tax rolls which were based on declarations from the planters understated the number of slaves.
3 Plantations without slaves have been omitted.
4 The best linear equation was (standard errors in parentheses):

$$B = 0.0395 + 0.0168 \text{ BA} - 0.0381 \text{ FW} - 0.0306 \text{ HN: } R^2 = 0.29$$
$$\quad\quad\quad (0.0056) \quad\quad (0.0165) \quad\quad (0.0205)$$

where B is the birth rate, BA the fraction of new-born children who were baptized, FW the fraction of women between 20 and 39 years, and HN

the fraction of slaves who were house slaves. A log linear regression yielded even less satisfactory results.
5 The best was (standard errors in parentheses):

$$M = 0.0714 + 0.0139 \text{ SA} - 0.0487 \text{ MGU} - 0.0413 \text{ KR}; R^2 = 0.17$$
$$(0.0122) \qquad (0.0199) \qquad (0.0186)$$

where M is the mortality rate, SA the fraction of the area which was used for sugar growing, MGU the fraction of the men who were between 20 and 50 years, and KR the fraction of the slaves who were creoles

The relation is weak and the significance level of the coefficients unsatisfactory, except for the age factor.

The log linear form gives in this case statistically a considerably better result:

$$\text{LnM} = 0.934 - 1.030 \text{ LnNS} - 0.574 \text{ LnCS} + 0.190 \text{ LnB}; R^2 = 0.46$$
$$(0.195) \qquad (0.211) \qquad (0.103)$$

where M is the mortality rate, NS the number of slaves on the plantation, CS the fraction of slaves who were below 5 years, and B the birth rate.

CHAPTER 13: **Slave Demography in the Danish West Indies and the Abolition of the Danish Slave Trade**

Svend E. Green-Pedersen

In recent years demographic analysis has become one of the most direct and busiest routes to increased understanding of slave societies. This reflects partly the historian's desire to gain insight into the functioning of these societies and in particular into the response of one group to another's attempt to control it. But it is also an indication that the data necessary to carry out such an analysis are more likely to be available for slave societies: masters in the slave colonies were both more interested in the vital rates of the work force and more able to collect the data than their equivalents in the metropolis, and the interests of the abolitionists were similarly biased, though for quite different reasons. In the Danish case, trends in the black population of the Danish West Indies before and after abolition of the slave trade contribute to an understanding of the demographic response of the Americas to abolition as well as to the motives behind the decision to institute abolition. In this paper I offer a brief review of Danish abolition, pointing to the centrality of demographic considerations in that decision, before using hitherto largely unpublished data from tax rolls to establish whether actual developments conformed to the expectations of the decision makers.

The historical debate on the abolition of Danish Negro slavery is not nearly as comprehensive as that on British abolition, but parallels nevertheless exist.[1] Thus the basic account of the abolition of the

231

Danish Negro slave trade, an article by C. A. Trier from 1905, shows many similarities to Reginald Coupland's account of the abolition of the British slave trade. In keeping with abolitionist tradition, they both interpret abolition as a moral victory over economic interest, and both have drawn on Thomas Clarkson's book of 1808 for their description of the abolitionist movement.[2] The first comprehensive revision of the Danish abolitionist tradition came later than the British revision, and it was not as violent. It was spearheaded by Jens Vibæk in his chapter on abolition in volume two of *Vore gamle Trope-kolonier* [Our old tropical colonies] in 1952–53. While Eric Williams asserted that Britain's slave trade was abolished for the sake of economic gain, Vibæk merely maintained that the abolition of the Danish slave trade rested "on a double basis: a humanitarian and an economic." There is general agreement among historians that the principal figure behind Danish abolition was Ernst Schimmelmann, minister of finance, who was also the owner of large plantations in the Danish West Indies. In view of Schimmelmann's attitude during the debate in the early nineteenth century on the postponement of the enforcement of the ban on Negro imports, Vibæk characterizes him as having "a problematic nature."[3] In an article in 1969, the present author modified Vibæk's criticism of Trier, and went on to emphasize that the Danish reform legislation was passed in 1791–92 because the Danish government at that time believed Britain was about to abolish her slave trade.[4]

The sharpest criticism of Vibæk's revision of Danish abolitionist tradition has come from the German historian Christian Degn in his book on the Schimmelmann family, a book based on studies of the Schimmelmann family records preserved in German and Danish archives.[5] Degn's account of Danish abolition tallies very closely with that of C. A. Trier in important respects. Like Trier, he emphasizes Ernst Schimmelmann's humane personality, characterizing him as both an idealist and an abolitionist.[6] But Degn takes issue with the revisionists without touching on the ideology of abolition, and thus his work differs from that of Roger Anstey and Seymour Drescher, his counterparts in the English historiography. This may perhaps be explained by the fact that the abolitionist ideology of the Danish Negro commission was a foreign import; the commission refers explicitly to the works of Falconbridge, Clarkson, and Frossard, as well as to a contemporary British parliamentary report.[7] Contributions from Danish abolitionists, notably Peder Paludan and Paul E. Isert, are not even mentioned.[8] There is a further difference between the Danish antislavery literature and the sources for the commission's report in that while the literary contributions are mostly modeled on French patterns, the commission relies heavily on British abolitionists.

Christian Degn has drawn attention to some reform plans for better treatment of the Negroes at the Schimmelmann plantations. They were of much the same kind as those attempted by other contemporary reform planters—e.g. Samuel Martin of Antigua—which were intended to establish a balance between births and deaths of the slave population. Such plans should also be seen in relation to the increasing price of slaves. Though Degn does not immediately link these plans with the demographic deliberations of the Danish Negro trade commission, he does emphasize that humanitarian considerations were decisive to Schimmelmann the idealist. In contrast to Christian Degn, the present author has emphasized that these reform plans are a necessary, but *not* a sufficient, prerequisite for an understanding of the demographic considerations of the Danish Negro trade commission. The political decision makers were in themselves not ill disposed to abolishing the slave trade for humanitarian reasons, but they were not prepared to sacrifice the assumed assets of the colonial plantations in doing so. It was thus not until they were convinced of the success of the attempts at social reform among the slaves that they finally decided they could afford to ban the import of slaves[9]—an interpretation, it should be noted, shared by Hans Christian Johansen in chapter 12 of this volume.

Were the expectations of the policy makers met? The main source for the study of demographic developments in the Danish West Indies is the West Indian tax rolls (*matrikler*), which were made for the purpose of the poll and property taxes. After the state had taken over the islands in 1755, the tax rolls were made annually and sent home to the Central Customs Department (*Generaltoldkammeret*) in Copenhagen. Their existence has been known for many years, and earlier writers have also made use of them.[10] In 1976 I succeeded in unearthing the tax rolls for Saint Thomas for the years 1755–56, 1758–66, and 1768–85, and for Saint Jan for the years 1755–66 and 1768–85. In addition, a number of contemporary extracts from the tax rolls were discovered.

In order to establish continuous series of demographic data, I have gone through the tax rolls for the first fifty years after the state took over the islands. The results are summarized in appendix table 13.A1. This period covers the golden age of Saint Croix, the largest of the Danish West Indian islands. The question of their reliability is of course of paramount importance. C. A. Trier was already aware of this problem, and he quoted the opinion of the contemporary colonial official, P. L. Oxholm, that the rolls were unreliable because they had merely been copied from one year to another. P. P. Sveistrup also had certain reservations about the accuracy of the tax rolls, but his claim that the rolls are almost totally lacking in information on the number of free Negroes seems dubious, especially for Saint Thomas.[11] Generally, one might assume that figures derived from tax rolls are biased downward, but empirical material so far employed does not seem to support this conclusion. Two further problems remain. One, pointed out by the national economist C. N. David, is that the number of recorded deaths and births excludes infants who died within their first year.[12] The other is that some taxable Negroes have been recorded in the tax roll as tax-exempt; for example, some able-bodied Negroes have been classified as Manquerons or Bosals.[13]

The development of the slave population in the half century from 1755 to 1804 may be seen in figure 13.1. The number of slaves almost doubled within the first two decades after 1755, when their population rose from less than 15,000 to between 28,000 and 29,000. The rapid increase after 1792 is explained by the edict on the slave trade of that year, which liberalized the import of slaves until 1803, when the ban on imports was to come into force. This had the effect of increasing the number of slaves by 25 percent in ten years—an increase in which all the colonies shared, despite the fact that the slave populations of Saint Thomas and Saint Jan, in contrast to that of Saint Croix, had grown scarcely at all during the 1755 to 1792 period.

Figure 13.2 shows the proportions of plantation slaves and town slaves on Saint Croix between 1755 and 1804, and indicates clearly the plantation base of the Saint Croix economy, with the proportion of slaves living in the towns of Christiansted and Frederiksted at no time exceeding 16 percent of the Saint Croix slave population. From figure 13.3, on the other hand, we see that the economy of Saint Thomas relied much less on plantations than that of Saint Croix. The percentage of slaves living in the town of Charlotte Amalie was twice as large as the percentage of town slaves on Saint Croix throughout the period, rising to a peak in 1797, when 34 percent of all slaves on Saint Thomas were town slaves. It should be mentioned that "town slave" and "domestic slave" are no more synonymous terms than are "plantation slave" and "field Negro." But it is clear, nevertheless, that the plantation slaves were worked much harder, especially in the sugarcane fields, than were the town slaves. Figure 13.3 also touches on the important problem of the social status of the free Negroes. It shows that while in 1755 the free Negroes of Saint Thomas owned 1

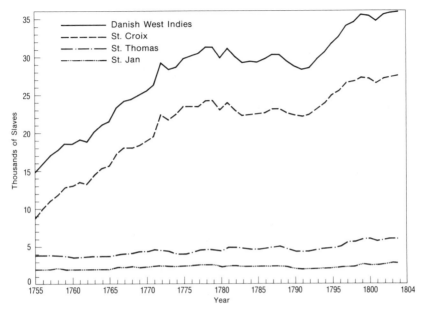

Figure 13.1 The Slave Population of the Danish West Indies, 1755–1804. Data from chapter appendix.

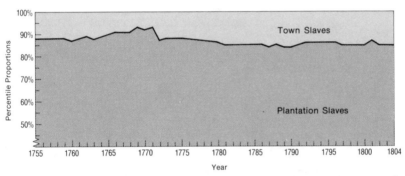

Figure 13.2 Percentile Proportions of Plantation Slaves and Town Slaves on Saint Croix, 1755–1804. Data from chapter appendix.

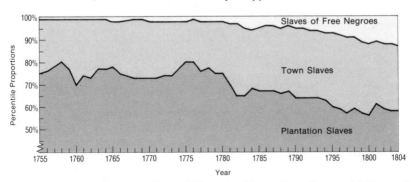

Figure 13.3 Percentile Proportions of Plantation Slaves, Town Slaves, and Slaves of Free Negroes on Saint Thomas, 1755–1804. Data from chapter appendix.

percent of all slaves, fifty years later they owned 13 percent. It thus seems beyond doubt that by 1804 the free Negroes of Saint Thomas constituted a middle class not altogether without property.

For the Danish West Indies as a whole, the number of free Negroes is not known before 1783, when they constituted 2.6 percent of the total Negro population of the islands. As may be seen from table 13.1, the percentage of free Negroes increased during the following two decades to 6.1 percent in 1804. The number of free Negroes on Saint Croix is not known before 1772, when they constituted 0.7 percent of the Negro population. By 1783 this number had increased to 2.3 percent, and it continued to grow for the following two decades, so that by 1804 free Negroes made up 5.8 percent of the Negro population. The number of free Negroes on Saint Thomas is known as early as

Table 13.1
Free Negroes of the Danish West Indies, 1783 and 1786–1804 (by percentage)

Year	Proportion of in Total Negro Population	Proportion of Adult Females Among	Proportion of Adult Males Among
1783	2.6		
1786	3.5		
1787	3.5		
1788	3.4		
1789	3.7		
1790	3.8		
1791	3.8		
1792	4.0		
1793	4.0		
1794	4.1		
1795	3.9		
1796	4.2		
1797	4.1		
1798	4.7	42.6	17.9
1799	4.6	47.1	18.6
1800	5.3		
1801	5.5		
1802	5.6		
1803	6.5		
1804	6.1		

Source: See note to appendix table 13.1.

1755, when they constituted 3.4 percent of the Negro population. By 1760 their number had risen to 4.1 percent. For the next twenty years their number was lower than in 1760, but in the early 1780s it increased once again, and by 1804 the free Negroes constituted 9.3 percent of the total Negro population of the island. The proportion of free Negroes on Saint Jan was remarkably small. In 1783 they made up a mere 0.3 percent of the Negro population of that island, and by 1804 they had only increased to 0.6 percent.

Table 13.1 also suggests that the larger proportion of the freed Negroes were females. For the two years when it is possible to compute the proportions of the sexes within the total number of adult free Negroes in the Danish West Indies, the percentage of females is more than twice that of males. On Saint Thomas the sex ratio may be computed almost without interruption for every year between 1755 and 1804. The proportion of females invariably exceeds that of males, and in most years the proportion of females is more than twice that of males. The explanation is doubtless that a large number of free Negroes were freed mistresses.[14]

In October 1776, during Governor General P. Clausen's term of office, an ordinance was issued which tried to regulate the affairs of the free Negroes. It laid down, *inter alia*, that every free Negro should have a certificate of liberty (*frihedsbrev*), issued by the governor general. The statistical evidence presented here indicates that the free Negro population grew in the years subsequent to the ordinance, and that by the time of the abolition of the slave trade they constituted a significant element of the population. It also indicates that the free Negroes were not altogether without property, since they owned around 10 percent of the slaves on Saint Thomas. During the nineteenth century the number of free Negroes grew rapidly, and at the same time they became the center of social unrest, though this was not a factor in the decision to abolish the slave trade. By the time slavery was abolished in 1848, the free Negroes constituted a large proportion of the Negro population.[15]

Figure 13.4 shows the development of the slave population and the white population in the Danish West Indies between 1755 and 1804. While the slave population more than doubled to some 35,800 in 1804, the white population grew only from some 1,900 to some 3,100. The already marked numerical disproportion between the white overlords and the black slaves thus became even more striking during this period. It should be mentioned, though, that the tax rolls do not include the white garrison of the islands. For instance, there were 120 white soldiers on Saint Croix in 1761, in addition to the 1,753 white inhabitants listed on the tax roll. And in 1771 there were 50 white soldiers on Saint Thomas and 30 on Saint Jan, in addition to the respective white populations of 434 and 117 listed in the tax rolls of these islands. In 1802 there were 458 white noncommissioned officers and private soldiers in the Danish West Indies, in addition to the 3,014 whites listed on the tax rolls.[16]

Nevertheless, it is understandable that the fear of a Negro rebellion was constantly lurking in the mind of every white. The Danish West Indian society has been aptly compared to "a pyramidal structure, whose summit, the ruling class, consisted of whites, with a stratified infrastructure of free coloureds, a mixed group of privileged slaves (domestic slaves, skilled slaves, etc.), and the base of the pyramid, the field negroes."[17] The great slave rebellion on Saint Jan in 1733 was fresh in people's memories, and the draconian punishments inflicted on those black slaves suspected of an attempt at rebellion on Saint Croix in 1759 should undoubtedly be seen against the background of the planter society's phobia of slave rebellions.[18]

What lends particular interest to the demographic material presented here is the fact that it comprises both birth and death figures of the Negroes.[19] For Saint Croix, this information is included in the tax rolls from 1780 on, whereas it is only included in the rolls of Saint Thomas and Saint Jan from 1793. The figures throw light on what Philip D. Curtin, in his pathbreaking article "Epidemiology and the Slave Trade," has called "the most striking demographic peculiarity of the South Atlantic System," viz., "its failure to produce a self-sustaining slave population in tropical America."[20] On the basis of the figures in the appendix, the rate of natural decrease of the slave population of Saint Croix during the twenty-five years from 1780 to 1804 averaged 1.1 percent annually.

Figure 13.5, which shows the mortality rate and the birth rate per 1,000 for Saint Croix from 1780 to 1804, indicates that tropical storms and epidemics were an important cause of the high mortality rate. It is thus seen that the mortality rate was frequently above the "normal" level. Incidentally, we know from other sources that in the very years 1782–83 and 1789 there were epidemics of smallpox and measles on Saint Croix, and that there were an epidemic and a crop failure in 1799 and 1800, respectively. In contrast, the birth rate per 1,000 is not only lower but also does not display much variation.[21]

In table 13.2 the percentage rate of natural decrease has been calculated for ten-year periods for the individual islands, insofar as the source material permits. This reveals interesting regional variations. On Saint Croix, during the last two decades before abolition, the

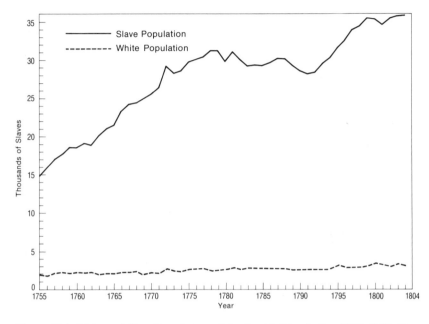

Figure 13.4 White and Slave Populations of the Danish West Indies, 1755–1804. Data from chapter appendix.

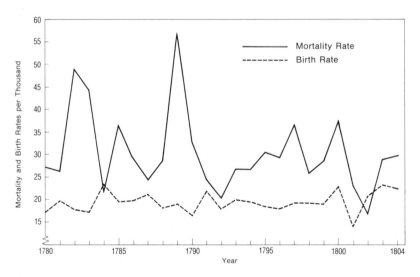

Figure 13.5 Mortality and Birth Rates (per 1,000) of Saint Croix, 1780–1804. Data from chapter appendix.

marked excess of mortality over fertility in the slave population suggests that the slave population was not on its way to becoming self-sustaining. The rate of natural decrease was lower on Saint Jan than on Saint Croix, while only on Saint Thomas was there an annual growth.

It would be tempting to explain the population decline of Saint Croix by the fact that the island had a higher proportion of plantation slaves than Saint Thomas, since it is generally assumed that slaves on large sugar plantations suffered from the highest mortality rate.[22] In addition, regional differences between Saint Thomas and Saint Croix might be explained by reference to Curtin's theory on the importance of epidemiological factors in the ability of the slave population to sustain itself by natural reproduction. At the beginning of European expansion there were three main areas, with different epidemic diseases, bordering the southern Atlantic: (1) Europe and North Africa, (2) tropical Africa, and (3) tropical America. People who moved from one of these areas to another were particularly vulnerable to new kinds of epidemic disease, just as they themselves carried new diseases into the area in question. In this connection, however, the point is that the decline in the slave population, according to Curtin, lessened as a gradually increasing proportion of the Negro population came to consist of Creole, rather than African, slaves, though this drop is also explained by the decline in average age as the older African population died off.[23] The proportion of Creole slaves was larger on Saint Thomas than on Saint Croix, since Saint Thomas had been colonized more than half a century before Saint Croix.

It is of interest to compare the Danish figures with rates of natural decrease of the slave populations of other West Indian islands. Richard B. Sheridan provides the following percentages for the rate of natural decrease on Jamaica:

1676–1700	3.1
1701–25	3.7
1726–50	3.5
1751–75	2.5
1776–1800	2.0

The corresponding figures for Barbados are even higher. Curtin estimates that the rate of natural decrease varied between 1 and 4 percent.[24] It may thus be concluded that if a comparison is made between the excess of deaths over births for the Danish West Indies, computed on the basis of the tax rolls, and figures from other West Indian islands, the Danish figures would appear to be relatively low, especially

Table 13.2
Annual Rate of Natural Reproduction of Slave Population (by percentage)

Period	Saint Thomas	Saint Jan	Saint Croix	Danish West Indies	Schimmel-mann's 4 plantations: la Princesse, la Grange, Caroline, and Thomas	Schimmel-mann's 3 plantations: la Princesse, la Grange, and Caroline
1773–82					− 1.1	− 0.8
1783–92			− 1.2			
1793–1802	0.5	− 0.3	− 0.9	− 0.6		
1816–24			− 1.1			
1825–34			− 0.5			
1835–44	− 0.8	0.4	− 0.7	− 0.6		

Note: The figures up to and including 1802 for Saint Thomas, Saint Jan, Saint Croix and the Danish West Indies have been taken from appendix table 13.A1. The figures for Schimmelmann's four plantations have been taken from a specification found among the records of the Negro trade commission in the Bundle "Dokumenter vedk. kommissionen for negerhandelens bedre indretning og ophævelse, samt efterretninger om negerhandelen og slaveriet i Vestindien 1783–1806," in Vestindisk-guineisk Rente- og Generaltoldkammer National Archives, Copenhagen. The figures have been paraphrased by Degn, *Die Schimmelmanns*, p. 79. In appendix G to the report of the Negro trade commission of 28 December 1791, also to be found in the above-mentioned bundle, the figures are given for three of the four plantations mentioned: the figures for the plantation "Thomas" have been excluded. The figures for the years 1816 onward have been taken from L. Rothe, "Om populationsforholdene i de danske vestindiske kolonier og fornemlig på St. Croix," (manuscript dated Copenhagen, 1847, pp. 6, 84, in Manuscript Collection VII D 5, National Archives, Copenhagen). Rothe, a West Indian civil servant, based his investigation on the tax rolls and census returns (see Merete Green-Pedersen, "Negerlovgivningen i dansk Vestindien," p. 9f., cited in Note 1 to text). Rothe asserts that the number of deaths before 1820 is too low, since some planters reported newly imported slaves in lieu of deceased slaves in order to conceal illegal imports. The following formula has been used in the calculations:

$$i = \frac{\left(\sum_{t=1}^{t=n} SF - \sum_{t=1}^{t=n} SD\right) 100}{\sum_{t=1}^{t=n} ST}$$

i = annual rate of natural reproduction of the slave population (in percent)
SF = number of slaves born
SD = number of slaves died
ST = total number of slaves

for the earlier periods. According to the tax rolls, then, the ability of the slave population in the Danish West Indies to sustain itself by natural reproduction seems to have been relatively good towards the end of the eighteenth century, although there was still an excess of mortality over fertility.

It is now necessary to relate these demographic findings to the deliberations of the commission that was set up in 1791 to study the abolition of the slave trade. In order to shed light on the general demographic development, the commission obtained from the Central Customs Department the tax roll figures for the Negroes on Saint Croix for 1780–90, including the figures of Negroes' births and deaths.[25] However, no figures for Saint Thomas and Saint Jan were obtained. On the basis of these data, the commission computed the annual mortality rate at 1 in 28 (35.7 per 1,000), and the birth rate at 1 in 51 (19.6 per 1,000). Special concern was caused by the low birth rate, and a number of reasons for it were stated, particularly the excessive proportion of males, unstable family relations, the lack of care for infants and pregnant females, and the large number of domestics. In short, the commission thought that the causes of the low fertility rate could be found in their unsatisfactory social conditions, and believed it possible to raise the fertility rate by improving the Negroes' standard of living.[26]

In this respect, the commission was in agreement with Thomas Clarkson's book *An Essay on the Impolicy of the African Slave Trade*, published in 1788, in which he observed: "I have now given a short history of no less than *twentysix* plantations. From these, and others in a similar situation, it will appear, that where there have been any favourable circumstances, such as the proper proportion of the sexes in one, gentle treatment in a second, any indulgence in point of labour in a third, and the like, *there* the slaves *have uniformly increased*: that where the contrary have taken place, *there* they have decreased, and *have been in want of supplies*."[27] Many of the examples referred to by Clarkson were adopted almost verbatim in the report of the Danish Negro trade commission.[28] The problem of encouraging the West Indian Negro population to reproduce itself by improving social conditions was one that occupied many reformist planters in the era of the democratic revolutions, notably Ernst Schimmelmann of the Danish West Indies, Samuel Martin of Antigua, Thomas Mills of Saint Kitts and Nevis, and John Pinney of Nevis.[29]

Ernst Schimmelmann's enthusiasm enabled the Danish commission to obtain statistical information from the Schimmelmann estates, which showed that a more humane treatment of the Negroes could produce improvements in their fertility.[30] The figures that the commission received came from the four Schimmelmann plantations of la Princesse, la Grange, Caroline, and Thomas, and covered the years 1773–82. The excess of mortality over fertility can be calculated at 1.1 percent on the basis of the figures received (see table 13.2). However, the commission used the figures for only three of the plantations, with the figures for the Thomas plantation omitted. The principal figures of the three plantations were put into appendix G of the commission's report. The rate of natural decrease calculated on the basis of these figures works out at 0.8 percent (see table 13.2). Since the commission's purpose in appendix G was to demonstrate that the fertility of the Negroes could be increased on model plantations (on the Schimmelmann estates the fertility rate was computed at 1 in 35 [28.6 per 1,000] as against 1 in 51 [19.6 per 1,000] on plantations generally), the suppression of the figures for the Thomas plantation raises the issue whether the commission was manipulating the figures it had obtained.[31] There is, however, one other possible explanation. The statistical data which the commission collected on normal plantations were exclusively from Saint Croix, and the three model plantations from which figures were quoted were expressly referred to in the heading of appendix G as "the Schimmelmann plantations on Saint Croix."[32]

It seems natural to conclude this comparative analysis of the considerations of the Negro trade commission and the factual demographic developments by trying to answer two important questions. Is it, to begin with, reasonable to assume that the commission had faith in its own economic arguments? and secondly, was there in fact a positive "natural reproduction" in the Danish West Indies in the nineteenth century?

Referring to the role of economic considerations in the British debate on the slave trade, Howard Temperley has said that it is "exceedingly difficult" to prove the role played by such arguments. He refers especially to Roger Anstey's demonstration of the fact that, at the passing of the 1806 bill to ban the British slave trade to foreign colonies, British abolitionists appeared as champions of the national interest and concealed their humanitarian motives. Temperley goes on to conclude, "As anyone familiar with the debate will testify, it is no more unusual to find humanitarians using economic arguments than to find their opponents using humanitarian ones."[33]

It should be stated that there is probably no final solution to the problem of the importance of the economic considerations behind the Danish edict of 1792 on the slave trade. I merely present those arguments which convince me that it is more justifiable to regard the demographic calculations of the commission as the decisive factor in satisfying the leading circles that they could afford to be humane, rather than to regard them as a mere cloak for humanitarians interested in concealing their real motives. I am thus supporting the economic interpretation insofar as the Danish government believed that the country could afford to carry out reform legislation. But I am not attempting to interpret the reform legislation as an excuse for economic gain. In the first place, the report of the Danish Negro trade commission was secret, and it seems fair to assume that in such a document arguments and motives are presented more freely than in, for instance, a parliamentary debate. Even if the demographic calculations of the commission were primitive, measured by present-day standards, and even if some of the use of the demographic material seems bewildering to us, we would hardly be justified in claiming that the commission deliberately wanted to present a distorted picture of slave demography in the West Indies.[34]

To this should be added that not only do the demographic and economic arguments of the commission correspond to those of contemporary abolitionists (Clarkson, for instance), but the whole tenor of the commission's report is consonant with contemporary capitalist ideas, such as those of Adam Smith, about freedom and prosperity going hand in hand.[35] As already shown by Trier, and later confirmed by the present author and by Degn, the secret report of the commission spoke of the abolition of slavery itself as the final aim. This vision of freedom, however, did not appear in a published extract of the report, largely because of apprehension about the planters' reaction.[36] The idea of prosperity was much easier to promote. This was placed in the preamble of the edict, which summarized the investigations of the commission in this way: "From the Results of these Enquiries, we are convinced that it is possible, and will be advantageous to our West-India Islands, to desist from the farther Purchase of new Negroes, when once the Plantations are stocked with a sufficient Number for the Propagation and the Cultivation of the Lands."[37]

Finally, the assessment of the importance of the economic considerations behind the drafting of the Danish edict depends on the overall interpretation by the historian of the statements and actions of the central characters. There is a consensus among historians that Ernst Schimmelmann, minister of finance, occupied a key position. As minister of finance, Schimmelmann drafted politico-economic reports, but he was not, as was William Wilberforce, the author of ideological pamphlets. Elsewhere, I have championed the view that the main theme running through Schimmelmann's policy was his desire to see the problem of the reproduction of the slave population solved before he carried out the definitive ban on slave imports. Schimmelmann therefore favored a *gradual* abolition rather than the *immediate* abolition promoted by Wilberforce and his circle. Richard Sheridan will suggest that the policy of the Danish minister of finance was thus a counterpart to the policy on the slave trade championed in 1791–92 by William Pitt, the British prime minister, and his close adviser Henry Dundas.[38]

The second main question concerns the slave demography of the Danish West Indies in the nineteenth century. Was there a positive rate of "natural reproduction" or not? Comprehensive demographic material also exists which helps to elucidate this problem, and on the basis of this material a West Indian civil servant drafted a report in 1847. The report makes it possible to calculate a series of figures for the excess of mortality over fertility for the slave population in the Danish West Indies during the first half of the nineteenth century (see table 13.2). The rate of natural decrease for the slave population of Saint Croix for the quarter century 1816–40 was 0.7 percent, compared to 1.1 percent during the period 1780–1804; the improvement would seem only marginal. There were even cases of increased rates of decrease. According to the tax rolls for the decade 1793–1802, the slave population of Saint Thomas displayed an annual increase of 0.5 percent as a result of natural reproduction, whereas in the period 1835–44 that island had an annual rate of natural decrease of 0.8 percent. On Saint Jan, on the other hand, the population had an excess of mortality over fertility of 0.3 percent during the years between 1793 and 1802, while between 1835 and 1844 there was a rate of natural increase of 0.4 percent annually.[39] The rate of natural decrease for Saint Croix was 1.2 percent between 1783 and 1792, and 0.9 percent between 1793 and 1802. Between 1816 and 1824 it stood at 1.1 percent. During the decades 1825–34 and 1835–44 it was 0.5 percent and 0.7 percent, respectively. For the Danish West Indies as a whole, the excess mortality over fertility was the same from 1793 to 1802 and from 1835 to 1844, viz., 0.6 percent, despite the fact that the age pyramid of the population must have been much closer to "normal" thirty years after abolition of the trade.

It may be said therefore that the reproductive ability of the slave population changed only insignificantly from the last twenty years of the eighteenth century to the three decades following the Napoleonic wars.[40] This somewhat surprising conclusion should be viewed against Stanley L. Engerman's statement that it "is probable that the

West Indian birth rates increased after the closing of the slave trade. . . ." And it may be added that in the third quarter of the nineteenth century Saint Croix was still afflicted by an excess of deaths over births. This is the background for the immigration of free colored labor, sponsored by Governor V. L. Birch and others, during this period.[41] But since the great reform plans of the Negro trade commission of 1791–92 were never carried out,[42] the absence of an improvement in the reproductive abilities of the Negroes in the early nineteenth century cannot be used to measure the effects of these plans.

The historical debate on the abolition of the Danish slave trade displays some parallels to its British counterpart, notably in its discussion on how much weight to attach to humanitarian as opposed to economic factors. Some historians have hailed the driving force behind Danish abolition, Ernst Schimmelmann, the minister of finance, as an idealist and abolitionist. On the other hand, it has been emphasized that the demographic calculations that were carried out on his initiative were in their essence an enquiry into whether the Danish government could afford to be humane. Since the debate on Danish abolition has largely turned on demography, it is natural to investigate the actual development of the Danish West Indian population. According to the surviving tax rolls the slave population of the Danish West Indies, when compared to the rest of the West Indies, had only a small excess of mortality over fertility towards the close of the eighteenth century, and on Saint Thomas it was in fact self-sustaining. The Negro trade commission made use of the figures of the tax rolls from Saint Croix, and interpreted them in the light of the contemporary assumption that a slave population could be made self-sustaining by social reform. This assumption was part and parcel of the abolitionist ideology, for example that of Thomas Clarkson, and it went hand in glove with contemporary capitalist ideology, and in particular with Adam Smith's idea that freedom and prosperity go hand in hand. Therefore it is not surprising that the Danish Negro trade commission of 1791 concluded that the Negro population of the Danish West Indies could be made self-sustaining if the slave trade was abolished gradually. Keeping in mind the demographic knowledge of the age, there is no reason to suspect the Negro trade commission of conscious manipulation of its statistical information. Finally, it may be added that in the 1830s and 1840s there was still an excess of births over deaths in the slave population in the Danish West Indies.

Appendix Table 13.1
Negro Population of the Danish West Indies, 1755–1804

Year	Saint Thomas Slaves Total	Births	Deaths	Free Negroes	Saint Jan Slaves Total	Births	Deaths	Free Negroes	Saint Croix Slaves Total	Births	Deaths	Free Negroes	Danish West Indies Total	Slaves Births	Deaths	Free Negroes
1755	3949			138	2031				8,897				14,877			
1756	3853			136	2041				9,956				15,850			
1757	3947			133	1991				11,031				16,969			
1758	3838			131	2078				11,807				17,723			
1759	3822			139	1983				12,792				18,597			
1760	3618			153	1991				12,956				18,565			
1761	3632			118	2020				13,489				19,141			
1762	3712			77	1969				13,236				18,917			
1763	3705			54	1986				14,425				20,116			
1764	3664			65	1974				15,392				21,030			
1765	3734			72	2024				15,699				21,457			
1766	3922			69	2164				17,198				23,284			
1767	4006				2192				17,970				24,168			
1768	4148			87	2303				17,952				24,403			
1769	4320			85	2215				18,332				24,867			
1770	4297			67	2302				18,884				25,483			
1771	4477			68	2432				19,401				26,310			
1772	4397			53	2431				22,251			157	29,079			
1773	4296			52	2324				21,698			361	28,318			
1774	3980			55	2293				22,350			336	28,623			
1775	3979			50	2355				23,384			368	29,718			
1776	4167			39	2398											
1777	4542			55	2482				23,403			382	30,427			
1778	4634			58	2454				24,067			371	31,155			
1779	4515			60	2497				24,226			366	31,238			

Appendix Table 13.1, *continued*

| | Saint Thomas | | | | Saint Jan | | | | Saint Croix | | | | Danish West Indies | | | |
| | Slaves | | | Free Negroes | Slaves | | | Free Negroes | Slaves | | | Free Negroes | Slaves | | | Free Negroes |
Year	Total	Births	Deaths		Total	Births	Deaths		Total	Births	Deaths		Total	Births	Deaths	
1780	4436			75	2285				23,037	398	625	374	29,758			
1781	4816			88	2388				23,803	470	623	408	31,007			
1782	4791			89	2371				22,856	407	1118	425	30,018			
1783	4700			248	2259			6	22,192	383	983	513	29,151			767
1784	4629			249	2306			6	22,326	518	485		29,261			
1785	4618			184	2258			34	22,359	437	816		29,235			
1786	4703			180	2322			21	22,539	444	658	863	29,564			1064
1787	4835			176	2293			34	22,996	487	561	884	30,124			1094
1788	4860			179	2289			7	22,971	419	656	889	30,120			1075
1789	4633			161	2200			8	22,470	426	1278	953	29,303			1122
1790	4342			175	1994			24	22,218	366	731	936	28,554			1135
1791	4254			176	1864			15	22,031	482	540	926	28,149			1117
1792	4279			201	1917			15	22,240	400	451	971	28,436			1187
1793	4498	62	15	209	2004	45	23	9	23,017	460	616	1010	29,519	567	654	1228
1794	4615	51	31	243	2008	31	18	10	23,719	463	633	1053	30,342	545	682	1306
1795	4722	53	9	198	2006	36	41	12	24,833	463	760	1070	31,561	552	810	1280
1796	4922	64	20	239	2109	29	34	15	25,445	458	748	1164	32,476	551	802	1418
1797	5383	76	28	252	2145	18	37	9	26,393	509	966	1186	33,921	603	1031	1447
1798	5474	25	17	274	2247	18	35	7	26,643	513	690	1413	34,364	556	742	1694
1799	5755	54	61	358	2503	37	61	10	27,127	515	776	1320	35,385	606	898	1688
1800	5887	51	31	714	2430	51	61	40	26,988	616	1009	1230	35,305	718	1101	1984
1801	5587	83	49	590	2535	44	41	29	26,454	373	614	1400	34,576	500	704	2019
1802	5814	77	85	635	2531	39	54	33	27,007	560	455	1434	35,352	676	594	2102
1803	5905	96	63	761	2650	54	45	61	27,161	634	788	1656	35,716	784	896	2478
1804	5882	60	48	602	2604	37	26	17	27,351	612	816	1694	35,837	709	890	2313

Note: The figures have been taken from the West Indian tax rolls which are preserved at the National Archives, Copenhagen, among the West Indian revised accounts. For Saint Thomas, the tax rolls have been preserved for the years 1755–56, 1758–66, and 1768–1804; for Saint Jan, for 1755–66 and 1768–1804; and for Saint Croix, for 1758–75, 1780–83, and 1786–1804. For the remaining years, the figures have been gleaned from contemporary extracts of the tax rolls. The figures for Saint Thomas for 1757 have thus been taken from a custumal labelled "Om Westindien," which is preserved in V-g Rtk. The figures for Saint Thomas and Saint Jan for 1767 are from pp. 342–43 and p. 339 respectively of another custumal (with a triangle on its spine), preserved in the same record holding. The figures for Saint Croix for 1755 have been taken from "Martfeld's Collections," vol. 3, preserved with the above custumals. The custumal with the triangle on the spine has also furnished the figures for Saint Croix for 1756–57 and 1777–79 (pp. 340–41, 529). The figures for St. Croix for 1784–85 have been taken from appendix D of the report of the Negro trade commission of 28 December 1791, preserved in the V-g Rtk bundle "Dokumenter vedk. kommissionen for negerhandelens bedre indretning og ophævelse samt efterretninger om negerhandelen og slaveriet i Vestindien 1783–1806."

In most instances the tax rolls contain summaries, from which the figures in the appendix have been taken. Where errors have been found in the summaries the figures have been taken from the actual tax rolls.

The contemporary tax roll extracts mentioned above also cover a large number of years from which the original tax rolls have survived. A comparison has proved that the extracts are correct, save for the unavoidable errors made in copying. The figures from some of these tax rolls have been used by a number of authors, including **Rolf Berger**, *Die Inseln St. Thomas und St. Croix* (Hamburg, 1934), pp. 115, 118; P. P. Sveistrup. *Bidrag til de tidligere dansk-vestindiske øers økonomiske historie* (Copenhagen, 1942), p. 15; J. O. Bro-Jørgensen, "Dansk Vestindien indtil 1755," in Johannes Brøndsted, ed., *Vore gamle tropekolonier*, 2d ed., 8 vols. (Copenhagen, 1966), 1:270–71; Jens Vibæk, "Dansk Vestindien 1755–1848," in Brøndsted, ed., *Vore gamle tropekolonier*, 2d ed., 2:102–3; Svend E. Green-Pedersen, "The Scope and Structure of the Danish Negro Slave Trade," *Scandinavian Economic History Review* 19 (1971):150, 157; Green-Pedersen, "The History of the Danish Negro Slave Trade, 1733–1807," *Revue française d'histoire d'outre-mer* 62 (1975): 204.

NOTES

The author wishes to thank Aase Bechsgaard, née Rothausen Nielsen, Grethe Bentzen, Jørgen Bach Christensen, Merete Green-Pedersen, Peter Hoxcer Jensen, Hans Christian Johansen, Henning H. Knap, and Richard B. Sheridan for allowing reference to be made to unpublished papers. He also wishes to thank Troels Dahlerup, Jørgen Elklit, Stanley L. Engerman, and Axel Kjær Sørensen for providing valuable suggestions. Finally, he wishes to thank Sheila and Jørgen Clausager for translating the paper into English. The sole responsibility for views expressed as well as for errors and omissions rests with the author.

1 The basic work on the abolition of Negro slavery in the Danish West Indies is H. Lawaetz, *Peter v. Scholten. Vestindiske tidsbilleder fra den sidste generalguvernørs dage* (Copenhagen, 1940). The following supplementary investigations may be mentioned: Merete Green-Pedersen, "Negerlovgivningen i dansk Vestindien 1755–1848, specielt med henblik på den engelske slaveemancipations betydning" (M.A. diss., Aarhus University, 1973); and Grethe Bentzen, "Debatten om det dansk-vestindiske negerslaveri 1833–1848 med særligt henblik på de igennem tidsskriftpressen og stænderdebatterne udtrykte holdninger" (M.A. diss., Aarhus University, 1976).

2 C. A. Trier, "Det dansk-vestindiske negerindførselsforbud af 1792," *Historisk Tidsskrift*, 7 ser. 5 (1904–5): 405–508; Reginald Coupland, *The British Anti-Slavery Movement* (1933; reprint ed., London, 1964); Thomas Clarkson, *The History of the Rise, Progress and Accomplishment of the Abolition of the African Slave Trade by the British Parliament*, 2 vols. (London, 1808; photographic reprint ed., London, 1968).

3 Jens Vibæk, "Dansk Vestindien 1755–1848," in Johannes Brøndsted, ed., *Vore gamle tropekolonier*, 2d ed., 8 vols. (Copenhagen, 1966), 2:162–89. A highly articulate criticism of the Danish abolitionist tradition may, incidentally, be found in Kelvin Lindemann's novel *Gyldne kæder* (Copenhagen, 1948). Referring to the transitional ten-year period before the enforcement of the ban on Negro imports, Lindemann writes that "with the dexterity of a conjurer Schimmelmann had created the illusion that this problematic procedure, which actually put a price on ruthless manhunting during the transitional period, was the triumph of humanitarianism" (p. 309). Lindemann's novel is a continuation of the novel *Huset med det grønne træ* (Copenhagen, 1942). The main character in these novels, which are (in Goethe's words) a mixture of "Dichtung und Wahrheit," is Paul E. Isert, the Danish abolitionist. See also Eric Williams, *Capitalism and Slavery* (1944; reprint ed., London, 1964), particularly chap. 8, "The New Industrial Order."

4 Svend E. Green-Pedersen, "Danmarks ophævelse af negerslavehandelen: Omkring tilblivelsen af forordningen af 16. marts 1792," *Arkiv* 3 (1969–71):19–37.

5 Christian Degn, *Die Schimmelmanns im atlantischen Dreieckshandel. Gewinn und Gewissen* (Neumünster, 1974). The book is treated in greater detail by Svend E. Green-Pedersen, "The Economic Considerations Behind the Danish Abolition of the Negro Slave Trade," in Henry A. Gemery and Jan S. Hogendorn, eds., *The Uncommon Market: Essays on the Economic History of the Atlantic Slave Trade* (New York, 1979), pp. 408 ff. Degn's book should be seen in the light of German research tradition, especially "die geistes-geschichtliche Methode"; it represents an attempt at depicting as an entity both the material and the spiritual cultures of the era of the slave trade.

6 Degn, *Die Schimmelmanns*, pp. 256, 261.

7 Roger T. Anstey, *The Atlantic Slave Trade and British Abolition, 1760–1810* (London, 1975); Seymour Drescher, *Econocide: British Slavery in the Era of Abolition* (Pittsburgh, 1977). On the commission's report, see Svend E. Green-Pedersen, "Economic Considerations," pp. 399 ff.

8 On these contributions, see Henning H. Knap, "Danish Anti-Slavery Literature before 1792" (paper presented to the Symposium on the Abolition of the Atlantic Slave Trade, University of Aarhus, October 1978).

9 Commenting on the abolition of British slavery, Michael Craton has written, "The Enlightenment had to demonstrate that slavery was not indispensable before idealism could come closer to success" (Craton, *Sinews of Empire: A Short History of British Slavery* [London, 1974], p. 254). In my opinion, the same holds true in the case of the abolition of the Danish slave trade. To complete the picture, it should be mentioned that Georg Nørregård and later Henrik Jeppesen connected the abolition of the slave trade with the incipient founding of plantations in Africa (Nørregård, *Danish Settlements in West Africa, 1658–1850* [Boston, 1966], pp. 172–85; Jeppesen, "Danish Plantations on the Gold Coast, 1788–1850," *Geografisk Tidsskrift* 65 [1966]: 48–88). However, in its report the Negro trade commission did not use this argument for the abolition of the slave trade; see Svend E. Green-Pedersen, "Economic Considerations," pp. 411 f.

10 The *matrikler* are a continuation of the *landlister* (tax rolls) from the period of the West India Guinea Company. As opposed to the *matrikler*, the *landlister* do not contain summary extracts, and for this reason are not so suitable for demographic statistical use. Waldemar Westergaard, *The Danish West Indies under Company Rule* (New York, 1917), appendices H and I, compiled vital statistics for a few years on the basis of the *landlister*. On the reliability of the *landlister* see J. O. Bro-Jørgensen, "Dansk Vestindien indtil 1755," in Brøndsted, ed., *Vore gamle tropekolonier*, 2d. ed., 1:271. For earlier writers who have made partial use of these figures, see note to appendix table 13.A1.

11 Trier, "Det dansk-vestindiske negerindførselsforbud," p. 472. P. P. Sveistrup, *Bidrag til de tidligere dansk-vestindiske øers økonomiske historie med særligt henblik på sukkerproduktion og sukkerhandel* (Copenhagen, 1942), p. 17, n. 2.

12 C. N. David, in *Nyt statsoeconomisk Archiv* 1 (1843):287 ff. See also Svend E. Green-Pedersen, "The Scope and Structure of the Danish Negro Slave

Trade," *Scandinavian Economic History Review* 19 (1971):150. Hans Christian
Johansen, in chapter 12 of the present work, uses data from the records
of the Negro trade commission for 1804. According to the instructions to
the governor general, this information was to be collected by civil servants,
since the tax roll figures which had been supplied by the planters were
believed to be too small. After adjusting for town slaves, which the commission ignored, the tax roll figures are higher by 2,192 slaves than the
commission's figures. Birth data for 1804 from the two sources are almost
identical—717 in the commission figures and 709 in the tax rolls. In Johansen's opinion, 102 stillbirths are not included in the 717 births (see p.
226). Stillbirths and births of children who died within their first year are
not included in the birth figures of the tax rolls either; see A. F. Bergsøe,
Den danske stats Statistik, 4 vols. (Copenhagen, 1853), 4: 606 f. According
to section 2 of the edict of 16 July 1778, Negroes born in the current year
were exempt from the poll tax.

13 The tax rolls usually divide Negroes into four main groups: (1) capable
Negroes—completely able-bodied and taxable individuals; (2) Manquerons and Bosals—Negroes with defects and newly imported Negroes; (3)
adolescent Negroes between twelve and sixteen years of age; and (4) children below twelve years of age (see Vibæk, "Dansk Vestindien, 1755–
1848," pp. 102 ff). On the subject of the tax rolls themselves and on tax-
ation, see also Thomas Riis's detailed introduction to the inventory of the
tax rolls in the Rigsarkivet [National Archives], Copenhagen (hereafter
cited as RA). The reliability of the classification of the Negroes in the tax
rolls is supported, *inter alia*, by the fact that in the development phase of
Saint Croix there were unusually large numbers of Manquerons; see
Jørgen Bach Christensen, "Kolonisamfundet på St. Croix i sidste halvdel
af det 18. århundrede, med særligt henblik på aristokratiet blandt plan-
tageejerne" (M.A. diss., Aarhus University, 1978), p. 53.

14 The social status of free colored mistresses is elucidated by H. F. Garde,
"Anna Heegaard og Peter von Scholten," *Personalhistorisk Tidsskrift*, 13th
ser. 6 (1958): 25–37; Garde, "Generalguvernør Adrian Benoni Bentzon
og hans vestindiske efterkommere," ibid., 14th ser. 4 (1962): 9–22; Garde,
"Samboinden Charlotte Amalie Bernard og hendes efterkommere indtil
5. led," ibid., 15th ser. 5 (1971): 211–27. Governor generals such as A. B.
Bentzon, Peter v. Scholten, and others lived in what Admiral H. B. Dahlerup in his memoirs termed common-law marriages with colored women
(*Mit livs begivenheder*, ed. Joost Dahlerup, 2 vols. [Copenhagen, 1908–9],
2:47). On the free Negroes, see Eva Lawaetz, *Free Coloured in St. Croix,
1744–1816* (Christiansted, St. Croix, 1979); and Neville Hall, "Slave Laws
of the Danish Virgin Islands in the later Eighteenth Century," in Vera
Rubin and Arthur Tuden, eds., *Comparative Perspectives on Slavery in New
World Plantation Societies* (New York, 1977), pp. 174–86.

15 Merete Green-Pedersen, "Negerlovgivningen i dansk Vestindien," p. 8
and passim; here it is seen, for instance, that by 1836 the number of free

Negroes on Saint Thomas had risen to 5,417, or about one-half of the total Negro population on the island.

16 Custumal with a triangle on its spine, p. 344, in Diverse dokumenter, 1754–1848, Vestindisk-guineisk Rente-og Generaltoldkammer [West Indian-Guinean Exchequer and Central Customs Department] (hereinafter cited as V-g Rtk.), RA. In the same place one can find a detailed computation of the ratio of white men capable of bearing arms to capable Negroes (see the custumal labelled "Forskellige oplysninger" [miscellaneous information], vol. 5, pp. 103r, 103v, 104r).

17 Bach Christensen, "Kolonisamfundet på St. Croix," p. 45. See also Elsa V. Goveia, *Slave Society in the British Leeward Islands at the End of the Eighteenth Century* (New Haven and London, 1965), p. 251.

18 Bro-Jørgensen, "Dansk Vestindien indtil 1755," pp. 229 ff.; Westergaard, *Danish West Indies*, pp. 165 ff., and "Account of the Negro Rebellion on St. Croix, Danish West Indies, 1759," *Journal of Negro History* 11 (1926): 50–61.

19 It must be noted that only the crude mortality rate is calculated, since the data presented here have not been standardized with respect to age and sex. We should note, too, that the sex ratios and age structures of the Danish possessions must have been distorted by the heavy importation of slaves in the decade before abolition. We cannot therefore address the interesting question of whether the slave population would have been self-sustaining if the sex ratios and age pyramids had been "normal."

20 Philip D. Curtin, "Epidemiology and the Slave Trade," *Political Science Quarterly* 83 (1968): 190–216; the quotation is from p. 213.

21 See Stanley L. Engerman, "Some Economic and Demographic Comparisons of Slavery in the United States and the British West Indies," *Economic History Review* 29 (1976): 269. Concerning the epidemics in the 1780s, see p. 35 of the report of the Negro trade commission of 28 December 1791 in "Dokumenter vedk. kommissionen for negerhandelens bedre indretning og ophævelse, samt efterretninger om negerhandelen og slaveriet i Vestindien 1783–1806," V-g RtK. Concerning the epidemic in 1799 and the crop failure in 1800 see Vibæk, "Dansk Vestindien 1755–1848," pp. 140, 186, where a drought in 1789 is also mentioned.

22 See Richard B. Sheridan, "Sweet Malefactor: The Social Costs of Slavery and Sugar in Jamaica and Cuba, 1807–54," *Economic History Review* 29 (1976): 247.

23 Philip D. Curtin, "Epidemiology and the Slave Trade," pp. 190–216. See also Philip D. Curtin, *The Atlantic Slave Trade: A Census* (Madison, 1969), pp. 28 ff. For a comment on Curtin, see B. W. Higman, *Slave Population and the Economy of Jamaica, 1807–1834*, (Cambridge, 1976), pp. 134–38.

24 Richard B. Sheridan, "Mortality and the Medical Treatment of Slaves in the British West Indies," in Stanley L. Engerman and Eugene D. Genovese, eds., *Race and Slavery in the Western Hemisphere: Quantitative Studies* (Princeton, 1975), pp. 285–310, and especially the table on p. 309; Curtin,

Atlantic Slave Trade, p. 28. Craton estimates that by 1807 the mortality rate in Jamaica was 3 percent, while the birth rate was 2.5 percent (*Sinews of Empire*, p. 196). Like my own, Sheridan's percentages have not been compounded; further, Sheridan has not employed figures of births and deaths, but figures of the population and the slave imports. The West Indian customs accounts have been preserved for Christiansted and Frederiksted for a sufficient number of years to make it possible, by interpolation, to compute the net import of slaves into Saint Croix during the years 1755–79 and 1780–1804 at 27,485 and 17,294 slaves, respectively (see Svend E. Green-Pedersen, "Scope and Structure," tables 1 and 2). The rate of natural decrease for Saint Croix, calculated according to Sheridan's method, is 2.8 percent and 2.1 percent for the periods 1755–79 and 1780–1804, respectively. The excess of deaths over births computed by this method exceeds by 1 percent the figure arrived at by using the figures of births and deaths in the tax rolls; this is probably due to the omission in the tax rolls of both the births and deaths of infants who died before they were one year old. On the other hand, these figures for the mortality rate approximate Sheridan's Jamaican figures. Curtin's percentages, in contrast to Sheridan's, have been calculated on the principles of compound interest. By applying the same formula as Curtin, I have computed the excess of mortality over fertility for the Danish West Indies, 1733–1803, at 2 percent. (Svend E. Green-Pedersen, "The History of the Danish Negro Slave Trade, 1733–1807," *Revue française d'histoire d'outre-mer* 62 (1975): 205.

25 The figures in appendix D of the report of the Negro trade commission, giving the number of Negroes on Saint Croix for the years from 1780 to 1790 inclusive, have been taken from the tax rolls; see the note to appendix table 13.A1.

26 For a more detailed summary of the opinions of the commission, see Svend E. Green-Pedersen, "The Economic Considerations," pp. 403 ff.

27 Clarkson, *Essay on Impolicy*, 2d. ed. (London, 1788), pp. 91–92; Clarkson's italics. Degn expresses a similar opinion, commenting on plantations owned by the Society for the Propagation of the Gospel: "The treatment of the slaves cannot have been very Christian, as the death figures were six times as high as the birth figures" (*Die Schimmelmanns*, p. 58).

28 Report of the Negro trade commission, 28 Dec. 1791, pp. 47–50.

29 For a more detailed survey, see Svend E. Green-Pedersen, "The Economic Considerations," pp. 409 ff.

30 Ernst Schimmelmann's work on this problem was also familiar in British abolitionist circles; it is mentioned in Clarkson, *Essay on Impolicy*, p. 89.

31 On the four Schimmelmann plantations the birth rate was 28.3 per 1,000, compared to 29.1 per 1,000 on the three plantations listed in appendix G; the corresponding death rates were 39.3 and 37.1 per 1,000, respectively. On the Thomas plantation alone the birth rate was 25.5 per 1,000, and the death rate was 60.1 per 1,000. It was thus a plantation with an extraordinarily high death rate that was excluded from the commission's figures.

The commission calculated the death rate on the plantations listed in appendix G at 1 in 27, compared to 1 in 28 on plantations generally. Had the Thomas plantation been included, the figures would have been 1 in 25, compared to 1 in 28. The consequences of the suppression of the Thomas figures are thus limited. A more serious objection to the calculations of the commission is the fact that it compared the birth and death rates of the Schimmelmann plantations in 1773–82 with the rates of ordinary plantations in 1780–90, without taking into account that the slaves were not exposed to the same epidemic diseases in the two different periods.

32 On the statistical data, see the note to table 13.2; on the use made of the data, see Svend E. Green-Pedersen, "The Economic Considerations," p. 404 ff.; on the Schimmelmann plantations, see Degn, *Die Schimmelmanns*, p. 59 ff., from which it may be seen that the Thomas plantation was situated on Saint Thomas, and that the two large plantations included in appendix G, la Princesse and la Grange, were situated on Saint Croix, while Caroline was on Saint Jan. Thus the heading of appendix G is somewhat misleading.

33 Howard Temperley, "Capitalism, Slavery and Ideology," *Past and Present*, no. 75 (May, 1977), pp. 96f.; Anstey, *Atlantic Slave Trade*, chap. 15. Anstey quotes a letter from William Wilberforce, and concludes that Wilberforce suggested that the 1806 bill be passed "behind the cloak of national interest" (pp. 365 ff.).

34 See Hans Christian Johansen, "The Reality behind the Demographic Arguments," chapter 12 of this volume.

35 On Adam Smith's evaluation of the profitability of slavery, see Adam Smith, *Wealth of Nations*, Everyman's Library no. 412, 2 vols. (London, 1960), 1:72, 345. *Wealth of Nations* was translated into Danish and published in Copenhagen as early as 1779–80 by Søren Gyldendal. It is not my intention to question the fact that the economic policy of the Danish government after 1784 was late mercantilistic; my theory is merely that the basic idea of the Negro trade commission, that freedom and prosperity go hand in hand, coincides with one of Adam Smith's ideas. On Danish late mercantilism, see Hans Christian Johansen, *Dansk økonomisk politik i årene efter 1784* (Aarhus, 1968), and the review of it by Svend Aage Hansen in *Nationaløkonomisk Tidsskrift* 106 (1968): 191 ff.

36 Trier, "Det dansk-vestindiske negerindførselsforbud," pp. 429 ff.; Svend E. Green-Pedersen, "Danmarks ophævelse af negerslavehandelen," pp. 25 ff.; Degn, Die *Schimmelmanns*, p. 287.

37 Quoted from Elizabeth Donnan, ed., *Documents Illustrative of the History of the Slave Trade to America*, 4 vols. (New York, 1969), 2:616.

38 Svend E. Green-Pedersen, "Economic Considerations"; Richard B. Sheridan, "Slave Demography in the West Indies and the Abolition of the Slave Trade," chapter 14 of this volume. Schimmelmann has been portrayed as by far the largest slave owner of the Danish West Indies (Vibæk, "Dansk Vestindien 1755–1848," p. 166; Degn, *Die Schimmelmanns*, p. 79). It should

be noted, however, that Bach Christensen, by using the tax rolls, has demonstrated that the Anglo-Saxon McEvoy family, measured on a family basis, was a greater slave owner than the entailed Schimmelmann estate (Det schimmelmannske Fideikommis) ("Kolonisamfundet på St. Croix," table xxii). See also Joseph Evans Loftin, "The Abolition of the Danish Atlantic Slave Trade" (Ph.D. diss., Louisiana State University, 1977), pp. 151 ff., in which it is claimed that a mutilated English version of the Danish edict on *gradual* abolition was used by the Wilberforce group because it wanted *immediate* abolition.

39 This positive rate of natural increase on Saint Jan in the 1830s and 1840s is confirmed by the parish registers of the Moravian brethren in Emmaus parish. According to these registers, 780 children were baptized in 1833–48, while 578 adults and children were buried. I am indebted to Karen Fog Olwig, Ph.D., for these data.

40 In the absence of data on the age and sex structure of the population, as well as on emigration and manumissions, the conclusion must remain tentative. We should note, however, that the effect of the slave trade on the first two of these variables should have become progressively weaker in the decades after abolition, before disappearing within a generation or so of the ending of the trade. Table 13.2 suggests that the slave population was declining independently of these effects. The fact that there was an excess of deaths over births on Saint Croix in 1814–15 may also be seen from Eva Lawaetz, ed., *A Report from Governor General P. L. Oxholm to the Royal West Indian Chamber in Copenhagen* [Det kongelige vestindiske Kammer], dated May 4, 1816 (Christiansted, St. Croix, 1977), p. 2. Fertility and mortality in the Danish West Indies were the subject of a debate between S. C. Sarauw, a West Indian civil servant, and C. N. David, the Danish national economist, in *Nyt Statsoeconomisk Archiv* 1 (1843): 253–93. The gist of David's position in the debate was the liberal capitalistic ideology of freedom and prosperity going hand in hand. David was personally engaged in the issue of slavery, since in 1843, inspired by Britain, he had formed an abolitionist committee together with J. F. Schouw, D. G. Monrad, N. F. S. Grundtvig, and Jean-Antoine Raffard; Schouw, Monrad, and Grundtvig were prominent Danish cultural personalities, and Raffard was minister of the French Reformed congregation in Copenhagen (see Grethe Bentzen, "Debatten om det dansk-vestindiske negerslaveri," pp. 68 ff.).

41 Engerman, "Economic and Demographic Comparisons," p. 272; Rolf Berger, *Die Inseln St. Thomas und St. Croix* (Hamburg, 1934), p. 96. See also Aase Rothausen Nielsen, "Immigrationen af arbejdskraft til St. Croix 1860–78. En analyse og vurdering af immigrationen samt dens betydning for arbejdskraftens sammensætning og vilkår" (M.A. diss., University of Copenhagen, 1973), pp. 27–28; Peter Hoxcer Jensen, "Indførsel af fri arbejdskraft til St. Croix 1849–76, med særligt henblik på immigrations og arbejdslovgivningen" (M.A. diss., University of Aarhus, 1978), and "Plantagearbejdernes vilkår i dansk Vestindien fra slaveemancipationen til

øernes salg" (prize essay, University of Aarhus, 1979). Fridlev Skrubbel-trang connects this excess of mortality over fertility with the high infant mortality ("Dansk Vestindien 1848–1880," in Brøndsted, ed., *Vore gamle tropekolonier*, 2d ed., 3: 105); see also *Statistiske meddelelser*, 3d ser. 6 (1883): 164–65.

42 As early as 1905, C. A. Trier gave a negative appraisal when he said that "the only measure to be carried out, by and large, of those planned in 1792, was the granting of loans for the purchase of negroes" ("Det dansk-vestindiske negerindførselsforbud," p. 472).

CHAPTER 14: **Slave Demography in the British West Indies and the Abolition of the Slave Trade**

Richard B. Sheridan

DEMOGRAPHIC TRENDS BEFORE ABOLITION

The upsurge of interest in the Atlantic slave trade and in New World slavery in recent decades has led to lively debates and to the publication of numerous scholarly monographs and articles. Much has been learned, for example, about how many slaves were transported, from what parts of Africa they were obtained, how many died on the Middle Passage, and to what destinations in the New World the survivors were delivered.[1] Demographers of slavery in the West Indies and elsewhere have shown how the patterns of fertility and mortality have varied among urban and rural slaves and in areas of different crop types, slaveholding sizes, labor requirements, disease environments, and other variables.[2] Rather surprisingly, few studies show how the economic, demographic, and epidemiological characteristics of the slave trade and of plantation slavery were interrelated, both in time and space, and why it was so difficult to break what might be called the symbiotic relationship between the slave trade and a viable plantation labor force. It will be my task in this paper to explore the nature of this so-called symbiotic relationship with special reference to the island of Jamaica, to show how the planters reacted to various restrictions imposed on the slave trade and to the policies of slave amelioration they were urged to adopt by the British government, and why little success attended the efforts to implement these policies, even after abolition of the slave trade.

259

Philip Curtin has shown how epidemiological factors influenced economic decisions and economic patterns, the demography of tropical America, and the preference for Africans over other workers on West Indian plantations. He points to differences of immunity and vulnerability to disease among peoples who came to the West Indian islands from geographically remote environments. The immunity that resulted from the mutual adaptation by human host and infectious organisms broke down when people moved across the ocean from one disease environment to another. Unfamiliar diseases attacked newcomers who came to the West Indies from environments which provided no source of immunity. Failure to produce a self-sustaining slave population in tropical America was the most striking demographic peculiarity of the South Atlantic System, in Curtin's opinion. Because slaves were cheap in Africa and the cost of encouraging family life and reproduction in the West Indies was high, planters generally preferred to buy new recruits from Africa rather than to encourage a high birth rate in order to produce a self-perpetuating slave gang. Africans not only tended to outnumber creoles on the plantations, but the planters' preference for male workers led to an excess of males over females and to a lower birth rate than would be expected for a balanced population.[3]

It is Curtin's contention that the demographic history of the sugar colonies tends to fall into a regular pattern over time. He finds that the ratio of slave imports to population was very high during the initial period of settlement, a period when a high rate of natural decrease was associated with the abnormal age and sex structure. However, the ratio of creoles to African-born increased and the total slave population leveled off as a given island or colony reached full production. But slave imports continued on a limited scale to make up the deficit between deaths and births. Eventually the black population reached a point of natural increase, as was the case with Barbados soon after 1807, and with Jamaica by the 1840s.[4]

My own studies have related the demographic experience of the sugar colonies to such factors as rates of economic growth, slave prices, slave resistance, intensity of cultivation, and amelioration policies. Early slavery in these colonies, which dates from about 1640 with the launching of the sugar industry in Barbados, was comparatively mild. It gradually gave way to near-monoculture slavery, which was characterized by the consolidation of smallholdings into sugar plantations, rising land values, annual cropping of cane land, soil depletion and its correction by heavy applications of fertilizer, dependence on imported foodstuffs and other supplies and equipment, and a slave population which failed to reproduce itself. The age of the democratic revolutions witnessed some amelioration of slave conditions as a consequence of the campaign to abolish the slave trade, rising slave prices, trade interruption and destructive hurricanes during the American Revolution, and the long and bitter slave rebellion which threatened to spread from French Saint Domingue to the British sugar colonies.[5]

The demographic characteristics of the laboring population of the West Indies can be illustrated by reference to the island of Jamaica. Writing in 1793, Bryan Edwards estimated that 200,000 of the 250,000 slaves in Jamaica lived on plantations; the remainder lived on smallholdings and in the towns.[6] According to Michael Craton, the proportion of slaves involved either directly or indirectly in the production of sugar might be calculated as high as 75 percent of all slaves, with the average integrated sugar plantation and its food-growing and cattle-grazing appendages containing about 240 slaves.[7] Instead of forming a perfectly symmetrical pyramid, the diagram illustrating the slave population on such a plantation assumed the shape of a lopsided Christmas tree. The low birth rate was represented by the narrow trunk, the bulging branches by the planters' preference for slaves in the fifteen to twenty-five age group who were recruited by means of the slave trade, and the narrow top of the tree by the relatively few older slaves. The tree was lopsided because of the imbalance of the sexes.[8]

During the era of the slave trade the African-born slaves not only suffered higher death rates than those born in Jamaica but they were also much less fertile. Craton estimates that the ratio of African-born to creole slaves in the island declined from over 90 percent in 1710 to about two-thirds in 1788 and to approximately one-half in 1807. Although slave cargoes consisted of about three males to every two females, there was a tendency for females to outlive males, which compensated, in part, for the unbalanced sex ratio. The annual Jamaican rate of population decrease was approximately 4 percent in 1701; it fell to under 2 percent in 1790, and to about 1 percent in 1808.[9]

Recent studies confirm the importance of the English slave trade to Jamaica. This trade, writes Herbert S. Klein, "is clearly the largest regional slave trade within the English-American context, and is comparable to the other leading 18th-century trades, the French and the Portuguese."[10] Klein finds that the age and sex ratios of the slaves brought to Jamaica were similar to those of Africans brought to the other important trading zones in the eighteenth century. The cargoes were dominated by males and adults, with the majority of slaves being men in their prime years of life. There was marked seasonality in the arrival of slavers, the key importing period being the months of November through March. Mortality on the Middle Passage, which ranged upward of 100 deaths for every 1,000 slaves leaving the African coast in the century before 1790, declined in the 1790s to 56 per 1,000 for the slaves carried in 301 British vessels. Klein attributes the decline in mortality to such factors as the parliamentary acts of 1788 and 1799 to regulate the slave trade, the use of more specialized ships (which contributed to the increased speed and efficiency of the trade), and the introduction of inoculation and other primitive health measures.[11]

MORBIDITY AND THE NEW WORLD ENVIRONMENT

The blacks who were forced to participate in the most massive intercontinental migration before the industrial era were uprooted from their African culture, often marched long distances to the barracoons on the coast, crammed into ships to cross that terrible belt of ocean known as the Middle Passage, and sold and distributed to plantations and mines, where they were seasoned for labor after their arrival in the New World. Debility, sickness, and death marked each step in the transfer from the African's homeland to the place of his or her forced labor. On the coast of Senegambia, for example, slaves awaiting shipment at times died of malnutrition as a consequence of drought, war, and financial collapse.[12] Slaves from the Bight of Biafra region, according to Klein, experienced the highest rates of mortality for Africans crossing in the Middle Passage. Because of their vegetable diet—principally yams and a little fish—the people from this part of Africa were said to be "weakly" and "liable to disorders."[13]

Since every Guinea ship was the meeting place of geographically remote disease environments, it is not surprising that the human cargoes of such ships became breeding grounds for diseases that originated in Africa, Europe, and the Americas. On the Middle Passage blacks and whites suffered from dysentery, diarrhea, ophthalmia, malaria, smallpox, yellow fever, scurvy, measles, typhoid fever, hookworm, tapeworm, sleeping sickness, yaws, syphilis, leprosy, and elephantiasis. Slaves also suffered friction sores, ulcers, and injuries and wounds resulting from accidents, fights, and whippings. Sir William Dolben told the House of Commons that the poor, unhappy wretches were chained together hand and foot and "crammed together, like herrings in a barrel." In this condition "they generated putrid disorders and all sorts of dangerous diseases" which frequently proved fatal.[14]

It was tragic that the slaves were transferred from the pestilential disease environment of the Guinea vessels to disease-ridden ports to await the day of sale. Sanitary arrangements were said to be unknown in the port of Kingston, where the greater part of the slaves entering Jamaica were landed; "dunghills abounded, and from these the ruts in the streets and lanes were filled up after every heavy rain. In the early morning negro slaves might be seen bearing open tubs from the various dwellings, and emptying their indescribable contents into the sea."[15] A close reading of the *Journals of the Assembly of Jamaica* reveals that few attempts were made to inspect and to quarantine ships entering Jamaica with slaves infected with smallpox and other contagious diseases.[16] Kingston, Jamaica, and presumably other British West Indian ports, lagged far behind Cartagena and other Spanish ports where slaves and slaving vessels underwent thorough health inspections; moreover, instead of being quartered in the towns of Spanish America, new slaves were kept on outlying farms and restored to health before they were sold.[17]

Sugar plantations in the slavery era were agro-industrial enterprises which combined cane growing with the manufacture of raw sugar. They employed hoe cultivators and draft animals in units of production which were large by comparison with plantations that produced such crops as cotton, indigo, and coffee. Slave morbidity and mortality on such sugar plantations were related both directly and indirectly to unhygienic conditions, accidents, suicides, punishment, diet, and work loads. Since sugar plantations were often situated in close proximity to the ports where Europeans and Africans intermingled, their inhabitants were vulnerable to communicable diseases. Plantations occupied relatively flat, lowland areas which were often poorly drained, and where stagnant water attracted disease-carrying mosquitos and flies. Since privies were seldom provided or used, slaves were prone to "go a bush" for nature's calls. Excrement and garbage strewn around the slave quarters attracted insects, rats, and vultures. Septic organisms were ingested by children who played in the grounds around the huts where fecal matter was abundant. Food and water supplies might be contaminated by the human, animal, and vegetable wastes which impregnated the soil with disease organisms. It was unfortunate that the slaves lived close to livestock pens where compost was made, and that they labored in highly manured cane fields. This was an environment probably without equal for generating the tetanus bacillus, one of the deadliest poisons known to man.[18]

Moving imported Africans from the disease environments of ships to those of ports and plantations was highly destructive to life and labor. Yet the demand for unskilled labor was at times so great that little preparation was made for the reception of new slaves. Planters were torn between putting new slaves to work immediately and taking measures to extend the life of their investment by assigning light tasks and providing health care—measures which were known as the "seasoning." They were tempted to resort to the former expedient because they were commonly supplied with slaves at the time they were wanted, and in the numbers needed.[19]

Planters were also torn between the comparative benefits and costs of buying new slaves and encouraging family life and reproduction so as to rear their own labor force. Dr. Jackson, who had practiced medicine in Jamaica, was asked by a committee of the House of Commons "whether it was more the object of the overseers to work the slaves moderately, and keep up their numbers by breeding; or to work them out, increasing thereby the produce of the estate, and trusting for recruits to the Slave Market?" He replied, "The latter plan was more generally adopted, principally, I conceive, owing to this reason, that imported Slaves are fit for immediate labor—slaves that are reared from childhood are liable to many accidents, and cannot make any return of labour for many years."[20]

Losses during the seasoning made a heavy drain on the newly imported slaves of even the best-managed plantations. Charles Leslie wrote in 1740 that almost half of the newly imported slaves died in seasoning, and several decades later Edward Long admitted that one-fourth of the newcomers were likely to die during the first eighteen months of seasoning.[21] Writing in 1790, William Beckford said that "let a purchaser of new Negroes be ever so successful in seasoning them, he does not think that he will be able with the most unremitting attention, and even with a superfluity of food, to preserve and domesticate, in three years, one out of four, who shall turn out a really industrious and efficient Slave."[22]

Apart from putting new slaves under the supervision of older, seasoned slaves from their own country, little attention was given to the seasoning of new recruits from Africa until the advent of the antislavery movement. Writing in 1764, Dr. James Grainger of the island of Saint Kitts found it a matter of astonishment that, among the many valuable medical tracts which had been published in recent years, not one had been "purposely written on the method of seasoning new Negroes, and the treatment of Negroes when sick." In his *Essay on West-India Diseases*, Grainger laid down rules for the feeding, clothing, housing, medical treatment, and labor of new slaves. He cautioned that no African could be seasoned to the climate of the West Indies until he had resided there "at least a twelvemonth." Above all, he warned against requiring new slaves to perform heavy field labor. "To put a hoe in the hands of a new Negroe, and to oblige him to work with a seasoned gang, is to murder that Negroe," Grainger exclaimed. He went on to say that "the African must be familiarised to labour by gentle degrees. This precept respects not only the aged, but even the young."[23]

THE ABOLITIONISTS' PRESCRIPTION

Thomas Clarkson wrote of a meeting of the Abolition Society on 7 June 1787, in which the ten members present reconsidered the object for which they had associated and the strategy best calculated to achieve their goals. The members agreed that there were two evils quite distinct from each other which it might become their duty to endeavor to remove. The first was the evil of the slave trade, whereby thousands of Africans were every year fraudulently and forcibly taken from their country, their relations and friends, and from all they considered valuable in life. The second was the evil of slavery itself, whereby the same Africans and their descendants were forcibly deprived of their rights and subjected to excessive labor and cruel punishment. Instead of seeking to remove the two evils simultaneously, the members agreed that by aiming at the abolition of the slave trade they would be "laying the axe at the very root." It was contended that if the planters were unable to procure more recruits from the coast of Africa they would treat their slaves more kindly, encourage them to marry and have children, see that the sick were properly attended to, provide adequate food and clothing, and take care that they were not overworked and worn down by the weight of severe punishment. Thus the planters would raise their own labor force and have no need for new slaves from Africa.[24]

The links between the slave trade and slavery were first investigated by the Privy Council Committee for Trade and Plantations in 1788. At the same time that the committee was taking evidence, Sir William Dolben's bill to regulate the slave trade was debated and enacted. Reacting to what it regarded as unjustified attacks by pro-abolitionist forces, a committee of the Jamaica House of Assembly submitted two reports to the Privy Council committee in October, 1788. The Jamaica committee approved the new slave trade regulating act and sought to dissociate the planters from the evils of the African trade. Moreover, the Jamaica committee sought to shift the blame for the natural decrease of the slave population. Deaths in the harbors of Jamaica between the arrival of a vessel and the sale of the slaves were charged to the slave trade, as were also deaths in the seasoning. Infant tetanus, which reputedly carried away one-fourth of the blacks within fourteen days of their birth, was a loss for which no medical treatment was known. Additional deaths were charged to destructive hurricanes, wars, and uncertain supplies of imported foodstuffs. The Jamaica reports were not altogether negative, for the committee believed that "the Increase of our Negroes by Generation" would in time be the beneficial consequences of the slave trade regulation act and a local act to improve the treatment of blacks.[25]

William Wilberforce, member of Parliament for Hull and leader of the Abolition Society, addressed the House of Commons in May, 1789, deploring the fact that it was more profitable for the planters to import black workers from Africa than to rear children to working age in the colonies. He contended that the number of slaves could be kept up by natural increase, and without any assistance whatever from the slave trade. About a month later Wilberforce told the Commons that the population decrease in the island of Jamaica "was but trifling, or, rather, it had ceased some years ago; and if there was a decrease, it was only on the imported slaves."[26] From data in the Privy Council report he calculated that the annual rate of population decrease was three-and-a-half percent from 1698 to 1730. Subsequently, the rate declined and amounted to not more than one percent from 1768 to 1788. Wilberforce thought this small rate of decrease could be accounted for by the hurricanes and consequent famines, and by the number of imported Africans who died in the seasoning. It was self-evident that deaths in the seasoning would cease if the slave trade was abolished.[27]

Voicing the judgment of his colleagues in the Society, Wilberforce told the House of Commons that abolition was the only certain mode of amending the treatment of slaves in order to secure their increase. He ridiculed the idea that the colonial legislatures could reform slavery by legal means when the evidence of slaves was in no case admitted against white men. On the other hand, if all hopes of supplies of slaves from Africa were cut off, "breeding would henceforth become a serious object of attention; and the care of this, as including better clothing, and feeding, and milder discipline, would extend to innumerable particulars, which an act of assembly could neither specify nor enforce."[28]

In the lengthy debate of 1792, Prime Minister William Pitt gave powerful support to the cause of his close friend William Wilberforce. He devoted a great part of his speech to proving from statistics that the population of the long-settled sugar colonies was increasing. In the case of Jamaica, he believed that the number of slaves who died in the seasoning made up of itself nearly the whole of the natural decrease of one percent per annum. Pitt maintained that if the slave trade was prohibited the disproportion between the sexes which hindered propagation would gradually diminish and a natural order of population be established.[29]

West India planters and merchants in England first joined with the slave traders of London, Bristol, and Liverpool in resisting the passage of the bill for regulating the abuses of the slave trade. They regarded the trade as a source of labor, and defended it as a necessity and a right which Parliament could not take from them without due notice and compensation. However, beginning in 1791, the West Indians began to dissociate themselves from the slave traders and to divert attention from abolition by stressing amelioration. Their plan was to introduce such regulations into the treatment of slaves as would secure their propagation, and thus make the need for the trade itself gradually wither away. The West Indians called for the amelioration of slave conditions by the local legislatures in the West Indies. Slave imports would be a necessary supplement to this policy of legislative amelioration until a viable breeding policy made imports unnecessary. According to Elsa Goveia, "The increased emphasis . . . placed upon conditions in the West Indies and upon positive policies to be carried into effect there reflected a significant change in the tactics of the West Indian group, who were now trying to suggest that they could offer alternative policies which would be more humane in effect than abolition."[30]

The role of mediator fell to Henry Dundas, one of Pitt's closest advisers. In his speech of 2 April 1792, he said that he meant to propose a moderate and middle way of proceeding. He believed that "the trade ought to be ultimately abolished, but by moderate measures, which should not invade the property of individuals, nor shock too suddenly the prejudices of our West India islands." Unlike the abolitionists, he thought the number of Africans then living in the islands was insufficient to maintain the population, and therefore he did not approve the idea of there being no more importations whatever.[31] Having gained a majority in the Commons for his resolution for the gradual abolition of the slave trade, Dundas moved on to draft an amendment which would specify the number of years the trade was to continue, and regulate the age and sex of the Africans who were transported to the colonies. He considered the cooperation of the West India merchants and planters as essential to his plan. He warned in his speech of 23 April 1792, that "if time was not given to encourage the merchants and planters to try fairly the scheme of rearing a sufficient number of native negroes to answer the purpose of cultivating the plantations, the trade would be carried on by foreign countries, and by our capitals [capitalists] and be an unregulated African trade."[32]

Dundas made two proposals with respect to the slave trade. One was to immediately abolish that part of the trade that was carried on for the service of foreign nations, which he claimed amounted to not less than 34,000 of the 74,000 slaves transported to the New World in British vessels. The other was to cut off the importation of aged Africans to the extent possible. Several reasons were advanced for regulating the age and sex of the blacks embarked from Africa. In the first place, young people were more likely to reproduce than were persons of advanced age. Secondly, young blacks would be subjected to fewer cruelties than oldsters before their embarkation. Thirdly, young slaves would contract and transmit fewer diseases than oldsters; it was a well known fact, Dundas asserted, that most of the calamities of the Middle Passage were owing to the diseases of old negroes. A fourth advantage was that young people were less attached to their homeland than those who were older, and would possess greater capacity to receive religious and moral instruction and to be seasoned for plantation labor. Finally, because young slaves would be less discontented than their elders, the colonies would be spared "much insecurity, tumult, and insurrection . . . which threatened the safety of our West India islands." But the Lords killed Dundas's amendment by inaction after it had been approved by the Commons.[33]

However, age-selective imports received the blessing of one colonial government. By the act of 23 December 1797, the Assembly of Jamaica levied a duty of ten pounds on every slave above the age of twenty-five years imported into the island. Governor Lord Balcarres of Jamaica said that long experience had shown that young blacks were more easily reformed of the "vicious habits" they imbibed in

Africa than old blacks, who were "generally among the first to excite and commence Acts of Disobedience and Rebellion."[34]

One repercussion of the parliamentary debate was the decision by the Danish government to abolish the slave trade carried on by its subjects. Svend Green-Pedersen writes that the Danish Slave Trade Commission and its leading figure, Ernst Schimmelmann, were convinced in the summer and autumn of 1791 that Britain was going to abolish the slave trade, and that this could create problems for the Danish slave trade. Accordingly, a royal edict of 16 March 1792 declared the Danish slave trade was to end on 31 December 1802. In order to encourage the import of females to serve as field hands and mothers, the edict abolished the duties and poll taxes on women and girls, but not on men and boys, during the ten-year extension of the slave trade.[35]

EXPANDING DEMAND AND THE WEST INDIAN RESPONSE

The hand of the British West Indians and their supporters was strengthened by events outside Britain and her colonies. The revolution in France had repercussions in the French Antilles which erupted into a massive slave revolt on Saint Domingue in 1791. The quick destruction of this largest and most productive plantation colony altered the structure of world markets. As the price of sugar and coffee increased, British planters increased their demand for slaves to expand the production of tropical staples. The expansion was not confined to the British empire, for Spaniards, Dutchmen, and Danes pushed their plantations, drawing heavily on the slaves supplied by British and American traders. The outbreak of the Anglo-French war in 1793 enabled Britain to capture the lion's share of the tropical trades and to launch military campaigns in the Caribbean region. Although the British expeditionary force sent to Saint Domingue was repulsed, the conquest of Trinidad and the mainland colonies of Demerara, Essequibo, and Berbice (later united in British Guiana) opened potentially valuable territories to British planters and slave traders.[36]

Jamaica's slave imports during the 1790s far exceeded those of any previous decade. They reached an all-time high of 23,018 in 1793, after which they ranged from 7,970 to 20,436 during the remainder of the decade. Bryan Edwards, member of Parliament for Southampton and a Jamaica proprietor, was informed by a correspondent in that island in the peak year, "Our harbours are full of Guineymen, yet the price keeps up enormously. . . . so long as the notion continues that the trade will be abolished, people will buy at any price, even to their own ruin, and the destruction of half the negroes, for want of provisions."[37] Massive purchases of new slaves were made by the proprietor of Worthy Park estate in Jamaica during the boom years. "Almost immediately the death-rate rose dramatically," write Michael Craton and James Walvin, "and at the end of the three years' seasoning of the new slaves almost a quarter of them had perished."[38]

During the sugar and coffee boom the abolitionists suffered parliamentary defeats on several occasions as the initiative shifted to the West Indians. On 6 April 1797, Charles Ellis, a Jamaica proprietor, brought forward a motion on behalf of the West India interest. He argued the case for gradual abolition by giving the West Indian legislatures responsibility for reforming slavery in such matters as the encouragement of religious instruction, childbearing, and the practice of monogamy. By means of legislative amelioration the slaves would be encouraged to increase by natural propagation until the slave trade was no longer needed. Ellis moved that an address be presented to the king, requesting him to recommend to the colonies the adoption of such measures as would obviate the causes that impeded the natural increase of the slaves, "gradually to diminish the Necessity of the Slave Trade and ultimately to lead to its complete Termination."[39] After Ellis's motion was passed, the Secretary of State wrote to colonial governors and legislatures that it was indispensably necessary to adopt legislative provisions that would lead to the religious and moral improvement of the slaves, give them due legal protection under the law, and encourage them to breed. By virtue of the power it conferred on the colonial legislatures, Ellis's law represented a major political victory for the West Indians and their supporters.[40]

Though it was not acted upon, William Pitt supported a compromise plan in 1799 to limit the importation of Africans to the annual decrease of the West Indian slave population, and to prohibit the clearing of new lands for cultivation with slave labor.[41] Upon learning of the plan, the Assembly of Jamaica was moved to appoint a committee to report on the state of the colony and to ascertain how far the proposed restrictions would affect the safety of the white inhabitants. The report of the committee vigorously defended the Assembly against its enemies in England, asserting that everything possible had been done to secure the comfort of the slaves that was consistent with their reasonable labor services and the safety of the white inhabitants. Though the measures of amelioration were said to have contributed to an increased number of blacks born and reared in the island, the report warned that these measures "must be adopted gradually in order to facilitate the effect and purposes intended."[42] The report insisted that the slave trade should continue, chiefly in order to supply the new coffee and sugar settlements. Data was produced by the committee to show that since the year 1792 at least 83 new sugar plantations had been settled. The coffee boom had an even greater impact, amounting to upwards of 700 new settlements worked by some 26,000 slaves.[43] The slave trade had been indispensable to the small coffee and other settlements in the interior parts of the island which had been established by former overseers, tradesmen, and bookkeepers. The white population, and also the ranks of the militia, had increased because of these new settlements. Indeed, it was alleged that the security of the island against both internal and external danger would be "rendered more effectual and permanent from the settling numerous plantations in the interior."[44]

Meanwhile, the abolitionists were gathering firsthand information which cast doubt on the success of the measures taken by the West Indian legislatures to implement Ellis's law to encourage amelioration. The source of the most damning evidence against the planters was James Stephen, the barrister and antislavery leader who lived at Saint Kitts, and from 1789 onward supplied Wilberforce with valuable information.[45] Wilberforce was later to write that his suspicion was confirmed that the amelioration laws had been intended by the colonial legislatures "for the protection of the Slave Trade, rather than of the slaves."[46] He was of the opinion that the slave codes were unenforceable "in those particulars of treatment, which are constant and systematic, such as underfeeding, overworking, and other general vices of management, whether arising out of degradation, absenteeship, speculation, the pressure of the times, or any other of the causes which have been specified. And it is these systematic vices which constitute the real evils of the condition of the bulk of our Slaves." Wilberforce warned that if local officials interfered in the day-to-day management of the slaves, it "would in practice be soon found productive, not only of discontent, insubordination, and commotions on private properties, but of the most fatal consequences to the safety of the whole colony."[47]

No doubt Charles Ellis and other absentees were too sanguine regarding the likelihood of gradual abolition. Though closely attuned to the movements of politics and economics in the metropolis, the absentees were often less well informed of conditions in the colonies. They apparently took little account of the expanding coffee sector of the Jamaican economy which absorbed the greater part of the new slaves. A report of the Assembly of Jamaica of 23 November 1804 said that the great body of imported Africans had been "distributed amongst tradesmen, jobbers, overseers, or persons employed in cultivating the smaller staples." The coffee plantations that were cultivated by Africans, almost all of whom had been purchased within the last twelve years, were still short of labor. Resident planters realized that their profits hinged largely on the ratio of effective laborers to the total number of slaves on a given plantation. Given access to the slave trade, a planter with 100 Africans in the prime of life would probably work 80 of that number. On the other hand, closure of the slave trade would reduce the number of effective workers even if the total population increased by natural means. It was estimated that in the course of twenty years, in spite of a projected natural increase of from 100 to 120 slaves, those able to work would decline from 80 to 40; the rest would consist of "invalids, the aged past labour, and children not yet fit for it."[48] No doubt the authors of this report indulged in special pleading.

The last years of the slave trade witnessed both an increase in numbers purchased and some evidence of sex-selective purchases. As an example of the latter type of purchase, one of the trustees of a sugar plantation in Jamaica wrote from Edinburgh, Scotland, to the plantation manager that it would be necessary to purchase twenty new slaves over a period of two or three years, "and they ought all to be young women so as to preserve the proper proportion between the male & female slaves upon the estate." Nearly a year later the manager was told to delay the purchase of the ten additional slaves for some months "unless you think it likely that the proceed[gs.] in the British Parl[t.] relative to the abolition of the Slave trade will have the effect of raising the price."[49]

Captain Hugh Crow, master of the *Kitty Amelia*, arrived in Kingston harbor with a cargo of slaves in the final months of the trade. He found sixteen other slave ships in the port and a glutted market.[50] The legal trade ended on 28 February 1808. Some seven years later a leading medical practitioner in Jamaica attributed "a great part of the decrease of negroes" in the ensuing years to the abnormally large imports in the final months of the trade, the poor physical condition of the slaves, and the fact "that a very considerable number of the proprietors of plantations, conceiving that they would be precluded from future purchases, strained their credit to the utmost in purchasing new negroes, for whom they had not the means of providing proper subsistence."[51]

CONCLUSION

Clement Caines, the Saint Kitts planter, imputed to the African trade such evils as the sterility of female slaves, deaths without number of black infants, premature decay and loss of the ablest blacks, together with the waste and misapplication of human labor.[52] To remove these and other evils various stratagems and measures were debated in Whitehall and the colonies. These included immediate versus gradual abolition, trade regulation, sex- and age-selective imports, and legislative amelioration with the object of substituting a plantation-reared labor force for recruits imported from Africa.

Despite their differences, abolitionists and absentee planters seem to have believed that it would be relatively easy for resident planters to encourage family life and reproduction, and to dispense with the slave trade as the supplier of plantation labor. They apparently neglected to consider the interests of resident planters who had established new coffee and other settlements. The labor of clearing forests for new settlements was unusually severe, and led to appeals from resident planters to keep open the slave trade to counteract the high mortality and increase the number of settlements. Moreover, abolitionists and absentees apparently neglected to calculate the cost of rearing a slave to working age, which included the loss of the mother's labor before and after delivery, lying-in and maintenance costs, interest foregone on capital invested in young slaves, and capital losses of children who died. According to a calculation of 1830, it cost nearly twice as much to rear a slave to working age in Jamaica as it did to purchase a newly imported slave in Cuba.[53]

Proponents of both legislative amelioration and immediate abolition seem to have believed that slave women would cooperate with a pronatalist policy which called for the awarding of premiums and labor and tax abatements to successful mothers, midwives, overseers, and proprietors. They thought that the slave population was likely to increase by natural means if the sexes were brought into balance and there was a growing proportion of creoles to African-born slaves. But Barry Higman finds fault with this argument. For Jamaica as a whole, he finds that there was a continued erosion of both the African and creole sections of the population after 1807.[54]

One African cultural survival which helps to account for the failure of the pronatalist policies was the practice of long lactation, and the taboo on sexual intercourse during the period of two or three years that the child was at its mother's breast. Slave women in the West Indies began to bear children at an earlier age than their sisters in the southern states of America, they gave birth at longer intervals, and they had fewer children who survived to maturity. Indeed, Stanley Engerman writes that the causes of the persistently low fertility in the West Indies are frequently attributed to "the cultural and psychological shock of enslavement and movement to the New World, and as a response to the conditions of life: an unwillingness to bring offspring into such conditions. To accomplish this end, it has been claimed, there was frequent resort to abortion and infanticide."[55] Not until the period following full emancipation in 1838 did the birth rate of black females in Jamaica increase sufficiently to achieve a net population increase.

APPENDIX

Appendix Table 14.1
The Slave Trade to Jamaica, 1701–1808 (5-year totals)

Years	No. of Ships	No. of Slaves Imported	No. of Slaves Re-exported	No. of Slaves Retained	Percentage Retained
1701–5[a]	51	11,206	2,698	8,508	75.9
1706–10	77	19,685	5,828	13,857	70.4
1711–15	94	23,391	10,743	12,648	54.1
1716–20	128	30,349	14,248	16,101	53.1
1721–25	144	36,157	16,484	19,673	54.4
1726–30	180	41,532	16,695	24,837	59.8
1731–35	179	40,465	20,098	20,367	50.3
1736–40	138	32,752	7,050	25,702	78.5
1741–45	135	30,846	5,397	25,449	82.5
1746–50	129	36,476	10,155	26,321	72.2
1751–55	198	40,892	4,843	36,049	88.2
1756–60	130	35,291	6,305	28,986	82.1
1761–65	168	42,002	7,101	34,901	83.1
1766–70	133	29,805	2,788	27,017	90.7
1771–75	206	46,877	6,534	40,343	86.7
1776–80	—	35,808	5,450	30,358	84.8
1781–85	—	49,498	11,528	37,970	76.7
1786–90[a]	—	34,943	10,278	24,665	70.6
1791–95	—	79,057	14,827	64,230	81.3
1796–1800	—	64,768	6,667	58,101	89.7
1801–5	—	38,271	7,069	31,202	81.5
1806–8	—	28,114	811	27,303	97.1
Totals		828,185	193,597	634,588	76.6

Sources: Period of 1702–75: Appendix to a memorial from Stephen Fuller, agent for Jamaica, to the Board of Trade, 30 Jan. 1778, Colonial Office 137/38, Hh 3,4, Public Record Office, London (hereafter cited as CO/PRO). Two other copies of this report, with some variance in the numbers imported and exported, can be found in the Papers of Edward Long of Jamaica and England, British Museum, Additional Manuscripts (hereafter cited as BM Add. MSS) 12,435, ff. 27–30. Period of 1776–87: Papers of Edward Long, BM Add. MSS 12,435, ff. 37–39. Period of 1789–98: Great Britain, *Parliamentary Papers* (hereafter cited as PP), 1803/4, vol. 10, pp. 175–39G, "Report of David Innes, Naval Officer, Kingston, Jamaica, Nov. 14, 1799." Year 1799: PP, 1801–2, vol. 4, pp. 378–79. Period of 1800–1808: *Journals of the Assembly of Jamaica* (hereafter cited as J. A. J.) 12 (1815):825, 23 Nov.

Note: These records were kept to assess the duties levied on slaves imported into and exported from Jamaica. They are lower-bound figures, since numerous slaves were reportedly smuggled into and out of Jamaica in order to avoid the duties.

ᵃNo data for the years 1701 and 1788.

Appendix Table 14.2
Annual Jamaican Slave Trade, 1789–1808, and Poll Tax Returns on Slaves, 1800–1815

Year	No. of Slaves Imported	No. of Slaves Exported	No. of Slaves Retained	No. of Slaves on which Poll Taxes were Paid
1789	10,129	2,193	7,936	
1790	13,466	2,163	11,303	
1791	14,397	2,559	11,838	
1792	14,761	2,663	12,098	
1793	23,018	1,915	21,103	
1794	14,590	3,041	11,549	
1795	12,291	4,649	7,642	
1796	7,970	2,727	5,243	
1797	10,827	2,813	8,014	
1798	10,488	710	9,778	
1799	15,047	412	14,635	
1800	20,436	5	20,431	300,939
1801	11,309	270	11,039	307,094
1802	8,131	2,554	5,577	307,199
1803	7,846	2,036	5,810	308,668
1804	5,979	1,811	4,168	308,542
1805	5,006	398	4,608	308,775
1806	8,487	166	8,321	312,341
1807	16,263	336	15,927	319,351
1808	3,364	309	3,055	323,827
1809				323,724
1810				313,683
1811				326,830
1812				319,912
1813				317,424
1814				315,385
1815				313,814

Sources: Period of 1789–98: PP, 1803/4, vol. 10, pp. 175–39G, "Report of David Innes . . . Nov. 14, 1799"; ibid., vol. 10, enclosure no. 13, Gov. Balcarres, to the Secre-

Appendix Table 14.2, *continued*
tary of State for the Colonies, 22 Mar. 1800. Year 1799: PP, 1801/2, vol. 4, pp. 478–79,
"Accounts presented to the House of Commons respecting the Trade to the Coast of
Africa for Slaves, etc." Period of 1800–1815: J. A. J., vol. 12 (1815), "Report from the
Committee on the Bill Introduced into the House of Commons in Great Britain for
Effectually Preventing the Unlawful Importation of Slaves," p. 825.

Appendix Table 14.3
Slave Population and Slave Imports, Jamaica, Selected Years, 1703–1800

Year	Estimated Population	Net Imports (annual average)	Net Imports as a Percent of Population
1703	45,000	2,225	4.9
1730	80,000	4,977	6.2
1750	120,000	3,907	3.3
1775	200,000	10,500	5.3
1800	300,000	15,368	5.1

Source: Period of 1702–75: Appendix to memorial from Fuller, 30 Jan. 1778, CO/
PRO 137/38, Hh 3,4; Papers of Edward Long, BM Add. MSS 12,435, ff. 27–30. Period
of 1800–1808: J. A. J. 12 (1815): 825, 23 Nov. See also R. B. La Page, *An Historical
Introduction to Jamaican Creole* (London, 1960), p. 74; George W. Roberts, *The Population
of Jamaica* (Cambridge, 1957), pp. 36–38.

Appendix Table 14.4
Slave Imports By Sex, Jamaica, 1764–74, 1779–84

	Males	Females	Total
Total of 121 cargoes	25,893	15,732	41,625
Percentage of total	62.2	37.8	100.0

Source: PP, *Accounts and Papers*, vol. 26 (1789), "Report of the Lords of the Committee
of Council for Trade and Plantations on the Slave Trade" (hereafter cited as Privy
Council Report), pt. 3.

Appendix Table 14.5
Average Sterling Prices of African Slaves Sold in Jamaica, Selected Years, 1723–99

1723–25	£15–£22[a]
1752–62	£30[b]
1772–75	£34. 10s. 3d.[c]
1793	£45. 16s. 10d[d]
1794	£46. 9s. 9d.[e]
1795	£42. 17s. 11d.[f]
1796	£51. 6s. 3d.[g]
1797	£51. 1s. 5d.[h]
1798	£58. 11s. 8d.[i]
1799	£72. 4s. 10d.[j]

Sources: For 1723–25, Treasury 70/958–9, Public Record Office, London; for 1752–62, PP, *Accounts and Papers*, vol. 26 (1789), Privy Council report, pt. 4; for 1772–75, Bryan Edwards, *History of the British West Indies* 2 (Dublin, 1793): 464; for 1793–99, J. A. J. 10 (1799): 436, 20 Dec.

[a] Sales of the Royal African Company
[b] Average of 71,115 slaves
[c] Average of 29 slave cargoes
[d] Average of 3,053 slaves
[e] Average of 1,691 slaves
[f] Average of 2,221 slaves
[g] Average of 807 slaves
[h] Average of 4,317 slaves
[i] Average of 2,009 slaves
[j] Average of 3,225 slaves

Appendix Table 14.6
Slave Population on York Sugar Plantation, Jamaica, 1777–1801

Year	No. Jan. 1	Births	Deaths	Purchased	No. Dec. 31
1777	487	14	31		470
1778	470	15	12		473
1779	473	12	12	—	476
1780	476	9	21		464
1781	464	14	19		459
1782	459	9	21		447
1783	447	18	18		447
1784	447	—	—		445
1785	445	11	17		439
1786	439	15	18	30	466
1787	466	9	23	10	462
1788	462	10	12		460
1789	460	11	20		451
1790	451	16	23	20	464
1791	464	8	17	10	465
1792	465	8	18		455
1801	442	14	9		447

Source: *The Gale-Morant Papers, 1731–1925, in the Library, University of Exeter*, in W. E. Minchinton, ed., *British Records Relating to America in Microform* (East Ardsley, Yorkshire: EP Microform Ltd., 1977).

Appendix Table 14.7
Slave Population on Worthy Park Plantation, Jamaica, 1783–96

Years	Total Population	Births	Deaths
1783	318	2	11
1784	316	10	18
1785	313	5	4
1786	307	—	—
1787	339	10	7
1788	338	9	12
1789	339	7	16
1790	345	—	6
1791	357	8	18
1792	359	13	14
1793	450	6	26
1794	528	8	56
1795	483	13	19
1796	470	8	22

Source: Michael Craton and James Walvin, *A Jamaican Plantation: The History of Worthy Park, 1670–1970* (Toronto, 1970), p. 130.

Appendix Table 14.8
Slave Imports and Poll Tax Returns on Slaves, Barbados, 1764–81

Years	Number Imported[a]	Number Taxed
1764	3,936	70,706
1765	3,228	72,255
1766	4,061	73,651
1767	4,154	74,656
1768	4,628	76,275
1769	6,837	75,658
1770	5,885	76,334
1771	2,728	75,956
1772	2,117	74,485
1773	1,269	74,206
1774		74,874
1775		74,410
1776		74,103
1777		72,578
1778		69,935
1779		68,295
1780[b]		68,270
1781		63,248

Source: PP, *Accounts and Papers*, vol. 26 (1789), Privy Council Report, pt. 3, Barbados, Evidence of John Brathwaite, agent for Barbados.

[a]John Brathwaite, who compiled these statistics, appended the following note: "I do not find, by the Paper from which this is copied, that any Slaves were imported during this Period, after the Year 1773. But there is no doubt a great many were sent from Barbadoes to Tobago, Demerary, &c." (ibid.).

[b]More than 2,000 slaves are reported to have been killed in the hurricane which struck Barbados on 10 October 1780.

Appendix Table 14.9
Annual Barbados Slave Trade and Poll Tax Returns on Slaves, 1788–1804

Years	No. of Slaves Imported	No. of Slaves Exported	No. of Slaves Retained	Slaves Taxed
1788	1,585	1,270	315	63,557
1789	556	490	66	63,870
1790	131	91	40	64,068
1791	426	310	116	63,250
1792	744	591	153	64,330
1793	1,438	1,107	331	64,556
1794	1,218	943	275	64,966
1795	2,059	1,729	330	64,470
1796	3,582	3,280	302	64,475
1797	3,462	2,895	567	64,520
1798	3,244	2,786	458	65,112
1799	1,968	1,491	477	67,247
1800	830	790	40	65,903
1801	—	—	—	65,561
1802	608	400	198	66,556
1803	3,177	2,948	229	67,812
1804	999	850	149	—

Source: "Correspondence of the antiquary John Pinkerton, with materials and notes accumulated by him," MS 1711, Pinkerton Papers, National Library of Scotland, Edinburgh.

Appendix Table 14.10
Births and Deaths on John Brathwaite's Windward Estate, Barbados,
January 1754 to December 1786

Years	Births		Deaths	
	Male	Female	Male	Female
1754	1	0	7	2
1755	1	2	6	2
1756	2	0	2	3
1757	1	2	3	2
1758	0	0	3	2
1759	1	1	5	4
1760	0	0	3	3
1761	2	3	6	2
1762	4	5	2	8
1763	2	2	1	3
1764	4	1	1	5
1765	4	1	2	2
1766	0	2	0	3
1767	2	2	4	2
1768	3	0	4	1
1769	3	3	1	2
1770	2	0	4	0
1771	2	2	3	3
1772	1	3	2	1
1773	3	0	0	1
1774	1	3	2	2
1775	2	0	2	1
1776	1	2	3	1
1777	2	5	4	2
1778	1	2	4	3
1779	1	6	1	2
1780	1	1	6	4
1781	0	2	4	3
1782	3	4	2	2
1783	1	1	2	3
1784	4	4	3	1
· 1785	4	3	4	3
1786	2	3	0	2
Total	61	65	96	80
Combined Total	*126*		*176*	

Source: PP, *Accounts and Papers*, vol. 26 (1789), Privy Council Report, pt. 3, evidence
of John Brathwaite.

Appendix Table 14.11
Slave Population on Codrington Plantations, Barbados, 1767–93

Year	Initial Population	Births	Deaths	Remaining Population
1767	336	—	—	—
1768	327	—	—	—
1769	321	—	—	—
1770	313	—	—	—
1771	313	—	—	—
1772	306	—	—	—
1773	310	12	14	308
1774	308	6	13	301
1775	301	6	8	299
1776	299	9	11	297
1777	297	10	26	281
1778	281	4	6	279
1779	279	14	11	282
1780	282	7	13	276
1781	276	6	7	275
1782	275	8	10	273
1785	273	17	11	279
1786	275	11	13	273
1788	273	8	12	269
1789	269	5	9	265
1790	265	4	6	263
1791	263	3	1	265
1792	265	7	6	266

Source: J. Harry Bennett, Jr., *Bondsmen and Bishops: Slavery and Apprenticeship on the Codrington Plantations of Barbados, 1710–1838* (Berkeley, 1958), pp. 73, 96.

Appendix Table 14.12
Estimated Annual Rate of Population Decline, Barbados and Jamaica, 1676–1800
(population and imports in thousands)

| | BARBADOS | | | | | |
	1676	1701	1726	1751	1776	1800
Estimated slave population	33.0	45.0	55.0	65.0	74.4	68.0
Total net slave imports for 25-year period	52.4	70.9	63.6	75.8	—	
Estimated annual rate of population decline for 25-year period	4.1%	4.9%	3.6%	3.8%	—	
	JAMAICA					
	1676	1701	1726	1751	1776	1800
Estimated slave population	9.0	43.0	75.0	121.0	200.0	300.0
Total net slave imports for 25-year period	54.0	86.1	132.0	176.6	228.8	
Estimated annual rate of population decline for 25-year period	3.1%	3.7%	3.5%	2.5%	2.0%	

Source: Richard B. Sheridan, "Mortality and the Medical Treatment of Slaves in the British West Indies," in Stanley L. Engerman and Eugene D. Genovese, eds., *Race and Slavery in the Western Hemisphere: Quantitative Studies* (Princeton, 1975), pp. 309–10.

NOTES

The preceding work was supported in part by the National Institutes of Health Grant *LM 01539* from the National Library of Medicine. I am indebted to Mr. Roderick McDonald for helping with the research for this paper.

1 Eric Williams, *Capitalism and Slavery* (Chapel Hill, N.C., 1944); Philip D. Curtin, *The Atlantic Slave Trade: A Census* (Madison, 1969); Roger Anstey, *The Atlantic Slave Trade and British Abolition, 1760–1810* (Atlantic Highlands, N.J., 1975); Roger Anstey and P. E. H. Hair, *Liverpool, the African Slave Trade and Abolition* (Liverpool, 1976); Herbert S. Klein, *The Middle Passage* (Princeton, 1978).

2 George W. Roberts, *The Population of Jamaica* (Cambridge, 1957); Michael Craton, *Sinews of Empire: A Short History of British Slavery* (Garden City, N.Y., 1974); Michael Craton, *Searching for the Invisible Man: Slaves and*

Plantation Life in Jamaica (Cambridge, Mass., 1978); B. W. Higman, *Slave Population and Economy in Jamaica, 1807–1834* (Cambridge, 1976); Richard B. Sheridan, *Sugar and Slavery: An Economic History of the British West Indies, 1623–1775* (Baltimore, 1974); Stanley L. Engerman, "Some Economic and Demographic Comparisons of Slavery in the United States and the British West Indies," *Economic History Review*, 2d ser., 29, no. 2 (May 1976), pp. 258–75.

3 Philip D. Curtin, "Epidemiology and the Slave Trade," *Political Science Quarterly* 83, no. 2 (June 1968): 190–216; William H. McNeill, *Plagues and Peoples* (Garden City, N.Y., 1977), pp. 176–207.

4 Curtin, *Atlantic Slave Trade*, pp. 29–30.

5 Richard B. Sheridan, "Africa and the Caribbean in the Atlantic Slave Trade," *American Historical Review* 77, no. 1 (Feb. 1972): 15–35.

6 Bryan Edwards, *The History, Civil and Commercial, of the British Colonies in the West Indies*, 2 vols. (Dublin, 1793), 2: 4, 471–72.

7 Michael Craton, "Jamaican Slavery," in Stanley L. Engerman and Eugene D. Genovese, eds., *Race and Slavery in the Western Hemisphere: Quantitative Studies* (Princeton, 1975), pp. 252–53.

8 Craton, *Invisible Man*, p. 61.

9 Ibid., p. 75; Craton, *Sinews of Empire*, p. 195; Michael Craton, "Jamaican Slave Mortality: Fresh Light from Worthy Park, Longville and the Tharp Estates," *Journal of Caribbean History* 3 (Nov. 1971): 5.

10 Klein, *Middle Passage*, p. 144.

11 Ibid., pp. 148–51, 155–60, 173–74.

12 Philip D. Curtin, *Economic Change in Pre-Colonial Africa: Senegambia in the Era of the Slave Trade*, 2 vols. (Madison, 1975), 1: 109–12.

13 Klein, *Middle Passage*, pp. 161–62; Elizabeth Donnan, *Documents Illustrative of the History of the Slave Trade to America*, 4 vols. (New York, 1965), 2: 589–90.

14 Great Britain, *Parliamentary Register* (Commons) 23 (London, 1788): 606.

15 W. J. Gardner, *A History of Jamaica* (London, 1909), p. 165; Edward Brathwaite, *The Development of Creole Society in Jamaica, 1770–1820* (London, 1971), pp. 6, 281.

16 The act of 5 May 1732 was the only quarantine act passed during the slavery era. It was entitled "An act to prevent the landing or keeping of negroes infected with small-pox in any of the three towns of St. Catharine, Port-Royal, and Kingston" (*Journals of the Assembly of Jamaica* [hereafter cited as J.A.J.] 3 [1732]: 85–90).

17 David L. Chandler, "Health Conditions in the Slave Trade of Colonial New Granada," in Robert B. Toplin, ed., *Slavery and Race Relations in Latin America* (Westport, Conn., 1974), pp. 51–67.

18 Tetanus, or lockjaw, is discussed in Richard B. Sheridan, "Morbidity, Mortality and Medicine," manuscript, pp. 29–30.

19 Elsa V. Goveia, *Slave Society in the British Leeward Islands at the End of the Eighteenth Century* (New Haven, 1965), p. 124.

20 Great Britain, *Parliamentary Papers* (hereafter cited as PP), *Accounts and*

Papers, vol. 29 (1790), "Minutes of Evidence: Select Committee of the House of Commons on the Slave Trade," p. 58, evidence of Dr. Jackson.

21 Charles Leslie, *History of Jamaica* (London, 1740), p. 328; Papers of C. E. Long, British Museum Additional Manuscripts 12,405, f. 357.

22 William Beckford, *A Descriptive Account of the Island of Jamaica*, 2 vols. (London, 1790), 2: 342.

23 James Grainger, M.D., *An Essay on the More Common West-India Diseases* (Edinburgh, 1802; 1st ed., London, 1764), pp. i–ii, 7–11.

24 Thomas Clarkson, *The History of the Rise, Progress and Accomplishment of the Abolition of the African Slave Trade by the British Parliament*, new ed. (London, 1839), pp. 175–78.

25 PP, *Accounts and Papers*, vol. 26 (1789), "Report of the Lords of the Committee of Council for Trade and Plantations on the Slave Trade," pt. 3.

26 William Cobbett, ed., *The Parliamentary History of England* (London, 1812–20), 27 (1789): 495–506, 576–99, 638–52; 28 (1789): 41–101. These debates are summarized in Clarkson, *History of Abolition*, pp. 350, 356, 439.

27 Clarkson, *History of Abolition*, pp. 439–41.

28 Ibid., pp. 444–46.

29 William Pitt's speech of 25 April 1792, in *Parliamentary Register* (Commons) 32 (London, 1792): 405–8; Clarkson, *History of Abolition*, pp. 473–77.

30 Goveia, *Slave Society in Leeward Islands*, pp. 22–23, 27.

31 Henry Dundas's speech of 2 April 1792, in *Parliamentary Register* (Commons) 32 (London, 1792): 225–30; Goveia, *Slave Society in Leeward Islands*, p. 30.

32 Henry Dundas's speech of 23 April 1792, in *Parliamentary Register* (Commons) 32: 333–48; Goveia, *Slave Society in Leeward Islands*, p. 30.

33 *Parliamentary Register* (Commons) 32: 336–38, 346–48.

34 J.A.J. 10 (1797): 64, 96, 293; Governor Lord Balcarres to the Duke of Portland, dated Jamaica, 24 Dec. 1797, in PP, *Accounts and Papers*, 1798/99, vol. 48, pp. 19–20.

35 Svend E. Green-Pedersen, "The Scope and Structure of the Danish Negro Slave Trade," *Scandinavian Economic History Review* 19, no. 2 (1971): 176–77; Donnan, *Documents of the Slave Trade*, 2: 616–17.

36 Goveia, *Slave Society in Leeward Islands*, pp. 20–21, 29–31, 37–39; Williams, *Capitalism and Slavery*, pp. 145–53.

37 Extract of an anonymous letter to Bryan Edwards in Westminster, dated Jamaica, 20 Feb. 1793, in Colonial Office 137/91, Public Record Office, London. Edwards forwarded this extract to Henry Dundas.

38 Michael Craton and James Walvin, *A Jamaican Plantation: the History of Worthy Park, 1670–1970* (Toronto, 1970), pp. 130–32, 172–73.

39 Cobbett, *Parliamentary History* 33 (1797): 269, 293–94; Anstey, *Atlantic Slave Trade*, pp. 327–28.

40 Goveia, *Slave Society in Leeward Islands*, p. 34.

41 Dale H. Porter, *The Abolition of the Slave Trade in England, 1784–1807* (New York, 1970), pp. 103–5.

42 "Report from the Committee chaired by Mr. L. Cuthbert," 20 Dec. 1799, J.A.J. 10: 415.

43 Ibid., pp. 438–40.

44 Ibid., pp. 413, 415; Seymour Drescher, *Econocide: British Slavery in the Era of Abolition* (Pittsburgh, 1977), pp. 57, 87–91.

45 Anstey, *Atlantic Slave Trade*, pp. 328–30.

46 William Wilberforce, *A Letter on the Abolition of the Slave Trade* (London, 1807), p. 231.

47 Ibid., p. 234.

48 "Report from the Committee chaired by Mr. Simon Taylor," 23 Nov. 1804, J.A.J. 11: 215–17.

49 William Robertson to Andrew Jardine in Jamaica, dated Edinburgh, 26 May 1804 and 1 Mar. 1805, in Trustee Papers of James Stothert of Dundee Estate, Jamaica, and Cargen, Dumfries, Scotland, GD 241/171/2, ff. 116, 149, Scottish Public Record Office, Edinburgh.

50 Averil Mackensie-Grieve, *The Last Years of the English Slave Trade: Liverpool, 1750–1807* (London, 1941), pp. 293–94.

51 "Report from the Committee chaired by Mr. William Shand," 17 Nov. 1815, J.A.J. 12: 806, examination of Dr. John Quier.

52 Clement Caines, *Letters on the Cultivation of the Otaheite Cane, etc.* (London, 1801), p. 267.

53 Richard B. Sheridan, "'Sweet Malefactor': the Social Costs of Slavery in Jamaica and Cuba, 1807–54," *Economic History Review*, 2d ser., 29 (May 1976): 239–44.

54 Higman, *Slave Population*, pp. 134–35.

55 Engerman, "Economic and Demographic Comparisons," pp. 270–74; Herbert S. Klein and Stanley L. Engerman, "Fertility Differentials between Slaves in the United States and the British West Indies: A Note on Lactation Practices," *William and Mary Quarterly*, 3d ser., 35 (April 1978): 357–74.

CHAPTER 15: **The Atlantic Slave Trade and**

the Development of

an Afro-American Culture

Franklin W. Knight

The variety of Afro-American cultures that may be found through-out the Americas derived from the existence for nearly four centuries of an organized commerce which brought millions of Africans from their homeland.[1] Nevertheless, the Atlantic slave trade was neither the first nor the sole conduit through which Africans arrived in the Americas. It is possible—though not highly probable—that Africans may have adventured (or misadventured) across the Atlantic Ocean before the voyages of Christopher Columbus and the other intrepid European explorers of the fifteenth and sixteenth centuries.[2] From the early sixteenth century, however, the African presence has been sustained. Africans accompanied the first Iberians as they laid the foundations of an integrated Atlantic world in the tropical and sub-tropical zones of the American hemisphere. The earliest Africans were acculturated Iberians, and while their role in the expansion of Europe was important, their significance as part of the larger African migration is decidedly tenuous.[3] It was the organized transfer of, and trade in, Africans which had the most significant effect on the initia-tion, expansion, and form of those cultures and societies which have usually been designated Afro-American.[4]

It is especially in terms of culture transfer, or the development and expansion of this distinctive Afro-American culture, however, that the organized transatlantic slave trade assumes importance. Before the organization and methodical transfer of millions of Africans between 1518 and 1870, those Africans and their descendants who had arrived earlier in the Americas had failed to have an autonomous cultural impact, or at best, had formed an integral part of the Spanish and Portuguese political and socio-cultural transformation of the indigenous societies and cultures.[5] In all probability those early Africans—as was the legal prerequisite—spoke Spanish and Portuguese and were Roman Catholic in religion; and they shared in almost all respects the mores and expectations of their fellow European adventurers and conquerors. Moreover, those early African pioneers lost their particular identity when they were gradually inundated by the later immigrants who were the desired commodity of the Atlantic slave trade.

This inexorable stream of Africans eventually produced Africanized communities in the Americas with reciprocal relationships between themselves and their host societies. Despite the notoriously disastrous conditions under which Africans and their offspring lived and worked, their communities formed significant portions of the local populations in those areas where export economies based on mining or on plantation staples such as tobacco, cotton, rice, coffee, and sugar flourished.[6] The African proportion of the local inhabitants varied enormously throughout the Americas at that time in the nineteenth century when the trade gradually ceased and the slave system collapsed.

In 1810, when wars of independence began to break up the Spanish mainland empire in the Americas, the Afro–Latin American component represented approximately 50 percent of a variegated population which was to be the frustration of the newly emergent states. When the slave system collapsed in the Antilles, the Afro-Caribbean populations ranged from more than 90 percent in Jamaica and Saint Domingue to approximately 50 percent in Cuba, Puerto Rico, Santo Domingo, and Saint Bartholomé. For purposes of comparison, Africans and Afro-Americans constituted only about 7 percent of the inhabitants in all the United States of America in 1860, and 33 percent of the Brazilian population in 1890. Regardless of the vicissitudes of history and economics, the Caribbean demonstrated the potential of an African population for survival, perseverance, and eventual demographic domination of a local society.

Crude population proportions (or even the gross totals of the African-based sector within any given territory) taken at specific dates are not especially informative for an analysis of the ways in which Africans and their descendants constructed their society and their specific culture. The Afro-American experience varied considerably across regions, as well as within relatively confined geographical areas.[7] The range of circumstances varied also. The socio-economic complex in which Afro-Americans participated in urban New York, or Philadelphia, or Baltimore varied considerably from that encountered in rural tidewater Virginia, or the cotton zones of Georgia, Alabama, and Mississippi. The constraints of western Cuba, with its predominantly sugar economy, were quite different from those of eastern Cuba, with its predominantly mixed economy, during the nineteenth century.[8] Larger islands such as Jamaica, Dominica, Guadeloupe, Martinique, Saint Vincent and Saint Lucia, with their mountains and other expanses of terrain generally unsuitable for plantation agriculture, possessed conditions far removed from the gently undulating smaller areas of Antigua, Barbados, or Saint Kitts, with their easy accessibility to the sea.[9] In Brazil the structure and lifestyle of the sugar plantations of the northeast differed considerably from those of either the coffee zones of São Paulo or the grazing belt of Rio Grande do Sul.[10]

The general environment—which may be conveniently termed an ecological zone—in which the Africans arrived and in which their descendants labored profoundly affected the culture and the anthropological attributes which were to characterize the Afro-American sector.[11] One explanation for the apparent uniformity of the Afro-Caribbean populations may be the prevalence of the sugar plantations and the association of the African populations with them. Indeed, Barry Higman's excellent study of early nineteenth century Jamaica confirmed what many observers had long suspected: that, *in general*, mortality rates and social disruption were more extreme among populations engaged in labor on sugar plantations than among those engaged in any other type of agricultural activity.[12]

With so many environmental factors involved, the proportion of Afro-Americans within any national or regional sample does not provide an immediately useful indication of either the number or residential density of that particular nonwhite segment. Both size and population density are important factors affecting the cohesiveness of any population as well as its cultural viability over a period of time.

The Afro-Argentine population in Buenos Aires provides a good illustration of this assertion.[13] In 1830, the African among the Buenos Aires population numbered about 8,000, accounting for approximately 30 percent of the inhabitants of the city. By 1910 the Afro-Argentines of Buenos Aires had managed to maintain their numbers—still approximately 8,000—but represented less than 1 percent of the urban population. But the changes in the nature and the experience of the Afro-Argentines amounted to far more than merely a proportional diminution. Both the sexual composition and the cultural distinctiveness of the group also underwent considerable metamorphoses. Around the middle of the nineteenth century, females outnumbered males, as they did in all normal immigrant groups. As large numbers of European—especially Italian—immigrants entered the country, they merged, cohabited, and intermarried with the Afro-Argentines. Within two generations the descendants of these two groups began to manifest an even greater cultural diversity and eclecticism than would have been possible within the boundaries of any conventional group cohesiveness.

The experience of the Afro-Argentines of Buenos Aires was comparable to that of other marginal groups with adverse sexual imbalances or precarious economic bases. The maroon society in Jamaica went through a similar experience.[14] As long as the maroon society was under attack from the colonial authorities, and as long as it offered a realizable alternative to plantation society slavery, the maroons had little difficulty in maintaining a cohesive structure, which served as a catalyst for the development of their particular variant of an Afro-American culture. The abolition of slavery, structural changes in the local island economy, and the demographic alteration among the maroons led to increasing exchanges and interchanges with the wider Jamaican community. Eventually the cultural distinctiveness of the maroons was largely lost. In an identical way the free African immigrants who came to Jamaica during the nineteenth century lost their distinctive West African culture, and the indentured East Indians and Chinese underwent cultural modifications after they had spent some time in the Caribbean.[15] Nevertheless, both the free Africans and the maroons (and the other major immigrants during the nineteenth century) made significant cultural contributions to the development of an Afro-Jamaican culture.

Population figures present still another problem. Neither during the period of slavery nor in the contemporary age do current figures provide any close, positive correlation between the volume of slaves deposited by the transatlantic slave trade and the subsequent population of Afro-Americans. Of all the American recipient areas, only Brazil had a population of Afro-Americans at the end of slavery which approximated its proportional participation in the slave trade.[16] Along with normal fluctuations in the volume of the trade, the peculiar combinations of local historical circumstances provided the catalysts that either facilitated or inhibited the development of an Afro-American culture.

In the mainland Spanish states of the Americas, after their political independence, the proportion of the Afro-American population varied considerably across as well as within the newly defined national boundaries. The Afro-American populations developed as virtually new clusters in areas of plantation activity notable for their absence of indigenous inhabitants. Such areas included the lowland regions of Venezuela, Colombia, Panama, and Costa Rica, where the Afro-Americans amounted to about 3 percent of the national populations. By contrast, Mexico, Guatemala, Honduras, Ecuador, Peru, Bolivia, Chile, Argentina, Uruguay, and Paraguay each had Afro-American populations of about 1 percent. Some lowland areas of Chile and Argentina were not incorporated in the plantation zones owing to "the tyranny of distance."[17]

Between the sixteenth and the nineteenth centuries, the Caribbean islands appeared to be ideal for the establishment of plantations using slave labor. The extent to which these islands became colonies of economic exploitation rather than refuges for the surplus populations of Europe may be gauged from the high percentages of the inhabitants who were African or Afro-American.[18] Some indications of this have already been given; but the point may be emphasized since the lowest nonwhite percentages of the Caribbean islands—those for Puerto Rico (48.5%), Bermuda (52%), and Cuba (56%)—equalled or exceeded the highest proportions of Brazil or the United States at the end of slavery in those nations.[19] What is surprising, however, is that the Afro-American populations of Brazil and the United States surpassed four million each (in 1880 and 1860 respectively), while the total for all the Caribbean islands in 1880 barely amounted to two million, with probably no more than an additional one million for all of mainland Spanish America.

With the exception of the Brazilian case, those populations stand in sharp contrast to the slave importation figures for the various regions. In terms of raw slave imports, Brazil received approximately 3.5 million Africans during the course of the slave trade (that is, between the years 1500 and 1850).[20] This total represented about 38 percent of the entire transatlantic trade for the period. The mainland Spanish American colonies bought about 600,000 Africans, or 6 percent of the volume sold throughout the Americas during that same period. The British North American colonies (which after 1776 became the United States of America) received about 450,000 slaves, or 4.5 percent of the total trade. The Caribbean islands and the Guianas, by contrast, received approximately 4.7 million Africans, accounting for about 47 percent of the trade. Clearly these proportions contrast sharply with the demographic situation at the end of slavery in the Americas, when Brazil and the United States together accounted for nearly 70 percent of the entire Afro-American population.

Reasons for the general growth or decline of the Afro-American populations are not difficult to ascertain. Across the Americas the free populations tended to increase naturally at the same rate, regardless of color, rank, or condition. Slave populations, on the other hand, showed a consistently similar pattern of decline throughout the Americas, with the singular exception of the United States.[21] The peculiar conditions of slavery, of the societies, and of the economies militated against the natural increase of the enslaved populations throughout the Caribbean and Brazil. Diet, disease, and the physical conditions of labor combined to depress the Caribbean and Brazilian slave populations far more severely than that of the United States. In order to maintain an adequate labor pool, therefore, slaveowners in Brazil and the Caribbean were forced continually to import new Africans.

The physical size of any territory and the economic importance of its primary products might be good indicators of the probable size of the Afro-American population at any given time. Size of territory or population, however, cannot provide an index to the distinctiveness of the Afro-American culture. The cohesiveness and vitality of the culture associated with any particular Afro-American community result more from the unpredictable functions of the historical trajectory of the area than from the physical size and demographic balance of the Afro-American component at any randomly selected period.

The transatlantic slave trade was a movement of peoples; it was only coincidentally a transfer of culture. Neither Africa, from which the slaves were taken, nor the Americas, where they finally remained, consisted of homogenous societies and cultures. African societies represented various cultures in a constantly changing environment. The Americas, too, reflected a restless kaleidoscope of societies and cultures before the nineteenth century. The group recruitment of African slaves was made more out of consideration of profits and vendibility than out of concerns for culture and community. African immigrants throughout the Americas, therefore, displayed a far greater degree of age- and sex-specificity than those of any other immigrant group. The chances of reconstituting particular ethnic groups in the Americas were slim but by no means nonexistent.[22] Nevertheless, with respect to culture, the importance lay not in the mere reconstitution of the ethnic group per se but rather in the timing and the conditions under which the regrouping took place. After all, the reconstitution of a specific ethnic group under the auspices of the slave trade did not, and could not, recreate the original conditions for the perpetuation of the basic African culture with any great degree of authenticity. To do so would have been exceptionally difficult for free individuals; for slaves it was virtually impossible.

Although a precise definition of culture is often unrelentingly elusive, we may, for convenience, accept culture as the system of values, beliefs, and general way-of-life of any group. Using this definition, we can delineate three areas in which the Atlantic slave trade affected the development and perpetuation of an Afro-American culture.

The first area concerns the volume and pace of introduction of the African slaves. For the first two centuries of the trade, the regional demand was relatively low throughout the Americas. Some slaves were supplied directly from Africa, others were shipped via Europe. The annual rate of introduction seldom exceeded 1,200 slaves per year. This relatively low regional demand tended to mask specific zones of periodic high concentration, such as Hispaniola during the sixteenth century, following the decimation of the native population. Low demand/supply patterns, however, coincided with certain characteristics of trade which would diminish or disappear later.

One such characteristic was the fastidiousness shown by purchasers in their choice of slaves. When buyers made deliberate selections based on the presumed efficacy of a distinct regional or ethnic type, they unconsciously contributed to the concentration of that particular group. Dense concentrations of ethnic and culturally cohesive groups permitted the establishment of a type of Americanized African culture (or Afro-American culture) that succeeding imported Africans found difficult or impossible to destroy.[23] Subsequent changes in the ethnic origins of slaves would not necessarily alter the variant African culture in the direction of the new majority, although in some cases a further modification of the old culture might take place.

The impact that the annual import rate had on the local society in 1600, when the import volume stood at 2,000 slaves, would be quite different from the impact of the 13,000 slaves imported annually in 1700, or the 55,000 imported annually by 1810. Greater volume reflected greater variations in ethnic origin. Moreover, when Africans arrived too rapidly, died too rapidly, or were held in cohorts of great sizes, socialization tended to be disrupted; the *bozal*, or new arrival, was too often the rule rather than the exception. Acculturation was probably more standardized in 1800 than in 1600—but the goals of the local society were probably quite different. This increased volume was probably both cause and consequence of the revolution in the American societies and economies, and Africans dominated the populations of those parts of the Americas because they were the chief engineers of this revolution. The viability of an Afro-American culture derived great impetus from the increased flow of Africans, and added a new dimension to the process of creolization taking place in plantation America.

The second area concerns the age and sex composition of the slave imports. The number, age, and proportion of women imported had important consequences for the Afro-American society.[24] For most of its existence the transatlantic slave trade was predominantly a commerce in males. The initial preference for males might have been attributable to the belief that men were more valuable than women and were more adept at clearing forests and accomplishing the onerous manual tasks required on the plantations. Recent publications— such as *Slavery in Africa* edited by Suzanne Miers and Igor Kopytoff, Philip D. Curtin's *Economic Change in Precolonial Africa* and Herbert S. Klein's *The Middle Passage*—have all cast doubts on the accuracy and simplicity of this belief. Conditions in Africa and Africans' attitudes toward their own people also influenced the sexual selection of those who were destined for the overseas slave trade. Until Europeans could penetrate African societies, their purchases of slaves remained a compromise between what they wanted and what the Africans would supply. Nevertheless, for whatever the reasons, approximately 80 percent of all slaves delivered during the early part of the trade were adult and adolescent males.[25]

Over a period of time, especially during the late eighteenth and early nineteenth centuries, the number and proportion of women increased. Some reasons for this change are not hard to find: the necessities of social control; the escalation in the price of young adult males; the international attacks on the slave trade in general; and the eventual realization that female workers could be equally as effective as men in doing the work on the American plantations. Moreover, as the locus of the trade shifted along the African coast, the additional marginal Africans—in the Miers and Kopytoff sense of that phrase— brought with the catchment area of the traffic, may well have been female.

During the final phase of the slave trade, therefore, the proportion of women and children steadily increased. Manuel Moreno Fraginals illustrated some changes in the sex distribution of slaves on selected Cuban estates—changes which, given the period, closely reflected the proportion of the sexes on sale in the slave markets of the island.[26] In his sample, the proportion of male slaves between 1748 and 1790 was 90.38 percent of the African labor force; between 1791 and 1822 this proportion fell to 85.03; between 1823 and 1844 it fell to 69.70 percent; and between 1845 and 1868 the decline bottomed out at 59.80 percent. The Cuban slave trade lasted the longest of any in the Caribbean, and it responded to the growing pressures to ameliorate and eventually to abolish the trade. One measure of this response can be traced in the proportion of females bought on the island. The female component in slavery increased from about 10 percent in the early stages of the trade to about 40 percent in 1868—presumably as an index of the mitigation of one of the worst evils of the trade.

Barry Higman's study, *Slave Population and Economy in Jamaica, 1807–1833*, demonstrates a pattern similar to that found in Cuba. Higman estimates that during the last phase of the slave trade to Jamaica, just before 1807, "the proportion of males imported [was] unlikely to have exceeded 60 percent of the total."[27] The Cuban trade, which continued much later than the trade elsewhere in the Caribbean, reflected this male-specific diminution. As Moreno Fraginals has written, "during the decade of the 1820s, four out of every ten immigrants were women; during the decade of the 1830s, the figure rose to five out of every ten . . . [and] around 1850 . . . out of every 15 immigrants, seven were women."[28]

The high proportion of male imports during the formative stages of American plantation societies may have had a depressing effect on the inclination of the slave populations to expand normally, although sexual imbalance alone would not have deterred a natural increase.[29] The reversal of the pattern during the later eighteenth and nineteenth centuries may have had a catalytic effect on the regularization and propagation of an Afro-American culture, since the increasing incidence of live births also increased the possibilities for infant socialization. More surviving infants—leading to an increased creolization of the population—expanded the opportunity to perpetuate the eclectic Afro-American culture.

But the trade also dovetailed with the phase of development of the American slave societies. As the plantation frontier stabilized, each slave society underwent subtle but profound changes in the demographic profile of its African and Afro-American (or creole) population. These changes were most pronounced in the sex balance, the age profile, and the creole proportion of each slave cohort, as well as in declines in the overall morbidity and mortality rates.[30] The mature slave society, therefore, manifested a general population pyramid approximating that of any free organic population group. The most startling change was the increase in the creole component of the slave sector. In the case of Cuba, the creole component increased from 11.53 percent in the later eighteenth century to 47.02 percent in 1868.[31] This change was also evident in all of the other predominantly plantation zones of the Americas.

Creolization had negative effects on slave imports. American slave importation figures tended to decrease in reverse proportion to the growth of a creole population of Afro-Americans. The most extreme case must certainly be that of the United States. The singularly phenomenal increase in the number of slaves—from the import figure of approximately 427,000 before 1790 to an Afro-American population of 4.5 million by 1864—certainly reduced the demand for slaves brought in from Africa. The consequence of creating an autonomous (self-sustaining) slave force was that the majority of the Afro-Americans in the United States were creolized in a society in which they formed a minority, and one in which they were bereft of the continual cultural reinforcement from Africa. The process of creolization affected the proportion of children in the population, social mores, occupational roles, and even the family structure and family relationships which were developed by that sector.[32]

Culturally, as well as psychologically, creolization varied according to whether Africans were in a minority, as in the United States of America, or a majority, as in most Caribbean plantation societies. The view of the world held by an Afro-American from the United States would have been, in some respects, slightly different from that of his counterpart in the French colony of Saint Domingue in 1792, or in the Spanish Colony of Cuba in 1860, or in the English colony of Jamaica in 1838.

The third area in which the slave trade affected the rise of an Afro-American culture had to do with the social and economic conditions of the specific host society and culture in which the slaves were eventually integrated. Both volume and age and sex characteristics responded reciprocally to the local conditions of the American societies, which fell within a continuum ranging from the settler society with significant European components to the exploitive plantation structures with their European minorities and lack of a stable, cohesive, European culture. Whether in a majority or a minority, the Europeans established and controlled, to a certain degree, the parameters within which the Africans retained, adapted, created, or forged their eclectic variant of a culture.

In the settler societies of Argentina, Brazil, Mexico, and the United States, African immigrants faced a vital, dynamic, and self-confident form of European society and culture. An African society survived, but it faced stiff and relentless competition from the mainstream or "high" culture. Regardless of the degree of success that it enjoyed among Afro-Americans, it was, at best, a subculture continually compared unfavorably with the culture of the majority. Elements of the African culture might be accepted and propagated by the dominant culture, but in general, where this was done, such elements lost their ethnic identity.

On the other hand, the paucity of non-Africans in the exploitive plantation societies meant that despite the elaborate attempts of the politically dominant groups to restrain or coerce the slaves into conformity, Africans and Afro-Americans—slave as well as free—had greater control over their individual and collective daily lives. The cultural weaknesses and deficiencies of the plantation elite provided an almost unique opportunity for Africans to fashion a society and a culture mostly on their own terms.[33] Indeed, Africans tended to influence speech, conduct, music, cuisine, art, and religion to such an extent that visitors often referred to plantation America as Afro-America.

The precise ways in which Africans adapted to the Americas, created communities, and set about articulating a shared culture varied considerably throughout the hemisphere, and reflected the variety of conditions they encountered, from the low density occupation of frontier grazing regions to the high density occupation of the cities and plantations. Sidney Mintz, Richard Price, and Harry Hoetink have contributed greatly to our understanding of this process in their recent writings.[34] They warn against making a linear connection via the Atlantic slave trade between African and American societies and cultures, or the tendency to oversimplify the genesis of an Afro-American culture. While Africa and the slave trade provided the basic ingredients, the final product depended on the collective contributions of Europe, America, and in some cases Asia. An Afro-American culture remains a dynamic amalgam of African and non-African elements, with an indelible "made in America" impression.

NOTES

1 The figures for the Atlantic slave trade have been, and probably will remain forever, in dispute. This paper relies on figures derived from the following sources: Philip D. Curtin, *The Atlantic Slave Trade: A Census*

(Madison, 1969); Stanley L. Engerman and Eugene D. Genovese, eds., *Race and Slavery in the Western Hemisphere: Quantative Studies* (Princeton, 1975); Henry A. Gemery and Jan S. Hogendorn, eds., *The Uncommon Market: Essays in the Economic History of the Atlantic Slave Trade* (New York, 1979); Enriqueta Vila Vilar, *Hispano-America y el comercio de esclavos: Los Asientos Portugueses* (Seville, 1977).

2 A number of books pursue this point. For one example, see Ivan Van Sertima, *They Came Before Columbus: The African Presence in Ancient America* (New York, 1977).

3 See Carl Sauer, *The Early Spanish Main* (Berkeley and Los Angeles, 1966); Lerome Bennett, Jr., *Before the Mayflower: A History of the Negro in America, 1619–1964*, rev. ed. (Baltimore, 1966), pp. 34–37; Leslie B. Rout, Jr., *The African Experience in Spanish American, 1502 to the Present Day* (London, 1976), pp. 15–26; Peter Boyd-Bowman, "Negro Slaves in Early Colonial Mexico," *The Americas* 26 (1969): 139–42.

4 Afro-American in this context means, generally, descendants of Africans found throughout the Americas; it is not restricted to the geographical confines of the United States. Where the more restricted implication applies, an attempt is made to make the identification clear.

5 See Gonzalo Aguirre Beltran, *La población negra de México, 1519–1810: Estudio etnohistórico*, 2d ed. (Mexico 1972); Magnus Mörner, *Race Mixture in the History of Latin America* (Boston, 1967); Frederick P. Bowser, *The African Slave in Colonial Peru, 1524–1650* (Stanford, 1974); Inge Wolff, "Negersklaverei und negerhandel in HochPeru, 1545–1640," in R. Konetzke and H. Kellenbenz, eds., *Jahrbuch für Geschichte von Staat, Wirtschaft und Gesellschaft Lateinamerikas* 1 (Cologne, 1964): 157–86.

6 Some population figures for the Antilles may be found in Franklin W. Knight, *The Caribbean: The Genesis of a Fragmented Nationalism* (New York, 1978), pp. 238–39.

7 See David W. Cohen and Jack P. Greene, eds., *Neither Slave nor Free: The Freedmen of African Descent in the Slave Societies of the New World* (Baltimore, 1972).

8 Franklin W. Knight, *Slave Society in Cuba During the Nineteenth Century* (Madison, 1970); Manuel Moreno Fraginals, *El ingenio, complejo económico social cubano del azúcar*, new ed. (Havana, 1978).

9 Michael Craton, *Searching for the Invisible Man: Slaves and Plantation Life in Jamaica* (Cambridge, Mass., 1978); Richard S. Dunn, *Sugar and Slaves: The Rise of the Planter Class in the English West Indies, 1624–1713* (Chapel Hill, 1972); Carl and Roberta Bridenbaugh, *No Peace Beyond the Line: The English in the Caribbean, 1624–1690* (New York, 1972); Cornelis Ch. Goslinga, *The Dutch in the Caribbean and on the Wild Coast, 1580–1680* (Gainesville, Fla., 1971); Elsa V. Goveia, *Slave Society in the British Leeward Islands at the End of the Eighteenth Century* (New Haven, 1965); Edward Brathwaite, *The Development of Creole Society in Jamaica, 1770–1820* (New York, 1971); François Girod, *La vie quotidienne de la sociéte' créole (Saint-Domingue au 18ᵉ*

siecle) (Paris, 1971); Luis M. Diaz Soler, *Historia de la esclavitud negra en Puerto Rico,* 4th ed. (Rio Piedras, Puerto Rico, 1974).

10 Emilia Viotti da Costa, *Da Senzala a Colonia* (São Paulo, 1966); Stanley J. Stein, *Vassouras: A Brazilian Coffee Country, 1850–1900* (Cambridge, Mass., 1957); C. R. Boxer, *The Golden Age of Brazil* (Berkeley, 1962); Warren Dean, *Rio Claro: A Brazilian Plantation System, 1820–1920* (Stanford, 1976).

11 See Harry Hoetink, *Slavery and Race Relations in the Americas: Comparative Notes on Their Nature and Nexus* (New York, 1973); Harry Hoetink, *The Two Variants of Caribbean Race Relations: A Contribution to the Sociology of Segmented Societies* (London, 1967).

12 Barry W. Higman, *Slave Population and Economy in Jamaica, 1807–1834* (Cambridge, 1976), pp. 105–115.

13 G. Reid Andrews, *The Afro-Argentines of Buenos Aires, 1800–1900* (Madison, Wis., 1980).

14 Barbara Klamon Kopytoff, "The Early Political Development of Jamaica Maroon Societies," *William and Mary Quarterly,* 3d ser., 35 (1978): 287–307. See also Orlando Patterson, *The Sociology of Slavery: An Analysis of the Origins, Development and Structure of the Negro Slave Society in Jamaica* (London, 1967), pp. 262–81; Richard Price, ed., *Maroon Societies* (New York, 1973).

15 On the free Africans, see Monica Schuler, *Alas! Alas! Kongo: A Social History of Liberated African Immigration to Jamaica, 1841–1867* (Baltimore, 1980); Vera Rubin and Arthur Tuden, eds., *Comparative Perspectives on Slavery in New World Plantation Societies* (hereafter cited as *Comparative Perspectives*) (New York, 1977), pp. 205–85.

16 For population figures, see Franklin W. Knight, *The African Dimension in Latin American Societies* (New York, 1974), pp. 44–49.

17 The phrase is taken from Geoffrey Blainey, *The Tyranny of Distance: How Distance Shaped Australia's History* (Melbourne, 1966).

18 Franklin W. Knight, "Patterns of Colonial Society and Culture: Latin America and the Caribbean, 1492–1804," in Jack R. Censer, N. Steven Steinert, and Amy M. McCandless, eds., *South Atlantic Urban Studies* 2 (Charleston, 1978): 3–23.

19 Knight, *Caribbean,* pp. 238–39.

20 Slave trade figures are from Curtin, *Atlantic Slave Trade,* pp. 47–49.

21 Eugene D. Genovese, *The World the Slaveholders Made: Two Essays in Interpretation* (New York, 1969).

22 Harry Hoetink, "The Cultural Links," in Margaret E. Crahan and Franklin W. Knight, eds., *Africa and the Caribbean: The Legacies of a Link* (Baltimore, 1979), pp. 20–40; Sidney W. Mintz and Richard Price, *An Anthropological Approach to the Afro-American Past: A Caribbean Perspective* (Philadelphia, 1976); Sidney W. Mintz, "The Caribbean Region," *Daedalus* 103 (1974): 45–71.

23 Hoetink, "The Cultural Links," pp. 20–40.

24 Herbert G. Gutman, *The Black Family in Slavery and Freedom, 1750–1925*

(New York, 1976); B. W. Higman, "Methodological Problems in the Study of the Slave Family," in *Comparative Perspectives*, pp. 591–96.

25 See Franklin W. Knight, "Sexual Composition and the African Slave Trade to the Caribbean" (Paper delivered at the Virginia State University Slave Trade Symposium, Petersburg, Va., October 4–5, 1979).

26. Manuel Moreno Fraginals, "Africa in Cuba: A Quantitative Analysis of the African Population in the Island of Cuba," in *Comparative Perspectives*, pp. 187–201.

27 Higman, *Slave Population*, p. 72.

28 Moreno Fraginals, "Africa in Cuba," p. 193.

29 Knight, "Sexual Composition," passim.

30 G. W. Roberts, "Movements in Slave Population of the Caribbean During the Period of Slave Registration," in *Comparative Perspectives*, pp. 145–60; Humphrey E. Lamur, "Demography of Surinam Plantation Slaves in the Last Decade Before Emancipation: The Case of Catharina Sophia," in *Comparative Perspectives*, pp. 161–73.

31 Franklin W. Knight, "Social Structure of Cuban Slave Society in the Nineteenth Century," in *Comparative Perspectives*, pp. 259–66.

32 Rubin and Tuden, eds., *Comparative Perspectives*, pp. 3–71.

33 Manuel Moreno Fraginals, ed., *Africa en America Latina* (Mexico, 1976); Crahan and Knight, eds., *Africa and the Caribbean*.

34 Mintz and Price, *Anthropological Approach*, pp. 1–64; Hoetink, "The Cultural Links," pp. 20–40.

Selected Bibliography

Index

Selected Bibliography

The following is not intended as an exhaustive list of sources but rather as a source of further information on the major themes of the present volume.

Alpers, Edward A. *The East African Slave Trade.* Nairobi, 1967.

Alpers, Edward A. *Ivory and Slaves in East Africa.* Berkeley, 1975.

Anstey, Roger T. *The Atlantic Slave Trade and British Abolition, 1760–1810.* London, 1975.

Anstey, Roger T., and P. E. H. Hair, eds. *Liverpool, the African Slave Trade and Abolition.* Liverpool, 1976.

Barnes, Gilbert Hobbes. *The Antislavery Impulse.* Washington, D.C., 1933.

Beachey, R. W. *The Slave Trade of Eastern Africa.* New York, 1976.

Bethell, Leslie M. *The Abolition of the Brazilian Slave Trade: Britain, Brazil and the Slave Trade Question, 1807–1869.* Cambridge, 1970.

Bethell, Leslie M. "The Mixed Commission for the Suppression of the Transatlantic Slave Trade." *Journal of African History* 7 (1966):79–93.

Bolt, Christine, and Seymour Drescher, eds. *Anti-Slavery, Religion and Reform: Essays in Memory of Roger Anstey.* Folkestone, England, 1980.

Brathwaite, Edward. *The Development of Creole Society in Jamaica, 1770–1820.* Oxford, 1971.

Buxton, Thomas Powell. *The African Slave Trade and Its Remedy.* 2 vols. London, 1839–40.

Clarkson, Thomas. *The History of the Rise, Progress and Accomplishment of the Abolition of the African Slave Trade by the British Parliament.* 2 vols. London, 1808.

Conneau, Captain Theophilus. *A Slaver's Logbook or 20 Years' Residence on the Coast of Africa.* Englewood, N.J., 1976.

Cooper, Frederick. *Plantation Slavery on the East Coast of Africa.* New Haven, 1977.

Coupland, Reginald. *The British Anti-Slavery Movement.* London, 1933.

Craton, Michael. *Searching for the Invisible Man: Slaves and Plantation Life in Jamaica.* Cambridge, Mass., 1978.

Curtin, Philip D. *The Atlantic Slave Trade: A Census.* Madison, 1969.

Curtin, Philip D. *Economic Change in Precolonial Africa,* 2 vols. Madison, 1975.

Curtin, Philip D. "Epidemiology and the Slave Trade" *Political Science Quarterly* 83 (1968):190–216.

Curtin, Philip D. "The Slave Trade and the Atlantic Basin: Intercontinental Perspectives." In N. Huggins, M. Kilson, and D. Fox, eds., *Key Issues in the Afro American Experience.* New York, 1971. Pp. 74–94.

Daget, Serge. "L'abolition de la traite des noirs en France de 1814 à 1831." *Cahiers d'étude africaines* 2 (1971):14–58.

Daget, Serge. "Long cours et négrier nantais du traffic illégal (1814–1833)." *Revue française d'histoire d'outre-mer* 62 (1975):90–134.

Davis, David Brion. *The Problem of Slavery in the Age of Revolution, 1770–1823.* Ithaca, 1975.

Deerr, Noel. *The History of Sugar.* 2 vols. London, 1949.

Degn, Christian. *Die Schimmelmanns im atlantischen Dreiechkshandel: Gewinn ind Gewissen.* Neumünster, 1974.

Donnan, Elizabeth. *Documents Illustrative of the History of the Slave Trade to America.* 4 vols. Washington, D.C., 1930–35.

Drescher, Seymour. *Econocide: British Slavery in the Era of Abolition.* Pittsburgh, 1977.

Eltis, David. "The British Contribution to the Nineteenth Century Transatlantic Slave Trade." *Economic History Review* 32 (1979):211–27.

Engerman, Stanley L. "The Slave Trade and British Capital Formation in the Eighteenth Century: A Comment on the Williams' Thesis." *The Business History Review* 46 (1972):430–43.

Engerman, Stanley L. "Some Economic and Demographic Comparisons of Slavery in the United States and the British West Indies." *Economic History Review* 29 (1976):258–75.

Engerman, Stanley L., and Eugene D. Genovese, eds. *Race and Slavery in the Western Hemisphere: Quantitative Studies.* Princeton, 1975.

Fage, John D. *A History of West Africa.* Cambridge, 1969.

Fogel, Robert W., and Stanley L. Engerman. "Recent Findings in the Study of Slave Demography and Family Structure." *Sociology and Social Research* 63 (1979):566–89.

Fogel, Robert W., and Stanley L. Engerman. *Time on the Cross: The Economics of American Negro Slavery.* 2 vols. Boston, 1974.

Fraginals, Manuel Moreno. *Africa en America Latina.* Mexico, 1976.

Fraginals, Manuel Moreno. *The Sugarmill.* New York, 1976.

Furtado, Celso. *The Economic Growth of Brazil.* Berkeley, 1962.

Gavin, R. L. "Palmerston's Policy towards East and West Africa, 1830–1865." Ph.D. diss., Cambridge University, 1958.

Gemery, Henry A., and Jan S. Hogendorn. "The Atlantic Slave Trade: A Tentative Economic Model." *Journal of African History* 15 (1974):223–46.

Gemery, Henry A., and Jan S. Hogendorn, eds. *The Uncommon Market: Essays on the Economic History of the Transatlantic Slave Trade.* New York, 1979.

Goulart, Mauricio. *Escravideo africana no Brasil.* Sao Paulo, 1950.

Higman, Barry W. *Slave Population and Economy in Jamaica, 1807–1834.* Cambridge, 1976.

Hopkins, A. G. *An Economic History of West Africa.* London, 1973.

Howard, Warren S. *American Slavers and Federal Law, 1837–1862.* Berkeley, 1963.

Humboldt, Alexander. *The Island of Cuba.* Translated from the Spanish, with notes and a preliminary essay, by J. S. Thrasher. New York, 1856.

Jakobsson, Stiv. *Am I Not a Man and A Brother? British Missions and the Abolition of the Slave Trade and Slavery in West Africa and the West Indies, 1786–1838.* Lund, 1972.

Johnson, Marion. "The Cowrie Currencies of West Africa." Parts 1 and 2. *Journal of African History* 11 (1970):17–49, 331–53.

Kelly, John Barrett. *Britain and the Persian Gulf, 1795–1880.* Oxford, 1968.

Klein, Herbert S. "Fertility Differentials between Slaves in the United States and the British West Indies: A Note on Lactation Practices and Their Possible Implications." *William and Mary Quarterly* 35 (1978):357–74.

Klein, Herbert S. *The Middle Passage: Comparative Studies in the Atlantic Slave Trade.* Princeton, 1978.

Klein, Herbert S., and Stanley L. Engerman. "Facteurs de mortalité dans le trafic franc d'esclaves au XVIIIe siècle" *Annales* 6 (1976):1213–24.

Klingberg, Frank J. *The Anti-Slavery Movement in England.* New Haven, 1926.

Kloosterboer, W. *Involuntary Labour Since the Abolition of Slavery.* Leiden, Netherlands, 1960.

Knight, Franklin W. *Slave Society in Cuba during the Nineteenth Century.* Madison, 1970.

Latham, A. J. H. *Old Calabar, 1600–1891.* London, 1973.

Lawaetz, H. *Peter v. Scholten, Vestindiske tidsbilleder fra den sidste generalguvernørs dage.* Copenhagen, 1940.

LeVeen, E. Phillip. *British Slave Trade Suppression Policies, 1821–1865.* New York, 1977.

Lloyd, Christopher. *The Navy and the Slave Trade: The Suppression of the African Slave Trade in the Nineteenth Century.* London, 1949.

Martin, P. M. *The External Trade of the Loango Coast, 1578–1870.* London, 1972.

Mathieson, William Law. *Great Britain and the Slave Trade, 1839–1865.* London, 1929.

Meillasoux, Claude, ed. *The Development of Indigenous Trade and Markets in West Africa.* London, 1971.

Miers, Suzanne. *Britain and the Ending of the Slave Trade.* New York, 1975.

Nørregård, Georg. *Danish Settlements in West Africa, 1658–1850.* Translated by Sigurd Mammen. Boston, 1966.

Northrup, David. "African Mortality in the Suppression of the Slave Trade: The Case of the Bight of Biafra." *Journal of Interdisciplinary History* 9 (1978):47–64.

Northrup, David. "The Compatibility of the Slave and Palm Oil Trade in the Bight of Biafra." *Journal of African History* 17 (1976): 353–64.

Northrup, David. *Trade Without Rulers: Pre-Colonial Economic Developments in South-Eastern Nigeria*. London, 1978.

Rebelo, Manuel dos Angos da Silva. *Relacoes entre Angola e Brasil*. Lisboa: 1970.

Reynolds, Edward. *Trade and Economic Change on the Gold Coast, 1807–1874*. London, 1974.

Rodney, Walter. "Slavery and other Forms of Social Oppression on the Upper Guinea Coast in the Context of the Atlantic Slave Trade." *Journal of African History* 7 (1966):431–43.

Rubin, Vera, and Arthur Tuden, eds. *Comparative Perspectives on Slavery in New World Plantation Societies*. New York, 1977.

Sheridan, Richard B. "'Sweet Malefactor': The Social Costs of Slavery and Sugar in Jamaica and Cuba, 1807–54." *Economic History Review* 29 (1976): 236–57.

Soulsby, Hugh G. *The Right of Search and the Slave Trade in Anglo-American Relations, 1814–1862*. Baltimore, 1933.

Stein, Stanley J. *Vassouras. A Brazilian Coffee County, 1850–1900*. Cambridge, Mass., 1957.

Temperley, Howard. *British Anti-Slavery, 1833–1870*. London, 1972.

Temperley, Howard. "Capitalism, Slavery and Ideology." *Past and Present*, no. 75 (1977), pp. 94–118.

Thomas, R. P., and R. N. Bean. "The Fishers of Men: The Profits of the Slave Trade." *Journal of Economic History* 34 (1974): 885–914.

Trier, C. A. "Det dansk-vestindiske negerindførselsforbud af 1792." *Historisk Tidsskrift*, 7th ser., 5 (1904–5): 405–508.

Verger, Pierre. *Flux et reflux de la traite des nègres entre le golfe de Benin et Bahia de Todos os Santos de 17e et 18e siècles*. The Hague, 1968.

Wallerstein, Immanuel. *The Modern World System: Capitalist Agriculture and the Origins of the European World Economy in the Sixteenth Century*. New York, 1974.

Walters, Ronald G. *The Anti-Slavery Appeal: American Abolitionism after 1830*. Baltimore, 1977.

Walvin, James, ed. *Slavery and British Society, 1776–1846*. London, 1981.

Ward, W. E. F. *The Royal Navy and the Slavers: The Suppression of the Atlantic Slave Trade*. London, 1969.

Ward, W. R. *Religion and Society in England, 1790–1850*. London, 1972.

Williams, Eric. *Capitalism and Slavery*. Chapel Hill, 1944.

Index

JACKET DESIGNED BY GARY GORE
COMPOSED BY GRAPHIC COMPOSITION, INC., ATHENS, GEORGIA
MANUFACTURED BY MALLOY LITHOGRAPHING, INC.,
ANN ARBOR, MICHIGAN
TEXT IS SET IN BASKERVILLE,
DISPLAY LINES IN BASKERVILLE AND CRAW MODERN

Library of Congress Cataloging in Publication Data
Main entry under title:
The Abolition of the Atlantic slave trade.
Proceedings of a conference held Oct. 16–19, 1978
at Aarhus University, Denmark.
Bibliography: pp. 303–306
Includes index.
1. Slave-trade—Europe—Congresses. 2. Slave-trade—
Africa—Congresses. 3. Slave-trade—
America—Congresses. 4. Abolitionists—Congresses.
I. Eltis, David, 1940–. II. Walvin, James.
III. Green-Pedersen, Svend E.
HT855.A26   382'.44   80–52290
ISBN 0–299–08490–6   AACR2